W9-CRN-036

Human
Evolution

Human

An Introduction
to Biological
Anthropology

C. L. Brace and
Ashley Montagu

Evolution

Second Edition

MacmillanPublishingCo., Inc.
NEW YORK

Collier Macmillan Publishers
LONDON

Earlier edition, entitled *Man's Evolution: An
Introduction to Physical Anthropology,*
copyright © 1965
by C. Loring Brace and M. F. Ashley Montagu.

Macmillan Publishing Co., Inc.
866 Third Avenue, New York, New York 10022

Collier Macmillan Canada, Ltd.

Library of Congress Cataloging in Publication Data

Brace, C   Loring.
  Human evolution.

  Published in 1965 under title: Man's evolution.
  Bibliography: p.
  Includes index.
  1. Physical anthropology. 2. Human evolution.
I. Montagu, Ashley   joint author. II.
Title.
GN60.B74   1977   573   76-5844
ISBN 0-02-313190-X

Printing: 1 2 3 4 5 6 7 8   Year: 7 8 9 0 1 2 3

Title page illustration: *Homo erectus* site at
Choukoutien, China. (Courtesy of the American
Museum of Natural History.)

To the Memory of
Theodosius Dobzhansky

Preface to the Second Edition

Biological anthropology is the study of human evolution. The evidence on which the field is based is drawn from a variety of areas: from our nearest nonhuman relatives—the living and fossil Primates, from variation in living human populations, and from our fossil precursors of the remote and recent past.

Since publication of the earlier version of this work, entitled *Man's Evolution: An Introduction to Physical Anthropology*, discoveries of fossils in the East Rudolf area of Kenya and in Ethiopia have greatly expanded our knowledge concerning the earliest developments in human evolution. As these are announced in the popular press, one often reads statements to the effect that "all previous theories of human evolution must now be abandoned." Announcements of this sort somewhat overstate the case. In fact, the new discoveries extend and expand our previous understanding, but, although they are of great significance, they do not quite live up to their revolutionary billing. With their aid, however, we have gained a better and more rounded, albeit still very incomplete, picture of what was going on toward the beginning of what can be recognized as the human line. Even as we write, further major East African finds are about to be announced, and it seems likely that still more will be discovered in the field season that will have been completed by the time these words appear in print.

If public recognition of progress in our understanding of human evolution tends

viii   to be captured by the drama surrounding the announcement of each newly discovered fossil, the reader should be aware that the other aspects of the field of biological anthropology have been at least as active. Discoveries in primatology, functional anatomy, physiology, and genetics, to name only the more obvious, have increased the scope of the field fully as much as the paleontological finds. But, as with the latter, these manifestations of growth have served principally to integrate and unify a field whose major dimensions were already generally recognized.

In this new edition we have thoroughly revised the material covered in the previous book. We have added three new chapters, "Population Genetics," "Primate Behavior," and "Race: The History of the Concept," along with many new illustrations and much new material in the text and readings. In recognition of the increasing perspective and maturity of the field, we present the new edition under a new title and subtitle that are more appropriate and more in keeping with the facts and the theories the book attempts to examine. The gratifying response to the earlier text emboldens us to hope that this new version will continue to serve the needs of the growing number of students of anthropology, both in its biological field and in its other branches.

The authors wish to thank Dr. Philip Gordon for reading the galleys, Kenneth Scott, our editor, and especially Joan Delaney of the production department at Macmillan.

C. L. B.
A. M.

Preface to the First Edition

This book presents an interpretation of the data of the human fossil record and of man's variation in the light of contemporary evolutionary theory. As such it attempts to articulate the available data with the evolutionary facts in such a manner as to make evolutionary sense of the facts of man's evolution. It has been our endeavor to present the reader with an operationally effective account of that evolution which not only makes sense but is also meaningful and verifiable, at least as verifiable as possible.

We believe that the facts ought to determine the nature of the theory, rather than the other way round. Adherence to this rule has served us as the guideline by which to find our way among both the thickets of the facts and the clouds of theories. We have endeavored also to bear in mind that theory-free statements of facts do not exist, and that therefore our own presentation of the facts is not altogether free of our theories. What we have striven to do is to make our particular evaluation of both the facts and the theories as fruitful as possible. This approach lends a theoretical and organizational consistency to the volume which, we feel, is lacking in many other works. It is possible, even probable, that some of the views expressed in the present volume may meet with criticism from professional physical anthropologists. Such criticism will be welcomed by the authors. Criticism is the life-blood of science. However, it should at once be said that this book is not designed to be a fully documented

x   attempt to change or modify the long-held viewpoints of professional anthropologists, but rather to afford the beginning student an easily comprehensible text which leaves him enlightened and undismayed by the conflicts, confusions, and unanswered questions which he is likely to encounter in so many other works.

In the present work many issues concerning which there is a wide diversity of opinion are discussed primarily from one point of view, namely, that there has been a progressive evolution of man which can, in its broad outlines, be traced more or less step by step, and that while that evolution has been reticulate we can, as in a scattergram, trace something of its central tendency. There may be some professional disagreement with this view, and to the nature of such possible disagreements we refer in the text. In the suggested readings works are included which present views diametrically opposed to ours.

With the beginning student in mind we have minimized the amount of traditional descriptive material, leaving this to some extent to be graphically presented in the illustrations. Instead, we have focused attention on an exposition of the processes affecting those traits which have responded to evolutionary forces, and have endeavored to give the reader a developmental account of change through time according to the logically comprehensible evolutionary principles.

It may, perhaps, be complained that we are omitting much of the uncertainty, complexity, and detail of physical anthropology. That may be a just complaint, but it is our strong feeling that a logical and consistent beginning constitutes a far better foundation on which to develop the subtleties of advanced study than one which presents a mass of conflicting data and interpretation to students who have not yet developed the competence or the sophistication to judge the issues for themselves.

The authors wish to express their warmest thanks to Mr. John Dennis Moore, their most efficient editor at Macmillan, who at every stage of the work has been most helpful, patient, and understanding.

C. L. B.
A. M.

Contents

Part One

General Biological Background

Introduction

The History of Evolutionary Thought and the Development of Biological Anthropology

Human Origins

If one concedes the fact that *Homo sapiens* possesses all the attributes of organic life, and especially of animal organic life, it follows that the course of human development should have proceeded in a manner not too different from that of the rest of the animal kingdom. Such a statement seems to us so self-evident it hardly requires emphasis, but this was not always so. Today it takes something of an effort to recall that the nature and development of organic life was viewed in a very different light a century and a half ago. At that time it was generally believed that plants and animals had simply been created in their present form. In accordance with the view that humans are also members of the world of organic reality, it was assumed that they too had been created in their present form.

Special creation does not scientifically explain the existence of life, since it is an idea outside the realm of verifiable

4   knowledge, but at least it does provide an answer to a question that humans inevitably ask. Until relatively recently, it was not particularly important that the answer be a correct one, since the problem to which the question was directed was not one of great importance in governing the behavior of humans toward humans.

The creation myths recorded in the writings of the major religions of the world, and, indeed, the verbal accounts from the religions of nonliterate peoples, indicate by their very arbitrariness the recognition by humans of their ignorance concerning the origins of the natural world of their everyday experience. Today the sciences of geology, paleontology, biology, and anthropology have contributed greatly to our knowledge concerning the course of organic development, and, rather than diminishing the wonder conveyed by the various creation myths, they have immeasurably enlarged and deepened that wonder. At the same time, they have not only left the basic moral teachings unchanged, but they have also provided solid evidence in their support.

Hence it should come as no surprise that religious thinkers and evolutionary scientists have no basic area of necessary disagreement. In fact, many contributions have been made to the understanding of organic evolution by investigators who were professionally committed to both religion and science. Much of our knowledge of fossil humans in Europe, where more is known of such fossil forms than in any other region of the world, has been the direct contribution of Roman Catholic priests supported by their church in their prehistoric researches.

For instance, much of our knowledge of Paleolithic art, archeology, and fossil humanity in Europe is derived from the labors of the Abbé Henri Breuil whose active career spanned the first half of the twentieth century. The work of Hugo Obermaier, also a Jesuit priest, was scarcely less important, and the most complete Neanderthal skeleton found to date, La Chapelle-aux-Saints, was the result of the efforts of the Abbés A. and J. Bouyssonie and L. Bardon.

A century and a half ago, however, the majority of scholars, lay people, and clergy felt that Christian scripture was more than a model for moral teaching. The general view was that the Biblical creation story literally recounted the prehistory of the world, that is, the history of the world before any written records. All attempts to view the present state of the world as the outcome of the operation of natural forces were viewed with suspicion, hostility and fear, as contrary to the teachings of the Scriptures. The suggestion that humanity itself might have developed in a similar manner was regarded as blasphemous.

A residue of this heightened concern felt by many when their own ancestry is in question is evident in the slip many people make when referring to Charles Darwin's epoch-making work of 1859, *The Origin of Species*. Almost everyone who can read and write is aware that all serious attempts to study human evolution date from the publication of Darwin's book, but many are not aware that Darwin's book scarcely made reference to humans, but restricted itself to a consideration of the evidence for evolution in general. Yet in the minds of many individuals, the title of the book is remembered as *The Origin of THE Species*, and it is supposed that *THE Species* upon which attention is focused is humanity. Nothing could be further from the truth.

While Darwin was aware that the principles set forth in his book could be applied in the investigation of human origins (the theme of his later work *The Descent of Man*, 1871), his concern in *The Origin of Species* was not with humanity at all. His primary purpose was to document his growing awareness that the species we observe around us were not simply created *de novo*. He had become convinced, by his extensive observations of variation and adaptation in related forms of living plants and animals, as well as by his increasing familiarity with the gradual change in living forms visible in succeeding layers of the fossil record, that all living things had achieved their present form by slowly occurring natural processes. Evidently the common tendency to interpolate the crucial article *THE* into Darwin's title is simply a bit of human egocentricity which, understandable though it may be, underestimates the larger scope of Darwin's actual intention.

We have mentioned that prior to Darwin the majority believed in special creation. The sensation that attended the publication of Darwin's book was due to the fact that the proponents of special creation felt their positions threatened by his mechanistic views. Ensconced in their citadels of infallibility, they felt themselves rudely shaken. Differences in social class and wealth were inherited in the world of Western civilization, and positions of power in church, school, and politics were monopolized by people with inherited wealth and social position. Understandably such people favored a world view that emphasized the divine and unchanging fixity of the *status quo — a status quo* with themselves at the top. Any expression of opinion regarding the world as subject to change in the natural course of events was viewed as a threat to the established order. When things are thought to be as good as they can be, any change is not infrequently considered a change for the worse. The conflict between "religion" and "science" reduces itself to social issues rath-

6   er distantly removed from any question of fundamental Christian morality.

In this respect, part of the impact of Darwin's work stems from the fact that he himself belonged to a socially prominent and well-to-do family. With such a background, any opinion he might offer would have received due consideration. Even a view thought to be contrary to the interests of his social class could not be ignored and brushed aside. As it was, his views were soberly and cautiously proposed and supported by an overwhelming amount of carefully considered evidence. Finally, the impact was heightened by the firm and convincing manner in which Thomas Henry Huxley — self-elected "bulldog" of Darwin — and Darwin's other supporters defended his position in contrast to the emotional, unethical, and rather un-Christian attacks by many of his critics.

If the mid-nineteenth century clash between "religion" and "science" was basically an issue of social philosophy, the strength of feeling generated on both sides bore testimony to the fact that it had been brewing for some time. It has already been stated that creation myths have adequately served most peoples as an explanation for the origin and existence of the world. Creation myths, however, do not account for changing worlds. They work only if the world to which they apply remains fixed from the point of creation to eternity. In western civilization creation myths were satisfactory enough till the end of the fifteenth century, but from that time on such myths became increasingly unsatisfactory to a small but growing body of thinkers.

Toward a Changing World

Columbus discovered America,* Magellan circumnavigated the globe, and the universe of humankind could never again be the same. This explosive increase in knowledge of peoples, places, and things produced changes in a no longer static world that did not fail to affect the lives and thought of humans. Economic and social changes followed shortly, and the result was the need for a philosophy that could comprehend a changing world. Naturally, no all-encompassing viewpoint could spring into being overnight, but, like so much else, it did initiate the beginnings of a change in thought that continues to this day.

One of the first examples of the development of the change in character and direction of thought, "The New Philosophy," as it

*Apropos of Columbus' "discovery" of America it has been remarked that when he started out on his voyage he didn't know where he was going, when he got to what is now called America he didn't know where he was, and when he returned to his home port he didn't know where he had been.

came to be called, is to be found in the writings of Francis Bacon (1561–1626). To encompass and give coherence to the vast increases in knowledge at the time, Bacon proposed systematic rules of observation whereby knowledge could be acquired. Little might be unraveled by this means concerning the nature of the world, but by being systematically collected, information would become available. Bacon, however, did not stop there. He urged, as William Gilbert (1540–1603) had done before him, the necessity of experiment.

And it was not long before a generation of "Bacon-faced" young investigators took up the challenge. One of these, Isaac Newton (1642–1727), worked out the laws by which he conceived certain fundamental processes of the world to operate. Newton's mechanistic insights, coming as they did toward the end of the seventeenth and beginning of the eighteenth centuries, were not of much use for the development of those branches of knowledge dealing with the study of life, since, although a great deal of information had been accumulated, it had not been collected systematically. For many, the world was still populated with dragons, unicorns, sea serpents, and a host of other mythical beings. What was needed was the rigorous application of Baconian principles to the world of animated nature, the phenomena of natural history.

The English comparative anatomist Edward Tyson (1650–1708), his coeval countryman the naturalist John Ray (1628–1705), and a number of their contemporaries devoted themselves to this task, but

Figure 1. Edward Tyson (1650–1708). Father of primatology, author of the first comparative anatomy of an ape, *Orang-Outang, Sive Homo sylvestris*, published at London in 1699. Painting by Edmund Lely. (Courtesy of the Royal College of Physicians, London.)

8

Orang-Outang, sive Homo Sylvestris:

OR, THE

ANATOMY

OF A

PYGMIE

Compared with that of a

Monkey, an *Ape,* and a *Man.*

To which is added, A

PHILOLOGICAL ESSAY

Concerning the

Pygmies, the *Cynocephali,* the *Satyrs,* and *Sphinges*
of the ANCIENTS.

Wherein it will appear that they are all either *APES* or
MONKEYS, and not *MEN,* as formerly pretended.

By *EDWARD TYSON* M. D.

Fellow of the Colledge of Physicians, and the Royal Society :
Physician to the Hospital of *Bethlem* , and Reader of
Anatomy at *Chirurgeons-Hall.*

LONDON:

Printed for *Thomas Bennet* at the *Half-Moon* in St. *Paul's* Church-yard ;
and *Daniel Brown* at the *Black Swan* and *Bible* without *Temple-Bar*
and are to be had of Mr. *Hunt* at the Repository in *Gresham-Colledge.*
M DC XCIX.

Figure 2. Title page of the first scientific treatise on the comparative anatomy of an ape, together with two essays on the folklore of the apes. Tyson's term *Pygmy* was used as a general term for monkeys and apes. The specimen he dissected was a juvenile male chimpanzee. The latter term was not used in England until 1738.

Figure 3. Karl von Linné (1707–1778), better known by the Latinized form of his name, Carolus Linnaeus. The father of taxonomy.

the man whose name is most prominently associated with this phase in the development of science was the Swedish naturalist Karl von Linné, better known by his Latinized name, Carolus Linnaeus (1707–1778). As a reflection of the thoroughness of his work, he is called a "systematist" to this day. In his immortal work, the *Systema Naturae*, first published in 1735 and in a tenth edition in 1758, he classified all known living organisms according to the greater or lesser extent of their similarities. Each form was designated by two Latin names, one for Genus, and one for species, hence the designation "binary nomenclature." From that day to this humans have been officially (and possibly somewhat prematurely) known as *Homo sapiens*.

Precise, controlled observation, as exemplified by Linnaeus, constitutes the foundation for all good natural science and remains so today. Analysis and interpretation have played an increasingly larger role in the public recognition and acceptance of scientific theories, beginning with the tremendous interest generated by the publication of *The Origin of Species*. But what is most notable in Darwin, whose interpretations are among the most convincing in

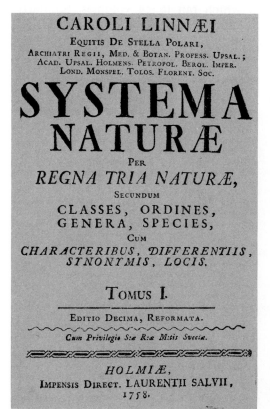

Figure 4. Title page of the definitive 1758 edition of the *Systema Naturae*, the foundation work of systematic biology.

science, is that they are based on an immense number of careful observations and systematically collected data.

Late in the eighteenth century, a number of savants, a small minority to be sure, began to suggest developmental schemes, based on the operation of observable forces, to account for the extensive similarities between many organisms for which precise observations had been recorded. The reaction to this was predictable. Those who had a vested interest in preserving the *status quo* of an unchanging world, created in the form they knew, were outraged. Since education was possible only for the relatively wealthy, it was inevitable that a majority of the educated should oppose the view of an evolving world. Yet, a few of the most able and devoted students of natural science were unable to resist explanations involving changes effected by natural forces.

Significantly, Linnaeus, in the last (1766) edition of his *Systema Naturae*, removed his former statement asserting the fixity of species. Linnaeus' eminent French contemporary, Georges Louis Leclerc, Comte de Buffon (1707–1788), commonly referred to as Buffon, had unequivocally clear and distinct ideas concerning change in the organic world, but these were buried in his massive *Histoire Naturelle des Animaux*, which ran to 44 volumes. Similarly, Charles Darwin's grandfather, the extraordinary Dr. Erasmus Darwin (1731–1802), in his *Zoonomia* (1794–1796), unambiguously expressed ideas that became the foundation of later nineteenth century evolutionary thinking, but his ideas were ahead of his time, and

Figure 5. Erasmus Darwin (1731–1802) at the age of 39. Author of *Zoonomia* (1794–1796) and other early evolutionary works. Grandfather of Charles Darwin. Painting by Joseph Wright. (Courtesy National Portrait Gallery, London.)

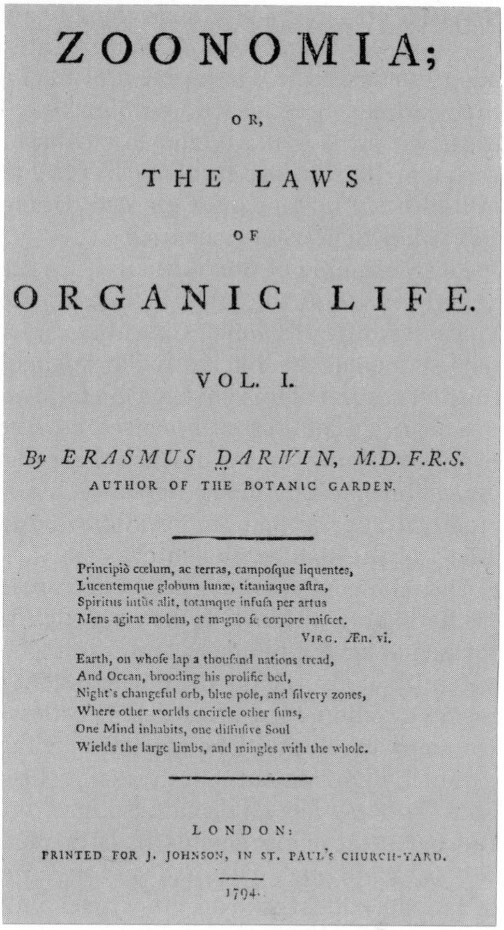

Figure 6. Title page of Erasmus Darwin's *Zoonomia* (1794).

ZOONOMIA;

OR,

THE LAWS

OF

ORGANIC LIFE.

VOL. I.

By ERASMUS DARWIN, *M.D. F.R.S.*
AUTHOR OF THE BOTANIC GARDEN.

Principiò cœlum, ac terras, campofque liquentes,
Lucentemque globum lunæ, titaniaque aftra,
Spiritus intùs alit, totamque infufa per artus
Mens agitat molem, et magno fe corpore mifcet.
VIRG. Æn. vi.

Earth, on whofe lap a thoufand nations tread,
And Ocean, brooding his prolific bed,
Night's changeful orb, blue pole, and filvery zones,
Where other worlds encircle other funs,
One Mind inhabits, one diffufive Soul
Wields the large limbs, and mingles with the whole.

LONDON:
PRINTED FOR J. JOHNSON, IN ST. PAUL'S CHURCH-YARD.

1794.

when not frankly ridiculed, were regarded as too speculative. Nevertheless, Dr. Darwin achieved sufficient recognition during his lifetime so that views of organic development were referred to as "Darwinism" even before the birth of his grandson in 1809. His book *Zoonomia; or, The Laws of Organic Life*, first published in 1794/96, and its third and best edition in 1801, is full of brilliant and original insights and is still very much worth reading.

Past and Future

Every age in human history contains a mixture of the elements of the past and the seeds of the future, but, in assessing previous periods, it is often difficult to put these in their proper perspective. Today the concept of evolution — the normal processes of cumulative change —

12 pervades all aspects of human thought and existence. We are aware that this was not always so, and scientists and historians have frequently engaged in the exercise of tracing modern world views to their earlier sources as we are doing here. The danger in this endeavor, however, is that we tend to attribute entirely modern views to earlier writers whose thinking has influenced the development of attitudes we now take for granted. Often our retrospective attribution is less than wholly accurate.

As an example of this difficulty, we may cite the assessment frequently made of the great French scholar Lamarck. Jean Baptiste Pierre Antoine de Monet, Chevalier de Lamarck (1744–1829) is often regarded as the first really thoroughgoing evolutionist. In fact, in the first edition of this book we too followed this interpretation. Serious historians of science, however, have noted that Lamarck was less of an evolutionist in the modern sense than many people have since given him credit for being. In reality, his views were developed principally to support one version of the divinely created world as rationalized in the eighteenth century.

The eighteenth century might be considered a kind of watershed in the history of ideas. It marks a high point in the self-conscious reverence for the thoughts and writings of the scholars of classical antiquity. It also marks the development of a pervading faith in the power of rational investigation. This flowering of the latter faith has led many to refer to the eighteenth century as "The Age of Reason" or the "Enlightenment." In the realm of the sciences, this faith in rational process has continued without break through the scientific and technical achievements of both the nineteenth and twentieth centuries, although it has had varying turns of fortune in other realms of human endeavor. The French revolution shattered the faith in human rationality for many people and the backlash was such that it affected many aspects of science in France for the duration of the nineteenth century. Currently in the United States the rational approach is under attack from both political radicals and political conservatives, although it continues to occupy a central position in the realm of the sciences.

In the self-consciously rational world of the eighteenth century, both scientists and philosophers viewed the world in terms of relative perfection. The scale ran from the simplicity of inorganic crystals to the utmost in divine complexity; from total lack of worth to the pinnacle of moral excellence in God. The components of the world were hierarchically arranged in an infinite number of links, "The Great Chain of Being," or in ladder-like form on what was called the "Scala Naturae." The position of humanity was regarded as a little lower than that of the angels, with the remainder of both organic and inorganic reality being relegated to a descending series of gradations below. "Nature's Gradation" in the transition between

one form and another represented the continuum of a graded series
of steps, each of which was the special creation of the Creator, immutable and unchangeable.

With their post-Renaissance reverence for the learning of antiquity, the scholars of the Enlightenment traced their rationalizations relating to the Great Chain of Being back to the philosophers of pre-Christian Greece, particularly Aristotle and his teacher Plato. The Platonic world view stressed the illusion of the perceived universe and regarded the perfection of reality as occurring only in the mind of God. Thus the perfect human or the perfect mouse is a divine idea (hence our concept of ideal), whereas the mice and humans of the world we know are merely imperfect manifestations. Linnaeus in the eighteenth century conceived it as a holy task to catalogue the categories of the organic world, achieving merit by displaying the wondrous multitude of the ideas in the divine mind.

But there was a paradox in the rational efforts of the thinkers of the Enlightenment. This paradox also stemmed from the writings of the scholars of ancient Greece, its seeds having been present in the formulations of Plato. Perfection existed in the mind of God, a mind of such infinite power that all conceivable thoughts must exist in it. If humans, then, with their less then perfect minds could think of something, obviously God could think of it too, and, if God thinks of something, it must therefore exist. Linnaeus himself had observed that variants in one plant or animal category often resembled individuals in another category almost as much as the presumed ideals of which they were imperfect manifestations. Perfect intermediate categories were in fact conceivable, and where conceivable, must perforce exist. A perfect divine mind meant a perfect world filled with everything imaginable. This richness has been encompassed in the concept called "Plenitude" and, as we have noted, constitutes one pole of the paradox of eighteenth century views, being logically incompatible with a view that conceived of the world as being made up of individual, immutable, and discrete entities.

The defenders of the Great Chain of Being grappled with this paradox, some such as Linnaeus stressing a hierarchy of discrete categories whereas others such as Buffon (and later, Lamarck) stressed plenitude in the form of infinitely graded continuity. Buffon, at one point, denied the reality of all elements of classification — species, genera, etc. — as artifacts imposed on an infinite gradation by finite and limited human minds. Later, threatened by a possible charge of heresy, he backed down. Scholars who emphasized plenitude expended considerable energy in the search for intermediate forms between established and accepted categories. These, the "missing links," they felt were necessary to demonstrate the perfection of the Great Chain. Ironically the concept of missing link was so completely recast in the evolutionary context of the late nineteenth century

14 that most educated people have quite forgotten the fact that it was originally developed in an effort to bolster a world view in which reality was fixed, immobile, and eternal.

Although a kind of rational dogmatism did characterize much of the intellectual ethos of the eighteenth century, observation did not by any means cease. Incongruent facts continued to accumulate and dissatisfactions led to attempts at revision and modification of the existing conceptual framework. One of these observations has given us a saying that survives to the present, although divested of the shock that it initially created. This was the extinction of the Dodo, giving us the phrase "dead as a. . . ." In a world in which reality depended on the existence of a divine mind, extinction was inconceivable.

But the Dodo was undeniably extinct, having been done in by Dutch sailors by the beginning of the eighteenth century. A large flightless pigeon-like bird, it had lived on the island of Mauritius, which was used as a water and provisioning station by European merchant vessels en route from South Africa to India. With no natural enemies and unable to fly, it was an easy victim of sailors craving fresh meat to vary their diet on a long sea voyage. Its consequent extinction may have caused mild gastronomic regrets among the sailors who plied the shipping routes to the Far East, but it created real mental anguish to the good philosophizers of Western Europe whose world view was badly shaken as a result. Although the Dodo was no more, was the mind of God any the less for the fact?

Although the concern that arose over the extinction of the Dodo may appear somewhat risible to some, its fate symbolizes something that is causing even greater anxiety today. The Dodo's extinction was the first such that penetrated the consciousness of the literate world. Many more creatures have since suffered the fate of the Dodo. Humanity by its astonishing proliferation has quite literally changed the face of the earth rendering life impossible for many other animals and plants and threatening its own long-term survival. Yet a version of the ancient faith that "God will provide" continues with little basic change. Suburbia rampant on a spreading asphalt plain, generating an atmosphere of smog and rivers of sewage, is just one of the more visible consequences of runaway human fecundity. Unless we take seriously the concern of the eighteenth century for the extinction of the world of which we are a part and develop a program of positive control over our conduct, there will be no future and we too will join the Dodo in the ranks of unsuccessful organic forms.

In any event, the defenders of the Great Chain of Being in the late eighteenth century attempted to introduce some tolerance for adjustment into their schemes. Individual efforts to change, strivings for perfectibility and also the reverse — degradation toward damnation — were considered by various thinkers. One such attempt was made by Lamarck. We remember this particularly for its incorporation of a view that had long been popular in the Christian world — that the striving for perfection ultimately will be rewarded. For humans, an approach toward godliness is the goal, but in "lower" organisms, that is, creatures lower in the Scale of Nature, striving might be rewarded by an approximation to the next higher step. Over a long period of time, Lamarck suggested, organisms could actually change rank, becoming transformed by their efforts to such an extent that they would be identified as entirely different species.

This scheme was indeed a bona fide attempt to develop a concept of organic evolution. Unfortunately it ran into trouble from both ends. To many of his contemporaries Lamarck's views represented a threat to established order. The idea that species could change was anathema to those who believed that the creatures of the world were formed in an instant, named by Adam in the Garden of Eden, and sent forth to populate the earth in their present form. Humanity, according to John Lightfoot (1602 – 1675) of Cambridge University, was created by the Trinity on 23 October 4004 B.C. On the other hand, to the scientists of the nineteenth century, Lamarck was clearly identified with the pious but misguided faith in the Great Chain of Being that characterized an earlier age. Darwin, for instance, was accused of failing to give adequate credit to his predecessors. Although he was not deeply involved in the history of ideas, he *was* familiar with the works of Lamarck. The criticism that he had not given Lamarck the credit it was claimed he deserved astonished Darwin since he could see little similarity between his scheme of adaptive interrelationships and an eighteenth century hierarchical view, even one with changeable links. Today, Lamarck is remembered principally for his view that characteristics developed during the lifetime of a particular organism could be transmitted to succeeding generations. This theory involving the inheritance of acquired characteristics has been conclusively refuted by twentieth century genetics.

Georges Cuvier

Although the scientific basis for the refutation of Lamarck's basic idea was not developed until nearly a century after his death, he was thoroughly discredited during his own lifetime by the mordant attacks of his rising young contemporary, Baron Georges Cuvier (1769 – 1832). Cuvier, with a theatrical and commanding personality, achieved great popularity as a lecturer and public figure and, by means of ridicule, influenced a whole generation of European scholars against the views of Lamarck. While it is true that the mechanism for moving evolution proposed by Lamarck has now been shown to be incorrect, it is too often forgotten that he clearly understood and documented the fact that evolution must have taken place.

On the positive side, Cuvier rigorously practiced the principles of observation exemplified in the work of Linnaeus and provided the foundations for the modern sciences of comparative anatomy and paleontology. Ironically, these two disciplines offer the most conclusive direct evidence for evolution. Furthermore, Cuvier produced a mass of work that destroyed forever the basis of the conception of a hierarchical Great Chain of Being.

Because of his work in paleontology, Cuvier was well aware of the sequences of time represented by superimposed layers of sedimentary rock. He was also aware of the graded changes in the fossilized forms of life contained within successive strata. Since he believed that all organisms were the result of special creation, he was forced to postulate a succession of special creations to account for the observable fossil record.

More than half a century earlier, Linnaeus had believed that all life now visible on earth dated from the time of the Biblical flood. Cuvier still held that view, but to it he added a succession of previous deluges and subsequent creations to account for the progression of changes visible in the fossil record. While he still attempted to view the world as fixed, rigid, and unalterable, it is evident that a major concession had been made. Change was recognized, even if it was considered to be of catastrophic and supernatural origin.

Concession, however, is hardly the same as creation in the scien-

Figure 7. James Cowles Prichard (1786–1848). Distinguished English physical anthropologist and alienist. Author of *Researches Into the Physical History of Mankind* (1813) and *The Natural History of Man* (1843).

tific world (it might be added that the successive catastrophes and creations invoked by Cuvier were not even his own ideas, having enjoyed considerable popularity for many years). The overall influence of Cuvier was to retard creative thinking, and it comes as no surprise, therefore, that a really convincing exposition of evolution and its mechanism (natural selection) was not to be a product of French scientific thought.

The final irony in connection with Cuvier's thought and influence concerns his reaction to questions relating to the possibility of the discovery of fossil humans. His pronouncement on this subject was *"L'homme fossile n'existe pas!"* Fossil humanity does not exist! As fate would have it, more evidence for the existence of fossil humanity has come from France than from any other part of the world.

Darwin's Revolutionary Work

It is generally granted that full-scale evolutionary thinking had its first convincing expression in the writings of Charles Darwin (1809–1882). Darwin's work represented the culmination of a sequence of intellectual development of quite respectable ancestry. European thinkers of the previous century had clearly expounded evolutionary views when human society was the subject of their concern. Rousseau, Condorcet, and Diderot, Kant, Herder, and Goethe, and Hume and Malthus from the French-, German-, and En-

Figure 8. Charles Darwin (1809–1882). Photograph taken in 1854 at the age of 45. Author of *The Origin of Species* (1859). (Courtesy of the British Museum, Natural History.)

18 glish-speaking worlds, respectively, had written of the natural development of social systems. Since the conditions of human society are so clearly controlled by our choice of activity, and since written history records great changes in human activities and societies, it is not unexpected that mutability and the forces effecting change should first be appreciated in the social sphere. So that Shelley could write at the beginning of the nineteenth century:

> Man's yesterday may ne'er be like his morrow;
> Naught may endure but mutability.

By the mid-nineteenth century sufficient thought and systematic observation had accumulated to make the time ripe for a synthesis by a powerful mind such as that of Charles Darwin. One could name a number of English scientific workers whose evolutionary views, closely resembling those of Darwin's, appeared during the half century prior to *The Origin of Species* (Blyth, Wells, Lawrence, Prichard, Lyell, Matthew, Chambers, Wallace), but this in no way diminishes the originality and importance of Darwin's great work.

Perhaps it is significant that such a development should occur in

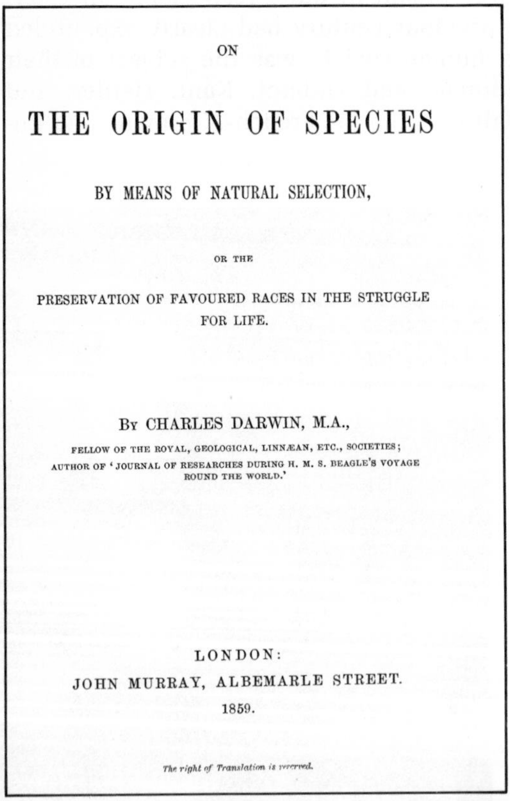

ON

THE ORIGIN OF SPECIES

BY MEANS OF NATURAL SELECTION,

OR THE

PRESERVATION OF FAVOURED RACES IN THE STRUGGLE
FOR LIFE.

By CHARLES DARWIN, M.A.,

FELLOW OF THE ROYAL, GEOLOGICAL, LINNÆAN, ETC., SOCIETIES;
AUTHOR OF 'JOURNAL OF RESEARCHES DURING H. M. S. BEAGLE'S VOYAGE
ROUND THE WORLD.'

LONDON:
JOHN MURRAY, ALBEMARLE STREET.
1859.

The right of Translation is reserved.

Figure 9. Title page of *The Origin of Species* (1859).

Figure 10. The back of Downe House and grounds, in the tranquility of which *The Origin of Species* was written.

England. There the Industrial Revolution originated and was already a hundred years old when Darwin's book was published. There changes in the social system had occurred by gradual rather than revolutionary means. Wealth and power could be attained by individual effort and no longer necessarily depended on inherited position. This is not to say that reverence for the *status quo* had disappeared, but the idea of progress, of change for the better, had become a genuine value for the first time. Darwin certainly was greatly stimulated by the expressed ideology of laissez-faire capitalism, and from it took over the idea of competition as a moving force in the world of nature. The result was that the principle of natural selection tended to be viewed in dramatic competitive imagery—"Nature red in tooth and claw," as Tennyson wrote.* Darwin himself never expressed it in quite such lurid terms, though he did, in *The Origin of Species*, frequently speak of "the warfare of Nature."

*Tennyson had read Lyell's 1837 *Principles of Geology* and Chambers' 1844 *Vestiges of Creation*.

Evolutionary Thought and Biological Anthropology

Darwin made evolution respectable. His work was presented in a sober and quiet voice with a mass of personally compiled and easily understandable supporting evidence, and with natural selection he furnished a guiding principle. This principle not only constituted an effective means by which evolution could occur, but it was such a simple, obvious, and inevitable process that, once understood, it became impossible to imagine a world in which evolution did not occur.

With these considerations in mind, Darwin's impact on both popular and scientific thinking easily qualifies him for the title "the father of evolutionary thought." As such, Darwin occupies a position of key importance in many more fields of interest than those merely limited to the field of biology. For example, the science of anthropology, the comparative study of the evolution of peoples and cultures, recognizes his particular importance, although Darwin would not have regarded himself as an anthropologist.

Biological anthropology, the comparative study of the evolution of man as an organism, has been most explicit in its recognition of Darwin's importance, since it is evident that all specifically evolutionary studies must claim him as an intellectual father. Recently, cultural anthropology has been approaching the study of the origin and development of culture from the evolutionary point of view, and, while ideas of social evolution go back to the eighteenth century, Darwin's work has been given increased recognition.

Even though evolutionary thinking now colors all interpretive

Figure 11. Darwin's study at Downe House in which *The Origin of Species* was written. Etching made by Axel Haig in 1882.

Figure 12. Thomas Henry Huxley (1825–1895) at the age of 58. Comparative anatomist, whose *Evidence as to Man's Place in Nature* (1863) and numerous other writings place him in the forefront of nineteenth century physical anthropologists. Painting by John Collier. (Courtesy National Portrait Gallery.)

generalizations in the biological sciences, including biological anthropology, many areas of specific and observational studies do not necessarily depend on an evolutionary viewpoint and historically have their roots in pre-Darwinian times. The accumulation of information contributing to a knowledge of basic human biology dates back to the collection of writings attributed to Hippocrates (c.460–c.370 B.C.), the Greek physician, and even before. Until quite recently, the accumulation of such knowledge was a more or less incidental by-product of the work of medical men. Historians of science can point to the work of the Renaissance anatomist and physician Andreas Vesalius (1514–1564) who laid the foundations for all subsequent investigations in human anatomy, but his contribution was most specifically to medical knowledge, however important it may have been for the advancement of basic human biology.

Blumenbach

The individual often given the title "father of physical anthropology" is Johann Friedrich Blumenbach (1752–1840), professor of anatomy at the University of Göttingen, Germany. As a pre-Darwinian

Evolutionary Thought and Biological Anthropology

Figure 13. Johann Gottfried Blumenbach (1752–1840). The father of physical anthropology. Author of *De Generis Humani Varietate Nativa* (1775).

savant, Blumenbach's work was not influenced by evolutionary concepts, although it is worth noting that he attempted to explain human differences by viewing them as adaptive responses to differing environments. His writings touch on all aspects of human variation —skeleton, internal organs, hair, skin, teeth, and similarities and differences when compared with nonhuman Primates. With the broad range of utilized knowledge characteristic of his eighteenth-century background, Blumenbach functioned more like a modern biological anthropologist than his increasingly specialized successors in the nineteenth century, despite his generally nonevolutionary viewpoint.

At first thought, it might seem as though the addition of an evolutionary orientation to the kind of interest in human biology, represented by Blumenbach, would have produced a science recognizable as biological anthropology, yet this did not immediately occur. To be sure, interest in human biology, and specifically in human evolution, greatly increased during the latter part of the nineteenth and the first part of the twentieth centuries, to the extent that the term "anthropology" in Germany, and particularly in France, refers to what is called more specifically "biological anthropology" in the English-speaking world. In spite of this heightened interest in human variations and their origins, the increasing specialization with-

Introduction

Figure 14. Sir Arthur Keith (1866–1955), anatomist and physical anthropologist, at the desk in Darwin's study. Author of *The Antiquity of Man* (London, 1925).

in the different areas of interest meant that professional students of human biology tended to be less and less well grounded in what are now called the social sciences. This growing compartmentalization has progressed so far that a feeling almost of antagonism has developed between natural and social scientists. Natural scientists, justly proud of the progress made in physics and chemistry during the last half century, have occasionally felt that such fields as general anthropology, sociology, economics, and the like are not true sciences, and the social scientists have tended to react by proliferating increasingly formidable terminologies of their own.

In America the field of anthropology owes its existence largely to the efforts of Franz Boas (1858–1942), who had been trained in the physical, natural, and social sciences at the doctoral level, and who clearly perceived the difficulties that would follow a dismember-

Figure 15. Franz Boas (1858–1942). Cultural and physical anthropologist. Author of *Changes in Bodily Form of Descendants of Immigrants* (1911) and *The Mind of Primitive Man* (1911) (Courtesy of the late Dr. Ernst Boas.)

Figure 16. William King Gregory (1876–1970). American paleontologist and distinguished contributor to our knowledge of the origin and evolution of the human dentition and of the primates. From the painting by Charles G. Chapman.

Figure 17. Aleš Hrdlička (1869–1943). American physical anthropologist. Author of *The Skeletal Remains of Early Man* (1930). (Courtesy of the Smithsonian Institution.)

ment of the science of humanity. Despite the occasional abrasiveness, the more successful departments of anthropology in the United States have continued to house both cultural and biological anthropologists.

Where biological anthropology, a name that is more in keeping with the scope of the modern discipline than physical anthropology, has remained within the medical domain, as is largely the case in Europe today, there has been less success in understanding the course of human evolution and its mechanics than is the case where biological and cultural anthropologists habitually rub elbows. The reason for this lies in the fact that the key to human survival is in human culture, and an understanding of culture past and present is necessary before there can be any adequate appreciation of the selective forces that have determined the course of human evolution.

Culture, the component of human possessions and human behavior derived from the activities and learning of previous generations, can be regarded as humanity's primary adaptive mechanism. An understanding of the evolution of any organism requires an appreciation of its adaptation, and hence the student of human evolution must be sensitive to the role played by human culture throughout the course of humanity's existence. This is a simple enough concept and quite obvious when stated, but, like so many other "obvious"

Evolutionary Thought and Biological Anthropology

26 concepts, it was not at all obvious until it was put into words. This has only been done within the last few years. So it is, that in spite of a full century of evolutionary studies, and the even longer accumulation of basic biological information, it is only now that a fully coherent picture of human evolution can be developed, and the field of biological anthropology can properly emerge from the union of its essential but diverse components.

Suggested Readings

APPLEMAN, P. (editor). *Darwin.* W. W. Norton, New York, 1970.
A superb collection of texts, backgrounds, contemporary opinions, and critical essays relating to Darwin and the Darwinian revolution. Almost seven hundred pages, and the paperback astonishingly inexpensive.

BRODERICK, A. H. *Father of Prehistory: The Abbé Henri Breuil: His Life and Times.* William Morrow, New York, 1963.
Henri Breuil, the leading prehistoric archeologist of his time, was born in 1877 and died in 1961. He thus spanned the periods of maximum archeological discovery in the nineteenth and twentieth centuries. This book tells his story, and since it is told by one who knew him well, it possesses both authority and understanding, and presents an illuminating history of archeology through the life and practice of one of its luminaries.

CASSON, S. *The Discovery of Man.* Harper & Row, New York, 1939.
A delightful history of man's research into his own origins, which traces the growth of both archeology and anthropology from their beginnings to modern times.

DANIEL, G. E. *A Hundred Years of Archaeology.* Macmillan, New York, 1950.
Deals with the development of prehistoric archeology in the period 1840–1940.

DARWIN, C. *On the Origin of Species.* John Murray, London, 1859.
There are many editions of this famous book. An inexpensive facsimile edition, with a valuable introduction by Ernst Mayr, was published in 1964 by the Harvard University Press.

———. *The Descent of Man.* 2 vols. John Murray, London, 1871.
A fundamental book.

EISELEY, L. *Darwin's Century: Evolution and the Men Who Discovered It.* Doubleday, New York, 1958.
A fine book on the discovery of evolution, written by an anthropologist.

ELLEGÅRD, A. *Darwin and the General Reader.* Gothenburg Studies in English, vol. 8, Göteborg, Sweden, 1958.

A study of the reception of Darwin's theory of evolution in the British periodical press, 1859–1872. Indispensable.

GLASS, B., O. TEMKIN, and W. L. STRAUS (editors). *Forerunners of Darwin: 1745–1859*. The Johns Hopkins University Press, Baltimore, 1959.
 Along with Lovejoy's book, the essays included present a view of the eighteenth century intellectual ethos, which is often overlooked by writers familiar principally with nineteenth and twentieth century sources.

GREENE, J. *The Death of Adam*. New American Library, New York, 1960.
 A history of the development of evolutionary ideas from Newton's day to their fulfillment in Darwin.

GRUBER, H. E. *Darwin on Man: A Psychological Study of Scientific Creativity Together with Darwin's Early and Unpublished Notebooks*. Transcribed and Annotated by Paul H. Barrett. E. P. Dutton, New York, 1974.
 A remarkable study of Darwin that combines a consideration of his family background with an analysis of his extensive but previously unpublished early notebooks to show how the formulation of evolution by means of natural selection gradually developed in his mind.

HADDON, A. C. *History of Anthropology*, 2nd ed. Watts, London, 1934.
 A brief and basic history of anthropology.

HARRIS, M. *The Rise of Anthropological Theory: A History of Theories of Culture*. Thomas Y. Crowell, New York, 1968.
 The most recent and by far the most thorough attempt to analyze and present the history of general anthropological theory.

HUNTER, D. E., and P. WHITTEN (editors). *Encyclopedia of Anthropology*. New York, Harper & Row, 1976.
 Excellent, and indispensably useful.

HUXLEY, T. H. *Evidence as to Man's Place in Nature*. Williams & Norgate, London, 1863.
 The 1896 edition is the best of this classic work, applying to man the principles that Darwin in the *Origin* had strategically not referred to man. A good reprint of the 1863 edition, with an introduction by Ashley Montagu, is published by the University of Michigan Press, 1959.

KING-HELE, D. *Erasmus Darwin*. Scribners, New York, 1963.
——. *The Essential Writings of Erasmus Darwin*. Hillary House, New York, 1968.
 A fine brief biography of a man of great genius whose far-ranging and original mind took the whole world of nature for his province, and whose evolutionary writings paved the way for the reception of his grandson's, Charles Darwin's, ideas.

28   The second volume presents a most attractive selection of Erasmus Darwin's writings, with a linking commentary by the editor.

LOVEJOY, A. O. *The Great Chain of Being*. Harper & Row, Harper Torchbooks, New York, 1960.
> This is a reprint of the original 1936 edition. It is an intellectual tour de force and one of the classics among writings on the history of science.

MEGGERS, B. J. (editor). *Evolution and Anthropology: A Centennial Appraisal*. The Anthropological Society of Washington, D.C., Washington, D.C., 1959.
> Eight lectures on the influence of evolutionary theory on the various branches of anthropology.

MILLHAUSER, M. *Just Before Darwin*. Wesleyan University Press, Middletown, Connecticut, 1959.
> A study of Robert Chambers' *Vestiges of the Natural History of Creation*, 1844, the book that prepared the way for Darwin's *Origin*.

MONTAGU, ASHLEY. *Edward Tyson, M. D., F.R.S. (1650–1708): And the Rise of Human and Comparative Anatomy in England*. American Philosophical Society, Philadelphia, 1943.
> A study of the development of evolutionary ideas written about the life of the man who wrote the first comparative anatomy of an ape and a man, and who was a cousin, seven generations removed, of Darwin!

———. *Darwin, Competition, and Cooperation*. Schuman, New York, 1952.
> A critical examination of the misuse of such terms as "The survival of the fittest," "The warfare of Nature," and "The competitive struggle for existence," and a consideration of the role of cooperation in evolution.

PENNIMAN, T. K. *A Hundred Years of Anthropology*, 3rd ed. Macmillan, New York, 1964.
> A good historical survey of anthropology.

SLOTKIN, J. S. (editor). *Readings in Early Anthropology*. Aldine, Chicago, 1965.
> A comprehensive anthology of pre-scientific writings on the nature, origin, history, and behavior of man.

STAUFFER, R. C. (editor). *Charles Darwin's Natural Selection*. Cambridge University Press, New York, 1975.
> As nearly as scholars have been able to reconstruct it, this, from his own previously unpublished (and published) work, is the "Big Book" that Darwin had been working on for three years when Wallace's paper of 1858 moved him to abandon it and produce the condensation published as *The Origin* in 1859. This together with Gruber's book documents the magnitude of Darwin's efforts, proving beyond dispute the nature and scope of his creative genius.

TOWNSEND, J. *A Dissertation on the Poor Laws.* University of California Press, Berkeley, 1971. With a Foreword by Ashley Montagu. Originally published anonymously in 1788 by "A Well-Wisher to Mankind," this is the first work in which the principle of natural selection is clearly enunciated. Its influence on Malthus was considerable, and thus indirectly equally so on Darwin.

Organic Continuity

On the Origin of Life

In order to appreciate the operation of natural forces in the production of cumulative organic change, i.e., evolution, it is necessary to understand something of the normal manner in which organic life is perpetuated. In an age when special creations and other supernatural phenomena were accepted as matters of course, it did not occur to people to question the assumption that flies, worms, insects, mice, in fact, life itself, arose by spontaneous generation in mud or trash or other organic refuse. The benevolent Belgian physician Jean Baptiste van Helmont (1577–1644) had even seen rats arise from bran and old rags. By the mid-nineteenth century, however, the investigation of the natural mechanics of the universe had proceeded to such a point that there was a growing tendency to attempt to explain the operation of all observable phenomena by logical, natural, and understandable means. Hence Darwin.

Among the various researches being pursued at that time, some of the most outstanding were those undertaken by the students and associates of the physiologist Johannes Müller in Berlin. Two of these, Jakob Schleiden and Theodor Schwann, are credited with making the scientific world aware of the importance of the cell as a basic building block in all organic life. This interest was epitomized by the statements of another of Müller's protégés who eventually became his successor, Rudolf Virchow, the founder of cellular pathology and later a distinguished physical anthropologist. Virchow explicitly regarded all organisms as being communities of cells, and he expressed what was to become a guiding biological principle when he said that all cells must arise from other cells. *Omnis cellula e cellula.*

Within a few years Pasteur had performed his famous experiments, which forever discredited spontaneous generation, and for the remainder of the nineteenth century the frontiers of basic biological research lay in investigations concerned with determining the mechanics of the cell. The egg was recognized as being a single cell, and it became increasingly clear that in order to understand organic growth and differentiation as well as organic perpetuation, the phenomena of cell division had to be investigated.

The Discovery of the Principles of Heredity

With the development of improved cytological staining techniques and microscopes of high quality during the 1880s, the various stages of ordinary cell division (mitosis) were observed. In the same period observations were made on the union of sperm and egg cells that universally precedes the accumulation of cell divisions involved in the growth and development of a single organism. The presence of chromosomes within the cell nucleus had been known for some time, but with the new staining techniques they could be more easily studied—the very name "chromosomes" means colored bodies—and it was realized that the precise number of chromosomes in the cells of any given plant or animal always remained constant. This, plus the realization that chromosomes were practically the only contribution made by the sperm in transmitting the male half of inheritance, led to the suspicion that the stuff of heredity, the basic genetic material, was located in these chromosomes.

As a final refinement, the Freiburg zoologist, August Weismann, predicted that the cellular division processes that produced the sex cells, the egg and the sperm, must include one stage where the process of chromosomal duplication, which normally accompanies cell division, was inhibited. He realized that if this were not true, then the union of sperm and egg at fertilization would double the number of chromosomes each generation. Observation quickly bore out this prediction, and the 1880s saw the demonstration and verification of the phenomenon of reduction division (meiosis) whereby the sex cells are furnished with only half the normal complement of chromosomes (the haploid set). Fertilization was then observed to restore the full (diploid) set to the developing zygote with half of its genetic material being contributed by each parent (see Figure 22).

By the 1890s, the basic phenomena of cell division and sexual reproduction were well known, and the time was ripe for the development of some scheme that could explain the transmission and assortment of characteristics under the control of heredity. A number of such schemes had already been proposed, among them the theory of "pangenesis" offered by Darwin, but the only one of these that was actually correct was almost completely unknown. These were the principles discovered by the Moravian abbot Gregor Mendel (1822–1884), who had published his work in 1866. This appeared in *The Proceedings of the Natural History Society of Brünn* (now Brno, Czechoslovakia) and although this was not a particularly important journal, it was available in most of the major European libraries. In spite of this, and in spite of the fact that Mendel carried on an extensive correspondence with the German botanist von Nägeli, sending him relatively detailed accounts of his experiments and ideas, his work and insights were completely ignored.

Darwin's work of 1859 formally initiated an era in which interest in the possibilities of evolution led to an increasing concern for information on the mechanics of organic perpetuation. Because of the involvement of evolutionary thought with the occurrence of accu-

Figure 18. Gregor Mendel (1822–1884). Moravian abbot, discoverer of the laws of heredity. (Courtesy of Professor Luigi Gedda.)

discovering the source of new variations. Darwin himself simply had faith in the sufficiently frequent origin of novelty — a faith supported by an immense amount of personal observation and accumulated evidence.

Darwin's Pangenesis

Critics pointed out that, even with new variants arising occasionally, they would breed with the existing population and the variation would become so diluted within a very short time that it would effectively be lost. This criticism worried Darwin enough so that he devoted a considerable amount of thought to meeting it, and, as a result, produced a theory of inheritance which, although incorrect, had one important element of similarity to that proposed by Mendel. This was the theory of pangenesis, which suggested that each cell of an organism gives off minute particles (Darwin called them gemmules) that are collected via the blood stream and stored in the gonads prior to transmission to the next generation. These particles then supervised the construction of cells similar to those that had produced them. While there were many insurmountable difficulties that eventually deprived this hypothesis of its effectiveness as an explanation of heredity, yet the concept that inherited characters are produced by the action of specific particles or units was essentially correct, and it solved the problems that arose when inheritance was assumed to be a "blending" of the maternal and paternal contributions.

The idea that heredity was particulate in its nature was one of the most important contributions of Mendel, and it is interesting to note that the powerful mind of Charles Darwin had also appreciated the fact that the apparently sporadic transmission of various traits could only be explained by assuming that the hereditary substance was made of discrete particles. The major flaw in pangenesis was the assumption that influences which altered the form of the cells would result in their giving off altered gemmules. This, in fact, was a statement involving the transmission of acquired characteristics and shows how Darwin came to fall into a Lamarckian position.

Mendel's Experiments

Mendel, however, was less concerned with the origin of variation than with the mechanics involved in the transmission of characteristics already a part of the hereditary endowment. Not that he was unaware of evolution or the implications of an understanding of the laws of heredity for evolutionary thought. His library contained a well-read copy of Darwin's work with his own marginal notations, and it is abundantly evident that Mendel's discoveries were not simply fortunate guesses, but rather the result of intelligent, well-planned, and brilliantly executed basic scientific research.

At a time when the origin of change was a major consideration, he was chiefly concerned with the ordinary facts of organic continuity, but it is not so much the subject of his inquiry that accounted for his failure to make an impression, as it was his method of approach. In retrospect this method scarcely seems remarkable since it involved assumptions that form one of the foundation stones of twentieth century science—quantification—but, at the time, this was so novel that virtually no one perceived the significance of what he had done.

While his records show that he performed breeding experiments on several kinds of plants, he is most famous for his work with the garden pea *(Pisum sativum)*. The choice of this humble plant was deliberate and reflects Mendel's intuitive grasp of the problem even before he began his experiments. He chose the pea since, as a self-pollinating plant, the various strains bred true indefinitely, and the only way in which different elements could be introduced was by artificial pollination. Furthermore, the several commercially available varieties possessed a series of traits that differed in easily distinguishable and simply inherited ways. He chose varieties distinguished by differences in seven simple traits that occurred either in one condition or another, for example:

> shape of the pea, whether wrinkled or round,
> color of the pea, whether green or yellow,
> length of the stem, whether tall or short,

and so on for the remainder.

When he cross-pollinated differing strains, he did something that biologists were not to do until another generation—he kept careful records and *he counted the results*. As a consequence, he discovered that the ratio of forms of whatever trait he chose remained constant from the second subsequent generation on. In the first generation after the cross, now referred to as the first filial or F_1 generation, he discovered that one form of whatever trait was being considered characterized all the plants. If, for instance, the parental generation included plants from both tall and short strains, he found that the entire F_1 generation was tall. When this was allowed to pollinate itself and produce a second filial or F_2 generation, he noted that three-quarters of the F_2's were tall but one quarter was short.

Subsequently, the aggregate offspring of all succeeding generations maintained this 3:1 ratio, but, when more detailed examination was made, it transpired that the short plants produced only short offspring when allowed to fertilize themselves. Also, one out of every three tall plants was capable of producing only tall offspring, while the remaining two-thirds of the tall plants produced both tall and short offspring in the 3 : 1 ratio. Thus, the external characteristics of his F_2 generation revealed only the two forms present in the original parental strains, but in terms of their potential, there were three kinds of plant present; one of which produced only short, one only tall, and the remainder able to produce both. Geneticists in the twentieth century have given these phenomena labels: the appearance is called the *phenotype*, the breeding potential is called the *genotype*. While Mendel did not use these terms, for our discussion it will be convenient to do so.

Mendel realized that his ratios could be most efficiently explained if one assumed that each trait was controlled by units, or factors, and if an individual inherited one such factor from each parent. In any individual, then, each trait would be controlled by a minimum of two such units. A Danish botanist was to christen these unit characters *genes* early in the twentieth century, and, again, we shall use the term for the sake of convenience.

Figure 19 diagramatically illustrates the preceding. In the parental generation, the true breeding tall strain has a double dose of the tall factor, or, in modern terms, is homozygous for tallness as is illustrated by a genotype of TT. The true breeding short strain is given the symbols tt to illustrate that, genotypically, it is homozygous for shortness. Since one half the genetic endowment of the offspring comes from each parent, and the tall parent can only pass on T, and the short parent t, inevitably the genotype of the first filial generation must be Tt, that is, mixed or heterozygous.

Now while the F_1 generation is genotypically mixed, it is phenotypically tall since, in *Pisum sativum*, the edible garden pea, tallness predominates over shortness. This is the phenomenon of dominance, and, in this case, the gene for tallness is dominant and the gene for shortness is called recessive. In all the characters in Mendel's experiment, one condition was dominant over its alternative, and Mendel believed he had discovered a general law of heredity, the law of dominance. Actually he did not take into account the fact that he had deliberately chosen characters that were expressed in an either-or fashion and had thus predetermined his results.

In later work with other plants, he noticed that in crossing certain strains of red and white flowers, the F_1 generation was pink. The F_2 generation then produced red, pink, and white offspring in the 1 : 2 : 1 ratio, and it was evident that the phenotype was an accurate indicator for the genotype. Such instances were called cases of partial dominance, and, in the vast quantity of genetic information that has accumulated since Mendel's time, it has become clear that the phenomenon of dominance does not warrant the status of a general law, as he had assumed.

Organic Continuity

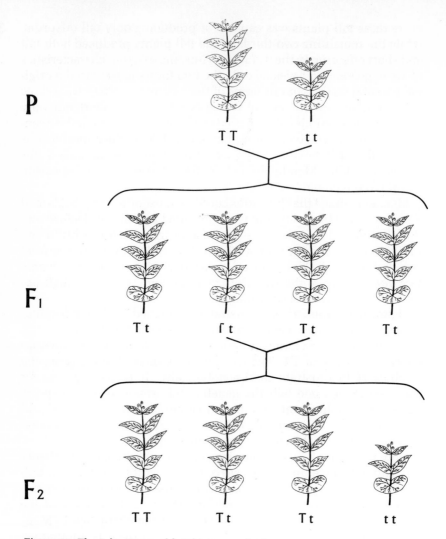

Figure 19. The inheritance of height in pea plants illustrating the Mendelian ratio. In the parental generation (P) one plant carries two "factors" for height *TT*, while the other plant carries two "factors" for shortness *tt*. The offspring in the first filial generation (F_1) each carry one "factor" from each parent *Tt*. In the second filial generation F_2 there will be 3 tall plants to every short plant because the "factors" will usually be distributed in the manner illustrated and because big *T* happens to dominate little *t*. It was from such painstaking observations of the transmission of particulate traits that Mendel was able to derive the basic laws of inheritance.

The other principles he deduced, however, have been proven by 37
the test of time and repeated experimental confirmation and are
basic to the understanding of all problems related to organic continuity and, ultimately, evolution. His basic contribution can be generalized in the following manner:

1. Heredity is particulate in nature, that is, the hereditary material
   of any organism is made up of discrete units. Today we call
   them genes.
2. The distribution of these units among the offspring of any particular mating is entirely a matter of chance.
3. The association of more than one of these units in a given individual or even in successive generations does not influence the
   unit itself. If any unit (gene) is segregated by chance (according
   to generalization number 2) it will be fully expressed despite
   the previous combinations in which it may have occurred.

Since the rediscovery of Mendel's work, some biologists have elevated various of these generalizations to the status of "laws." Actually, according to strict logic, the first one could be regarded as a major
principle or law, and the next two as conditions or corollaries, since
their expression depends on the existence of the units. Unfortunately during Mendel's lifetime neither the basic nature of cellular reproduction nor the power of a quantitative approach to biological
problems was sufficiently understood for the scientific world to
have recognized the value of his work. He died in 1884, a respected
and beloved ecclesiastical figure, head of the powerful monastery of
Altbrünn, widely known for his struggle to preserve the rights of the
monastery against the encroachments of Habsburg tyranny, and totally ignored by the world of science.

The Rediscovery of Mendel's Work

In 1900, more than fifteen years after Mendel's death and some thirty-five years after his fundamental work had been reported, the accumulation of knowledge in the various branches of biology had
advanced to the point where the quantitative predictions of a Mendelian kind of formulation could be appreciated. Inevitably, when
the world is ready for a discovery, someone makes it, and the readi-
ness of the biological world for a quantitative genetic formulation
was indicated by the fact that three separate workers independently
came to the same conclusions as a result of similar courses of research. What is even more interesting, each, having realized the
import of his discovery, combed the botanic literature to see whether
there was any support for such a formulation, and each independently rediscovered Mendel's classic publication and gave Mendel

full credit for the initial discovery. The Dutch botanist Hugo de Vries, the German botanist Karl Correns, and the Austrian botanist Erich Tschermak announced their independent and nearly identical discoveries within the space of four months in papers read before the German Botanical Society, and, as a result of their insistence, the quantitative picture of heredity that underlies twentieth century biology is called Mendelian genetics.

The Development of Genetics

During the decade following the rediscovery of Mendel, it was discovered that his predictive scheme worked for many organisms and not just for peas. Mendel's "factors" were given the name of *genes* by the Danish botanist Wilhelm Johannsen (1857 – 1927), and it was recognized that chromosomes, as observed under the microscope, behaved in somewhat the same way Mendelian theory predicted that genes should behave. It was soon realized, however, that there were many more genes than chromosomes. The suggestion was offered that chromosomes were structures which carried the genes, and the experimental work that followed provided ample confirmation. Microscopic investigations of cell structure, cytology, joined with quantitative breeding investigations to create the field of cytogenetics, which has given us a far better understanding of the working of heredity than either field could have done separately.

If genes were carried on the chromosomes and chromosomes were constantly transmitted from one generation to another, then presumably those genes that occurred on the same chromosome would be transmitted as a linked group and would not assort at random as strict Mendelian theory would claim. In individual cases this was partially confirmed, but, for populations as a whole, the complete randomness of Mendelian theory was observed. The solution to this problem and to many others was provided by the work of Thomas Hunt Morgan (1866 – 1945) and his associates at Columbia University. Beginning in 1910, Morgan carried out a series of brilliant experiments using *Drosophila melanogaster*, commonly known as the fruit fly. Hitherto much of the basic information concerning heredity came from work on plants, but the selection of *Drosophila* greatly accelerated things. Thousands of flies can be raised in the laboratory at very little cost, and they produce a new generation every two weeks. *Drosophila* possesses one other great advantage, although this was not discovered until the 1930s, and this is the fact that the salivary glands of the larval form have cells with gigantic chromosomes some one hundred times longer than those of other cells. Subsequently this meant that the hard-won conclusions of early *Drosophila* research could be checked microscopically.

By 1915, Morgan's group had observed that certain specific traits were almost always transmitted together. It was postulated that chromosomes were linear arrangements of genes with the loci for traits inherited together being adjacent. This tendency to be transmitted together was called genetic linkage, and it was found that there were four linkage groups for *Drosophila* that corresponded to the four chromosome pairs. There are twenty-three such pairs in man, one of these pairs consisting of the sex chromosomes. The components of this particular pair are unmatched, one being the X and the other the Y chromosome. A Y chromosome in association with an X chromosome determines the sex of the individual as male. An X chromosome associated with another X chromosome determines the sex of the individual as female.

CROSSOVER

Since there were different degrees of the regularity with which traits in the same linkage group (i.e., chromosome) were transmitted to-

Figure 20. Thomas Hunt Morgan (1866–1945). One of the founding fathers of modern genetics. (Courtesy of the New York Academy of Medicine.)

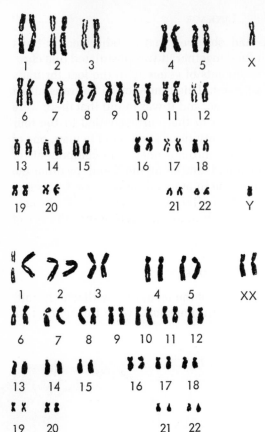

Figure 21. The chromosomes of the human male (above) and the human female (below). (Courtesy of Dr. Kurt Hirschhorn.)

gether, Morgan postulated that this must be related to their positions on the chromosome. Closely linked characters are controlled by genes that occur side by side. At first it seemed that Mendel's criterion of independent assortment was therefore invalid, but information from whole populations showed that this was not true. Morgan realized that at some time during reduction division when the sex cells were being produced, parts of the halves of chromosome pairs must get tangled and exchanged—a process called crossover. Experiments showed that crossover could occur anywhere along the length of a chromosome pair with equal probability. Evidently if one gene locus (position on the chromosome) is right next to another gene locus, crossover will only rarely dissociate the two, but if one investigates genes whose loci occur at opposite ends of the chromosome, any crossover to which the chromosome is subject will separate them.

Within a large population, crossover occurs often enough so that there is no evident association between the various genes on a single chromosome, and since, in evolutionary genetics, it is the survival of

General Biological Background

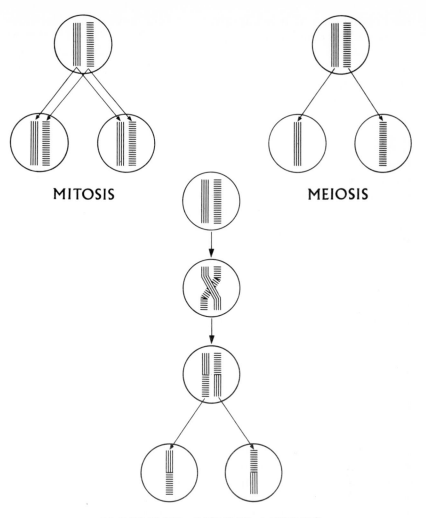

MITOSIS

MEIOSIS

CROSSOVER DURING MEIOSIS

Figure 22. Mitosis, meiosis, and crossover. In crossover, illustrating how genes on homologous chromosomes can be interchanged. In mitosis there is a duplication of each chromosome so that the daughter cells have one each. During meiosis each chromosome arranges itself in longitudinal contact with the one derived from the opposite parent. In this way each gene is brought into place opposite its corresponding gene (synapsis or conjugation). These chromosomes become closely entwined about each other lengthwise. It is during this crossover process that segments of each chromosome break off and become attached to the broken ends of the opposite chromosome. In this way genes that were originally located in a maternal chromosome become part of one that originally came from the father. Crossover, then, provides a major source of genetic variability.

Organic Continuity

the population which is important, it would appear that Mendel's original claim concerning the random assortment of unit characters was correct as far as evolution is concerned. For individual family lines, linkage between loci is an important phenomenon, but, when enough family lines are included in a population, crossover will assure Mendelian randomness.

SEX LINKAGE

Ordinary genetic linkage as it has been presented here should not be confused with the phenomenon referred to as sex linkage. This latter refers to loci found on that part of the X chromosome which is not matched by the associated Y chromosome. Since there is no Y chromosome locus corresponding to those on the nonhomologous part of the X chromosome, any abnormal gene occurring there will be expressed without inhibition. In humans, for instance, genes for red and green color blindness occur on the nonhomologous part of the X chromosome. If a male has such a gene on his X chromosome, it will be expressed since the Y chromosome has no corresponding locus or potentially suppressing gene. A female, however, has two X chromosomes, and, if one has an abnormal gene, there is a good chance that the corresponding locus on the other will possess a normal gene that will inhibit its expression. Two abnormal genes on the other hand will be expressed. This is why red and green color blindness is found more frequently in males than in females. The mechanism has been called sex linkage.

By the 1920s, the picture of hereditary transmission was quite well understood, although, for various sociopolitical reasons, it was eventually rejected by Russian biologists who, until recently, regarded particulate genetics as an especially evil bit of capitalist mythology. To be sure, until 1969 no one had ever seen a gene, but then neither has anyone even now actually seen a neutron or the nucleus of a hydrogen atom, and yet the Russians showed no reluctance to accept the fact of their existence and use them in the construction of a formidable weaponry. More recently the Russians have decided to accept the existence of the gene and modern genetics.

The Origin of Change

Because of the wealth of biological phenomena that has occupied the attention of research workers, it has taken biologists a full half century longer than it took physicists to come to grips with the structure of their basic particles. The nature and mode of action of the gene is only now becoming understood. In Morgan's time, however, the grosser effects of genes and chromosomes became generally known, but this did not at first explain the origin of change. Morgan, in exploring the mechanics of organic perpetuation, could not see how this could fit evolutionary interpretations, and for some years he rejected evolutionary thought.

Then in 1927, one of Morgan's former students, H. J. Muller, announced that he had produced permanent heritable changes in the genetic material of *Drosophila* as a result of subjecting them to X-rays. Spontaneously occurring heritable changes had been noticed at the turn of the century by de Vries, one of the rediscoverers of Mendel, and he had called them mutations, suggesting that these were the sources of evolutionary novelty. It was eventually realized that de Vries' changes were rare and rather unusual alterations and not the normal means by which evolution occurred, so the term mutation was given to the simple alterations in single genes observed by Muller. The simple but permanent nature of the change, and the means of its production, led Muller to postulate that a gene was actually a single molecule—reason enough why one had never been seen. Time has shown that Muller was substantially correct, but the proof had to await the development of refinements in research technology and the accumulation of results from a field which had yet to be born—molecular biology.

MOLECULAR BIOLOGY

Research in this direction started slowly and has been picking up speed ever since. Early in the 1930s, workers at the University of California purified and crystallized a virus, the simplest living thing. For some time, viruses were regarded as being possible examples of "naked genes," that is, genes without organisms attached, so there was great interest in the analysis of the crystallized viral material. Subsequent findings have shown that a virus is *not* a naked gene, but this initial theory accounts for the widely held misconception that the basic genetic material is "nucleoprotein" since the analysis of crystallized virus showed that it was entirely composed of only two substances, nucleic acid and protein. At its most basic, living matter is composed of protein and nucleic acid, and there is some justification in the statement that the most significant progress in biological research for the past several decades has come as a result of discoveries relating to the structure and modes of operation of these two classes of substances.

Among other things, the advances in basic biology during the 1940s can be traced to the use of more rapidly breeding experimental organisms. From Mendel's garden peas to Morgan's fruit flies, attention was now turned to bacteria, specifically *Escherichia coli*, the harmless colon bacillus normally found in the human large intestine. With a new generation being produced every twenty minutes, breeding experiments can be carried out in one day which would have required two years if fruit flies had been used, and in the neighborhood of 2,000 years if a subject had been used with approximately the span required for a human generation. In three years, *Escherichia coli* produces nearly as many generations as have occurred for humanity during the last million years.

DNA

In the mid-1940s it appeared that the simplest genetic changes, the smallest mutations, caused simple changes in the mode of operation of single enzymes. Enzymes themselves are proteins, the most complex of organic molecules, and for a while, as the result of work on *Neurospora*, bread mold, it was postulated that one gene controlled one enzyme. This turned out to be a little too simple; but it had become increasingly obvious that the main function of a gene is the control of protein synthesis. Then in 1952, by experiments with the colon bacillus and with a virus that infects it (a bacteriophage) it was proven that the material which carries the hereditary information is a nucleic acid, specifically deoxyribonucleic acid, generally referred to as DNA. The stage was now set for one of the most important breakthroughs in the history of science, the discovery of the exact structure and mode of action of the basic genetic material.

Until the last decade, it had been felt that the discovery of the significance of the gene was to biology what quantum mechanics was to physics, but it is now apparent that the use of the concept "gene" as a simple unstructured particle was similar to the conception of the atom as a solid irreducible particle, which prevailed in pre-twentieth century physics. In 1953, James D. Watson and Francis H. C. Crick, working in the Cavendish Laboratory at Cambridge University, proposed a structure for deoxyribonucleic acid, DNA, which has had an impact on the biological sciences comparable to the effect that nuclear theory had on the physical sciences at the beginning of this century. It is an interesting and not unilluminating fact that the Cavendish Laboratory was also the scene of some of the most fundamental work in the development of nuclear physics.

Nucleic acids, like proteins, are polymers. The term polymer (many unit) refers to the fact that these molecules are constructed of relatively simple units attached end to end in the form of a long chain. For proteins, the basic units are *amino acids*. There are some twenty amino acids, and all the varied and complex protein molecules are formed by differing numbers of these twenty amino acids in specific orders. Nucleic acids also are formed by sequences of basic units, but in their case, the constituent units are organic bases called *nucleotides* and there are only four of them. One of the problems that plagued investigators for some time was how to use these

Figure 23. Model of a portion of the DNA molecule, showing the two interlocking polynucleotide chains. Only a few of the thousands of turns in the double helix are shown. Each outer helix consists of five carbon-sugar molecules S (deoxyribose), alternating with P phosphate groups— hence, a pair of sugar-phosphate (deoxyribosephosphate) chains wound in a double helix. The helical polynucleotide chains are united by the closely-fitting paired nitrogenous bases AT adenine-thymine and GC guanine-cytosine connected by hydrogen bonds (the double lines). A, Adenine; C, Cytosine; G, Guanine; P, Phosphate; S, Sugar; T, Thymine; =, Hydrogen bonds. It has been estimated that if the helical chains (or sugar-phosphate backbones), or tapes, as they are sometimes called, in the human body were placed end-to-end, they would reach beyond the moon. Each unit phosphate-sugar-base represents a nucleotide; hence, each helix is a polynucleotide chain.

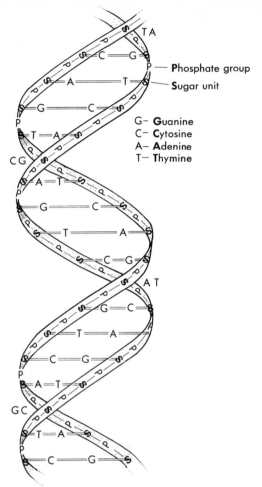

— Phosphate group
— Sugar unit

G— Guanine
C— Cytosine
A— Adenine
T— Thymine

four building blocks to construct a model that would give a clue not only to the means by which it duplicated itself, but also to the process whereby it could direct the building of protein molecules from the twenty building blocks of which they are constructed. The Watson-Crick model provided the solution to these problems, a solution for which Watson and Crick shared the Nobel prize with M. F. H. Wilkins of the University of London in 1962. It should be added here that there are many who feel that the late Rosalind Franklin, whose work greatly contributed to making the Watson-Crick model possible, should also have shared in the Nobel award.

It was known that the four bases of which DNA was composed were adenine, cytosine, guanine, and thymine, and that these attached to a helical structure made of repeating units of a sugar (de-

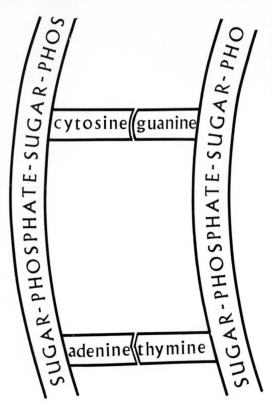

Figure 24. The sequence of subunits in a DNA molecule showing the alternation of sugars and bases in the backbone and the way nucleotide parallel strands couple with each other.

oxyribose) and phosphoric acid. Further, it was known that the amount of adenine present was always the same as the amount of thymine, and the amount of cytosine was always the same as the amount of guanine. Watson and Crick proposed that the DNA molecule was a double helix, with two phosphate-sugar chains linked via the bases attached to the sugars. The adenine attached to the sugar of one chain paired with the thymine attached to the sugar of the other chain. With guanine and cytosine behaving in similarly complementary fashion, evidently one chain was the mirror image of the other.

One of the most important characteristics of the basic genetic material is its ability to make exact copies of itself in cell division after cell division and in generation after generation. The Watson-Crick model suggests that the two strands of the usual double helix must separate during each cell division, with one half going to each daughter cell. There, the guanines pair with cytosine, the adenines with thymine, and the single helix lays down its mirror image exactly reconstituting the form of the DNA molecule of the original cell. There are still some formidable problems to be overcome in de-

General Biological Background

tailing the manner in which this process works, but undoubtedly these problems will eventually be solved.

At first it seemed even more difficult to perceive how this model could relate to protein synthesis, since it appeared extraordinary that all of the information necessary for the building and operating of an entire organism could be present within the nucleus of a single cell and written down in a code with only four symbols. Nevertheless, the discoveries of the last decade have shown that this is indeed the case. Shortly after their initial proposal, it was suggested that if the four nucleotides of DNA were to correspond somehow to the twenty amino acids of protein, then the nucleotides must occur in groups of at least three in order that there be enough unique combinations. Four taken two at a time yields only sixteen (or 4^2), while four taken three at a time makes sixty-four, which is more than enough. The group of three adjacent nucleotides is referred to as a nucleotide triplet or occasionally as a *codon*.

There were other problems, too. For example, DNA occurs largely in the nucleus, while protein synthesis takes place in minute bodies called ribosomes situated in the cytoplasm. The ribosomes, however, are also the sites where the greatest quantity of the other form of nucleic acid occurs. This is ribonucleic acid, or RNA, which differs in a minor way from DNA. Apparently RNA is laid down on the model of DNA in the nucleus, and from there it moves out into the ribosomes where it directs the synthesis of proteins from the available amino acids in the cytoplasm. Since most proteins are enzymes, which catalyze and control subsequent reactions, the production of

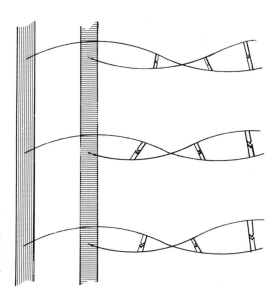

Figure 25. Proposed chromosome-DNA relation. A possible model for the way in which the double helix DNA molecules relate to the double structure of a chromosome.

proteins in the ribosomes influences the speed at which more protein enzymes are produced. This process, of course, is cumulative and accounts for the fact that tissues differentiate during growth, although the same genetic potential is to be found within the DNA of each cell nucleus of a given organism.

The hypothesis that the four nucleotides taken three at a time — a four-letter alphabet from which words only three letters long are constructed — providing explanation of the means by which the synthesis of protein is coded in the structure of nucleic acid, received brilliant confirmation by the experimental work of two groups in 1962. Research teams at New York University and at the National Institutes of Health in Maryland artificially hooked together nucleotides to form synthetic RNA molecules of known structure. These molecules were then put into an amino acid soup, and in the presence of the necessary enzymes, they managed to synthesize proteins whose structures depended upon the sequence of RNA nucleotides. Still more recently, biologically active DNA has been synthesized in the laboratory, and one group has succeeded in putting together a DNA molecule that codes for a specific enzyme. They have in fact created a "gene" in the laboratory.

Many problems still remain to be cleared up, for instance, the exact relationship between the basic genetic material, DNA, and the chromosome, which is a linear structure of a protein nature. Also the exact mechanics by which the helical DNA molecule unwinds itself and then synthesizes its mirror image remains unknown. Yet with the basic foundations provided by the research of the recent past, there is every reason to expect that the problems that remain will be solved in the relatively near future.

The reader may have noticed that throughout our discussion of nucleic acids and proteins, we have not used the term gene. Rather we have preferred the vaguer phrase "basic genetic material." The concept of the gene, as it developed through the era of Morgan and his followers, was based on the minimal units affected by crossover. During the 1940s, there was some thought that a gene might correspond to a single enzyme. Then, in the case of the important human blood protein, hemoglobin, it was discovered that the difference between normal and abnormal forms of the molecule, inherited as a single gene trait, was simply due to the difference in the identity of one single amino acid unit out of the 600 units present. According to what we have said then, the gene in question should be the nucleotide triplet responsible for the amino acid at that particular site in the protein chain. The difficulty lies in the fact that a change in only one nucleotide can account for the difference in the amino acid called for, but if another nucleotide in the triplet is substituted instead, no change is made in the effect. Some nucleotide alterations act like single gene changes, but under certain circumstances, other such alterations do not. This only serves to illustrate the fact that the concept of the gene is a little too crude to be used effectively when one reaches the molecular level. For much of agricultural, medical, and evolutionary research, however, it remains as effective as when it was developed by Mendel a century ago.

There are many today who predict a time when humanity will be able to exercise some control over its own heredity. While one may cautiously assert that this does not appear likely within the immediately foreseeable future, yet no one even as recently as the late 1940s could have predicted the spectacular progress made by biochemical genetics in the decade following 1953. With these and other lessons clearly in mind, we shall pursue the better part of valor and refrain from making any predictions at all.

Suggested Readings

ANFINSEN, C. B. *The Molecular Basis of Evolution.* Wiley, New York, 1959.
  One of the most provocative attempts yet undertaken to relate the new findings of biochemistry to the fields of genetics and evolution.

BOYER, S. H. IV. (editor). *Papers on Human Genetics.* Prentice-Hall, Englewood Cliffs, N.J., 1963.
  A collection of some of the most significant contributions to modern human genetics.

CARTER, G. S. *A Hundred Years of Evolution.* Macmillan, New York, 1957.
  A survey of the changes of thought in evolutionary theory since the publication of Darwin's *Origin.*

DUNN, L. C. (editor). *Genetics in the 20th Century.* Macmillan, New York, 1951.
  Essays by twenty-six leading authorities on the progress of genetics during its first fifty years.

GILLISPIE, C. C. *Genesis and Geology.* Harvard University Press, Cambridge, 1951.
  A study in the relations of scientific thought, natural theology, and social opinion in Great Britain, 1790–1850.

HARRIS, H. *The Principles of Human Biochemical Genetics.* Am. Elsevier, New York, 1970.
  Demonstrates how many of the traits with known inheritance exist at the level of single molecules.

50 LUDMERER, K. M. *Genetics and American Society: A Historical Appraisal.* The Johns Hopkins University Press, Baltimore, 1972.
Social prejudice can determine what people will accept as "proven fact," and this shows that even professional scientists are not immune.

MEDVEDEV, Z. A. *The Rise and Fall of T. D. Lysenko.* Translated by I. Michael Lerner. Columbia University Press, New York, 1969.
The chilling story of what can happen when academia becomes politicized.

OLBY, R. *The Path to the Double Helix.* University of Washington Press, Seattle, 1975.
Along with Watson's personal account, Olby provides a general picture of the difficulties that have been overcome in developing the basis for our current understanding of the structure of the gene.

PROVINE, W. B. *The Origins of Theoretical Population Genetics.* University of Chicago Press, Chicago, 1971.
A thoroughly readable account of the problems that had to be overcome before genetics and Darwinian evolutionary theory could be encompassed within a single framework.

SAYRE, ANN. *Rosalind Franklin and DNA.* W. W. Norton, New York, 1975.
A supplement to Watson's *The Double Helix* recounting the role played by Rosalind Franklin in providing the clues to the structure of the DNA molecule.

SUTTON, H. E. *Genes, Enzymes, and Inherited Diseases.* Holt, Rinehart and Winston, New York, 1961.
Presents evidence for the basic nature of inherited traits.

WATSON, J. B. *The Double Helix.* Atheneum, New York, 1968.
In science as in politics, aspiration to top status sometimes leads to an understandable but not altogether elevating scramble for success. Watson provides an unblushing but fascinating account of his pursuit of the Nobel Prize.

————. *Molecular Biology of the Gene.* Benjamin, New York, 3rd ed, 1976.
A thorough and authoritative work.

Chapter 2

Principles of Evolution

Natural Selection

The great contribution of Charles Darwin, in addition to providing the evidence for the evolutionary explanation of the origin of the diversity of organic life, lay, more specifically, in the fact that he proposed the mechanism by which evolution could work. That mechanism is natural selection. To the embarrassment of the natural scientist and the annoyance of the student, natural selection is peculiarly difficult to encompass within a *simple* definition. Yet despite the difficulty in reducing it to a simple definition, there is virtually unanimous agreement in the use of the principle. The physical scientist encounters similar difficulties in defining entropy, a concept that is as useful and well understood in his confraternity as natural selection is in the biological one. The anthropologist's concept of culture is similarly useful and equally difficult to encompass within a simple definition.

By natural selection, the biologist means the aggregate of environmental forces that condition the chances for species survival, in two words, "differential fertility." In the course of time, those variants within a species that are better fitted for survival, in the face of the various environmental forces, will leave a larger progeny than the less well adapted individuals. Heredity being what it is, the offspring of the better adapted individuals will tend to exhibit characteristics similar to those that made their parents successful, and, providing that the selective forces have not altered, this will continue to favor the transmission of those characteristics. As a result of natural selection, the variant of today may become the average of tomorrow, at which time, more successful variants may arise by chance and forecast still further change for the species in question.

Nineteenth century advocates of evolution by means of natural selection, living in what has been called "The Age of Violence," tended to view the process in rather more violent terms than is customary today. For example, such terms as "the warfare of Nature," "struggle for existence," and "survival of the fittest" became established usage. Today, however, many biologists have pointed out that reproductive success is the final determiner of what the future of a species shall be, and the ability to leave adequate numbers of descendants does not necessarily depend on size, robustness, or intelligence. Individuals with well-developed procreative powers, who are otherwise merely adequate for survival, will have far greater influence on succeeding generations than the strong and vigorous but less fertile. The nineteenth century emphasis on the survival of the fittest should therefore be modified to read "the survival of the fit." The "fittest" are likely to be too rigidified to be able to exhibit the necessary flexibility called for by changes in the environment.

While Darwin's opponents could not deny the documentation he produced for the operation of selective forces, they could and did attack him for his assumptions concerning the origin of the variations that were essential if evolution by means of natural selection were to work. Darwin, with the insight built upon a lifetime of careful observation, simply took it on faith that the necessary variation arose by natural means. Long after his death and after the rebirth of the science of genetics, the source for this variation was finally located in those minute modifications of the gene, namely, mutations. In the late 1920s, long before the exact nature of a mutation was known, it was the generally accepted view that "mutations are the raw materials of evolution." They do indeed produce the variation on which naturally occurring forces operate to effect the accumulation of organic change, i.e., evolution.

Although environmental forces are responsible for exerting the selection that produces adaptive responses in organic life, this does not mean that similar environments in different areas necessarily engender identical forms of life. For a variety of reasons, apparently similar selective forces may engender quite different responses. One of the most frequent reasons why this is so is the fact that all organisms bear the traces of their previous evolutionary history, and since this is often radically different, the base on which the forces operate is different enough to have quite diverse results.

General Biological Background

To take an extreme example, the requirements for successful survival of a highly mobile organism in an aquatic ecological niche (an
ecological niche is the total life way of an organism) are limiting
enough to produce a great superficial resemblance between successful sea-going vertebrates. Whether these are whales or fishes or the
extinct Mesozoic Ichthyosaurs, they all possess streamlined bodies
propelled by powerful tails. Yet there are some striking differences.
The fishes, for example, propel themselves by means of side-to-side
tail movements while whales and dolphins, with their horizontal
tails, move them up and down. Both methods are remarkably efficient, and, at first, it might not seem apparent why one was selected
rather than the other. Why the first fishes adopted a side-to-side
movement nearly 500 million years ago is a question upon which we
can only speculate since we do not possess the fossil evidence for
precursors of the first fishes, but the reason why the whales, who after all are remote descendants of the earliest fishes, chose the up-
and-down motion is apparent when the history of pre-whale development is appreciated.

Whales are mammals with the typical mammalian warm blood
and elevated metabolism. The elevated metabolism developed as an
adaptation enabling the early mammals to inhabit a cool terrestrial
ecological niche where normally cold-blooded reptiles were less
likely to be effective. In order to maintain the elevated metabolism,
regular food intake was required and regular food intake necessitates
a reasonably efficient means of locomotion. Whereas reptiles, being
less well adapted to terrestrial locomotion, still preserve the lateral
position of their limbs, they tend to crawl with the aid of side-to-side
motions of the entire body. This is a slowed-down version of what
fish do in the water, and it is less efficient than the characteristic
mammalian form of terrestrial locomotion where the limbs are
moved in a front-to-back plane directly under and supporting the
weight of the body. To aid this movement the mammal typically
flexes and extends the backbone in the same plane of motion as the
limbs. While mammals are ultimately descended from the early fishes by way of amphibians and reptiles, the pressures conditioning
early mammalian development ensured it that the typical movement
of the backbone in aiding locomotion was in a vertical rather than a
horizontal plane.

Once this development had occurred, it affected all subsequent
mammalian history, and when one line reinvaded the oceans in the
Cenozoic, its method of meeting the requirements for success in an
oceanic ecological niche was conditioned by these previous adaptations. Powerful propelling movements of the tail could be accomplished with fewer changes in the skeletomuscular system by ensur-

ing that the tail was horizontal and the movements up-and-down, rather than by developing a vertical tail with side-to-side movements.

The superficial similarity between whales and fishes is technically a case of convergence. The selection exerted by the environment is strong enough to produce such an effect, although sufficiently radical differences remain to avert any possibility of confusing the two forms.

Genetic Drift

Evolutionary change can also occur by chance. In small populations (about 100 individuals) the *relative* amount of any given individual's contribution to the next generation is much greater than would be the case where the population size is up in the thousands or more. A mutation transmitted in a small population would have a much better chance of becoming generally established than it would in a large population, but at the same time the probability that any given character might fail to be transmitted would also be much greater. The gain or loss of genes simply due to the operation of chance on the reproductive mechanics of small populations has been called genetic drift. Since it simply depends on the accident of transmission, it is unrelated to natural selection, although the fixing or loss of characters in the genetic endowment of a population may ultimately have evolutionary significance.

As for moving evolutionary change in any persistent direction, genetic drift (often called the Sewall Wright effect in honor of the American geneticist who proposed it) has probably played an unimportant role. Since it is the result of chance only, it is necessarily nondirectional. Genetic drift can accomplish the separation of two populations of the same species that have been isolated from each other for a long time. If, for instance, two populations become separated when a rise in sea level floods the connection between their areas of habitation, then it is possible that the random accumulation of insignificant changes over the generations may proceed to the point where mutual fertility is reduced or absent when contact is reestablished. Once this degree of reproductive isolation is reached and it is no longer possible to exchange genetic material by hybridization, then the two populations have reached the level of specific difference and there are two new species. In this way, genetic drift may have played a role in speciation and to some extent in the progressive evolution of some groups.

The selective effect of similar environments on closely related forms may very well ensure that these continue to resemble each other, although they have been separated for long periods of time.

One of the classic cases is represented by the monkeys. Both New World and Old World monkeys are recognizably monkeys and quite similar in their adaptation to life in the trees of a tropical forest. However, they have been separated for fifty million years, and neither group looked like monkeys when the separation took place. The fact that they separately reached the Monkey Grade of development is a striking example of parallelism, and while this is not a particularly important principle, it does illustrate the effect that the continued operation of similar selective forces will have on similar basic organisms, despite the influence of genetic drift and other factors tending to produce differences.

Specialized vs. Unspecialized or Adaptation vs. Adaptability

All species must adapt to their environments if they are to survive, and if the environments change, the species must adapt to the changes. This is accomplished in several ways. Some organisms become closely adapted to the particular conditions of their environment. When this adaptation is particularly close, it is termed specialization. For instance, the marsupial koala bear of Australia is specialized for existence on a diet of eucalyptus leaves, which is fine if nothing happens to the eucalyptus trees. Specializations frequently enable organisms to make highly efficient use of a particular resource, but occasionally they mean that this efficiency is attained at the expense of adaptability. The fossil record is littered with the bones of animals that became overspecialized in one way or another and failed to adapt when conditions changed.

SPECIALIZATION

At this point we should interject a note of caution. There has been a tendency among paleontologists in the past to record those features of extinct animals that differentiate them from their modern counterparts, label these features "specializations," and attribute their extinction to such "specializations." This has been particularly evident in the literature dealing with fossil humans where every bump on the skull has at one time or another been called a specialization and cited as a reason for excluding the fossil in question from human ancestry. With this tendency, there has gone the assumption that any specialization is limiting and therefore of doubtful value. The reduced number of digits in a horse's foot is excellent for high-speed locomotion, but it necessarily precludes any manipulative ability. In this case, the specialization is limiting, but the specialized molar teeth of horses have no such disadvantages. With their highly complicated enamel and dentine layering, and the open, continuously growing root, the horse can eat highly abrasive foods for upward of twenty years without wearing the teeth to the gums. While horse molars are wonderfully specialized, they do not prevent the animals from eating virtually anything they choose. Perhaps the most remarkable specialization in the animal world is the human brain, yet it is just this specialization which has allowed humanity to devise the means for surviving in a variety of environments possible for no other mammal.

In contrast to specific adaptation, another trend that has been developed with great success by certain organisms is the emphasis on adaptability. Adaptability can be achieved in two ways. Either an organism can possess a morphology suitably generalized so that it can get along adequately in a variety of environments — witness the variety of habitats and diets successfully utilized by the brown rat — or it can preserve the genetic potential for producing variants capable of getting along under specifically differing conditions.

POLYMORPHISM

The reader will recall that the F_1 generation of the cross between two pure-breeding strains preserves all the genetic material of both parental lines. The offspring of the F_1, i.e., the F_2, will show the original parental conditions as well as the hybrid or heterozygous state. The preservation of several manifestations of a particular characteristic within the range of variation of a particular species is called polymorphism (many + form + ism). The continuing forces of selection dictate the changes each manifest character possesses for survival, and the proportion between them is kept in balance. Recent investigations have shown that balanced polymorphism is a relatively common means of preserving the adaptability of a species.

There is another aspect of balanced polymorphism. In many cases the heterozygous condition is the best adaptation. While the heterozygotes have the greater chances for survival (this is sometimes referred to as "hybrid vigor"), in obedience to Mendel's observed 1 : 2 : 1 ratio, 50 per cent of each succeeding generation will be homozygous. Natural selection, then, determines the proportion between the survivors, and the polymorphism is therefore in a state of balance. As we shall see when we discuss human variation later on, one of the best known examples of balanced polymorphism exists in the human hemoglobins. The operation of natural selection in discouraging the survival of the various homozygotes often appears to be a rather startling evolutionary waste, but then, in the completely opportunistic workings of evolutionary forces, the fate of certain individuals is unimportant provided that enough of the adaptively adequately endowed survive to propagate the species. This is clearly

must produce in each generation simply in order that the fish population continues to maintain itself.

PREADAPTATION

Evolution, being opportunistic as well as cumulative, frequently
takes advantage of structures developed under certain circumstances
and uses them as the base for adaptation to changed environmental
circumstances. Such a condition is referred to as preadaptation.
Preadaptation, the reapplication of structures originally developed
for other purposes, has accounted for some of the otherwise remarkable developments in evolution, although this should not be taken to
indicate that there was any such preordained plan. The four fins of
the early Paleozoic fishes were a preadaptation for later life on land,
although it should be stressed that their initial appearance was simply to enable the fish to function more efficiently in the water. It was
simply a matter of chance that it was later possible to modify fins
into the legs of the earliest land tetrapods.

Another example of preadaptation is exemplified by the whales
and dolphins we have previously mentioned. When their land-
dwelling ancestor was made over for an efficient aquatic method of
locomotion, the up-and-down capabilities of the spinal column were
utilized and adapted as the mechanism for moving the propelling
flukes of the developing tail. In this case, the type of movement had
originally been developed for effective terrestrial locomotion and
was then remade, as it were, for aquatic propulsion. As such, the
direction of spinal column movement can be regarded as a preadaptation for its subsequent use upon re-entry into an oceanic environment. Again we stress that there was no preconceived purpose involved.

Long before the development of human beings, their Primate precursors passed through a phase in which the characteristic mode of
locomotion was brachiation — hanging beneath tree branches and
proceeding hand over hand. This meant that the body developed to
function in a vertical rather than a horizontal posture, and, as far as
humans are concerned, this was a necessary preadaptation to the later adoption of an upright posture on the ground. Actually every organism is a complex of made-over characters, which accounts for the
fact that organic adaptations are so frequently complex and ineffi-
cient. Humans, as we shall see, are made-over apes. The term preadaptation, however, should be reserved for those structures that can
be reapplied in new contexts. The postural preadaptation developed
by humanity's arboreal ancestors represents an appropriate example,
as does the hand-eye coordination that successful tree living also
produced.

From time to time in evolutionary history, adaptations have arisen which have proven so successful that they have allowed a considerable expansion of the population in the areas inhabited by a particular group of organisms. When such an adaptation is so effective that it allows the possessors successfully to enter previously unoccupied or poorly filled ecological niches, then the result is what is called adaptive radiation. Birds, for example, inhabit a wide variety of ecological niches, but basically this all stems from the initial development of the ability to fly.

In the history of the development of evolutionary thought, the adaptive radiation of a particular group of finches played a crucial role, for it was this which impressed the young Charles Darwin with the importance of natural forces in shaping developments in the organic world. As the naturalist aboard the British brig H.M.S. *Beagle* on its voyage around the world, Darwin spent five years building up

Figure 26. The bills of birds furnish a good example of adaptive radiation. (Courtesy of G. Hardin, from *Biology: Its Human Implications*, and W. H. Freeman and Company.)

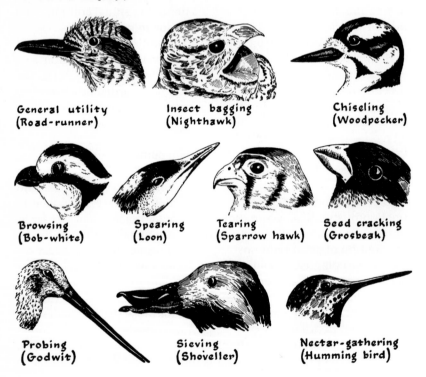

General utility
(Road-runner)

Insect bagging
(Nighthawk)

Chiseling
(Woodpecker)

Browsing
(Bob-white)

Spearing
(Loon)

Tearing
(Sparrow hawk)

Seed cracking
(Grosbeak)

Probing
(Godwit)

Sieving
(Shoveller)

Nectar-gathering
(Humming bird)

the fund of knowledge that was eventually to form the basis for his immortal work. In 1835, the *Beagle* visited the Galápagos Archipelago — a string of rocky islands some 600 miles west of the coast of South America. There Darwin was fascinated by the various morphological differences exhibited by the local birds, particularly the finches.

Superficially these appeared to be drab and uninteresting little birds, but closer inspection revealed that the different species had undergone modifications in the beak that enabled them to occupy ecological niches ranging from those of insect eaters similar to warblers, to woodpeckers, to parrot-like ones. All these differences were in addition to variations on the normal seed-eating niche characteristic for finches. It occurred to Darwin that the absence of natural predators and the absence of the usual occupants of these various ecological niches was a function of the long geological and geographic isolation of the islands, and that the chance arrival of stray finches, blown from the mainland long ago, allowed them to exploit these niches without the normal competition. Since availability of food was the main limiting factor, those variants that could take advantage of normally unfinchlike sources of nourishment would flourish. This would account for the fact that these otherwise quite similar birds differ markedly in their food-getting structures, their beaks. In exploring the picture of the adaptive radiation of the Galápagos finches and similar radiations of the other Galápagos animals, Darwin developed the basis for what he was later to generalize and apply to all life as the theory of evolution by means of natural selection.

The Probable Mutation Effect

In later sections we shall briefly treat the sequence of adaptive radiations that eventually prepared the way for the appearance of humans. We have already stated that the major determiner of the course of organic evolution has been natural selection working on the variations supplied by genetic mutation. We have also noted that genetic drift accounts for differences that arise by chance, although it does not allow for development in any consistent direction. For many years, biologists have noted that directional changes have occurred during the course of evolution but in such a way that they could be accounted for neither by natural selection nor by genetic drift, which could not have acted consistently enough to produce the changes.

The changes we refer to are changes of a reductive nature, at least this is what they appear to be upon first inspection. Viewed through time, a trait that had once been prominent appears to become reduced in later generations. More accurately, we should say that it fails to develop to its former level, but the failure to develop is not particularly selected *for* by environmental pressures.

The classic example is presented by the depigmented and eyeless creatures inhabiting underground rivers and pools in caves. Insects, crustaceans, molluscs, and fishes that have lived for thousands of years in lightless environment all show a reduction in, or failure to develop, those structures relating to life in a world requiring adaptation to solar radiation. Sensory receptors such as eyes are reduced or absent. Similarly, pigment, whether for camouflage or to prevent the tissue damage that can be caused by ultraviolet light, is absent.

The case of eye reduction is particularly instructive because comparative study gives us a good impression of the graded steps by which complete ocular absence can come to be. Studies of various cave fishes show a spectrum of ocular development ranging from a structurally present but nonfunctional eye to complete absence of any eye tissue at all. The first reductive steps can be seen in those creatures in which the eye is present but the optic nerve is nonfunctional. Next follow forms in which the eye is present but lacks a developed retina. Further steps can be observed in those forms that have incompletely developed corneas or lenses. Still further examples of reduction are displayed in those creatures in which histological study of the eye region can identify small unorganized patches of lens-, cornea-, or optic nerve-type tissues. For the student of evolution, it is instructive to note that visual organ development is most rudimentary in those fishes that inhabit caves of the greatest apparent geological antiquity. While it is evident that pigmentation and eyes can serve no useful purposes under such conditions, nevertheless it is difficult to think of any particular advantage in their elimination. This is an extreme case, but the fossil record abounds with examples of structures that have become reduced as a result of their ceasing to be as important to the survival of their possessors as when they were originally developed. The problem for those concerned with explaining the mechanics of evolution was to discover a means by which such changes could occur, without resorting to a Lamarckian view involving the inheritance of acquired characteristics and without doing violence to the known facts of genetics.

In the late 1920s, when evolution began to be interpreted with the aid of the developing field of genetics, a number of scientists, such as the English statistician R. A. Fisher, realized that the vast majority of mutations are actually detrimental to their possessors. It has been estimated that only one in every 50 to 100 thousand replications of a gene will result in its failure to copy itself exactly — hence a mutation — and, out of these, less than 1 per cent will prove advantageous. No wonder, then, that evolution is a slow process.

At the same time that these facts became known, the American geneticist Sewall Wright, who developed the concept of genetic drift, also realized that the vast majority of mutations will result in physiological inactivation. Recalling that the primary role of the basic genetic material is in supervising protein synthesis, and that the vast majority of proteins are those organic catalysts called enzymes, it is not hard to visualize why most mutations should result in physiological inactivation, and how this has effected the reduction of various structures that have ceased to be of adaptive value.

MUTATION PRESSURE

Sewall Wright realized that mutations, accumulating unopposed, would produce physiological inactivation as expected, and this, in turn, would interfere with the growth of those structures that depend on normal physiological function. The pressure of unopposed mutations thus could produce structural reduction simply by the accumulation of mutations alone, or, as we shall be expressing it in the next chapter:

$\Delta\, q$, or change in gene frequency,

can be caused by

uq, which is the mutation (u) from the original gene (q)

written as

$$\Delta\, q = uq.$$

Some biologists over the years have assumed that the term "mutation pressure" meant an unusual or abnormal *rate* of mutation, but Wright was simply interested in the effect of the *normal* mutation rate. However, Wright did not feel, as some had tried to interpret him, that mutations could accumulate unopposed. Basically, he felt that this was unlikely for two reasons. First, he conceived of the term mutation pressure as including both mutation away from the original gene (uq) and mutation back to it (v) from whatever in the gene pool is not q (expressed as $1 - q$). Backward mutation then would be $v(1-q)$. The complete expression of gene frequency change (Δq) as a result of mutation pressure then would be:

$$\Delta\, q = uq - v(1 - q).$$

Allowed to go unobstructed, this would reach an equilibrium beyond which no permanent change could occur as a consequence of the effects of mutation alone.

PLEIOTROPY

The second reason Wright felt that the effects of mutation alone could not produce cumulative genetic change was his assumption

62   that each gene had more than one effect. This phenomenon, called *pleiotropy* (many + turning), would imply that even if the forces of selection controlling the maintenance of a given trait were to be eliminated, the gene accounting for the trait would not be free to vary since it would still be subject to the selective forces relating to the other trait(s) it controls.

We suggest that neither the pleiotropy nor the backward mutation phenomenon is sufficient to discount the possibility of change occurring by the accumulation of mutations alone. Mutation at its simplest and most basic level is the modification of a single nucleotide in a nucleic acid chain. Reverse or backward mutations, needed to restore the function altered or abolished by the first mutation, require, as suggested by one geneticist, "a very precise chemical change," and, as a consequence, "they are very rare." In fact, the probability of chance alteration of a series of nucleotides in a given region of a nucleic acid molecule is greater than the chance of mutation back to the original condition of any one of them, making the concept of a backward-forward mutation equilibrium considerably less valuable than is often assumed. Cumulative change, then, can occur as a result of mutation alone, although the expression may be somewhat more complicated than the simple $\Delta q = uq$.

The argument that pleiotropy will not allow random change to take place in a given gene suggests that even if selection relating to one of the traits it controls is eliminated, this is most unlikely to be true for the other traits it controls. But, it should be noted, even if change occurred in a single gene that produced an advantageous manifestation in a single trait, the genetic change would almost certainly produce alterations in the other traits controlled, and the likelihood is high that these changes would be selectively disadvantageous. If pleiotropy were the all-pervasive phenomenon claimed, then positive Darwinian evolution by means of natural selection would be impossible.

Since the evidence for Darwinian evolution is simply overwhelming, there must be a flaw in the assumption of universal pleiotropy. Pleiotropy has been documented in many instances, but, as knowledge about the mechanics of gene action has increased, it appears to be much more complex than the somewhat mysterious black-box model suggested a generation ago. Now that we know that genetic change, at its simplest, involves alteration of single components of known molecules, we can consider the consequences of such events with a bit more insight.

Genetic mutations involve changes in one or more nucleotides in the triplets (codons) of which a DNA molecule is composed. Since the role of the codon is the specification of an amino acid unit, which is then towed to the site of protein synthesis, any such alteration will probably result in the acquisition of the wrong amino acid.

General Biological Background

This then is assembled along with the other amino acids to produce **63** an enzyme altered at this one site. In turn, the most likely result is that the enzyme will not work at all, or, if it does work, it will not work as well as it normally should, and the reaction of which it is a part will be only partially completed. If there are a series of structures dependent on the completion of this reaction, then it is evident that the change that prevents its completion will have multiple effects — pleiotropy in the old sense. On the other hand, a great many enzymes have very specific activities, and random changes in their structure will alter these activities and no others.

In either case, the probable result of the most likely mutations will be physiological inactivation as Wright and others perceived long ago. Organic structures are the end products of growth processes controlled by enzyme action, and the probable enzymatic (physiological) inactivation, which is the result of mutation, generally means that the growth process necessary to produce normal structure is not completed, i.e., structure is reduced. We have labeled this process the Probable Mutation Effect (PME). It is a kind of labored academic pun suggesting that the probable effect of those mutations that probability suggests will be most likely to occur will be structural reduction (whether the structure is the form of a single molecule, an enzyme chain, or a visible organ).

In a normally adapted organism, the failure of one of its normal structures to attain complete development usually means that the chances for the survival of that organism are reduced. This was what Fisher meant when he noted that most mutations are detrimental.

However, when a species enters a new ecological niche, or there is a change in the environmental pressure affecting its survival, then there are going to be certain structures that are no longer quite so important. Any chance mutation affecting such a structure will *not* be selected against. As we have seen, most chance mutations produce reductions, and the accumulation of mutations in time will result in the reduction of the structure in question.

For fishes that have inhabited a lightless environment for hundreds of thousands of years, the presence of eyes or of pigmentation is of no importance. Mutations can occur affecting eye or pigment structure without any disadvantage to the fish, and the accumulation of such mutations over the generations dooms the adaptively unimportant characters to eventual reduction. While the blind and depigmented fish are the classic and extreme example, there are many somewhat less dramatic instances which indicate that the probable mutation effect has been a minor but constant force in shaping evolutionary history. Again, our discussion of human diversity will suggest the role that this has played in the course of human evolution.

Evolutionary theorists have been somewhat wary about accepting the implications of the PME. For one thing, there has been an enthusiasm, practically amounting to dogmatism, on the part of some geneticists, for explaining every aspect of morphology and all biological change as results of natural selection alone—to the exclusion of any other mechanism. Some have even come close to suggesting that we must accept the primary shaping role of natural selection even when we can find no logical reason for it. This argument suggests that, in such instances, the right research simply has not yet been designed. At times, however, the argument smacks of a sophistry approaching blind faith. Certainly this seems to have been the case for those geneticists who have refused even to admit the theoretical possibility of genetic drift, and it would also seem to be true for some of those who have been skeptical of the PME.

In another instance there has been an attempt to explain the reductive phenomena dealt with by the PME by using an extension of more orthodox selective force theory. Where the PME has sought to account for the reduction of no-longer-necessary features by what is really a version of entropy—the tendency for things to run down— there are those who have suggested that the saving in metabolic energy effected by a creature that fails to develop a useless trait will give it a slight competitive edge over those creatures that continue to grow the trait in question even though it does them no good. However, even this argument becomes a bit strained when it tries to suggest that a significant amount of energy is saved by the cave fish that develops only a vestigial patch of retinal tissue compared with the fish that develops both a vestigial patch of retinal and a vestigial patch of lens tissue. The energy-saving argument becomes even harder to sustain when one can point out that a minor but systematic reduction in tooth size has occurred during the last several thousand years in precisely those human populations that have been engaged in producing a food-energy surplus. For our part, it seems simpler to attribute this to the PME.

We have spent some time in developing the case for the PME, partially because it has been somewhat neglected in other books, but principally because we suspect that it has played an increasingly important role in the course of human evolution. As the reader will perceive, we develop this further in the latter part of our discussion of "The Stages of Human Evolution" and in "Human Variation and Its Significance," Chapters 9 and 12.

In Retrospect

The impact evolutionary thinking had on the complacency of the nineteenth century was unsettling. Many educated people simply could not bring themselves to examine the theory of evolution dis-

passionately, and still more experienced the uncomfortable feeling **65**
that it was indecent to apply such principles in an attempt to understand the development of humanity. It is said that after the 1860
meeting of the British Association for the Advancement of Science
held at Oxford on June 30, the Canon of Worcester Cathedral, upon
his return home, informed his wife that the horrid Professor Huxley
had announced that humans were descended from the apes. Where-
upon his wife is said to have exclaimed: "Descended from the apes?
My dear, we will hope that it is not true. But if it is, let us pray that it
will not become generally known." Alas for the dear lady the facts,
in spite of her prayers, have become generally known.

SEXUAL SELECTION

In fact, many people who accepted general evolutionary thinking
did not believe that natural selection was adequate to explain the
evolution of humans, and among these skeptics was none other than
Charles Darwin himself. During the decade following the publication of the *Origin,* he collected information relating to human diversity, and in 1871 he published *The Descent of Man, and Selection in Relation to Sex*, in which he stressed the role played by
sexual selection in human evolution. This approach stresses the role
played by human choice in influencing the frequency of the variants
that would be transmitted. Some biologists still believe that such features as beards, fat-padded mammary glands, and various remarkable facets of Hottentot anatomy can only be explained in this way. It
has been assumed that the strongest and most vigorous males would
choose the most attractive females as mates and therefore assure the
perpetuation of their particular traits.

Such a view was understandable in Darwin's day, but enough anthropological information has since accumulated to render such
interpretations quite outmoded. Today, it is evident that what constitutes "desirability" varies greatly from culture to culture. Even
within a single tradition, such a behavior can scarcely be expected to
remain constant over the periods of time required to affect evolutionary development. In addition, the degree to which members of nonliterate societies approach the culturally prescribed ideals of sexual
attractiveness has virtually no influence on reproductive behavior.
Those who are physically able indulge in sufficient sexual activities
to present all with equal opportunities for reproduction. Ability as a
hunter, trapper, food and water finder is more important than features of morphology that may be regarded as sexually desirable. Finally, marriage in most nonliterate societies is not free, but rigidly
determined by regulations over which the individual generally has
no control.

Certainly, throughout the greater part of human evolution, sexual

Principles of Evolution

66 selection cannot have been of any importance. Some have noted that, with the lowering of mortality during childbirth produced by modern medicine and the standardization of human ideals of "beauty" as a result of the activities of magazines, motion pictures, and television, perhaps some sort of sexual selection is in fact being practiced at the present time. With more women than men in the world, it is true that greater percentages of women remain unmarried than previously — presumably the men select the more "desirable" women for marriage partners. The effect of this is easily offset by the fact that the declared paragons of female pulchritude limit the actual extent of their reproductive activites to the point where the mammarian monstrosities of Hollywood fame tend to have had more husbands than children. However much they may inspire imitation by young people, their actual contribution to the future betterment of humankind is disproportionately small. Hence, "serial monogamy" or "sequential polygamy" is not without its eugenic effect.

One final point deserves mention before we leave the subject of evolutionary principles, and this concerns the sources of control over the direction of evolutionary development. Some scientists, even at this late date, find it difficult to believe that natural selection working on normally occurring mutations has been sufficient to produce the observed evolutionary developments. Some have resorted to an explanation called orthogenesis — straight-line evolution, or development that continues by its own momentum in a single direction without any visible cause. Occasionally a vital force is assumed, while others have tried to defend the idea of a momentum tending to continue a direction of development set in motion originally by selective forces.

These ideas deal with the unknowable, and since they rely on essentially mystical assumptions, they have been rejected by most modern students of evolution. There is overwhelming agreement that natural selection, utilizing the raw material produced by mutation, has been able to create the diversity visible in the organic world as well as the changes hinted at in the fossil record. Less agreement exists concerning the roles of the probable mutation effect and genetic drift, although it is recognized that these have been far less important than natural selection.

In summary, then, we may say that natural selection is the process of diversification of adaptations in a population, and the product of evolution is a diverse but well-adapted population. Evolution, in short, consists of the changes that occur in genotypes, and having a great store of such diverse potentials makes for evolutionary adaptiveness.

Finally, it should be said that while in theory evolution is relatively well understood, in practice there remain a great many problems awaiting the application of as yet undeveloped research techniques and the additions to our knowledge that will come from the efforts of **67** future generations.

Suggested Readings

ALTNER, G. (editor). *The Human Creature.* Doubleday, Anchor Books, New York, 1974.
  Highly informative and readable on the evolution and nature of man.

AUERBACH, C. The chemical production of mutations, *Science,* vol. 158, 1967, pp. 1141–1147.
  Illustrates the unlikelihood of specific reverse mutations.

CAMPBELL, B. G. (editor). *Sexual Selection and The Descent of Man 1871–1971.* Aldine, Chicago, 1972.
  A helpful discussion by eleven authorities.

DARWIN, C. *The Descent of Man,* 2 vols. John Murray, London, 1871.
  Darwin impressively, but not altogether successfully, in the case of humans, presents the evidence for evolution by sexual selection.

DOBZHANSKY, TH. *Genetics of the Evolutionary Process.* Columbia University Press, New York, 1970.
  A splendid survey of the major developments in the study of the genetics of the evolutionary process. A quite fascinating book, and highly readable.

HARDIN, G. *Nature and Man's Fate.* Holt, Rinehart and Winston, New York, 1959.
  A readable and thought-provoking application of evolutionary principles to man.

HUXLEY, J. *Evolution: The Modern Synthesis.* Harper & Row, New York, 1942, 1964.
  The 1964 edition contains a new introduction bringing this standard work on the evolutionary process up to date since it was first published in 1942.

KING, J. L., AND T. H. JUKES. Non-Darwinian evolution, *Science,* vol. 164, 1969, pp. 788–798.
  A controversial but stimulating discussion of protein components disputing the importance of selective control.

LACK, D. *Darwin's Finches.* Cambridge University Press, London and New York, 1947.
  A study of adaptive radiation in a small self-contained group of birds.

68 MAYR, E. *Systematics and the Origin of Species.* Columbia University Press, New York, 1942.
A fundamental work on the origin of species.

————. *Animal Species and Evolution.* Harvard University Press, Cambridge, 1963.
A full exposition, synthesis, summation, and critical evaluation of the present state of knowledge of the biology and genetics of animal species and their role in evolution. The chapter on man as a biological species will be of special interest to readers of the present volume.

MEDVEDEV, Z. A. *The Rise and Fall of T. D. Lysenko.* Translated by I. Michael Lerner. Columbia University Press, New York, 1969.
The grim and frightening story of what can happen when "relevance" of scientific activity is determined by politicians rather than by scientists and rational research.

MOODY, P. A. *Introduction to Evolution,* 2nd ed. Harper & Row, New York, 1962.
One of the best all-round general introductions to the subject of organic evolution.

OHNO, S. *Evolution by Gene Duplication.* Allen and Unwin, London, 1971.
A controversial work which leaves room for the operation of the Probable Mutation Effect.

SIMPSON, G. G. *The Major Features of Evolution.* Columbia University Press, New York, 1953.
A sound and sophisticated presentation of evolutionary theory.

————. *The Meaning of Evolution,* revised ed. Yale University Press, New Haven, 1967.
The best book on the subject.

————. *This View of Life.* Harcourt Brace Jovanovich, New York, 1964.
A highly stimulating series of essays especially relating to the evolution of man.

General Biological Background

Population Genetics

The forces of selection act on individuals, and organic continuity depends on the successful life and reproduction of individual organisms. While students of evolution occasionally tend to forget the fact that the crucial events of organic perpetuation occur at the individual level, nevertheless it should be kept in mind that the individual alone is not sufficient. At the behavioral level it is clear that some kinds of animals (including humans) increase the chances for individual survival through combined activities. The supportive nature of group behavior—implied in the phrase "safety in numbers"—is evident for many species, but this is not what we had in mind when we said that the individual alone is not sufficient. Rather, the sufficiency to which we refer is the genetic endowment of the individual.

True an individual may be endowed by heredity with the capacity to meet all the challenges that life will throw its way, but there is always the possibility that a situation will arise which it simply cannot handle. Perhaps such a hypothetical situation will face the offspring of our imagined individual, whether one, two, or many generations removed. If these offspring are genetically identical with their assumed progenitor, the result will obviously be extinction.

The world is not a static one and circumstances are continually arising that threaten the survival of previously well-adapted creatures. Faced with changes in survival requirements, changes in adaptation are evidently necessary. As has already been noted, genetic mutation can provide for alternate adaptations, but mutations are relatively rare events, occurring approximately once in every hundred replications of a given gene, and there is no assurance that a mutation—let alone a favorable one—will occur coincidental with a change in survival conditions. Actually, as the makers of pesticides have become aware, some micro-organisms with a reproductive time requirement on the order of minutes rather than days or weeks (or longer) can produce enough generations of individuals with sufficient rapidity so that mutation alone is adequate to furnish the basis for adjustment when conditions change, but for organisms with more complex adaptations and longer life spans mutation is simply not enough to provide an adequate base by itself.

While it remains true that mutation does provide the raw material on which selective forces operate to produce the observable changes characterized as organic evolution, this is not something that happens obligingly upon demand. Above the rapidly reproducing micro-organismic level, adaptive potential is ensured by sexual reproduction. In the face of the current possibly lethal human population expansion, it might be regarded as inappropriate to sing the praises of sexual reproduction, but, with the exception of the imminently disastrous human manifestation thereof, we can point to the survival benefits it has conferred on other creatures.

Given a mode of reproduction that requires the participation of two kinds of partners (males and females, as though it needed explanation) the mechanism is established for a potential genetic diversity that (to mix metaphors) is light years removed from the situation in which an individual tends to produce carbon copies of itself. Each parent contributes half its genetic endowment to the gametes (egg or sperm); this endowment, when united in the diploid zygote, represents a genotype that in combination is different from the genotype of either parent. Not only that, the process of meiosis can produce an enormous variety of gametic combinations. Remember that in meiosis—let us say, the production of an egg—only one half of each parental diploid chromosome is contributed to the daughter cell, but just which half is a matter of chance. For example, in the human situation with 23 chromosomes, a mother could contribute either half of the first chromosomes (1, or 1'), and so on through all 23 (for the 23rd or sex chromosome it would be X, or X'). Successive eggs in their haploid state could be 1', 2, 3 . . . 22, X; 1', 2', 3 . . . 22, X; . . . 1', 2', 3' . . . 22', X'; and 1, 2', 3 . . . 22, X; 1, 2', 3' . . . 22, X; . . . 1, 2', 3', . . . 22', X'; and so on. Given nothing more than the diploid nature of the parent and the process of meiosis, each person can produce 2^{23} different kinds of gametes—or more than 8 million differing kinds of egg or sperm per individual. To produce a viable offspring an egg and a sperm must unite, expanding the possible combinations to a truly astronomical figure. The different possible combinations that can be produced by a single mated pair is more than 60 trillion. No wonder then that no two children produced by separate acts of fertilization by a single couple ever look exactly alike. (Identical twins do not count here since they are the products of single instances of fertilization—two separate individuals from a single fertilized egg.) Adding still further to the variation that results from a sexual mode of reproduction is the still more complicated results of crossover during meiosis.

It is evident that with all this variation being produced each generation, some individuals will be better suited to the prevailing living circumstances than others. The continuation of a single familial line depends on the fact that some offspring will have a better chance of surviving and reproducing than others. More than a century ago, Darwin recognized that all organisms, even slow breeding ones, produce far more offspring than is necessary simply to replace the parental generation. He also recognized that there was variation among the offspring, both between themselves and between each and its parents. Knowing nothing about the principles of genetics, mutation, or the variation-generating process of meiosis, he could not account for the source of the variation he observed. Variation he observed none the less, and, along with the production of more offspring than necessary for simple replacement, this he realized was the source of the change through time that constitutes organic evolution.

From the discussion, it should be obvious that sexual reproduction by a single mated pair can produce almost limitless variation simply by recombining the genetic material present in both parents. But if potential parents themselves cannot cope with changing conditions and fail to survive long enough to reproduce, then they leave no offspring in spite of the fact they they might have possessed genetic material which, in other combinations, could have formed an adequate basis for survival. Further still, the potential "almost limitless variation" in the offspring is based on the finite genotype of the parents, and radical departure from the parental condition is unlikely. This is what accounts for familial resemblances.

With all the biological advantages that sexual reproduction confers on any given family line, it is evident that organic continuity would be a tenuous thing if it were dependent on a single individual or even a single mated pair. However, with the genetic resources of several dozen pairs of individuals and the nearly infinite combinations their matings can produce, the continuity of much of what they genetically possess *as a group* is considerably more likely. This is the basis for the view supported by many professional geneticists that the basic unit of evolution is that group of individuals among whom genetic material is regularly circulated, a group variously called "local population," "breeding population," "Mendelian population," or *deme*.

The assumption is often made that, within such a local breeding population, each individual is equally likely to breed with any other individual and that genes are distributed completely at random, a condition referred to as *panmixia*. In fact, because about half of any population is composed of individuals of like sex, which cannot breed together (each requiring a breeding partner of opposite sex), and because genes tend to be transmitted in chromosome-long blocks, panmixia is rarely approximated at any given time. Not only that, but the semi-isolated demes of which many species are composed often do not have geographically determined breeding barriers and members of adjacent demes may occasionally (or even regularly) contribute to genetic leakage — gene flow — across supposed population boundaries. As we shall expand upon later, this lack of reproductive isolation is crucial to our conclusion that the concept of race is of no use in understanding the nature and mechanics of human biological variation.

In spite of these limitations, the concept of breeding population and the models and quantified logic of population genetics have contributed greatly to the understanding of organic evolution. In part, these contributions have resulted from the consideration of populations of genes rather than populations of individuals. In a large enough population over a long enough period of time, the effects of crossover during meiosis and chromosomal reshuffling each generation will assure the operation of the Mendelian principle of random assortment. Focusing on the genes alone — the gene pool — of a population, scientists have developed mathematical models to demonstrate the effect on the frequencies of genes in a gene pool of such influences as specific mutation rates or specific selective force intensities as well as other factors. The basis for this particular focus is the realization that evolution, at bottom, is change in the genetic constitution of a population.

Genetic Equilibrium

In 1908, both the British mathematician H. G. Hardy and, working independently, the German physician Wilhelm Weinberg developed a simple quantitative model that explained how a given gene frequency is maintained from generation to generation when a population is in a state of equilibrium. According to the Hardy-Weinberg law, percentages of given genes are maintained in simple algebraic fashion. For a trait controlled by a single locus, the proportions of the two alleles will be maintained in the form of a simple binomial expansion.

Take the example of the garden pea, for instance, where the genes for tallness were labeled T and t. If these letters are assigned to their frequencies, then the genetics of stature in the edible pea can be dealt with in standard Hardy-Weinberg form. By convention p stands for the frequency of gene T and q for the frequency of gene t. These frequencies are used in the form of percentages so that they must total 100 per cent. Put simply, in this instance, $p + q = 1.00$.

Since the discussion concerns Mendelian or breeding populations, and one of their assumed characteristics is that they breed only with themselves, the reproduction of the genotype, algebraically, is

$$(p+q)^2$$

and

$$(p+q)^2 = p^2 + 2pq + q^2.$$

It should be recalled that the example of pea plants started with two individuals who then were bred together to produce the observed Mendelian ratios. Each individual contributed equally to the succeeding generations, or, genetically, 50 per cent. Since one was genetically TT (and phenotypically tall) and the other was tt (and phenotypically short), the gene pool at the beginning was half T and half t, or, using the terms we have just introduced, p (the gene frequency of T) is .5 and q (the gene frequency of t) is also .5.

Recall that $p + q = 1$, so in this case

$$.5 + .5 = 1.$$

No matter how large the population becomes, if it breeds only by utilizing its own gene pool the percentage of genes — gene frequencies — should remain the same, hence

$$(p+q)^2 = (.5+.5)^2$$

and

$$(.5+.5)^2 = .25 + (2 \times .25) + .25 = .25 + .50 + .25 = 1.0.$$

If the gene frequency of the initial population were to change, again, the percentages would remain constant. For instance, if we started with one tall and one short plant but the tall one was heterozygous, Tt (tall because T is dominant over t), then with individuals Tt and tt we would have gene frequencies for T and t of $p = .25$ and $q = .75$.

$$(p+q)^2 = (.25)^2 = 2(.25 \times .75) + (.75)^2$$

Population Genetics

$$p^2 = .0625$$
$$2pq = .3750$$
$$q^2 = .5625$$

And this sums up as   1.0000

These are the gene frequencies under stable conditions with no other factors exerting any influence. This also indicates the phenotypic percentages under the same conditions. With both TT and Tt being phenotypically tall, we can simply add their gene frequencies $(p^2 + 2pq)$; these being .0625 and .3750, we find that 43.75 per cent of our population is phenotypically tall. The percentage that is phenotypically short (tt) will equal q^2 or .5625. In other words, if the gene pool of a population has 75 per cent short genes where tallness is dominant, slightly over half the individuals will actually appear short.

Since the phenotype is easier to discern than the genotype, being the portion of the organism one actually observes, the problem usually involves trying to figure out gene frequencies from known population appearances and breeding behavior. For instance, in the example above, it can be observed that short is recessive to tall. To find out the gene frequency of t (in other words, q), we simply count the percentage of short individuals in the population, which gives us q^2. Taking the square root of q^2 gives the frequency of the gene t. Since $p + q = 1$, obviously $1 - q = p$ and we have the frequencies of both the alleles.

In like fashion, the Hardy-Weinberg equilibrium works if there are more than two alleles, as for example in the human $A B O$ blood group system. Frequencies for the three genes are labeled p, q, and r, where $p + q + r = 1.00$. Again their distribution in a breeding population can be figured as $(p + q + r)^2$, which works out to be

$$p^2 = AA$$
$$2pq = AB$$
$$2pr = AO$$
$$q^2 = BB$$
$$2qr = BO$$
$$r^2 = OO$$

Sometimes it is convenient to study one gene in a multiple allele system by lumping everything else into a single category. If we focus on the gene frequency of the B allele in the human $A B O$ system, we are interested in q. All the rest, which properly are p and r, can be considered "not q," or $1 - q$. This allows us to use the simple binomial form of the Hardy-Weinberg law:

General Biological Background

$$[q+(1-q)]^2 = q^2 + 2q(1-q) + (1-q)^2.$$

Things become more complicated in practice when geneticists actually try to calculate gene frequencies in multiple allele systems from observed phenotypes, which is one reason why studies have been concentrated on traits under relatively simple genetic control.

Changes in Equilibrium

The Hardy-Weinberg model, as we have shown, accounts for the maintenance of initial gene frequencies in a population. In spite of all the nearly limitless combinations generated by meiosis and magnified by each such unique combination mating by chance with another, the actual frequencies of the genes in the population gene pool will remain unchanged. If evolution can be defined most simply as a change in gene frequency, then it is obvious that the Hardy-Weinberg model by itself describes a situation that is the very opposite of evolution. For a brief period early in this century some biologists in fact felt that the findings of geneticists, exemplified in the Hardy-Weinberg equilibrium, had proven Darwin wrong.

Both in the laboratory and in the wild, small but very real changes in population gene frequencies could be demonstrated. As time has gone on, the investigation of these small changes—microevolutionary studies—has constituted an increasingly important part of biology in general and biological anthropology in particular. Following the discovery of mutations by Muller in 1927, the algebra for calculating their impact on a gene pool was proposed almost simultaneously by the British scientists R. A. Fisher and J. B. S. Haldane and the American biologist Sewall Wright. By agreement, change in gene frequency per generation is represented by a capital Greek delta (Δ). Several factors in addition to mutation can contribute to gene frequency change. The forces of selection can systematically reduce the chances for survival and replication of a given gene; a regular influx of different genes can occur if immigrants are added to a population; and, especially in small populations, chance alone can play a part in determining gene frequency.

Change (Δ) in gene frequency (q) between one generation and the next is expressed as Δq, which is equal to the difference between the gene frequency of the initial generation considered (q_0) and the gene frequency of the first subsequent generation (q_1). Expressed symbolically,

$$\Delta q = q_0 - q_1.$$

If this change is due simply to the action of mutation away from the gene whose frequency is denoted by q and we denote this mutation rate by u, then gene frequency change is simply the product of the initial gene frequency (q_0) and the rate at which change is occurring (u), or,

$$\Delta q = u q_0.$$

From the discussion it will be seen that the gene frequency in the next generation (q_1) will be that of the parent generation (q_0) modified by the amount of change away from that figure produced by mutation $(u q_0)$, or

$$q_1 = q_0 - \Delta q = q_0 - u q_0.$$

To obtain this altered gene frequency (q_1), one can either calculate the amount of change and subtract it from the initial frequency $(q_0 - u q_0)$ or produce the same results by multiplying the initial frequency by a figure that is less than unity by the amount equal to the mutation rate. In other words,

$$q_1 = q_0 - u q_0 = q_0 (1 - u)$$

If we build on this new gene frequency (q_1), change by mutation in the next generation will be

$$q_2 = q_1 (1 - u)$$

and since

$$q_1 = q_0 (1 - u).$$

we can get

$$q_2 = q_0 (1 - u)^2$$

With mutations accumulating for n generations,

$$q_n = q_0 (1 - u)^n.$$

If nothing occurs to alter the course of this process, q will approach 0 and the gene for which it represents the frequency will disappear from the population.

Early in the history of quantitative approaches to heredity, a special case of the picture of gene frequency change by mutation was advanced as a general model. Specifically, when mutations away from a particular allele were considered, the reverse condition was also assumed; i.e., mutations back to the original condition were assumed to be occurring simultaneously. In order for the reverse mutation to reach the gene with frequency q, it has to start from the frequency of what is not q, or $1 - q$. The rate of this reverse mutation

is conventionally called v. With u representing the mutation rate $\qquad$
away from q, and v representing the mutation rate toward q, the total
change will be

$$\Delta q = v(1-q) - uq.$$

If these competing mutation rates are allowed to operate for
enough generations, an equilibrium will eventually be reached in
which mutations away from the gene in question will be balanced by
mutations toward it. The *rates* will remain the same, but it is evident that a small percentage of a large number will be the same as a
larger percentage of a small number and, when this condition is
reached, the backward and forward mutations will occur with equal
frequency. Stated simply,

$$\Delta q = 0, \quad \text{or} \quad uq = v(1-q).$$

Evidently the proportion of the two alleles q and $1-q$ (which is
the p of our earlier examples) in a population at equilibrium equals
the proportion of their rates of mutation each to the other, so that

$$\frac{q}{1-q} = \frac{v}{u}$$

To obtain the actual frequencies of the genes in question when
equilibrium has been reached, this can be written as

$$q = \frac{v}{v+u} \quad \text{and} \quad 1-q = \frac{u}{v+u}$$

It is now apparent, however, that this rather neat representation of
genetic change based on mutation alone was an oversimplification of
the molecular reality. In the past, the presence or absence of a gene
was determined by relatively gross effects. Was an enzyme working
or was it not? Dysfunction could be caused by the addition or deletion of a single nucleotide in the DNA molecule, which supervises
the assembly of the protein, since both events result in the assembly
of strings of incorrect amino acids. Function can be restored for all
major intents and purposes by the respective deletion or addition of
an adjacent nucleotide, or, at least, one in the same general region of
the DNA template, and, to the observer, it would look like a reverse
mutation. In reality, however it is not. The complexity of components at the molecular level that combine to produce what is observed as a single gene effect was not anticipated in the formulas of
classic population genetics. The intellectual rigor brought to the
study of evolution by quantification was enormously beneficial and,
in most instances, fully justified. In the case of the backward-forward mutation rate formulation, however, there has been a tendency
for students to put more faith in the model than in biological reality.

One of the most successful applications of the logic of population genetics has been in the assessment of the consequences of selection. To see how this works one must consider the concept of fitness, indicated by the symbol W. Fitness has been defined as a relative phenomenon. For instance the likelihood of survival of a given genotype (individual) is figured in relation to the likelihood of survival of other genotypes. The assumption is made that when any two genotypes are compared, one will be more fit than another. In comparing the various genotypes of a population, one will be discovered that is more fit than any other. Its fitness value is regarded as unity for comparative purposes, and the fitness of each other genotype is expressed as a percentage. With 1.0 representing the most fit genotype, other fitness values will range down to 0.0 for a genotype that has absolutely no chance for survival. This latter is called a "lethal" genotype.

Let us take as an example the genotypes for stature in the garden pea – this may be tiresome, but at least it is familiar and therefore convenient. There are three such genotypes, TT, Tt, and tt. If we assume for the sake of argument that genotype TT has the greatest fitness, we assign it a fitness symbolized by W_0 where $W_0 = 1$. The other genotypes will have fitnesses of W_1 for Tt and W_2 for tt. Since we have assumed that TT is most fit, we deduce that something is selecting against the survival of the other genotypes to the extent that W_1 and W_2 are each less than W_0. The selection against each of these genotypes (i.e., each coefficient of selection) is designated s so that s_0 is the coefficient of selection operating against TT. Since this has a fitness of 1.0 and by definition is not being selected against, the coefficient of selection s_0 is 0. The other coefficients of selection, s_1 and s_2, are less than unity by an amount equal to the percentage that the fitness value of each genotype, respectively, W_1 and W_2, is of the most fit genotype. Specifically,

$$s_0 = 1 - \frac{W_0}{W_0} \qquad s_1 = 1 - \frac{W_1}{W_0} \qquad s_2 = 1 - \frac{W_2}{W_0}$$

While dealing with fitness, we should mention that, given the fitness of the several genotypes, we can compute the fitness of a population. The "mean" or average fitness, designated $\overline{W}$, is the sum of the various genotype proportions each multiplied by the appropriate fitness value. Recall that, for our erstwhile pea plants, the proportion or frequency of gene T is represented by p and of gene t is represented by q so that, without selection, the gene frequencies for the two stature alleles is

$$p^2 + 2\,pq + q^2 = 1.$$

We also defined the fitness of each genotype as

$$W_0 \qquad W_1 \qquad W_2$$

Therefore, mean fitness will be

$$\overline{W} = p^2W_0 + 2pqW_1 + q^2W_2.$$

Note that, since both W_1 and W_2 are less than 1.0, mathematically $\overline{W}$ will be less than unity. But if we let the gene frequency change proportional to the fitness of the various genotypes, it is clear that the genotype with a fitness of W_0 (equal to 1.0 by definition) will be greater than the average $(\overline{W})$ and hence the genotype proportion will increase as the less fit genotypes decrease. After a generation of selection, genotype frequency will be

$$\frac{p^2W_0}{\overline{W}} + \frac{2pqW_1}{\overline{W}} + \frac{q^2W_2}{\overline{W}} = 1.0.$$

Let us plug some hypothetical figures into this framework and see what happens. If we start off assuming that half the genes in the pea population are for tall and half for short, we have $p = .5$ and $q = .5$. Now if we assume a fitness of 1.0 for W_0 (p^2), .95 for W_1 (pq), and .90 for W_2 (q^2), we find

$$\overline{W} = (.5^2 \times 1.0) + (2 \times .5 \times .5 \times .95) + (.5^2 \times .90)$$
$$W = .25 + .475 + .225$$
$$\overline{W} = .95,$$

which is the average fitness of the population.
To see what happens to our genotype frequency after one generation,

$$TT = \frac{p^2W_0}{\overline{W}} = \frac{.25}{.95} = .263 \ (+),$$

$$Tt = \frac{2pqW_1}{\overline{W}} = \frac{.475}{.95} = .5,$$

$$tt = \frac{q^2W_2}{\overline{W}} = \frac{.225}{.95} = .237 \ (-).$$

Evidently the frequency of genotype TT has increased and that of tt has decreased. Note also that the relative frequencies of genes T and t have also changed. If, for instance, we wish to know how the frequency of gene t has changed we can compute it directly from the above figures. Since genotype Tt is half t, we add half its frequency to the frequency for tt to find the gene frequency for t after a generation of selection. This then becomes

$$\frac{pqW_1}{\overline{W}} + \frac{q^2W_2}{\overline{W}} = \frac{q(pW_1 + qW_2)}{\overline{W}} = .25 + .237 \ (-) = .487 \ (-).$$

Our new gene frequency for t, symbolized as q_1, has become .487 $(-)$. Recall that gene frequency change is

$$\Delta q = q_0 - q_1.$$

In this case,

$$\Delta q = .5 - .587 \, (-) = .013.$$

This is the absolute amount of gene frequency change. We should note that t is being selected against so Δq in this instance is really a negative figure.

It is also possible to compute changes in gene frequency by dealing with the fitness of a gene itself and not the whole genotype. Again we take the relative fitness of the best adapted gene as 1.0. As an arbitrary point of departure in the present instance, we have assumed that, in our two gene (T, t) system, t has a lower fitness. Therefore T, with the greater survival value, has a fitness of 1.0. The fitness of the other gene t is less to the extent that it is being selected against. Since this selection is designated s, the fitness of t will be $1 - s$. Previously we used the figure .9 for the fitness of the tt genotype, but we should recall that this was really the fitness for a frequency of q^2 and not for q itself. This latter figure would have to be $\sqrt{.9}$, or nearly .95. Since fitness is relative to the amount of selection against a particular condition (0 for the most fit, therefore with no selection against T, fitness $= 1.0 - 0 = 1.0$), the fitness of t must be $1.0 - s$, where s is the selection against t. The proportion of t after selection, then, will be $q \, (1 - s)$.

After selection has operated for a generation, the amount of p will be unchanged since it is not being selected against, whereas q, as we have noted, is reduced by $(1 - s)$. In the new generation, then, the amount of the two genes will be $p + q_1$ where $q_1 = q \, (1 - s)$, i.e., $p + q \, (1 - s)$. But since q has been reduced by selection, $p + q$ no longer adds up to unity by the amount $1 - sq$. If this amount is considered the denominator of the frequency figure, then the criterion of unity can be preserved, so

$$\frac{p}{1 - sq} + \frac{q(1 - s)}{1 - sq} = 1.0.$$

The change in frequency for gene t after one generation of selection will be

$$\Delta q = q_0 - q_1 = q - \frac{q(1 - s)}{1 - sq} = \frac{sq(1 - q)}{1 - sq}.$$

We obtained this before when we approached the change in gene frequency from the point of view of assessing the fitness of the various genotypes rather than the genes themselves. Hence, we can write

General Biological Background

$$\Delta q = q - \frac{q(pW_1 + qW_2)}{\overline{W}} = \frac{sq(1-q)}{1-sq}.$$

Since the gene t is being selected against, Δq is actually a negative figure. We could build this into our equation by setting it up so that $\Delta q = q_1 - q_0$, but if we simply keep this in mind there should be no confusion. This is not simply done as an inviolable convention because the same kind of algebra can be applied to demonstrate the effects of selection *for* a given gene rather than against it. In the case we have presented in which selection is reducing the frequency of t, it is apparent that, continued over enough generations, the gene would be completely eliminated just as it would be in the case of unopposed mutation.

Gene Flow

Mutation and selection in the long run are the principal factors that produce evolutionary change. However, as one should be aware from our illustrations of their operation, the process is a slow one. This being the case, there are a number of circumstances in which their influence can be retarded or even countered. The chances of allele apportionment in small populations can result in either fixation or loss of a given gene. Environments themselves can change, thus altering the nature of fitness of genes and genotypes. Furthermore, populations do not always stay put, breeding infinitely in splendid isolation as our models have tacitly assumed. Local populations frequently maintain intermittent contacts with other local populations of the same species and regularly exchange genes proportional to the amount of their contact. If this situation is the rule rather than the exception, as we suspect was the case for most of the span during which human evolution took place, then the concept of breeding population becomes more than a little difficult to apply.

The model remains a useful tool, however, and can continue to be valuable if the effects of gene flow between local populations are taken into consideration. For instance we can let m equal the rate of mixture between two populations that differ in the percentage of a certain gene. Taking the t allele of our long-suffering pea plants again, we use q to designate its frequency in the population being studied and Q to represent its frequency in the population contributing material across the population boundary. Change, that is, Δq, will be proportional to the migration or mixture rate m as well as the difference in gene frequencies in the populations considered represented as $q - Q$. Each generation the new frequency q will be determined by how much Q is being added, symbolized by mQ, and by the proportion left over, subtracting for mixture, of the original q, which is written as $(1 - m)\,q$. Put together, the new frequency of q is

$$q_1 = mQ + (1 - m)q,$$
$$= mQ + q - qm,$$
$$q_1 = q - m(q - Q).$$

Recalling that $\Delta q = q_0 - q_1$, we find

$$\Delta q = q - q - m(q - Q),$$
$$\Delta q = -m(q - Q).$$

So far we have treated the effects of mutation, selection, and gene flow separately. Since they all contribute to changes in gene frequency, i.e., to evolution, it should be possible to combine them in a single equation. One form of this equation is

$$\Delta q = \pm \frac{sq(1 - q)}{1 - sq} - uq - m(q - Q).$$

Selection can be either for or against a given gene as our $\pm$ sign indicates. The mutation part could also include an expression of reverse mutation rate. Given a positive coefficient of selection, provided that the other two elements are not larger, the equation can be elaborated to an equilibrium. This, of course, will be altered if either gene flow or fitness changes.

What we have developed in this chapter is the simplest possible exposition of the operation of population genetics. Before closing, we should warn the reader that simplification may very well distort reality, occasionally to an unreasonable extent. For instance, in the models we have discussed we have focused on the forces that affect the frequency of a single gene. This is a drastic reduction from the concern expressed at the beginning of this chapter for populations of genes or whole gene pools. We should not forget that fitness is a property of the genotype as a whole and not of single genes. Within a given genotype, genes can interact in ways that are quite unpredictable given only information about the distribution of the gene itself or even a whole gene pool without information on the clusters or genotypes of which the population is composed. Models have been constructed to take some of these complications into account, but the mathematics becomes increasingly formidable and the amount of insight tends to drop accordingly. What we have presented here should be sufficient to provide a conceptual base for what we shall be presenting in later chapters.

Suggested Readings

CAVALLI-SFORZA, L. L., AND W. F. BODMER. *The Genetics of Human Populations.* W. H. Freeman, San Francisco, 1971.
    An exhaustive, up-to-date, and acclaimed treatment of the subject.

FISHER, R. A. *The Genetical Theory of Natural Selection.* Reprint of the 1930 edition, with revisions. Dover, New York, 1958.
   This classic work was the first exposition of population genetics available to a general readership.

LEVINE, R. P. *Genetics.* Holt, Rinehart and Winston, New York, 1962.
   A good standard exposition of the field of genetics in general.

LI, C. C. *Population Genetics.* University of Chicago Press, Chicago, 1955.
   One of the most highly regarded presentations of the subject. It puts less emphasis on the more formidable mathematical aspects of population genetics than does the work of Fisher and Wright.

————, *Human Genetics: Principles and Methods.* McGraw-Hill, New York, 1961.
   A good demonstration of relatively simple population genetics theory using human examples.

McKUSICK, V. A. *Human Genetics*, 2nd ed. Prentice-Hall, Englewood Cliffs, N. J., 1969.
   A thoroughly up-to-date presentation of human genetics with a good but brief section on the quantitative or populational aspects.

METTLER, I. E., AND T. G. GREGG. *Population Genetics and Evolution.* Prentice-Hall, Englewood Cliffs, N. J., 1969.
   Far and away the best introductory work on population genetics. Comprehensible to the mathematically unsophisticated and clearly applied to an evolutionary context.

MOODY, P. A. *Genetics of Man*, 2nd ed. W. W. Norton, New York, 1975.
   Presents the field of genetics with an eye toward the history of the field.

MOORE, JOHN A. *Heredity and Development.* Oxford University Press, New York, 1963.
   The stress on the complexity of translating genotype into phenotype is a valuable counter to the focus on genotype by many students of population genetics.

SINNOTT, E. W., L. C. DUNN, AND TH. DOBZHANSKY. *Principles of Genetics.* McGraw-Hill, New York, 1958.
   A good exposition of the field of genetics before the impact of molecular biology. Valuable because this is the general view held by most practitioners of population genetics.

STERN, C. *Principles of Human Genetics.* 3rd. ed., W. H. Freeman, San Francisco, 1973.
   A well-rounded coverage of the subject.

84 WILLIAMS, G. C. *Adaptation and Natural Selection.* Princeton University Press, Princeton, N.J., 1966.
  A stimulating discussion of the roles of the individual and the group in relation to the operation of natural selection.

WRIGHT, SEWALL. *Evolution and the Genetics of Populations. Volume I: Genetic and Biometric Foundations.* University of Chicago Press, Chicago, 1968.

Volume 2: Theory of Gene Frequencies. University of Chicago Press, Chicago, 1969.
  No one is more qualified than Wright as one of the founders of the field to deal with the formidable mathematical and biological complexities of such an undertaking.

Chapter 4

Taxonomy and Primate Classification

Classification

Before the advent of modern genetically based evolutionary studies, taxonomy (literally, the arrangement of names) constituted the foundation of the biological sciences. The eighteenth century systematists spent their lives devising and revising systems of names to encompass all living organisms. The most complete of these is Linnaeus' system, which, with some modifications, survives to the present day. While the form remains substantially the same, the reasoning behind it has undergone change. Prior to Darwin, taxonomy primarily served to demonstrate the order inherent in creation and was regarded as an end in itself. Today, rather than constituting a picture of the ordained and eternal, formal classification is best considered to represent a summary of evolutionary distances and relationships. Occasionally philosophers of science will attempt to equate the relationships and complexities of the physical and organic worlds with the infinite and eternal of the religious philosophers, and perhaps they have a point, for the immense but logical complexity of organic evolution as revealed by a complete taxonomy is indeed great and wonderful. In this sense, perhaps, there is still some value in regarding classification as being partially justified as an end in itself.

Our primary concern, however, is with

the practical results of taxonomy and with the problems involved in constructing an adequate classification. Except at the species level, the units and levels of classification are purely arbitrary and primarily reflect the accumulated opinions of ten generations of classifiers. Even at the species level there are problems that result in the continuous use of compromise and expediency. For example, the continuous evolution of a single line produces an accumulation of changes in time that demands adjustment of the specific designation, but at precisely which point the change in name should go into effect is an unanswerable question. The same sort of question occurs where geographic isolation separates members of an original species. In time, differences in selective pressures and the accidents of genetic drift would change them enough to prevent the possibility of interbreeding, but such a point would be reached after a full continuum of reducing interfertility, and the actual instant when species differentiation occurs is simply an arbitrary decision made by a taxonomist.

With these difficulties in mind, the taxonomic unit species is still a basic and useful concept and the definition we shall use is this:

> *A species is comprised of all those organisms that interbreed to produce viable fertile offspring.*

Some authors prefer the stipulation that the organisms "regularly interbreed" indicating that those populations which experiments show are interfertile but geographically isolated in nature should not be included in the same species. For evolutionary purposes it is true that in such a case the initial step toward speciation has occurred. On the other hand, certain authors feel that "those organisms which are capable of interbreeding . . ." should define species, since this refers to anatomical and physiological fact. In our definition, we have attempted to avoid these two extremes by being deliberately vague and using a phrase that could be interpreted either way. These restrictions only allow a limited amount of quibbling and furnish us with a basic evolutionary unit.

The Binomial System

At the core of the system standardized by Linnaeus and adopted by all subsequent biologists is the binomial (two-name) classification. The terms of the binomial classification are genus and species. Reference to a particular organism in a proper scientific work includes the mention of both its generic and specific names. Man,* (it should

---

*The sexism of this period was such that the entire article devoted to "Woman" in the first edition of the *Encyclopaedia Britannica*, published in 1771, consists of six words: "The female of man. See HOMO."

General Biological Background

have been "humanity"), for instance, is *Homo sapiens;* dog is **87**
Canis familiaris; cat is *Felis catus*, and so forth. Whether used together or separately, the terms should be italicized. The initial letter
of the generic designation is always capitalized, whereas that of the
specific designation is always lower case. Higher taxonomic categories are not printed in italics although the initial letter is capitalized.

As indicated above, the only nonarbitrary taxonomic unit for all
practical purposes is the species. However, there has been some attempt to define genus by removing the stipulation that breeding
should produce fertile offspring. For example, if members of good
but separate natural species can be induced to breed and produce
offspring, but the offspring are not fertile, then it is evident that there
must be some natural relationship between the parental species.
Some biologists would regard this as the criterion for their placement within a single genus. The health and vigor but sterility of that
well-known hybrid, the mule, furnishes a case in point. Though it
has neither pride of ancestry nor hope of posterity one could guess
without any further information that its parents belonged to different
species of the same genus, and such indeed is the case. Both horses
and donkeys belong to different species of the genus *Equus*, being,
respectively, *Equus caballus* and *Equus asinus*. Lions and tigers
also belong to a single genus — *Panthera leo* and *Panthera tigris*
— and one would expect a lion-tiger cross to be viable but sterile.
Again, the expectation is borne out.

Difficulties arise, however, when one attempts to extend this criterion. In the wild, matings between members of different species but
the same genus do not normally occur, and even in the rare instances
where they may have happened, reliable scientific recordings and
follow-up studies are simply nonexistent. Most of the known instances of cross-specific breeding have taken place in the artificial
circumstances of captivity, and even these represent only a small and
unsystematic proportion of the possible combinations. We know
about the lion and the tiger, but what about the lion and the leopard
(Panthera pardus)? Where cats of the genus *Felis* are concerned,
we know that the domestic cat *(Felis catus)* is capable of breeding
with the European wildcat *(Felis sylvestris)*. The offspring, however, are fertile. Going up the line, it is not so certain that the housecat is capable of breeding with the largest member of the genus, the
American mountain lion *(Felis concolor)*, and, could it do so, the
probability of its producing viable offspring seems remote.

Other examples simply compound the confusion, and ultimately
one is forced back to the "opinion of a competent systematist," a
method on which scientists have traditionally relied. If it is difficult
to establish objective criteria for defining the genera of living animals, obviously it is even more difficult to make reliable generic distinctions between the animals of a bygone era. For prehistoric
creatures, even the assignment of species can be a major problem, as

we shall see when we deal with the scraps of evidence for the earliest known human-like creatures.

Taxonomy

Taxonomically the larger and more inclusive divisions are compounded of closely related clusters of the immediately lower divisions, but no criteria have been offered for their exact definition. The standard list of major taxonomic categories with the appropriate name for the placement of humans is as follows:

Kingdom	**Animalia**
Phylum	**Chordata**
Class	**Mammalia**
Order	**Primates**
Family	**Hominidae**
Genus	*Homo*
species	*sapiens*

Most of these categories can be further subdivided, and one sees such terms as Superfamily, Subphylum, Infraorder, and the like. These are produced by adding the prefixes Super-, Sub-, and Infra- to the terms in the list above. When category splitting involves refinements at the Family level, there is a convention that helps the reader to identify the level being referred to. A Superfamily term ends in -oidea, a Family term ends in -ïdae, and a Subfamily designation ends in -inae. To use a Primate example, New World monkeys belong to Superfamily Ceboidea; the largest Family is the Cebidae; and this includes, as one of its Subfamilies, the Cebinae.

In the discussion that follows, we shall deal exclusively with the more important subdivisions of the Order that includes humans and their nearest relatives, i.e., the Order Primates.

Most authorities agree in splitting the Order into two suborders, although their exact names occasion some disagreement. The classification we are using is based on that proposed by G. G. Simpson, although the reader should be aware that neither we nor Simpson himself now follow the scheme exactly as it was originally proposed. The two suborders are Prosimii and Anthropoidea. The Prosimians include the tree shrews, lorises, lemurs, and tarsiers. Anthropoidea includes monkeys, apes, and humans. The differences between the varieties of Primates are so numerous that it is reasonable to ask what it is that defines the Primates as an Order. Until recently, taxonomists were inclined to require certain basic characteristics of any organism if it were to warrant inclusion within a particular category. This procedure was a carryover from pre-Darwinian thinking and was based upon the idea of fixed, eternal, and preordained distinctions. If it were possible to make taxonomic judgments on the basis of such rigid requirements, it would make matters easier for the student as well as for the professional scientist, but, unfortunately, there are always exceptions to any rigid scheme, and among the diverse and generalized members of the Order Primates there are sufficient exceptions so that no rigidly defined lists of traits are adequate to define them.

A solution to this dilemma has been offered by the English anatomist and primatologist Sir Wilfrid E. Le Gros Clark, who distinguishes the Primates from the other Orders of Mammals on the basis of a number of evolutionary trends. Our discussion is largely based on that of Le Gros Clark.

The tendencies that characterize the Order Primates involve two areas of the overall anatomy, the locomotor apparatus and the head, and manifestations of the tendencies listed below in both of these areas signify that the possessors are Primates.

I. Limb structure characterized by
  A. Retention of generalized or primitive mammalian organization
    1. Retention of a well-developed clavicle (collarbone) allowing great mobility of the pectoral appendages (arms).
    2. Retention of the primitive vertebrate pentadactyl (five-fingered) appendages.
  B. Emphasis on grasping ability
    1. Enhanced mobility of all the digits, but especially of the thumb and big toe.
    2. Presence of nails, rather than claws, indicating the development of pads of well-endowed tactile sensory tissue at the ends of the digits.
II. Cranial organs characterized by
  A. Development of the powers of vision
    1. Varying degrees of binocular ability.
  B. Expansion of the choice-making organ—the brain, especially in the cerebral cortex
  C. Reduction of the muzzle
    1. Reduction in importance of the sense of smell and its related organs.
    2. Reduction in the dentition coincident with its reduced importance as a defensive and manipulative organ. This involves reduction in the primitive mammalian number of teeth and simplification of crown cusp patterns.

The significance of these tendencies will be discussed later when we deal with the evolution of the Primates as seen through the interpretation of the fossil record. At the moment, it is sufficient to note that these are all related to the fact that, early in the age of mammals,

90 the Primates adapted to an arboreal (tree-living) ecological niche.

It is not our intention to discuss the living members of the Primates in any kind of detail, fascinating as that may be; however, in order to convey some idea of the relationships, forms, and habitats of the various Primates, a brief consideration of the Superfamilies will follow. For the classification of the Primates see Table 1, pp. 118–119.

Order	*Primates*
Order	**Primates**
Suborder	**Prosimii**
Infraorder	**Lemuriformes**
Superfamily	**Tupaioidea**
	Lemuroidea
	Daubentonioidea
Infraorder	**Lorisiformes**
Infraorder	**Tarsiiformes**
Suborder	**Anthropoidea**
Infraorder	**Platyrrhini**
Superfamily	**Ceboidea**
Infraorder	**Catarrhini**
Superfamily	**Cercopithecoidea**
	Hominoidea

Prosimii

TUPAIOIDEA

This Superfamily today occupies an equivocal position. After a long taxonomic sojourn among the insectivores, it was promoted to the status of the most primitive of the Primates. This new situation has met with serious criticism from many authorities. Among the tree shrews, to give the tupaiids their common name, placentation is unlike that in any Primate, and there are fundamental differences in ankle and wrist bones, the cartilaginous skull, musculature, viscera, and many other features. It has been suggested, therefore, that the tupaiids be removed from the Order Primates and placed with the lepticid-like insectivores. But if that is done it will not alter the fact, upon which all authorities agree, that the tupaiids constitute the closest relatives of the Primates.

Several forms of tree shrew are known, ranging from India east and south through Southeast Asia and the Indonesian Archipelago. They are small scurrying creatures, living on a variety of insects, although they do eat some fruits and seeds and occasional small mammals, mice for instance. They tend to live in bushes and on the lower branches of trees rather than in the arboreal niche proper.

General Biological Background

Figure 27. Tree shrew (*Urogale everetti*), Philippines. (Courtesy of Dr. Ralph Buschbaum.)

Tree shrews possess claws on *all* digits, unlike Primates who generally possess flattened nails on their digits. From whatever taxonomic category we choose to view them, the tree shrews constitute a remarkable living example of a form transitional between the Primates and the primitive, generalized, mammalian stock that the Order Insectivora represents. The tree shrews afford us a clue to the nature of the first step away from the basic mammalian stem toward the evolution of the higher Primates and ultimately humankind.

LEMUROIDEA

The lemurs proper, the most primitive of living Primates with the exception of the controversial tree shrews, exist only on the island of Madagascar and neighboring smaller islands off the east coast of Africa. There they have been isolated for more than half the age of mammals, and, in the absence of competition from both carnivores and "higher," more efficient Primates, they have undergone something of an adaptive radiation of their own. Living lemurs vary in size from the tiny mouse lemur (*Microcebus*) with a body length of four or five inches (with its fluffy tail added it still totals less than a foot in length) up to the stump-tailed *Indri*, which is about three feet

Figure 28. Brown Lemur (*Lemur fulvus*). (Courtesy of the Zoological Society of Philadelphia.)

tall when standing on its hind legs and is about the bulk of a middling-sized dog.

The lemurs have monkey-like limbs with flattened nails on their digits — all except the second toe, which preserves a convenient claw for scratching purposes. The cranial development, however, represents a compromise. The brain is larger than that of other mammals of comparable size, but it is not up to monkey standards. The reduction of the snout has not proceeded to the degree it has in monkeys, and with the bare patch of moist skin — the rhinarium — the sense of smell is retained to a greater extent. Sensory whiskers remain on the muzzle, over the eyes, and on the wrists indicating that the sensory equipment of the primitive terrestrial mammal persists. The lemurs also retain the ability to move the ears toward sources of sound, an ability long since lost by higher Primates in spite of the fact that it is retained by some humans who can manage to "wiggle their ears."

Finally, the lower incisors and canines of modern lemurs, instead

General Biological Background

of being set vertically in the jaw, project straight forward. Used in conjunction with the lips and tongue, this "dental comb" serves as a device for picking through and grooming the fur, an activity performed by the fingers in the more dexterous higher Primates.

The Mozambique Channel, which separates Madagascar from mainland Africa, is more than 200 miles wide at its narrowest and has a geological antiquity that extends back to long before the existence of the Primates. We do not know how the first mammals got there but presumably they drifted across on rafts of vegetation or trees that were washed out to sea. Once they got to Madagascar, they diversified to fill the various available ecological niches. In the case of the lemurs, the functional similarities to very remotely related mainland forms provide some striking examples of parallelism and serve as eloquent testimony to the shaping powers of natural selection. Unfortunately the isolation was terminated about two thousand years ago by that most destructive of Primates — *Homo sapiens* — and some of the most instructive examples of parallel evolution among the lemurs became the victims of this invasion. Among these was the large arboreal browser *Megaladapis*. Native legends and accounts, together with the description of a mid-seventeenth century French explorer, mentioning a monkey-like creature the size of a young cow, almost certainly refer to *Megaladapis*. No mention of it is made in the systematic treatises of the eighteenth century naturalists, and it would seem that *Megaladapis*, like the dodo, became extinct about two hundred and fifty years ago.

Megaladapis illustrates how one group of lemurs adapted to the niche of a bulky arboreal browser in the manner of the marsupial koala of Australia; another form adjusted to terrestrial living by developing locomotor efficiency. This was *Hadropithecus*, a quadrupedal running form, that shows an adaptation parallel to that of the patas monkey in the open plains of the southern Sahara, the Sudan, and adjacent areas of the African mainland. *Hadropithecus* also was unsuccessful in the face of competition from the invading terrestrial Primate *Homo* and became extinct before the advent of writing on Madagascar, so our knowledge of its existence and its form is confined to the mute testimony of the pieces of skeleton that have been found.

Representing another extreme of the lemur adaptive radiation is yet another recently extinct creature *Palaeopropithecus*. The arms were longer than the legs, and with the curvature of hand and foot bones and the form of toe and finger joints suggesting that both hands and feet served as permanent hooks, one interpretation holds that they clambered and suspended themselves by their arms — brachiated — in the manner of modern anthropoid apes, especially the chimpanzee and the orang. Another interpretation, noting the differences in neck muscle attachments, suggests that they characteristically hung in the manner of sloths. Still another, influenced by the fact that their remains have been found in conjunction with lake-bed deposits, has viewed them as specialized for an aquatic existence, but this would seem more than just a bit far-fetched. With hook-like hands and elongated arms, they were surely arboreal clamberers, whether in the sloth or ape-like mode.

Daubentonioidea

This Superfamily is represented by only a single species, the curious and specialized aye-aye. Unimportant for building a systematic picture of Primate evolution, it is nevertheless a curious and interesting creature. It represents, in fact, a part of the lemur adaptive radiation of Madagascar, where the isolation of this refuge area allowed creatures to survive that would long since have been eliminated by natural selection had they been faced with competition from the main stream of mammalian development. Other environmental refuge areas—the Galápagos Islands with their birds and reptiles and Australia with its marsupials—have harbored similar evolutionary curiosities.

The Madagascar aye-aye has diverged to such an extent from the rest of lemur evolution that at one time it was even classed as a rodent. Now it is recognized as a lemur but belonging in a separate Superfamily of its own. It has enlarged rodent-like incisors while the rest of the dentition is greatly reduced, claws on all the digits except the thumb, and a greatly elongated third finger of the hand. This latter is related to its dietary specialization. Its main item of food is a wood-boring grub, which it locates in branches by the sound. Having located a grub burrow, the aye-aye gnaws an opening with its spe-

Figure 29. Aye-Aye (*Daubentonia madagascarensis*), an aberrant primate from Madagascar. (Courtesy of the Zoological Society of Philadelphia.)

cialized incisors and then inserts the long third finger like a flexible
wire probe. With this it impales the grub, extracts it, and then pops it
into its mouth—lunch. Not really an important Primate, but an interesting one, alas with poor prospects for survival—again as a result of
human expansion. At the beginning of the present century, the aye-
aye ranged from the northernmost tip of Madagascar half way down
the east coast, but today they number among the rarest and most
endangered animals on earth with an estimated number of no more
than fifty surviving specimens.

<h2 style="text-align:center">Lorisiformes</h2>

Lorises are the mainland equivalents of the lemurs. Anatomists have
listed enough distinctions between lemurs and lorises to separate
them into different Infraorders, but because of the similarity in their
sensory and motor equipment, they occupy an ecological niche similar to that of the Madagascar lemurs. They range throughout the bush
and forest parts of Africa, India, and Southeast Asia, but since these
areas are also the locations of the more successful Anthropoidea, the
restrictions on loris form and activity have been much more stringent. Among other things, most lorises have sought refuge in nocturnal activities. Admittedly some true lemurs are nocturnal, but the
diurnal arboreal ecological niche on Madagascar is also occupied by
lemurs. On the mainland, however, competition from the monkeys

Figure 30. Loris. The potto *(Perodicticus potto).*
(Courtesy of the Zoological Society of Philadelphia.)

means that most Prosimians are nocturnal or semi-nocturnal (twilight operators).

On Madagascar, the lemur Superfamily is divided into Families Lemuridae and Indrisidae. The latter show a slight proportional enlargement of the hind legs and a tendency to progress by jumping rather than by the quadrupedal scampering characteristic of the Lemuridae. This distinction between the jumpers and the more orthodox quadrupeds is present in even more exaggerated form among the Lorisiformes, a group divided into the Families Lorisidae and Galagidae. The anatomy and the physiology of the lorises and pottos, for instance, are related to a slow and deliberate mode of progression. This is obviously prudent for a nocturnal creature in an arboreal environment; it is a trait so well developed that some are able to creep up unperceived on sleeping birds and in this manner add fresh animal protein to their diet. By contrast, the galagos, commonly called "Bush babies," display enlarged hind legs obviously related to jumping. Some accounts have described the galagos as specialized for hopping, and many a reader has retained the impression of small kangaroo-like creatures bobbing quaintly from branch to branch. Until recently, the devoted zoo-goer lucky enough to spot a galago would normally see little more than a small fur lump whose most dramatic activity was the occasional blinking of a sleepy eye. For those whose good fortune has included a visit to African scrub forest and brush country, the emergence of the Bush babies at dusk will remain a fascinating event. Their frenetically active scamperings are punctuated by sling-shot-like leaps projecting the little creatures ten, fifteen, and more feet across open spaces between trees.

TARSIOIDEA

The entire Infraorder Tarsiiformes with its one Superfamily is represented by the single Genus *Tarsius*. The Tarsiers display a unique combination of primitive and advanced features that has given taxonomists trouble for years. A case could be made for regarding them as the most primitive of the Suborder Anthropoidea, as deserving of a special Suborder of their own, or, as is generally felt, the most advanced of the Prosimians.

The center of this taxonomic wrangle is a creature "the size of a small kitten" that inhabits parts of the Indonesian Archipelago, Borneo, and the Philippines. Its name, tarsier, refers to the elongation of the tarsal portion of the foot. This provides the added leverage that allows the little tarsier to make spectacular leaps more than four feet straight up — a remarkable performance for such a small animal. This specialization along with the specialization of the eyes for nocturnal activities and modifications in the dentition prevents the living tarsier from being a good representative of a transition between

Figure 31. Tarsier *(Tarsius syrichta)* from Mindanao, Philippines. (Courtesy of the Zoological Society of Philadelphia.)

the Prosimians and the Anthropoidea although it approaches more closely to filling this role than any other living Primate. In structure and habits it is the counterpart of the galago of Africa, another example of the effects of natural selection on creatures that inhabit similar ecological niches in different parts of the world.

Anthropologists of an earlier generation suggested that the vertical clinging and leaping of the tarsier provided a model that might cast light on the origin of a habitually erect body posture. With a tarsier-like ancestor displaying such a preadaptation, claims were advanced that the long-legged vertical human body plan could have evolved straight from an Eocene prosimian without going through a monkey- or ape-like stage. While there is no fossil evidence for such an occurrence, and the gap between a tarsier and a human is wide indeed, the supporters of this view point to *Indri* on Madagascar as showing how this could have been bridged. The Indris, largest of living lemurs, is a vertical clinger and leaper with a very short tail. When on the ground, it often moves bipedally. It should be stressed that no one is advancing the Indris as an actual human ancestor. Rather, the case is made that if such a large vertical clinger and leaper could evolve independently on Madagascar, there is no reason why a parallel development could not have occurred on the mainland in a form that later went on to give rise to the higher Primates including humans. It is a thought-provoking speculation and it would be unwise to dismiss it out of hand, but at the moment there simply is no evidence for it.

Anthropoidea

CEBOIDEA

This is the only Superfamily in the Infraorder Platyrrhini, the New World monkeys that range from southern Mexico down into the tropical parts of South America. Until the arrival of the American Indians beginning a few tens of thousands of years ago, the only Primates in the Western Hemisphere belonged to the Superfamily Ceboidea. The best indications point to a separation from the Primates of the Old World of more than fifty million years. During that time, the New World monkeys have undergone an adaptive radiation which in many ways parallels that of Primates in the Old World.

Two Families are encompassed by the Ceboidea, the Callithricidae and the Cebidae. The Callithricidae include the marmosets: scurrying, scampering, squirrel-like creatures, which functionally might be called the Prosimians of the New World. The Family Cebidae is composed of the New World monkeys proper and includes the only monkeys in the world that can actually hang by their tails. Not even all of the Cebidae have prehensile tails, and even in the case of *Cebus* itself, the capuchin or organ grinder's monkey (the popular name for the best known of the Cebidae), the tail is not as well developed a weight-supporting organ as it is in the howler monkey or in the woolly and the spider monkeys.

The howler monkey is aptly named, for the enlarged hyoid bone in the throat of both sexes, but especially well developed in males, serves as a vocal resonating chamber, and the creature can produce a simply phenomenal volume of noise — audible for several miles on a quiet day. However, from the point of view of the student of primate evolution, the most interesting of the New World monkeys is the spider monkey. Not only does it possess the most thoroughly prehensile tail of any primate, but, it also is the only monkey in either hemisphere that makes more than occasional use of the mode of progression characteristic of the apes — brachiation. As a consequence of this adaptation there has been some selection for modifications of the pelvis, chest, shoulders, arms, and hands, which show a striking degree of convergence toward the form visible in the same parts of

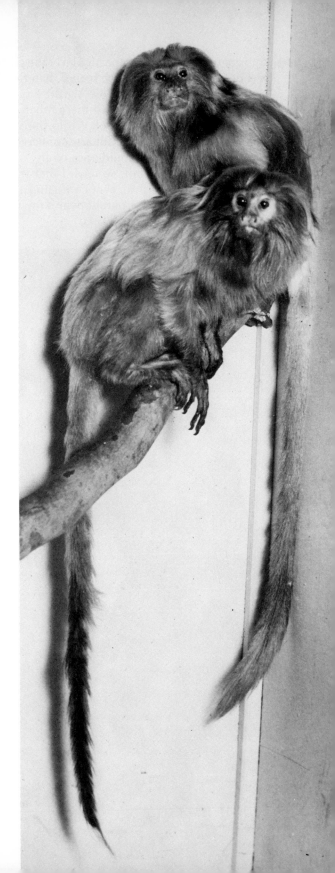

Figure 32. Golden Marmosets (*Leontocebus rosalia*). Female (front) and male (back). (Courtesy of the Zoological Society of Philadelphia.)

the anatomy of the apes, particularly the gibbon, which, as the small-est of the apes, is not much bigger than the spider monkey. The spi-der monkey is the only New World monkey in which the thumbs have been reduced often to a mere tubercle, the hand functioning as a kind of quick-release hook.While the spider monkey, as an inter-esting example of evolutionary convergence, comes closest to the structure of the anthropoid apes of any of the New World monkeys, the possession of a tail, so useful that it is practically a fifth hand, would prevent one from ever confusing a spider monkey with a gen-uine ape. Despite the parallelism shown in the evolution of New

Figure 33. Cebus. White-throated capuchin monkey (*Cebus capucinus*). (Cour-tesy of the Zoological Society of Philadelphia.)

Figure 34. Spider monkey. Geoffrey's spider monkey (*Ateles geoffroyi*). Note the enormously developed prehensile tail and absence of a thumb.

World monkeys, none ever invaded the terrestrial ecological niche and no really bulky forms evolved.

CERCOPITHECOIDEA

The Infraorder Catarrhini includes monkeys, apes, and humans, and the Superfamily Cercopithecoidea is its monkey division. The single Family Cercopithecidae includes all the Old World monkeys. This in turn is further subdivided into the Subfamilies Cercopithecinae and Colobinae, each of which includes many Genera. The Cercopithecinae embraces the mangabeys, guenons, baboons, and macaques, i.e., all the monkeys one generally associates with the Old World and particularly with Africa. Many, such as macaques

Figure 35. Baboon. The mandrill *(Mandrillus sphinx).* (Courtesy of the Zoological Society of Philadelphia.)

Figure 36. Green monkey *(Cercopithecus aethiops sabaeus).* (Courtesy of the Zoological Society of Philadelphia.)

and baboons, are partly or wholly terrestrial, and as a consequence, tend to have longer muzzles and larger canine teeth than New World monkeys. Some of the baboons get to be quite large in size and, the males particularly, are equipped with formidable canine teeth — necessary defensive equipment for a relatively slow-running quadruped only secondarily adapted to terrestrial living. Members of the Subfamily Cercopithecinae extend as far south and east as the Celebes and as far north and east as Japan, but they are most numerous in Africa.

The Subfamily Colobinae includes the leaf-eating monkeys, the langurs and the proboscis monkey, and is concentrated in Southeast Asia and India, although a few are found in Africa. They are characterized by the possession of complex sacculated stomachs, which enable them to derive adequate nourishment from their bulky but relatively un-nutritious diet of leaves and shoots (the nuts, fruits,

Figure 37. Mona monkey (*Cercopithecus mona*) with young. (Courtesy of the Zoological Society of Philadelphia.)

berries, insects, eggs, etc., of the cercopithecine diet have relatively much higher nutritive values). In addition, the presence of many cellulose-digesting bacteria in the digestive tract suggests that, like the terrestrial ruminants, they can utilize structural carbohydrates as a major energy source. Indeed they have been successfully raised in captivity on a diet of fresh alfalfa. The Colobinae are primarily arboreal and, with their gastric specialization, are farther from the evolutionary line that led to the great apes and humans than are the other Old World monkeys.

HOMINOIDEA

Anthropoid apes and humans. Finally we reach the Superfamily to which we ourselves belong, and, since it is of greater concern to us, it is worth giving a more complete classification of it and dwelling for a while on each of its genera.

Superfamily **Hominoidea**
  Family **Pongidae**
    Subfamily **Hylobatinae**
      Genus *Hylobates*, the gibbon
             Symphalangus, the siamang
    Subfamily **Ponginae**
      Genus *Pongo*, the orang-utan
             Pan, the chimpanzee
             Gorilla, the gorilla
  Family **Hominidae**
    Genus *Homo*, humans

All the members of this Superfamily, unlike any other Primates, are utterly devoid of external tails; all are now or show clear evidence that their ancestors were brachiators, and, as such, show various degrees of structural adaptation to an erect posture; all have the same numbers of incisors, canines, premolars, and molars, and have the same cusp patterns on the molars and second premolars; and all show varying degrees of cerebral expansion when compared with the other Primates. Because they are so close to us, our interest is heightened and our objectivity often diminished. The repeated reassessment of the details of their classification and the sometimes acerbic disagreements between scientists who study them bear witness to somewhat excessive emotional involvement—a problem that becomes more acute the closer we come to the study of humankind.

There are enough disagreements relating to the classification of the Hominoidea so that the above scheme is offered tentatively. For example, there are some who regard the gibbons as sufficiently different to warrant a separate Family for them, the Hylobatidae, instead of regarding them as a Subfamily of the Pongidae.

Hylobates and Symphalangus. The siamang is actually just an enlarged version of the gibbon inhabiting Java and Sumatra, and there has been some considerable recent feeling to the effect that siamangs do not warrant a separate genus for themselves, i.e., some primatologists now include them in genus *Hylobates.* The siamang inhabits Sumatra and the mountains of Selangor State in the Malay Peninsula. But since it is not otherwise notable, it will not be treated separately. The gibbons are the most numerous of the anthropoid apes as well as the most spectacular arboreal acrobats. Exclusively tree-living, they owe at least a part of their acrobatic ability to the fact that they are by far and away the smallest of the anthropoid apes. While adult stature nearly reaches three feet, body weight ranges from not quite fifteen pounds down to well under ten pounds. Obviously the build is exceedingly slender, with the limbs — especially

Figure 38. White-handed gibbon *(Hylobates lar).* (Courtesy of the American Museum of Natural History.)

106 the arms—being enormously elongated in proportion to the general bulk. With such anatomical equipment, the gibbons are brachiators without peer, flourishing in the forests of Southeast Asia and Indonesia and ranging all the way from sea level up to the frost line in the foothills of the Himalayas.

The brachiating specialization of the gibbon has clearly gone beyond the point reached by humanity's own remote brachiating ancestor. In the gibbon, the fingers are so elongated that they can only be opposed to the thumb by bending them sharply toward the palm, and, even then, the opposition is weak and ineffective. Evidently to gain such superb powers of locomotion, they have sacrificed a considerable amount of manipulative ability.

Pongo. The orang-utan is the larger of the two Asiatic anthropoid apes and, like the gibbon, is for the most part arboreal, in contrast to the two African apes, which are largely terrestrial. Today the orang is restricted to the swampy forests of western Borneo and the very northwestern tip of Sumatra, the same species being found in the two areas despite their separation. Extensive fossil remains show that, in the recent past, the orang was common throughout Borneo, Java, Sumatra, and mainland Southeast Asia as far north as China.

It seems likely that its present restricted habitat is at least partially due to competition from the most formidable Primate of them all, humankind. In the recent past, humanity has spread and multiplied in Southeast Asia and Indonesia as a result of the utilization of controlled food resources, i.e., agriculture. Even the most primitive slash-and-burn mobile cultivators had a major impact on the extent of fully developed tropical rain forest. With the disappearance of the rain forest, the orang disappeared also. Gibbons, being small and light, are not so seriously affected by the fact that cut and burned

Figure 39. Two immature Sumatran orang-utans (*Pongo pygmaeus*). (Courtesy of the Zoological Society of Philadelphia.)

rain forest is replaced by brush and bamboo, but one need only make **107**
an attempt to imagine several hundred pounds of orang-utan strug-
gling to brachiate in a bamboo thicket and the present limitations of
the area inhabited become understandable.

Ironically, the growing realization that the orang faces imminent
extinction has actually hastened its disappearance in the wild. Many
zoos, becoming increasingly aware of its rare and endangered status,
have been willing to pay premium prices to obtain specimens. This
has led to a flourishing series of poaching and smuggling operations.
Since catching a live and uninjured adult a hundred feet and more
up in the canopy of a tropical rain forest is an extremely difficult
feat, the poachers generally look for mothers with infants, shoot the
mother, and capture the youngster. The result has been a disastrous
reduction in the number of breeding females even in those areas that,
ecologically, could still support wild orang populations. Compound-
ing the tragedy is the fact that only a pathetic few of the young apes
secured by these means survive the trials of capture and transport to
reach quarters where they receive adequate care. Recent successes in
zoo breeding programs raise the hope that orangs may be able to survive in captivity, but the prospects for the wild population are increasingly gloomy.

Physically the male orang stands somewhat less than five feet in
height and weighs about one-hundred and sixty-five pounds, although large males are over five feet and two hundred pounds, making them second in size only to the gorilla. In captivity some individuals get to be well over three hundred pounds, although these are
grossly overweight.

Females, on the other hand, average only half the bulk of the
males, being under ninety pounds. The arms are enormously long—
over eight feet in span for a large male—and, in conjunction with
their thorough adaptation as arboreal brachiators the bones of both
the hands and the feet are curved into permanent hooks. However
excellent this may be for supporting bulky bodies with a minimum
of muscular effort, it severely limits manipulative ability. These facts
and many others are known about orangs, but we have relatively little information about their mode of living in the wild. This is partly
due to their solitary habits, but mostly because the remaining areas
inhabited make observation difficult. The creatures live hidden in
the leafy parts of big trees far above the forest floor, and, as if that did
not make things difficult enough, for part of the year the forest floor
is neck deep in water so that a boat would be necessary. Hence relatively little is known of the family life and social habits of the orang,
and, with the tremendous current expansion of the human population in Southeast Asia, it is apparent that serious efforts must be
made to secure this information before it is too late.

The orang is more of an enigma than any of the other anthropoid

Figure 40. Sumatran orang-utan (*Pongo pygmaeus*) with infant. (Courtesy of the Zoological Society of Philadelphia.)

apes since less is known about its life in the wild. One of the enigmas concerning the orang is the meaning of their pronounced sexual dimorphism. In gorillas, baboons, and other Primates where marked sexual dimorphism occurs, the reason is not hard to discover. In virtually every instance, the group in question is terrestrial rather than arboreal, and the size, muscularity, and special dental development of the males play an important role in maintaining group cohesion and in defense against threatened predation. The orang in contrast has been thought to be one of the most exclusively arboreal of all Primates, rarely descending to the ground. This is, in fact, not quite true. While females remain largely arboreal, mature males may spend six or more hours traveling and foraging on the ground and do

General Biological Background

most of their long-distance traveling along the forest floor. Biruté Galdikas-Brindamour, who made these observations, also observed a subadult male asleep on the ground for 45 minutes during the day. He had merely bent a sapling under him as he lay down. Subsequently she observed three actual "ground" nests. In these instances the nests were built on logs that had fallen less then a yard off the floor.

Why then should the male orang possess such formidably enlarged canine teeth and muscular strength out of all proportion to the demands of an arboreal mode of existence? Some have suggested that perhaps orangs lived a very different kind of life in the very recent past before humanity pushed them to their present refuge areas, but this is not a very helpful guess. Fossil orang remains coincide with the area formerly covered by rain forest. Their present diet is of the fruit, nut, and leaf variety found only in rain forests, and their locomotor anatomy is obviously specialized for climbing and not much else. To be sure, the modern zoo-goer will see captive orangs moving in clumsy quadrupedal fashion across cage floors, sometimes using their arms like crutches, sometimes moving in amoeba-like fashion by extending now one appendage now another and pulling themselves along, or in extreme instances curling themselves up into long-haired orange balls and simply rolling. None of it is very efficient, however, and it does not take a sophisticated observer to realize that the orang simply is not designed for terrestrial locomotion. However different their ecology was before human pressures altered it, one can be sure that the terrestrial component was minor indeed and certainly not sufficient to account for their present sexual dimorphism.

A cogent explanation for sexual dimorphism among orangs has been offered by Biruté Galdikas-Brindamour. She observed that all adolescent females preferred large mature males as sexual partners to the smaller subadult males who were their more frequent companions. This female preference combined with male competition suggests that since the larger males would have an obvious advantage in sexual competition they would be more likely to be reproductively the most successful. The females, requiring no such size because it gives them no reproductive advantage, would remain small. In addition, a small female can find food more easily than a large one.

Until very recently, it was generally thought that, except for a mother with a dependent youngster, orangs pursued solitary lives, coming and going in the rain forest canopy with nearly complete indifference to the presence or absence of other orangs. Such, however, is far from being the case. Determined efforts are currently being pursued to study orangs in their natural habitat before they disappear. These studies show that mature males control areas of undisturbed forest that include the territories of several separately living females. Part of the male effort at territorial control is vocal, and the male bellow evidently carries for more than a mile. A female in estrus will approach in response to the signal, while the reaction of nonestrus females is a prudent withdrawal.

Adult males, especially old ones, spend a fair amount of time foraging on the forest floor, and apparently sometimes make their sleeping nests there. Under these circumstances, one could argue that greater size would have a higher fitness (W), but it still seems likely that the achievement of large size was a response to conditions in the forest canopy and that observed terrestrial activities are only a secondary consequence.

Not only do female orangs show a response to the male voice, but other males do so as well, demonstrating considerable agitation. And when a male actually catches sight of another male, it is enough literally to provoke a screaming rage. Actual fights between males have not been observed, but the great bulk and musculature of an adult male orang plus its enlarged canine teeth may very well be related to the ability to control areas of forest canopy and ensure access to receptive females. In short, the bellow may not be all bluff.

Mature orangs have been described as morose and phlegmatic, and doubts have been voiced about their intelligence compared to that of their more demonstrative cousins the chimpanzees. However, most mature specimens are seen in the sanitary but bleak confines of their zoo cells, where their behavior is a correspondingly stunted and truncated version of what it potentially could be. More perceptive studies and observations suggest that their ingenuity is at least on a par with that of their more celebrated African relatives.

Pan. Of all the anthropoid apes, the African chimpanzee is the best known, although most of this knowledge was based on chimps in captivity, and only recently, as the outcome of a prolonged and successful attempt to study them in their African habitat, has reliable information been obtained concerning their ways of life under natural conditions. Male chimpanzees weigh in the neighborhood of one hundred and ten, and females just under ninety pounds on the average, with a wide range of fluctuations. In the past, this wide range of size, shape, and color led to the creation of several species of chimpanzees from what represented no more than individual differences within the normal range of variation.

Although the differences of opinion are still far from being settled, many authorities suspect that there are only two species of chimpanzee, a full-sized one ranging from Gambia at the very westernmost tip of Africa throughout the forested areas of West Africa and the Congo drainage basin, and a pygmy chimpanzee just south of the great bend of the Congo river itself. It is not yet certain, however, whether the pygmy chimpanzee is a genuine separate species, or whether it is simply the small end of a line of normal chimpanzee

variation. If the latter is found to be the case, there would be but one
species of chimpanzee throughout the whole range, an area larger
in extent than the area inhabited by any other anthropoid ape.

In contrast with the Asiatic anthropoid apes, which are almost
exclusively arboreal in habitat and specializations, the African apes
make regular use of a terrestrial habitat. This is particularly true of
the gorilla, which, because of its size when adult, is almost completely terrestrial, but even the smaller chimpanzee spends between
one third and one half of each day on the ground. In arm, shoulder,
and trunk structure, both apes are classed as brachiators despite
their secondary adaptation to quadrupedalism when terrestrial locomotion is required.

In their arboreal activities, the chimpanzees (and the gorillas when
young) behave as their structure would indicate and brachiate as
expected. While the immediate fossil precursors of gorillas and
chimpanzees are not known, it is believed by most investigators that
they must have been more thoroughly arboreal than either is today,
and that they utilized brachiation as their mode of progression, otherwise the development of the brachiating build in the modern representatives would be difficult to explain.

In discussions of brachiation, there is sometimes a tendency to
exaggerate the emphasis on arm swinging. Gibbons, to be sure, do

Figure 41. Chimpanzee (*Pan
troglodytes*). (Courtesy of
the New York Zoological Society.)

exhibit an extreme case and, for a fair proportion of their more rapid arboreal movements, do indeed use the arms alone. Orangs also do so although to a lesser extent. Occasionally chimpanzees and even gorillas can be seen moving hand over hand, suspended by the arms alone, but — and this is true for orangs as well — the normal mode of arboreal progression is a sort of four-handed clambering involving a variety of locomotor styles. Bipedal walking as well as quadrupedal walking on top of branches, quadrupedal suspension in sloth-like fashion beneath branches, some true brachiation, but most frequently reaching and grabbing by one long arm followed by the feet and the other hand where convenient, all these and other forms of locomotion occur. One can guess that this arose as a feeding adaptation where the arms were used first to pull food from branch tips to mouth, and later actually to pull the ape from one branch to another.

The chimpanzee possesses a particular fascination for lay people and scientists alike, representing a form more nearly resembling humanity's probable prehuman ancestor than any other living Primate. Although it is less highly specialized either for arboreal living, as are the Asiatic anthropoids, or secondarily for terrestrial quadrupedalism, as are the gorillas, yet the chimpanzee may have gone just a little farther in the brachiating direction than our prehuman ancestors. The chimpanzee hand is long and strong, but the thumb is short, opposition to the fingers is awkward, and the muscular definition that would allow fine finger movements is sacrificed in favor of the ability to flex the fingers all together as a powerful weight-supporting hook.

The chimpanzee, however, should not be regarded as a creature doomed by limiting specializations. Though it possesses less manual dexterity than many monkeys, its manipulative ability is nevertheless greater than that of any other ape and its ingenuity exceeds that of any Primate with the exception of humankind. Recent prolonged field observation by Dr. Jane van Lawick-Goodall at the Gombe Stream Reserve in Tanzania and Dr. and Mrs. Vernon I. Reynolds in the Budongo Forest in Uganda have greatly increased our knowledge of chimpanzee behavior in their natural habitat. Their studies have revealed that chimpanzees utilize an astonishing variety of food resources, and Drs. van Lawick-Goodall and Geza Teleki have recorded repeated incidents of deliberate hunting. This, however, should not be regarded as support for the image of the blood-thirsty "killer ape" so dear to the heart of some would-be science popularizers, since most chimpanzee hunting behavior appears to be more a matter of the opportunity of the moment rather than something conceived in advance. Infant baboons, bushpigs, or bushbucks, when encountered by chance are treated as edible, as are lone monkeys. In fact, the human inhabitants of chimpanzee country are watchful of their own infants. Dr. van Lawick-Goodall, although completely accepted and regarded as harmless by the chimpanzees, nevertheless **113** has kept her own small son within the safety of a stout cage at times during his visits to the Gombe Stream Reserve.

Perhaps the most remarkable addition to our knowledge about chimpanzees is the discovery that they actually modify natural objects to be used as tools. A slender twig or stalk of grass is carefully stripped of projections, moistened with the lips, carefully inserted into the middle of a termite's nest, then withdrawn; the attached termites are licked off and eaten with relish, providing a good source of protein for the chimpanzee. Knowledge of this procedure obviously is not gained through inherited instinct, but must be learned by imitation. Here, then, is an activity that must have been discovered in some previous generation and has become part of a transmitted tradition. Such behavior is cultural behavior, and it follows that chimpanzees possess the rudiments of culture. In contrast to humans, however, culture is not the *primary* adaptation of the chimpanzee. Humans deprived of their culture are totally helpless, while the cultureless chimpanzee would still have a better than even chance of survival.

Gorilla. It may appear somewhat surprising, but the very existence of the gorilla was not suspected until almost the midpoint of the nineteenth century. Africa was among the last of the world's great land masses to be explored; hence, despite the gorilla's great bulk, its habitat in the more remote and inaccessible parts of the continent guaranteed a seclusion from all but the relentless push of twentieth-century *Homo sapiens.*

The appearance of the gorilla—large and black and hairy—presented a perfect image upon which the Victorians could project and thus "substantiate" the alleged inherent beastliness of humanity, in which they so perfervidly believed. As such, the poor gorilla was invested with the attributes of ferocity that were assumed to belong to this repressed animal nature, and all kinds of bizarre and frequently unsavory legends were created to fit the gorilloid image. Recent detailed and excellent field study has shown that the actual facts of gorilla behavior are about as far removed from the lurid fancies of the popular accounts as it is possible to be. In reality, the gorilla is so involved in the process of acquiring enough of the low-nutritive-value food of its characteristic diet to nourish its vast bulk that it has little time for the varied and interesting activities that account for so much of the fascination of chimpanzee behavior. In fact, gorillas tend to be incurious, unimaginative, peaceful, and dull.

The gorillas of Africa are found in two regions separated by some 700 miles and are considered to belong to corresponding subspecies. The western or lowland gorilla, inhabiting the forests of the Cameroons and Gabon in the north and westernmost parts of the Congo basin, was the first to be discovered. As the type species and subspecies of the Genus *Gorilla*, the full formal designation is *Gorilla gorilla gorilla*. Early in the twentieth century, the mountain gorilla was recognized as being distinct and has been named *Gorilla gorilla beringei*. This population inhabits a narrow area at an elevation of over ten thousand feet in the cold damp forests of the mountains at the very eastern edge of the Congo basin.

Zoologists suspect that the separation of gorillas into eastern and western groups may be of recent origin, reflecting, as in the case of the orang, the impact of the spreading influence of humans. In the recent past, then, gorilla distribution may have been continuous from the Virunga volcanoes and Mt. Kahuzi in the Great Lakes region of Central Africa all the way across the northern Congo basin to Rio Muni, the Cameroons, and Nigeria in the west. Contrary to the popu-

Figure 42. Lowland young gorillas (*Gorilla gorilla gorilla*). Male (left) and female (right). (Courtesy of the Zoological Society of Philadelphia.)

lar racist assumption that this area was the aboriginal homeland of native African populations, it has only been penetrated by people in significant numbers within the past two thousand years. The climate is too damp for grain crops, and stone axes do not make it easy to cope with a full-fledged tropical rain forest. The development of adequate cultivated root crops and an iron technology does not go back more than two thousand years in equatorial Africa, and it is only within that time span that slash-and-burn agriculturalists have been able to move into the forested areas of West Africa and the Congo.

Actually since mature gorillas do not climb to get their food, they tend to avoid the mature rain forest areas since nothing much grows on the dimly lighted forest floor. This is in marked contrast to chimpanzees who do climb to reach their food and consequently exploit the resources up in the mature forest canopy. Gorillas on the other hand prefer areas of secondary growth and those marginal places where, because of swampy or rocky conditions, the forest is only incompletely developed.

With the expansion of secondary growth areas following the incursion of slash-and-burn agriculturalists, one might think that ideal gorilla habitats have increased in the last two thousand years. As far as the gorilla is concerned, however, this has been more than offset by the actions of the incoming farmers. It is not surprising that our close primate relatives like to eat the same foods as we do, even if the bulk of their diet may differ, and a dozen hungry gorillas in a banana patch can create havoc in a very short time. Congolese farmers, then, regard gorillas as destructive pests and hunt them when they come in contact with them. Furthermore since the diet of tropical forest agriculturalists tends to be very close to the border of protein insufficiency as far as human requirements are concerned, added meat is highly prized when available. From the point of view of local farmers, gorilla hunting not only eliminates an agricultural pest but also provides a protein supplement to an otherwise marginally adequate diet. As a result, gorillas now survive in only a fraction of their former range, and those that remain live a threatened existence.

There are a number of problems and tantalizing hints suggested by the suspicion that the now-isolated gorilla populations were once continuous. We now regard them as subspecifically distinct, but how would we treat them if we were faced with the restored continuum? This is not just a trivial problem relating to a rare and untypical creature for, as we shall see later, we face the same kind of question when dealing with human variation both through time and across geographical areas. In the case of the gorilla, there is just enough remaining of the former suspected continuum so that some interpretation can be suggested. The mountain gorillas in the east have longer and heavier bodies with somewhat shorter stockier

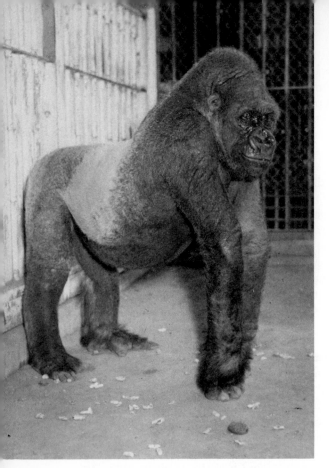

Figure 43. Adult male lowland gorilla (*Gorilla gorilla gorilla*). (Courtesy of the Zoological Society of Philadelphia.)

limbs. This, along with their much thicker fur coats, may be related to the conservation of body heat, reflecting the fact that their mountain habitat is distinctly colder than that of the lowland gorilla. If distribution were still continuous, we might expect to see a cline or gradient of trunk and limb proportions ranging unbroken from the lowland extreme to the mountain one.

In the mountain gorilla also, for a given jaw and skull size, the molar teeth are considerably larger and higher crowned and the chewing muscle attachment areas are expanded. Compared with the molars, however, the front teeth of the mountain gorillas are distinctly smaller. The mountain gorilla diet includes larger proportions of bark, roots, stems and other such abrasive items than the lowland gorilla diet, and the forces of selection have evidently maintained large cheek teeth. The higher proportion of fruits in the diet of the lowland gorilla has allowed the cheek teeth to reduce somewhat but has maintained large front teeth. In this respect, the lowland gorilla approaches the condition of the chimpanzee (and also the orang) where the incisors at the front end of the dental arch are relatively

General Biological Background

greatly enlarged to handle the tough rinds of the fruits that comprise
the bulk of their diet.

Interestingly enough, there is a recently described gorilla population that is intermediate between the mountain and lowland extremes. This is a group of *eastern* lowland gorillas, which has even been given another subspecific name by some students, *Gorilla gorilla graueri*. These live in the Utu region of the eastern Congo basin far closer in actual distance to the mountain gorillas than to the western lowland gorillas nearly seven hundred miles away. The body proportions of *G. g. graueri* are more like the lowland gorillas of the west, but their dental proportions are intermediate between the mountain and lowland extremes, and it would appear that their diet is intermediate as well.

This relict population suggests to us that if the former gorilla distribution were restored, we would see clines or gradients of traits ranging unbroken from one extreme to the other, but that the cline in one trait might not coincide in actual area with the cline in another. We shall meet this problem of crosscutting or noncoinciding clines in continuous populations later on when we deal with human populations since it forms the basis for our claim that the race concept is an inadequate means of dealing with the reality of human biological variation. The suspicion that noncoinciding clines may once have characterized gorilla biological variation suggests the possibility that the application of subspecific designations was not an adequate procedure for gorillas either. At present, however, gorilla populations are noncontinuous and subspecific naming can be defended.

The variation in gorilla ecology and adaptation along with the obvious fact that gorillas are more closely related to chimpanzees, as judged by a whole series of features, than to any other primate has led some authorities to recognize this at a higher taxonomic level. It has been suggested that both the gorilla and the chimpanzee should be included in the same genus, and since the chimpanzee was recognized and formally named first, its generic name should be used. That would make the gorilla *Pan gorilla*, while the chimpanzee would remain *P. troglodytes*. Cogent arguments have been made both pro and con, but the issue has not yet been resolved. Until it has, we shall provisionally adhere to the traditional usage and retain *Gorilla* as a formal generic label.

Gorillas, as the largest living Primates, are bulky creatures, although the real massiveness is predominantly a property of the males. Female gorillas tip the scales somewhere in the neighborhood of two hundred pounds, but males average twice that size. Normal male stature is somewhere between five and six feet with large males occasionally reaching well over six feet and a weight of over five hundred pounds. In captivity some gorillas have become quite obese and have weighed well over six hundred pounds.

Taxonomy and Primate Classification

Table 1
Classification of the Living Primates

Order	Suborder	Infraorder	Superfamily	Family	Subfamily	Genus	Common Name
	Prosimii	Lemuriformes	Lemuroidea	Lemuridae	Lemurinae	*Lemur*	Common Lemur
						Hapalemur	Gentle Lemur
						Lepilemur	Sportive Lemur
					Cheirogaleinae	*Cheirogaleus*	Mouse Lemur
						Microcebus	Dwarf Lemur
						Phaner	Fork-Crowned Dwarf Lemur
				Indridae		*Indri*	Indris
						Lichanotus	Avahi
						Propithecus	Sifaka
			Daubentonioidea	Daubentoniidae		*Daubentonia*	Aye-Aye
		Lorisiformes	Lorisoidea	Lorisidae		*Loris*	Slender Loris
						Nycticebus	Slow Loris
						Arctocebus	Angwantibo
						Perodicticus	Potto
				Galagidae	Galaginae	*Galago*	Bush Baby
						Euoticus	Needle-Clawed Bush Baby
		Tarsiiformes	Tarsioidea	Tarsiidae		*Tarsius*	Tarsier
				Callithricidae	Callithricinae	*Callithrix*	Plumed Marmoset
						Leontocebus	Tamarin
						Cebuella	Pygmy Marmoset
						Mico	Naked-Eared Marmoset
						Marikina	Bald-Headed Tamarin
						Tamarin	Black-Faced Tamarin
						Oedipomidas	Pinché
					Callimiconinae	*Callimico*	Goeldi's Marmoset
					Aotinae	*Aotes*	Douroucouli
						Callicebus	Titi

						Genus	Common name
Primates	Anthropoidea	Platyrrhini	Ceboidea	Cebidae	Pithecinae	*Pithecia*	Saki
						Chiropotes	Saki
						Cacajao	Uakari
					Alouattinae	*Alouatta*	Howler
					Cebinae	*Cebus*	Capuchin
						Saimiri	Squirrel Monkey
					Atelinae	*Ateles*	Spider Monkey
						Brachyteles	Woolly Spider Monkey
						Lagothrix	Woolly Monkey
		Catarrhini	Cercopithecoidea	Cercopithecidae	Cercopithecinae	*Macaca*	Macaque
						Cynopithecus	Black Ape
						Cercocebus	Mangabey
						Papio	Baboon, Drill
						Theropithecus	Gelada
						Cercopithecus	Guenon
						Erythrocebus	Patas Monkey
						Mandrillus	Mandrill, Drill
					Colobinae	*Presbytis*	Common Langur
						Pygathrix	Douc Langur
						Rhinopithecus	Snub-Nosed Langur
						Simias	Pagi Island Langur
						Nasalis	Proboscis Monkey
						Colobus	Guereza
			Hominoidea	Hylobatidae	Hylobatinae	*Hylobates*	Gibbon
						Symphalangus	Siamang
				Pongidae	Ponginae	*Pongo*	Orang-utan
						Pan	Chimpanzee
						Gorilla	Gorilla
				Hominidae		*Homo*	Human

While they are equipped with a strength to match their bulk, it is obvious that a quarter-ton of gorilla is going to think twice before attempting to brachiate carelessly from tree to tree. Simply finding branches or even trees to support so much weight requires careful selection. Young gorillas, and to a lesser extent grown females, do utilize trees and construct their nighttime sleeping nests in them, but the adult males generally remain on the ground, sleeping at the bases of the trees in the branches of which are the nests of the younger and smaller animals. As with the chimpanzee, the chief natural enemy, apart from parasites and infections, is the leopard. The size and strength of the male as well as the formidable canine teeth are useful in defending gorilla groups, since even these imposing animals are not immune from leopard predation.

In terrestrial Primates generally the male is much larger than the female and equipped with larger canine teeth, whereas in the more arboreal Primates the sexes tend to be much more equal in size. In the gibbon, for instance, there is scarcely any size difference, although the size difference—sexual dimorphism—of the orang does not fit this generalization, as has been noted in our previous discussion.

As a terrestrial animal of respectable bulk, the problem of weight support has led to some interesting adaptations in the gorilla. Particularly in the mountain gorilla, which is the less arboreal of the two subspecies, the foot has been modified to a remarkable extent in the human direction. The big toe has greatly reduced powers of opposition, the other toes are much reduced, there is something of a heel, and the sole is supported by dense fibrous tissue in a marked convergence toward the human condition. The mountain gorilla foot more

Figure 44. Body proportions in fully grown apes and man. From left to right: orang-utan, chimpanzee, gorilla, and man. (Courtesy of Professor A. H. Schultz.)

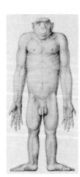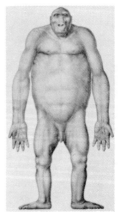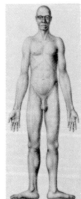

closely resembles a human foot than it does the foot of any other Primate including the chimpanzee, which is more closely related to the gorilla than is any other Primate.

But the gorilla is a quadruped, and the hand, too, has been modified for weight support. The short forearm flexor tendons, remnants of the gorilla's brachiating past, prevent the hand from being extended palm down on the ground. The weight-supporting part of this hand-hook, then, becomes the knuckles, properly the dorsal surface of the second phalanges of digits two through five. The proximal phalanges (the first segments of the fingers proper) are kept more or less in line with the metacarpals (in the palm), the wrist, and the forearm. In both the chimpanzee and the gorilla the metacarpals of the palm are so long that in knuckle-walking stance the thumb does not reach the ground. The weight-supporting dorsal surface of the second phalanges possesses specially thickened skin—the knuckle pad—comparable to the weight supporting surface on the soles of the feet. Bony and ligamentous strengthening for this weight-bearing role has necessarily had to proceed further in the gorilla than in the chimpanzee with the result that manipulative ability is still further reduced. There is a continuing discussion concerning the origin and significance of the knuckle-walking characteristic of the two African apes. Since both groups share this unusual form of locomotion, it has been used to argue for their close phylogenetic relationship, a position that seems reasonable. However, there is no evidence to support the claim sometimes advanced that the human line once went through a knuckle-walking stage.

Impressive as the gorilla is, it is clear that humanity's precursors could not have descended from a line in which size had developed to such a degree. The gorilla's bulk is a key to its safety as a terrestrial vegetarian, but it has necessitated weight-supporting changes that effectively eliminate the possibility that the descendants of such a creature could ever become human. Such a possibility could not be so easily discounted for the chimpanzee. If people were to vanish suddenly, the niche exploited by the genus *Homo* would be left unoccupied, and more than one recent student has suggested that there would be nothing to prevent the chimpanzee from developing in a truly hominid direction. Humans may indeed vanish quite suddenly as a consequence of their own conduct, but the sad probability remains that they will either have already destroyed the last surviving group of wild chimpanzees, or that they will render their world uninhabitable by their self-destruction.

We perceive, then, that the Primates constitute an Order characterized by great variability, the earliest members of which are of considerable antiquity. More than six hundred species of the Order have been described, and it is of more than passing interest to note that this speciation has occurred largely among the non-hominoid Pri-

122 mates, the prosimii and the New and Old World monkeys. The great apes have tended toward a comparative conservatism in virtually every way. In a world where ever more rapid change is increasingly the norm, this would appear to be dubious strategy for survival.

Suggested Readings

BOURNE, G. H. *The Ape People*. Putnam, New York, 1971.
  A very readable account of the apes and ape research.

BUETTNER-JANUSCH, J. (editor). *Evolutionary and Genetic Biology of the Primates*, 2 vols. Academic Press, New York and London, 1963/64.
  A valuable survey of contemporary research on the Primates written by specialists in each field.

CALMAN, W. T. *The Classification of Animals*. John Wiley, New York, 1949.
  A brief introduction to zoological taxonomy.

CLARK, W. E. LE GROS. *The Antecedents of Man*. Quadrangle Books, Chicago, 1960.
  An introduction to the evolution of the Primates.

DEVORE, I. (editor). *Primate Behavior*. Holt, Rinehart and Winston, New York, 1965.
  An invaluable source-book reporting the field studies on the behavior of monkeys and apes.

EIMERL, S., AND I. DEVORE. *The Primates*. Life Nature Library, Time Inc., New York, 1965.
  A brief, beautifully illustrated and attractively written introduction.

HOOTON, E. *Man's Poor Relations*. Doubleday, New York, 1942.
  An informative account of the Primates.

JENKINS, F. A., JR. (editor). *Primate Locomotion*. Academic Press, New York, 1974.
  The most recent and authoritative research on the subject.

MAYR, E., E. G. LINSLEY, AND R. L. USINGER. *Methods and Principles of Systematic Zoology*. McGraw-Hill, New York, 1953.
  A standard text on taxonomy.

NAPIER, J. R., AND P. H. NAPIER. *A Handbook of Living Primates : Morphology, Ecology and Behaviour of Non-Human Primates*. Academic Press, New York, 1967.

The most recent and authoritative treatment of the Primates as a whole. **123**

REYNOLDS, V. *The Apes: The Gorilla, Chimpanzee, Orangutan and Gibbon — Their History and their World.* E. P. Dutton, New York, 1967.
Excellent reporting on field observations both by the author and other students of great ape behavior both in the wild and in captivity.

SCHULTZ, A. H. *The Life of Primates.* Universe Books, New York, 1969.
An authoritative and scholarly work by a scientist who has devoted a long and productive lifetime to the study of primate biology and morphology.

SIMPSON, G. G. *Principles of Animal Taxonomy.* Columbia University Press, New York, 1961.
By a master of the subject.

SWINDLER, D. R., AND C. D. WOOD. *An Atlas of Primate Gross Anatomy: Baboon, Chimpanzee and Man.* University of Washington Press, Seattle, 1973.
The most ambitious graphic presentation available.

TUTTLE, R. (editor). *The Functional and Evolutionary Biology of Primates.* Aldine-Atherton, Chicago, 1972.
Reports on current problems in primate biology by the most active workers in the field.

VAN LAWICK-GOODALL, J. *In the Shadow of Man.* Houghton Mifflin, Boston, 1971.
A unique account of the most famous and fundamental study of chimpanzees under natural conditions by the investigator responsible for it.

WASHBURN, S. L. (editor). *Classification and Human Evolution.* Aldine, Chicago, 1963.
A most valuable series of contributions, by different specialists, relating to the classification of the *Hominoidea*.

Primate Behavior

Chapter 5

Why Study Primate Behavior?

Why study Primate behavior? The answer should be obvious, but as with so many things one believes to be obvious, a straightforward statement is often of value in determining the focus of the question. Simply stated, we are interested in studying Primate behavior for the possible light it may throw on the origin and evolution of human behavior. Humans after all are Primates, and a full-scale study of Primate behavior would include a focus on the human as well as the nonhuman parts of the behavioral spectrum. Human behavior, however, is an enormously complex subject involving the study of language, customs, politics, economics, and history, to say nothing of psychology and even physiology. Obviously, a full consideration of this is beyond the limits we have set for ourselves in this book, although the study of Primate behavior falls well within the study of the biological evolution of humanity.

An awareness of the dimensions of human behavior can be very illuminating. Adaptation involves active adjustment to a changeable world, and such adjustments are essentially behavioral. And if, as we have every reason to believe, humans have evolved from an ancestor not unlike one or another of the Old World Primates, then a knowledge of their behavior should provide a valuable base for assessing the evolution of human behavior.

We hasten to add that no living Primate can be expected to duplicate the behavior of the remote prehuman ancestor in every aspect, for the same reasons that no living Primate can be used as a model for the exact physical structure of our prehominid forebears. This is because contemporary nonhuman Primates have been in existence as long as humans, and longer in the case of some forms known from fossil layers that predate the appearance of humans. Any form that has been in existence for a span of some millions of years has obviously been successful in adjusting to the forces of selection during that time. Such adjustments constitute evolutionary changes and make it most unlikely that any successful species has remained absolutely static. While the form and behavior of some nonhuman Primates may be *similar* to conditions that once characterized various prehuman ancestors, they will not be identical.

Since the dawn of written history, both consciously and unconsciously, Primates have been used as referents to the human condition, although in many cases they have served more as symbols of humanity's preconceptions about itself than as genuine sources of insight. Noble characteristics are attributed to the sacred langurs by the modern Hindus; the ancient Egyptians worshipped the Hamadryas baboon as exemplifying vitality and exuberant sexual vigor—considered a great virtue; while Christians through the ages have considered "the ape" as the embodiment of beastliness, including exuberant sexual vigor—considered a great vice.

Wisdom, foolishness, altruism, trickery, responsibility, and lasciviousness have all been projected upon unsuspecting Primates at one time or another. The attribute so chosen is often a reflection of the values, whether positive or negative, of the culture making the projection. Even in this supposedly scientific age, for instance, we have more than a lingering suspicion that the enormous enthusiasm shown among professional modern "monkey watchers," as students of Primate behavior are sometimes called, for the investigation of sexuality and dominance reflects, at least in part, dimensions of importance to the post-Freudian Western World.

On the other hand, it would be unwise to regard everything attributed to the nonhuman Primates as "projection." The very fact that they have so frequently been the objects of projection can itself be explained by the recognition that, both structurally and behaviorally, they do in fact display greater similarities to the human condition than is true for any other group of animals. If we mentally try to correct for these two tendencies—whether taking the behavior of modern primates too literally as representing that of our prehuman ancestors, or projecting peculiarly human foibles into our contemporary nonhuman relatives—then we would maintain that the study of nonhuman Primate behavior *can* tell us something about the genesis of the human condition.

Initially, the basic adaptations that set off Primates from the rest of the mammals were related to their exploitation of the tropical arboreal ecological niche. In a later chapter, we shall discuss the development of some of the anatomical features that evolved as a result of this initial adaptation. Here we should note that, where physiology and behavior are concerned, all living Primates bear the stamp imposed by adaptation to life in the trees. This is even true for the Primate whose departure from an arboreal ancestral state has been most marked and of longest duration, the Primate that calls itself human. While there are instances where individual Primate groups may differ in one trait or another from the generalized arboreal model, a pattern of characteristics always remains that can only be explained by referral to the influence, either present or past, of an arboreal way of life. This is manifested physiologically and behaviorally in the primary sensory orientation toward the world, in features of a gastrointestinal, growth, and reproductive nature, and in general mental characteristics as well.

Sensory Orientation

Take, for instance, the primary sensory orientation toward the world. Bats orient largely by the sense of hearing; some fish and insects depend heavily on chemical sensing (although whether we would equate this with either or both of the separate smell and taste senses of the higher vertebrates is a moot point); certain subterranean creatures rely to a great extent on the sense of touch; while Primates, like birds, basically are visually oriented creatures. In the Primate case, this was an almost inevitable result of the early expansion into the arboreal ecological niche.

Place a primitive mammal in a tree, and even if all its senses are at an approximately equal level of development, it will obviously rely most heavily on its ability to see. A gambol through the tree tops would be a risky thing at best if one attempted to locate the next branch by sniffing it out, and listening for it would surely be even less rewarding. Feeling for it might work, but it would be a slow process, and the creature relying on this method of orientation would have a substantially reduced fitness (W) when competing with a visually oriented organism. It is of passing interest to note, however, that there is one group of Primates that does depend for its orientation on touch; at least it does so to a greater extent than other Primates. These are the lorises (see Fig. 30). As one might guess, they are slow moving, but since they are nocturnal, they do not compete directly with their visually oriented relatives who are relatively helpless in the total or near-total absence of light.

This brings up a point of some importance. A fully effective ex-

acuity that can only be utilized at times of relatively full illumination. To determine what is edible and whether or not it is ripe, keen color perception is desirable. As with many birds, there is a concentration of color-receiving cells, cones, in the center of the Primate retina. Cones, however, do not work in dim light. The cells that do, on the other hand, the rods, do not register color, which is why everything looks gray to us at dusk. In general, Primates have excellent and acute color vision and good depth perception but are relatively night-blind.

Basic to an understanding of the behavior of all the higher primates including humans is a recognition of the crucial shaping effect the arboreal environment had on the way the world is perceived. Although humans are the most thoroughly terrestrial of all modern Primates and have a terrestrial ancestry that goes back to four million years and perhaps more, they still, like their ape and monkey relatives, live in a largely visual world. This world is principally diurnal, three dimensional, and, as the film credits say (reflecting our Primate heritage), perceived in "glorious technicolor."

Dietary Adaptation

Exploitation of the arboreal ecological niche involved gastrointestinal changes as well as a restructuring of the primary sensory orientation. The earliest Primates in the fossil record and some of those living ones judged most "primitive" can be regarded as slightly modified insectivores. Full-scale expansion in the arboreal ecological niche, however, was made possible by a shift in dietary focus from insects to plant foods. Most kinds of Primates, both Old World and New World, depend almost entirely on plant products. For the most part, these are comprised of fruits, shoots, berries, and nuts, which justifies the statement that, from a dietary point of view, the primary Primate adaptation is frugivorous.

This basic frugivorous adaptation has been conspicuously departed from by two groups of Primates, and to a lesser extent, by still another. One of those exceptions is the Colobinae who have specialized in a leaf-eating diet. While this is a most interesting adaptation that features energy extraction from structural carbohydrates (cellulose, for instance) quite similar to that of the terrestrial ruminants (cows or antelopes), it is, nevertheless, a relatively recent and special development that casts no light on the development of the human species or any other Primate. The partial departure from the frugivorous pattern mentioned previously is the baboon group with its focus on grass roots and other edible bulbs, and perhaps we could even regard the gorilla as an exception, with its focus on bedstraw, wild celery, thistles, nettles, and bamboo shoots. All these groups will, however, eat nuts, fruits, and berries when they can get them.

The other group that represents a major departure from the basic frugivorous pattern is the human species. To be sure, there are people and, in fact, whole cultures, that regard themselves as "vegetarian," but this is a development that has taken place largely since the dawn of written history. The archeological record suggests that the average human diet has included animals as food for about a million years. Some groups, such as certain Eskimos, eat nothing but animal-derived food, but this extreme, like the vegetarian one, is such a recent development that it has relatively little significance as an indicator of the average human diet throughout the time span in which the genus *Homo* has existed as a recognizable entity.

These extremes do illustrate the extraordinary range of diets on which human populations can thrive. This range is far greater than that for any other Primate and may represent one of the basic reasons for the success of the Primate *Homo*—that is, where "success" is measured by the relative increase in numbers of individuals. The expansion of the human dietary range has been accomplished principally by extending it into the realm of animal foods. Monkeys and baboons have been observed to kill and eat baby birds and gazelles, respectively, when they are encountered, although the encounters are usually quite accidental and not very common. Chimpanzees also have been known to kill and eat young baboons, bushbucks, and bushpigs, and, in one instance, a group of chimpanzees was seen deliberately going after a colobus monkey in a tree. This too was killed and eaten. In spite of these observations, it is well documented that no Primate aside from humans has a regular or significant animal component to its diet.

With a dietary range running from completely vegetarian to completely carnivorous, we know that humans are unique among the Primates and that their uniqueness is illustrated by the extent of that range in a meat-eating direction. The question arises, however, concerning just what is the appropriate diet of humankind. What diet are humans adapted to? Several approaches have been taken in answering this question. Some have suggested that the human is principally an ape with a larger than usual dependence on learned behavior. As such, then, humans have been regarded as basically frugivorous creatures who have learned to eat meat. The argument is that meat is not a "natural" food for humans. Studies on modern hunting and gathering populations where the products of the hunt comprise about 20 per cent or less of total food intake are offered in partial support of this argument.

At the other extreme are the arguments that humans are really "killer apes" with a built-in blood lust. Supporting this interpreta-

tion are various cited examples such as: the example of overfed   **129**
"masculinity" waddling off to the woods each fall to blast away at
anything that moves; the large and growing number of animal species extinguished by human effort; history written in terms of human
carnage (or glorious battles, depending on your viewpoint) including
recent wars where "progress" is measured in the form of body count;
and many others. Not really a support for this view, but an argument
that its opposite has been overdrawn, is the recognition that modern
hunters and gatherers are not typical of the conditions under which
humans lived for most of their existence. Most of these modern examples live in ecologically undesirable, or from our point of view,
refuge areas, having been pushed there by modern food-producing
peoples. Game in such regions is far less plentiful than it was in the
average human habitat through most of the Pleistocene.

   We have a suspicion that the killer-ape school of thought is in fact
simply a reworking in modern language of the concept of original
sin, which has long enjoyed such a prominent position in Christian
tradition. In fact, it is advocated by its proponents with some of the
grim enthusiasm that characterized the particularly intense version
manifest in the Calvinistic concept of the innate depravity of humanity. The favor that it has found in some quarters and the furor it has
stirred in others are probably in part due to the fact that it offers in the
name of "science" a new version of the old and familiar concept of
original sin.

   If the examples we have cited appear contradictory, perhaps it is
because the human dietary adaptation is neither complete nor clear-
cut. Certainly human digestive physiology differs from that of all
other Primates in important ways, while resembling it in other respects. Humans like other Primates (and guinea pigs too) cannot synthesize ascorbic acid. We suspect that the loss of this ability was
because the frugivorous diet of our common ancestors supplied it in
sufficient quantities so that there was no selection against the accumulation of mutations disrupting the synthesizing machinery. In
time, the ability was lost entirely, but this was only disadvantageous
late in human history when such artificial circumstances as long sea
voyages and consequent dependence on dried and nonfresh foods
resulted in scurvy. The use of citrus fruits and especially limes to
counteract their inability to synthesize ascorbic acid earned the Primates in the British navy the designation "Limeys," an honorific
now extended to all English Primates.

   In addition to this general Primate lack, humans share an unusual
gustatory enthusiasm with their simian brethren, which also reflects
the arboreal frugivorous heritage. This is our extraordinary sweet
tooth. Supposedly, this is particularly pronounced during human
childhood, a suggestion that might be sustained by those who have
recently had the misfortune to serve as referee at a juvenile birthday

party. Presumably also, this enthusiasm in some cases drops with the onset of maturity when those traits are finally developed that evolved most recently and that most clearly serve to distinguish humans from their Primate relatives. If the reduction in the craving for sweets is, in fact, a criterion for mature humanity, then the eruption of the dairy-freeze phenomenon across the face of the affluent society—"glop shops" as those with a love-hate relationship refer to them—clearly bodes ill for the future.

If humans still share these traits with their frugivorous forebears, they differ just as sharply in others. The whole basic pattern of food intake in humans is most un-Primate-like. There is no intrinsic reason why we should eat three or four or five meals a day except for our cultural conditioning in such periodicities. Some human groups eat only two meals a day, others only one, and still others have a formal meal only when the hunters bring back something substantial. But whatever the pattern, the concept of assembling for the set purpose of gastronomic gratification followed by a period of noneating is singularly unlike that of any other Primate. The average Primate, as one zoologist put it, leads a life of "nonstop" snacks. He further noted that in the feast and fast phenomenon, and in the food-sharing that accompanies the eating part of it, humans behave much more like carnivores than Primates. In this as in other features, however, the human adaptation, as we have already said, is neither complete nor clear-cut. While we have maintained our essentially carnivore-type eating pattern, the television set and the packaged food industry have combined to reinstitute the old Primate urge to nibble, with the result that the burgeoning beltlines of the affluent, once a phenomenon particularly identified with middle age, might better be called the smorgasbord spread.

While one might argue that, in our eating behavior, we vary from the Primate pattern to the carnivore pattern to both as a result of learned behavior, there is a corollary which, we think, indicates that there is a genuine difference in digestive physiology between humans and other Primates. Not only is the nonstop nibble the characteristic Primate eating pattern, but the nonstop elimination of the unusable intake is also a characteristic Primate pattern as anyone who has had to clean up after a pet monkey well knows. By and large, human defecation is a once-a-day phenomenon unlike the every-few-minutes manifestation in other Primates. Although we have noted with something less than wholehearted enthusiasm the re-emergence of Primate eating patterns where sweets and snacks are concerned, we can at least be thankful that no such similar relapse has yet been observed where feces production is involved. Lest pride in our anal control be overdone, we should note that the sheer increase in human population is threatening to swamp the world with our sewage. Those curious little fibers that marine ecologists have recently been finding in the Gulf Stream have turned out to be remnants of toilet paper.

Prognosis for the future, however, is not our concern in this chapter. Rather, the point we wish to make is that humankind is separated from the rest of the Primates by differences in the digestive system that have far-reaching implications. Humans can regularly go for long times between eating or eliminating. Most human populations eat meat, and it is possible to survive on animal food alone. This suggests to us, even if we knew little else, that the crucial difference between humans and their closest Primate relatives is related to human adaptation to hunting as a major part of their subsistence activities.

Reproduction and Growth

The rabbit has long been deplored as a symbol of fecundity and there is no doubt about its ability to multiply. Each rabbit, however, takes about six months to reach a sufficient level of maturity to enter the reproductive rat race (to mix one's mammalian metaphors). In the same period of time its modest cousin the mouse will have long since matured, bred, reached the status of great-grandparenthood and generated more than one hundred seventy additional mice — providing that nothing interferes with the process. If a month to reach breeding age, a month-long gestation period, an equal sex ratio and an average litter size of six are assumed, a single new-born mouse pair, behaving normally, is capable of leaving more than a third of a million descendants during the course of a single year. The life of the average mouse, however, whether or not it is nasty and brutish, is indubitably short. Many potential mice never get born, and many who do fail to achieve reproductive age before being converted into a midnight snack for a hunting cat, owl, fox, or mousetrap.

All of this is by way of contrast with the reproductive potential of the average Primate. Among the higher Primates (monkeys, apes, and humans), only one offspring is produced each year after sexual maturity is reached. Furthermore, Primates, in contrast with most other mammals, take many years to reach their adult status. Even the major predators, such as wolves, lions, and bears, behaviorally among the most complex of the non-Primate mammals, reach reproductive age between two and three years. Many monkeys take between three to five years, the great apes take between eight and twelve, and humans between thirteen and nearly twenty years depending on conditions of health and nutrition. One might well ask, in the face of such awesome rodent reproductive ability, how have the Primates been able to survive at all?

Primate Behavior

Survive they have, however, and one of them, ironically *Homo,* the slowest breeding of them all, is multiplying at such a rate that he threatens to make the earth uninhabitable for *any* creature including himself. The key to this success, if "success" it be, lies in the fact that each individual Primate at birth has a far greater chance of growing to reproductive age than is true for each individual rodent. In fact, at any point during its life a Primate's survival chances are better than those of a rodent. To be sure, there are fewer potential predators in the arboreal ecological niche, but this argument becomes less true when one includes the terrestrial Primates. Several things are involved. An adult Primate, depending to a greater extent on learned behavior than blind instinct, can deal more effectively with the complexities of the world, giving it a higher probability of making the right choice in any given situation. This ability, in part, may well have been selected for in the arboreal habitat where decision making simply to get around is more frequent and constant than is true on the ground where the proverbial one false step does not automatically mean a disastrous drop.

Learned behavior, as a means of coping with problems, takes longer to develop to a reliable level than the "gut reaction" approach that depends more on physiological maturation than reasoning based on experience. During the period in which a creature is learning to cope with the challenges of the world, it would be relatively vulnerable if it were entirely dependent on its own efforts in the struggle for survival. Compensating for the prolonged vulnerability of the learning period is an equally prolonged extension of maternal care. In mice, the period of infant dependence on maternal care is only a matter of weeks. In the larger carnivores this stretches to about two years and, in the higher Primates, it runs from three or four years up to about two decades for humans. Not only is the length of the dependence period vastly extended proportional to the extent of reliance on learned behavior for survival, but the nature of the dependence differs in kind. The responsibilities of mother mouse cease at weaning but a mother monkey will continue to play a protective role for another year or two. In apes the post-weaning protective period is longer still and, in humans it lasts five times or more as long as the actual duration of nursing.

Prolonged maternal protection reduces the environmental pressures that, in rodents, favor the earliest possible physiological maturation. During this prolonged protected period, the growing Primate can learn the workings of the world by a kind of experimental approach. This trial-and-error form of behavior we call play, or in the case of higher Primates and even humans, "monkey business." It is significant that the length and intensity of the play period is proportional to the amount of adult behavior of the learned variety rather than of the more "instinctive" kind.

The distinction between instinctive and learned behavior is far less sharp than it was thought to be a generation ago. For instance, we tend to think of the sudden withdrawal from painful stimulus — the hand from the hot stove, for instance, or the blink of the eye at the approach of a projectile, bug or whatever — as "innate." In fact, however, such behavior does require a trial or two before it is properly set. The learning period may be brief, but it does occur. After that, however, the behavior involved does become nearly involuntary, taking place more or less automatically following the occurrence of the stimulus. For our purposes here, however, we have divided the behavioral spectrum into learned and innate components. We recognize the arbitrary nature of doing this. In a more developed and sophisticated treatment, this would clearly be insufficient, but with this warning it has utility at the introductory level.

Social Behavior

The mere fact that the growing Primate spends a period of years dependent on a parent or, to turn it around, an adult spends several years playing protector for each offspring, would ensure that a goodly portion of the life of each Primate has to be considered in the context of its behavioral relationships with other Primates. Evidently the higher Primates are social animals and, not surprisingly, monkey watchers have devoted an increasing amount of attention to Primate social behavior.

Early students had not enjoyed the opportunity of watching the dynamics of natural Primate groups and the question of what served as the bonds uniting and maintaining Primate social groupings was initially answered in terms of certain assumptions about human nature and of one particularly unfortunate and abnormal instance of baboon group behavior. This latter could hardly be called "social" behavior since it was antisocial in the extreme.

The unfortunate example derives from the saga of the Hamadryas baboon colony at Monkey Hill in the London Zoo during the late 1920s. Monkey Hill is an oval enclosure, one hundred feet long by sixty feet wide, and, at the time, it had a population of nearly sixty male Hamadryas baboons. Thirty females were introduced to this group with disastrous consequences. No wild baboon population has been observed with as many males in a single group, and, even if it were possible, it could never occur in such a small space and with such a totally inadequate number of females. Normally in wild groups, the males, numbering between one and ten on the average, are hierarchically arranged. In dry country where forage is scarce, Hamadryas groups tend to be composed of a single adult male, a couple of adult females, and a couple of immature animals. In better watered terrain, the number of males per group rises to between five and ten (and apparently more in some cases) with about twice that number of adult females. Immature animals occur in about the same numbers as the grown females. Where there are two or more adult males in a group, they are ranked in a hierarchy or pecking order, with the dominant one at the top enjoying first access to food and sexually attractive females, but also being charged with principal responsibility for maintaining group integrity, whether this involves defense against predators or keeping subordinates in line.

With the introduction of the female baboons at Monkey Hill, the most powerful and aggressive males set about gathering as many females as possible into the harem groups that constitute the normal aggregates in the wild. A male Hamadryas baboon is a powerful creature, twice the size of a female, and equipped with formidable canine teeth. Predictably many of the females became the focus of attention of two or more of the previously deprived males and, just as predictably, many of the females were literally torn to pieces. Within two months, half of the introduced females had been killed in fights. When the experiment in coeducational living was finally abandoned, the five surviving females were removed leaving the remaining thirty-four males as the baboon colony on Monkey Hill at the London Zoo.

As one anthropologist suggested, if a group of thirty women were turned loose in a prison containing twice that number of adult male convicts and all left to work out their destinies without supervision, it would not be surprising if something similar would be the outcome.

The story of the baboons at the London Zoo was written up by the young British anatomist Solly Zuckerman as *The Social Life of Monkeys and Apes*, 1932, and read with a fascinated mixture of horror and delight. The timing of this book and the nature of the example cited above were both particularly unfortunate, although completely by coincidence. By the early 1930s, cultural anthropologists had published a substantial number of field studies showing the wide variety of human behavior considered normal in the various parts of the world. Evidently different cultures could condition the raw material of humanity to behave in radically different ways, and the educated citizen of the Western World faced the fact, for the first time, that the ideals of Western civilization might not alone embody the highest canons of excellence in the spectrum of human behavior.

This came on the heels of the First World War, which had profoundly shaken the confidence of a world that had been brought up in the somewhat naive conviction of Victorian rectitude. More importantly, it coincided with the growing acceptance of the findings of Viennese psychoanalyst Sigmund Freud. Not only did these suggest that the unconscious played a greater role in human behavior

than had previously been realized, but also that the basic sexuality of **135**
human nature could not be overlooked. Sex had been a taboo subject
for the proper Victorians, but with the shattering of their self-right-
eous serenity and the discovery of cultural relativism, the Freudian
emphasis was accepted with growing enthusiasm by the post-war
generation. Trends often seem to acquire a momentum of their own,
which certainly appears true in this case. We suspect that the current
blatant glorification of sex, and the development of Freud's thera-
peutic unlocking of the unconscious to the stage now advocated by
the popular phrase "let it all hang out" would absolutely astonish
the good doctor were he to return for a brief visit.

The publication of the saga of Monkey Hill, coming in the early
1930s, offered a little something for everyone. If culture so conditioned people that their basic nature was repressed into the unconscious, then to the post-war sophisticates, the study of cultureless
Primates should provide valuable insight into the unvarnished nature of Primate—and by extension, human—nature. To many, the
baboons of the London Zoo epitomized basic Primate behavior, so to
speak, in the raw. To the moral survivors of an earlier day, they
seemed rather too raw, confirming the old Calvinist insistence on
the innate depravity of humanity and arguing for the maintenance of
a traditional set of rules by which the baser aspects of human nature
could be kept under control and people thus prevented from doing
each other in. Others, no less impressed by what they felt to be a
demonstration of basic Primate nature, took a more Freudian tack
and argued that dire consequences would follow the attempts to
push human sexuality and aggressiveness completely back into the
unconscious.

Artificial Conditions and Unsound Inferences

Whatever the merits of either position, they are both based on the
unfortunate acceptance of the behavior of the baboons on Monkey
Hill as models of normal Primate behavior. Even the recognition
more than a decade later that the situation was more analogous to
human convicts in a prison failed to consider just what an abnormal
picture of behavior this was, and it has taken many subsequent
studies of baboons in the field (interestingly enough, initiated by
Zuckerman himself) to begin to set the record straight. Baboons are
pugnacious and, during the breeding season, they are just as interested in sex as any other creature (more than some, less than others)
but, in the wild, life is not just one long orgy punctuated by attempts
to do in anyone else getting into the action.

In sum, not only were the baboons of Monkey Hill an abnormal
model of Hamadryas baboon behavior, but they were also taken as
the unfortunate objects for the projection of human attitudes about

136   themselves. As the sacred baboons of the ancient Egyptians, they had been symbolic of sexual vigor. The literate post-Victorians of Europe and America, somewhat more conscious of history than many of their counterparts today, were well aware of the baboons' ancient reputation for sexuality and projected their own erotic imaginings on the poor beasts, whether their heightened interests led them to fear and repression, or whether they rejected the repressions of yesteryear with an almost equally exaggerated flaunting of the phallic.

Within the next decade, observations on a colony of rhesus macaques, which had been established on Cayo Santiago, an island off Puerto Rico in the Caribbean, appeared to confirm the conclusions relating to sexuality and aggressiveness that many had drawn from the episode in the London Zoo. During the same period, however, a study was conducted and published on the howler monkeys of Barro Colorado, an island in the Panama Canal Zone, but this presented quite a different picture. Unlike the baboons or the macaques, the howler monkeys were less obsessed by sex and appeared to be much less aggressive, lacking a clear-cut dominance hierarchy.

Noting that the howler monkey was the first New World Primate to be studied and that both the baboon and the macaque were Old World monkeys, some interpreters drew the conclusion that the difference in sex and dominance behavior represented a basic difference between the Old and the New World Primates. Further, noting that humans are modified Old World Primates, it was hinted that beneath the veneer of civilization, humans were probably just as given to exuberant sexual vigor and aggressive strivings for dominance as Monkey Hill baboons. Some have even gone so far as to suggest that humans owed their pre-eminence in the animal world to just this assumed Primate heritage.

However, as more studies have been made and as information has been collected on Primate behavior under natural conditions, it became obvious that these conclusions were premature. One mistake that had been made was the assumption that the monkeys' enthusiasm for sexual activity, like the human one, was a year-round phenomenon. On the contrary, in the nonhuman Primates there is a definite breeding season during which most sexual activity takes place. If they are observed out of season as happened in one of the early studies of New World monkeys, sexual activity may be drastically reduced or entirely absent.

The Freudian discovery of sexuality pervading the unconscious had led to the assumption that sex was the basic bond that held Primate groups together. As it turns out, nonhuman Primate groups maintain their identity even during the substantial portion of the year during which sex does not act as a cohesive bond. Not only that, those Primate groups in which sexual activities are relatively infrequent and sex drive apparently low — the gorilla for instance — also maintain their identity as groups.

Where the subject of aggressiveness has been the focus, there has been a growing suspicion that these early findings, while far from yielding reliable conclusions, were in fact on the track of something. Summarizing the results of much subsequent work, it would appear that the dichotomy is not so much Old World/New World as it is arboreal versus terrestrial. Studies on New World monkeys dealt necessarily with arboreal groups since there are no terrestrial Primates native to the Western Hemisphere. Both the baboons and macaques of the Old World, however, represent nearly complete readaptations to at least a partial terrestrial mode of life.

This departure from the original Primate habitat, the arboreal ecological niche, coincides with certain morphological and behavioral changes that are almost certainly relevant to our interest in trying to reconstruct the probable course of development by which humans emerged from their nonhuman predecessors. Unlike their arboreal relatives, the terrestrial Primates show a marked degree of sexual dimorphism. Among the most thoroughly terrestrial, the males are twice as big as the females, possess considerably larger canine teeth, and are very much stronger. Added to this formidable physical equipment is a matching level of aggressiveness and, from an anthropocentric point of view, just plain meanness. The value of this is obvious when one realizes that even a large and hungry leopard will be most reluctant to face the phalanx of four or five adult male baboons that form the core of the typical troop. Even now the sexual dimorphism visible in modern humans suggests that it played a role in group defense in the past analogous to its role in the other terrestrial Primates, and it is interesting to note that the skeletal remains of the earliest hominids suggest that sexual dimorphism was more pronounced then than now. At a time when human cultural means of defense were crude in the extreme, the survival value of this, as in the baboons, is obvious.

If mutual defense plays a more significant role in maintaining the cohesion of Primate social groups than sexuality per se, it is joined by another factor that is often overlooked. We mentioned this in the section on Reproduction and Growth but largely in relation to the development of the individual rather than from the standpoint of its importance to the maintenance of the group. This factor is the prolongation of the learning period and its consequences. As the growing Primate learns about the world, one of the things it learns is that its world, particularly in its most secure form, normally includes the presence of other Primates of the same species. Not only do growing youngsters learn to perceive the world as members of a group, they learn to differentiate the members of that group according to the roles they play, and they, reciprocally, learn to play certain roles toward them.

Years of patient study by devoted monkey watchers have been necessary before the dynamics of within-group and between-group social behavior could be worked out. Some of the most revealing recent insights have come from studies on the rhesus monkey colony on Cayo Santiago, Puerto Rico. Although the situation is not fully equivalent to studying Primates in the wild since food is provided and animals are occasionally withdrawn for laboratory work elsewhere, there is the advantage that the animals are tagged, making positive identification possible, and further, that birth records and therefore maternal-offspring (and, hence, sibling) relationships are known. Observed patterns of behavior have been checked against known genealogical relationships with most interesting implications.

The Structuring of Relationships

In some instances, particular grown males have been observed "grooming" particular mature females. In grooming, one monkey picks through the fur of another with its fingers. Normally animals of lower status will groom those of higher status more than the reverse as a means of demonstrating and maintaining good will. In the cases where the adult male, rather than being the recipient, is actually the donor of grooming behavior toward an adult female, a check of the records reveals that, biologically, this is a mother-son relationship that has endured beyond immaturity. Further observation shows that the likelihood of mating behavior between the two is substantially reduced, even when the female is in estrus. Evidently a monkey can learn to play a role in relationship to another monkey and will continue to do so in spite of the physiological changes that occur in time. In this we may possibly see something of the origin of the incest taboo.

Similar mechanisms work in structuring some of the other relationships within a given group. For instance, maturing female rhesus macaques eventually enter the dominance hierarchy of the adult females in the troop. Allowing for the fact that the phenomenon of estrus periodically but temporarily changes female rank, each young monkey tends to be accorded a rank approximately equivalent to that of its mother rather than having to fight its way up on its own. It might be stretching things to suggest that we have here the roots of hereditary status differences, but, again, it is apparent that the young monkey tends to exhibit behavior appropriate to the role it was brought up to play.

Male status is not achieved in quite the same way, but, as in the

above examples, what has been learned in the social context of **139**
its early years does become important in its later behavior. In
1959–1961, when Dr. George Schaller undertook the first successful
study of gorilla behavior in the wild, he observed that when two gorilla bands met on the trail, they behaved in a way that led him to
suspect that their relationships had long since been settled in previous encounters. Gorilla groups revolve around single mature males
and apparently their personalities and their previous experiences
determine what groups do when they meet. Sometimes they mingled
peaceably for a time, later separating amicably. Sometimes one or
the other hurried away after contact. Dr. Schaller suspected that the
determining circumstances lay in experiences predating his year of
observations, but, of course, there was no way he could prove it.

In the case of the rhesus monkeys of Cayo Santiago, the years of
record keeping have proven to be of some help. As a male monkey
approaches maturity, apparently its changing physiological state
proves disruptive to the previous role structure of the group. It tends
to spend more and more time at the peripheries of the group, and
eventually it joins another group. The interesting thing is that it does
not join just any group. Its entry into whatever new group it joins is
via another male monkey, already a member of the group, that acts as
his "sponsor." Its dominance rank then starts as equivalent to that of
its sponsor. When the records are checked, the sponsor is often found
to be an older sibling that had previously left the natal group. If not a
sibling, the records show that it most likely had been an older member
of the juvenile play group in the natal band. In either case, the two
monkeys had previously worked out a relationship over some time
that becomes re-established on switching groups. The factors governing subsequent group switchings by fully adult males, which
have been observed in both wild gorillas and wild macaques (Northern India), are unknown, but presumably they are simply an extension of the dimensions of learned relationships we have already discussed.

As a footnote to group maintenance and individual group switching, it is interesting to note that in the nonhuman Primates it tends
to be the males that switch bands, whereas in human groups, particularly those at subsistence technology levels, it tends to be the females, although this is not by any means a rigid rule. In either case,
the biological result is gene flow and the prevention of genetic isolation and accounts for the broad territorial expanse of single species
where ground-living Primates such as baboons and humans are concerned. Apropos of the incest taboo, Dr. C. Packer in 1975 reported
eight years of observation on three study groups of anubis baboons at
Gombe National Park in Western Tanzania, in which out of forty-one
individuals thirty-nine males and one adult female and her juvenile
daughter transferred to other groups. Apparently every male trans-

fers at some time during its life, probably spending its reproductive life in a troop other than its natal one.

TERRITORIALITY

We mention territoriality as a separate category only because so much has been made of it in the recent past. Humans have been credited with an instinctive drive to control territory, and much of the argument has been clouded by emotion and a kind of mystique. Others have countered with the suggestion (which we prefer) that territoriality is best considered an extension of the same factors that control social behavior. The long Primate learning period ensures familiarity and satisfactory relationships not only with the other Primates encountered, but with the geography occupied during that time as well. A creature dependent for its survival on a large component of learned behavior will be reluctant to abandon the familiar for the unknown. The familiar includes known sources of food, water, and refuge as well as the other members of the group on which one's security depends.

For an arboreal Primate, these resources can generally be found within a single square mile. Terrestrial Primates tend to require between three or four and fifteen or more square miles. The amount of land required to sustain a group that depends, at least in part, on hunting is greatly expanded, measuring from the tens to the hundreds of square miles. Evidently the still greater extent of learned behavior that distinguishes humans from their Primate relatives allowed them to familiarize themselves with the vastly greater territorial range that became necessary as the switch to hunting took place early in human development.

AGGRESSION

When the societies of nonhuman Primates are studied it is found that aggressive behavior, on the whole, plays a cohesive role. Its principal function appears to be to keep the amount of divisiveness and aggression to a minimum. Far from desiring to inflict injury the aggressors seek to reduce the amount of aggression accompanied by a minimum amount of injury to others and as little social disruption as possible. The fighting is, for the most part, ritualized—i.e., the principals go through the motions of aggression rather than its actual performance. In this manner ritualized fighting limits the consequences of aggressive encounters between conspecifics, and the social mechanisms controlling aggression between individuals and groups clearly help preserve the species. Even in extraspecific encounters bluffing and display may be positively selected.

General Biological Background

There can be little doubt that such nonlethal aggressive behavior has positive selective value, but to jump from this conclusion, as many have done, to say that humans have been the subject of the same selective pressure, constitutes a *non sequitur*. Humans have had a very different kind of evolutionary history from that of other Primates, and while natural selection has by no means been suspended in its action on humans, that action has been directed toward a different set of conditions. In humans cooperation and altruism have been at a much higher selective premium than in other Primates. Competition has by no means been attenuated, although it should be evident that cooperation and altruism are each forms of competition, in which under certain conditions they become highly selectively valuable.

Surveying human societies we find that there are few in which some form of aggressive behavior, however slight, does not occur. The range of variation is striking, varying from the wholly unaggressive Tasaday food collectors of Mindanao in the Philippines to the highly violent societies of the civilized world such as the United States. This great variability suggests that violent behavior is largely learned. How else could one account for the marked differences in the expression of violence? The genetic explanation will not bear scrutiny. The evidence suggests that as a consequence of natural selection in the unique environments in which humans have spent the greater part of their evolutionary history they became polymorphously educable. Humans can learn virtually anything—among other things, to be virtually either wholly or largely unaggressive, and all the forms of behavior in between. We do not accept the view that the genes represent the equivalent of the theological doctrine of predestination. So that whatever humanity's genetic potentialities for aggression may be, and we know that many such potentialities exist, their organization and expression will largely depend on the environmental stimulation they receive. If this is so, then there is every reason for optimism, for if we understand the conditions that produce aggressive behavior, by changing those conditions much can be done to reduce the expression of such behavior. Today we know a fair amount about these social conditions; what we now need is to do something about them.

There are many other aspects of Primate behavior that are both interesting and well studied, and no doubt we can be faulted for omitting much of interest. We hope, however, that this chapter has demonstrated how the latest possibilities of human behavior are already evident in the nonhuman Primates, and that an extension of the principles of evolution to the behavioral realm and its biological bases could easily explain the origin of the human condition.

ARDREY, ROBERT. *The Territorial Imperative. A Personal Inquiry into the Animal Origins of Property and Nations,* New York, Atheneum, 1966.
> Noted for its mystique more than its logic, this is of interest principally because it shows what can happen when a nonscientist brings his preconceptions as well as his writing skills to bear on a problem about which he is incompletely informed.

BERNSTEIN, I. S., AND T. P. GORDON. The function of aggression in Primate societies. *American Scientist,* vol. 62, 1974, 304–311.
> An excellent account.

CROOK, J. H. (editor). *Social Behaviour in Birds and Mammals.* Academic Press, New York, 1970.
> Subtitled "Essays on the Social Ethology of Animals and Man," this book should be regarded as fundamental reading for all students of primate, and especially, human behavior.

DE VORE, I. (editor). *Primate Behavior: Field Studies of Monkeys and Apes.* Holt, Rinehart and Winston, New York, 1965.
> The first major collection of field studies in the recent renaissance of field studies in Primate behavior.

DU CHAILLU, PAUL B. *Explorations & Adventures in Equatorial Africa.* London, John Murray, 1861.
> This is the book, a bestseller in its day, which popularized the myth of "the ferocious ape." It is in many ways a worthy book and will always remain one of the great adventure stories in the language.

EIMERL, S. AND I. DE VORE. *The Primates.* Life Nature Library, Vol. 23. Time Inc., New York. 1965.
> A brief, well-written and beautifully illustrated presentation of the Primates.

FOX, R. In the beginning: aspects of hominid behavioral evolution. *Man,* Vol. 2, 1967, pp. 415–433.
> A provocative essay, although the biological conclusions are negated by a failure to take into account the fundamentals of population genetics.

HOLLOWAY, R. K. *Primate Aggression, Territoriality, and Xenophobia.* Academic Press, New York, 1974.
> An indispensable book of important original contributions.

JAY, P. C. *Primates: Studies in Adaptation and Variability* Holt, Rinehart and Winston, New York, 1968.
> An outstanding collection of papers on Primate behavior and its implica-

JOLLY, A. *The Evolution of Primate Behavior*. New York, Macmillan, 1972.
A balanced, well-written, and aptly illustrated account.

KUMMER, H. *Primate Societies: Group Techniques of Ecological Adaptation*. Aldine-Atherton, Chicago, 1971.
Much of what we know about the relation of specific kinds of primate social behavior to particular ecological circumstances is based upon the extensive field work of Hans Kummer.

FOSSEY, D. Making friends with mountain gorillas. *National Geographic*, vol. 137, no. 1, 1970, 48–67.
———— More years with mountain gorillas. *National Geographic*, vol. 140, no. 4, 1971, pp. 574–585
Beautifully told and illustrated, by far the best accounts of mountain gorillas we have.

GALDIKAS-BRINDAMOUR, B. Orangutans, Indonesia's "People of the Forest." *National Geographic*, vol. 148, no. 4, 1975, pp. 444–473.
A delightful, beautifully illustrated, and informative account of the Bornean orang.

HORR, D. A. The Borneo Orang-utan: population structure and dynamics in relationship to ecology and reproductive strategy. *Primate Behavior*, vol. 4, 1975, pp. 307–323.
An excellent field study.

VAN LAWICK-GOODALL, J. *My Friends the Wild Chimpanzees*. National Geographic Society, Washington, 1967.
First hand reporting on chimpanzees in the wild, although it is marred by sentimentality and an unscientific viewpoint. Excellent pictures.

LORENZ, K. *On Agression*. Harcourt Brace Jovanovich, New York, 1966.
A summary treatment by one of the pioneers in the systematic study of animal behavior who has never been able to shake a set of culturally induced assumptions concerning the nature of human nature.

MICHAEL, R. P., AND J. H. CROOK (editors). *Comparative Ecology and Behavior of Primates*. Academic Press, New York, 1973.
A collection of reports on field work by many of the principal scientists actively pursuing work in primate behavior.

MONTAGU, ASHLEY. *The Nature of Human Aggression*. Oxford University Press, New York, 1976.

144   A critical examination of the views of Konrad Lorenz, Robert Ardrey and other "innate aggressionists."

———. (editor). *Man and Aggression.* 2nd ed. Oxford University Press, New York, 1973.
    An anthology of critical studies of Lorenz's and Ardrey's views.

MORRIS, D. (editor). *Primate Ethology.* Aldine, Chicago, 1967.
    A valuable collection of original contributions.

MORRIS, R., AND D. MORRIS. *Men and Apes.* McGraw-Hill, New York, 1966.
    A fascinating, well-researched, and entertainingly written account of humanity's interest in its Primate relatives.

MORRIS, D. (editor). *Primate Ethology.* Aldine, Chicago, 1967.
    A valuable group of contributions to the study of the behavior of monkeys, apes, and children.

OTTEN, C. M. (editor). *Aggression and Evolution.* Xerox College Publishing, Lexington, Mass., 1973.
    A representative array of contributions providing a wide coverage of the subject.

SCHALLER, G. *The Mountain Gorilla.* University of Chicago Press, Chicago, 1963.
    A splendid field study of the ecology and behavior of *Gorilla gorilla beringei.*

———. *The Year of the Gorilla.* University of Chicago Press, Chicago, 1964.
    A delightful and readable account by a zoologist who was the first person with the patience and the courage to spend a year, unarmed, in gorilla country observing the largest of the Primates at home in the mountains of Central Africa.

WASHBURN, S. L. (editor). *The Social Life of Early Man.* Aldine, Chicago, 1961.
    A collection of papers devoted to understanding Primate behavior and the genesis of human behavior.

Part Two

The Fossil Record

Chapter 6

Dating Problems and the Cenozoic Geological Sequence

The Geological Time Scale

Before we can deal with the antiquity of humanity and with its precursors, some kind of perspective is necessary concerning the dimensions of geological time and the age of life on earth. During the height of the controversy that attended the advent of evolutionary thought, the eminent British physicist Lord Kelvin attempted to establish the age of the earth by mathematical projections based on rates of heat loss. While Kelvin was not insistent on a precision of more than within several tens of millions of years, by the end of the nineteenth century he was confident that the correct figure was probably nearer twenty than forty million. Contrast this with our realization today that the detailed history of life on earth as revealed in the fossil record is more than twenty-five times as long, and with our suspicion that the age of the earth itself may be on the order of 250 times as long as Kelvin postulated.

Our present estimates, however, are based on time determinations made with the aid of a knowledge of the phenomena of radioactivity and their significance.

The existence of radioactivity was not even suspected until very near the end of the nineteenth century, so for a period of about fifty years there was a considerable gap between earth age estimates made by geologists and those made by physicists. Within the time span allowed by Kelvin, Darwinian biologists could not construct a picture of organic evolution any more than could geologists picture the building of contemporary physiography by means of observed rates of erosion and deposition.

The twentieth century discovery that nuclear reaction produced the heat generated by the sun eliminated the whole theoretical basis for the time estimates made by Kelvin and his followers and showed that although his mathematics, which had caused so much despair among the Darwinians, were perfectly correct, the assumptions on which they were based were untenable. As it turned out, the geologists had been much more nearly correct in their appraisals, although the sedimentation rates on which their estimates were based could not be subjected to any degree of mathematical precision or elegance and were necessarily somewhat crude. Kelvin's specific assumptions had been wrong, but his realization that accurate age estimates could only be based on quantitative treatment of the properties of the basic materials of which the universe is constructed was quite correct. It is to the continuing efforts of physicists in attempting to refine the bases for such quantitative treatment that we owe our present knowledge of the age of the universe, of the duration of life on earth, and of the antiquity of humanity.

Radioactivity

The investigation of the characteristics of radioactivity has had an explosive impact on the life of the twentieth century. Rather paradoxically the technology that has given us a more or less accurate idea of how long we have been in existence also has moments when it threatens to put a term to that existence. At the moment we are concerned with those properties of matter that enable us to measure time.

In all creation, among the most stable things known are the various rates of decay of radioactive elements; while radioactive elements have been called "unstable," the *rate* of their instability is quite constant, and eventually this decay stops when the radioactive element is completely transformed into a stable element and all further change ceases. With decay proceeding at an unvarying rate, the stable end product accumulates in proportion to the amount of the radioactive substance and the length of time during which the process has been going on. If nothing has artificially occurred to upset the quantities of substances present, the ratio between the remaining radioactive element and its stable end product should be directly related to time. In practice there are several limitations, for instance, the half-life (the amount of time it takes any given quantity of a radioactive element to decay to half what it was) of various radioactive elements varies all the way from a few seconds up to billions of years. Too short or too long a half-life means that the accurate measurement of the ratio of unstable to stable elements built up during the period of interest to geologists and prehistorians will be difficult or impossible to compute. Furthermore, either one or both elements may be subject to removal or addition by the action of weathering or chemical reaction, aside from the fact that most radioactive elements are so rare as to be virtually useless for dating purposes.

Dating by Radioactivity

Despite all these difficulties, a few radioactive elements have been successfully used, and it is with the aid of these that our entire picture of the absolute age of the various strata of the earth has been constructed. Uranium 238, with a half-life of 4.51 billion years, is one of the most useful of these. One of the stable elements into which uranium is transformed is lead, and by measuring the uranium to lead proportion in an unweathered igneous rock, the geophysicist can arrive at an accurate figure for the time elapsed since the uranium-containing mineral within the rock crystallized. The rate of decay of uranium is so slow, however, that not enough of it is transformed to yield accurate measurements for any time period of less than several million years. Therefore, however useful uranium determinations may be for determining the age of the various earlier epochs of the Cenozoic or the periods of the Paleozoic and Mesozoic, they are of no help at all in attempting to date events within the last several million years. For the student of human evolution this is rather a pity since it is within this time span that humanity's evolution has occurred.

For events within the last fifty or sixty thousand years, the use of radioactive carbon, C14, has proven most successful, but for anything much older, this is of no use since its half-life is so short $(5,730 \pm 40 \text{ years})$ that very little is left after this much time, and accurate measurements are not possible. But for determining the dates of the late Neanderthals and the development of modern humans, C14 has been invaluable. At the moment, techniques involving the use of Potassium 40 have yielded some dates for the Middle and Lower Pleistocene and further refinements are eagerly awaited since this is the time span during which many of the most crucial events in human evolution occurred. Many interpretations involving the known fossil record will stand or fall on the basis of the determinations being made at the present and to be made in the near future with the Potassium-Argon (K/Ar) technique.

There are a number of other techniques that have been used to establish the absolute ages of prehistoric deposits, although most of these, for one reason or another, have been of limited use, and there are doubts concerning the practicability of some. Almost certainly, new techniques will be developed, and before long we may be able to establish dates for many prehistoric strata and check them by more than one means. Without providing a description of the governing rationale, we can note that such techniques as proactinium-thorium, fission track, and thermoluminescence have been successfully used, and amino acid racemization shows promise of being useful.

Subdivisions of Geological Time

With this brief discussion of the techniques of absolute time designations as a basis, Figure 45 shows the various accepted subdivisions of the stretch of geological time during which life has advanced from its invertebrate origins. The numbers indicate tentative dates for the onset of the division to which they correspond. Although the dating techniques are called "absolute," the figures must remain tentative since further refinements may alter them by several millions of years. Despite this uncertainty, it is generally felt that at least the right order of magnitude is being expressed — always bearing in mind that Kelvin said the same sort of thing more than a century ago when he proposed a radically different time scale for the entire age of the earth, not merely for the span of organic life in the fossil record. Our confidence in these more recent estimates is increased by the fact that physicists, geologists, and evolutionary biologists are now in mutual agreement in accepting dates of this magnitude, and the consensus is that the future will bring no really radical alterations.

Vertebrate Evolution

While there is scattered evidence for the existence for some invertebrate forms in the Pre-Cambrian, the really reliable picture of the unbroken continuity of organic forms right up to the present day does not begin until the Cambrian period early in the Paleozoic era, and even then there is no evidence for the presence of animals with backbones. Hints of the presence of primitive fishes occur in the Ordovician, but it is not until the Silurian that we find the first complete fossil of a kind of jawless fish, the Ostracoderm. This appears

ERA	PERIOD	EPOCH	TIME
Cenozoic	Quaternary	Recent	(10,000)
		Pleistocene	3
	Tertiary	Pliocene	5
		Miocene	25
		Oligocene	40
		Eocene	60
		Paleocene	80
Mesozoic	Cretaceous		120
	Jurassic		180
	Triassic		200
Paleozoic	Permian		285
	Carboniferous		350
	Devonian		400
	Silurian		450
	Ordovician		500
	Cambrian		600

MILLIONS OF YEARS

Pre-Cambrian

Figure 45. Geological time table.

to have developed in fresh water streams and it seems likely that some form of Silurian Ostracoderm was the ancestor to all subsequent vertebrate life, including humanity itself.

Widespread terrestrial uplifting during the Devonian so altered the environment in which the Ostracoderms had lived that these fish were forced to undergo a variety of adaptive changes in response to the requirements of the changing environment. The uplift and desiccation reduced the security of fresh water streams, and, as a response, some of the fishes underwent modifications enabling them to invade the oceans, where they underwent further changes, which culminated in the oceanic fishes of today.

More important to our story, however, are the fishes that met the

Dating Problems and the Cenozoic Geological Sequence

Figure 46. Swift-moving ostracoderm from the Late
Silurian of Norway (*Pterolepis nitidus*). (Courtesy
of the American Museum of Natural History.)

challenge of reduced water levels in the streams of their origin. Of
these, the most significant are the Crossopterygians, which developed muscular lobes at the bases of their fins that could serve as
props for helping push the fish from one puddle to another in the
beds of the drying streams. While these adaptive changes enabled
these fish to remain in their watery niche, it also meant that more
time was being spent on dry land, and with the development of
lungs and nostrils, the Crossopterygians actually became transformed into crude amphibians by the end of the Devonian.

The succeeding Carboniferous saw a return of the moist, damp
lowlands, and it was during this time that the amphibians enjoyed
their heyday, undergoing adaptive radiation in the lush swampy
environment that was to give rise to much of the coal used today.
Terrestrial uplifting started at the end of the Carboniferous and
uplifting inevitably produces desiccation. Amphibians—compromise land animals at best—cannot endure prolonged existence in a
dry environment. Part of their respiration is carried on by the moist
glandular skin and should they be too long in the dry air, they become completely dried up. Furthermore, amphibians require the
presence of standing water for purposes of breeding. Their eggs must
be laid in water and the larval tadpole stage of development must
occur there before they have reached the point where temporary
excursions can be made on land.

The hint of uplift at the end of the Carboniferous was a prelude of
what was to come, but it was sufficient to produce an important
adaptive response in some of the amphibians. A dry protective skin
was developed so that the creature could remain indefinitely out of
water, and protective coatings for the eggs were developed so that it
was no longer necessary to return to water to reproduce. Effectively,
then, some of the amphibians had become primitive reptiles and the

Figure 47. Crossopterygian fish, the Coelocanth (*Latimeria chalumnae*), a living fossil from the Jurassic or earlier, thought to have been extinct since then, but discovered to have survived in 1954 when the first specimen was caught off the east coast of South Africa. Many others have since been caught. (Courtesy of the American Museum of Natural History.)

Figure 48. A crossopterygian lobe-finned fish (*Eusthenopteron*), of Devonian age, compared with a labyrinthodont amphibian (*Diplovertebron*) of Devonian age. It is from this kind of crossopt that the first labyrinthodont amphibia are believed to have evolved. (Courtesy of the American Museum of Natural History.)

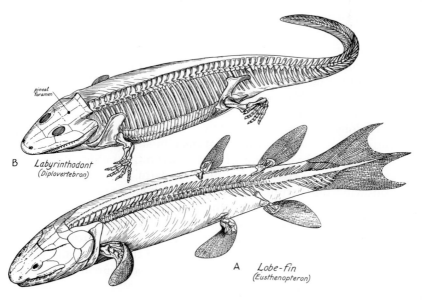

Dating Problems and the Cenozoic Geological Sequence

foundation was laid for the extensive development of terrestrial animals that was to come in the Permian and the following Mesozoic.

During the Permian, major geological changes occurred greatly altering the face of the earth. These are referred to collectively as the Appalachian revolution and involved the upthrust of the entire Appalachian mountain chain from an area that for millions of years had been intermittently awash. These changes were the consequences of the break-up of what had once been a single huge continent, Pangaea. As with the other great upthrusts of geological history, two major climatic changes occurred. First of all, the rise of extensive land masses and the interruption of air flow by high mountains created large areas with a dry climate. Reptiles, whose development enabled them to solve the problems of desiccation, took advantage of this developing ecological niche and commenced the adaptive radiation that was to produce the bizarre and spectacular forms of the Mesozoic, the Age of Dinosaurs (Fig. 49).

The second consequence of uplift is often overlooked, but, in our picture of the forces shaping the development of terrestrial life, it is at least as important. This is the fact that extensive uplift necessarily produces large areas of land that are not only high but also cool. There is relatively extensive evidence for glaciation in the Permian nearly 230 million years before the great Pleistocene Ice Age was to have its impact on the development of humanity. The existence of a large Permian life zone that was cool and moist provided the challenge to one branch of the developing Reptile class, which was successfully met by the Therapsids.

Successful survival in a cold climate requires that an organism maintain its body temperature above that of the surrounding environment. Generation of body heat in turn requires continued and regular fuel intake and this requires an efficiency of locomotion and the mechanics of capturing and eating food well above that generally thought of as being characteristic of reptiles. In their limb structure, tooth differentiation, and the separation of the breathing and eating passages, the Permian mammal-like reptiles, the Therapsids, clearly show that they were developing an elevated metabolism and had taken a long step in the direction of true mammals to which they eventually gave rise. So it was that the climatic developments of the Permian initiated a direction of organic evolution culminating in the mammals that were later to dominate the earth.

Following the Permian, however, worldwide climate improved and the ensuing Mesozoic saw the adaptive radiation of the reptiles that filled most of the available ecological niches. Herbivorous and carnivorous dinosaurs roamed the land, aquatic forms became adapted to the oceans, flying forms invaded the air, and the largest terrestrial animals that ever lived, the Sauropods, pursued a semiam-

Figure 49. Mesozoic reptiles: dinosaurs. *Stegosaurus* in the foreground, *Tyrannosaurus* in the middle ground, and *Brontosaurus* in the water. Painting by R. Kane. (Courtesy of the American Museum of Natural History.)

phibious life in the swamps where a part of their vast bulk was supported by water. The Mesozoic was the Age of Reptiles proper, and although the mammalian development triggered by the preceding Permian continued in the form of a number of small true mammals, these were relatively unimportant at the time and remained in the background.

At the end of the Mesozoic, for reasons we can only guess, the large dominant reptiles all disappeared. Some have postulated that the cooling of the climate heralding the beginning of the Cenozoic was the crucial factor, but this leaves unexplained the fact that the large reptiles had vanished *before* the changes in climate occurred. Some have suggested that the origin and spread of modern seed plants in the middle of the Mesozoic may have accounted for the extinction of the characteristic Mesozoic vegetation on which the herbivorous reptiles were dependent, and that without their food supply, and failing to adapt to a new one, they became extinct. This would have caused the extinction also of the carnivorous dinosaurs that preyed on them and the whole chain of reptilian existence could have been upset. Perhaps this was the cause or perhaps it was something else; in any event, the ruling reptiles vanished toward the end of the Mesozoic, leaving a world of unoccupied ecological niches into which the mammals would radiate in the ensuing Cenozoic.

Dating Problems and the Cenozoic Geological Sequence

156   The few inconspicuous mammals that had survived throughout the Mesozoic provided the base for the adaptive radiation that commenced at the beginning of the Tertiary, and among the first orders to appear in the Paleocene was the order Primates. Today, of course, Primates include higher monkeys, apes, and humans, but in the early Cenozoic they were a primitive lot that scarcely represented much of an advance beyond a late Cretaceous insectivore.

Suggested Readings

BROTHWELL, D., AND E. HIGGS, (editors). *Science in Archaeology.* Basic Books, New York, 1963.
> A comprehensive survey of progress and research, especially good on dating methods.

BUTZER, K. W. *Environment and Archeology: An Ecological Approach to Prehistory*, 2nd ed. Aldine-Atherton, Chicago, 1971.
> An authoritative reconstruction of Pleistocene physical environments and man-land relationships at different stages of prehistory.

CARTER, G. S. *Structure and Habit in Vertebrate Evolution.* University of Washington Press, Seattle, Washington, 1967.
> A readable account of the 'success story' of the vertebrates, giving a functional account of the major changes in their evolution.

COLES, J. M., AND E. S. HIGGS. *The Archaeology of Early Man.* Praeger, New York, 1969.
> A comprehensive and valuable survey.

FLINT, R. F. *Glacial and Quaternary Geology.* John Wiley, New York, 1971.
> Definitive coverage.

HOLE, F., AND R. F. HEIZER. *An Introduction to Prehistoric Archeology.* Holt, Rinehart and Winston, New York, 1965.
> A most useful systematic introduction to the history, method, and theory of archeology.

MICHAEL, H. N., AND E. K. RALPH. *Dating Techniques for the Archaeologist.* M.I.T. Press, Cambridge, 1971.
> A thorough review of the dating techniques that can be applied to the time span during which recognizable human beings have been in existence.

MICHELS, J. W. *Dating Methods in Archaeology.* Souvenir Press, New York, 1973.
> A useful work.

OAKLEY, K. P. *Frameworks for Dating Fossil Man,* 2nd ed. Aldine, Chicago, 1966.
A comprehensive summary of data for relative and absolute dating, with an inventory of the dating of all fossil human remains.

ROMER, A. S. *Vertebrate Paleontology.* 3rd ed., University of Chicago Press, Chicago, 1966.
Very readable.

Pre-Pleistocene Primates

chapter 7

The Four Grades of Primates

In our consideration of the development of life on earth we have progressively narrowed our concern, proceeding from the simple recognition of "Life" in the Pre-Cambrian to Vertebrates in the Ordovician, through Amphibia, Reptilia, Mammalia, and now more specifically Primates. Until this present focusing, our picture has tended to touch on the more dramatic aspects of the organic world, but with the appearance of Primates at the beginning of the Cenozoic, it is our task to limit our attention to them rather than to continue chronicling the major events of organic evolution. Actually, from our point of view, the appearance and development of Primates could properly be regarded as a major event, but, at the time, it was not particularly dramatic.

The discovery of fossil Primates played something of a role in the development of evolutionary thought in the nineteenth century since the founder of the science of paleontology, Cuvier, in his attempt to dispel the concept of evolution as an explanation for sequence in the fossil record, had not only claimed that fossil humans did not exist but that fossil Primates of any kind were impossible. In 1836, just four years after Cuvier's death, the first fossil monkey had been found, and just a year later, one of Cuvier's own disciples, Edouard Lartet, found the fossil *Pliopithecus*, a possible precursor of modern apes.

Despite the interest devoted to the unravelling of Primate evolution, there have been a number of obstacles in the way of complete success in this endeavor. In the first place, Primates are not comparable to the great herd animals and they have never been particularly numerous in any one spot. Furthermore, most of them have been relatively small creatures so that the probability of a Primate being preserved as a fossil has never been very good. Finally, Primates have tended to live in tropical forests where conditions for fossilization are poor. Because of these problems, the Primate fossil record is disjointed and incomplete, and if this were all we had to go on it would be difficult to chronicle Primate evolution prior to the appearance of humans. As we shall see later, the fossil evidence for humans, while not without its own problems, is much more satisfactory.

The one thing that makes it possible to venture tentative interpretation of the course of Primate evolution prior to the Pleistocene are the inferences that can be made from a thorough comparative study of the living Primates. Up to a point, we can regard the living Primates as a frozen picture of Primate evolution in the Cenozoic, with the various major taxonomic groupings representing the various stages of Primate evolution as they appeared. We must stress, however, that this approach can only be used with caution since there is no guarantee that our various representative groups of living Primates have not undergone significant modifications since they first appeared in the Tertiary. Humanity has continued to evolve and it is abundantly clear that the other Primates have not obligingly stood still to aid us in our interpretations. With this caution then, a combination of the direct evidence from the fossil record and inferential evidence from living Primates can provide us with a much better idea of the course of Primate evolution than could the exclusive use of either one of these approaches.

Among the living Primates there are representatives of four grades in their adaptive radiation with the fourth grade being represented by humans alone. As we shall see in Chapter 9, humanity has developed through a series of four stages since its first appearance, but since it has remained within the same ecological niche and since the stages succeed each other with the earlier ones becoming transformed into the later ones, never more than one being in existence at any one time, the series of stages in human evolution cannot themselves be called an adaptive radiation. For the Order Primates as a whole, their four grades, Prosimian, Monkey, Ape, and Human, do represent an adaptive radiation since they did develop to take advantage of differing ecological niches and while each appears at a different time during the Cenozoic and develops out of the preceding grade, all four continue to exist today. We shall treat them in order of their appearance.

The living Prosimians represent less of a change from the ancestral mammalian pattern than the higher Primates do, so it is not surprising that the earliest creatures that are recognizably Primates are effectively at the Prosimian grade of organization. The first Primates took to the trees with the sensory equipment of terrestrial animals. In terrestrial (ground-living) as opposed to arboreal (tree-living) creatures, the senses of smell and hearing are relatively more acute than is visual ability. The hindrance to vision that grass, brush, and other vegetation offers means that the ability to see acutely is less important to a small terrestrial creature than the ability to detect invisible danger. On the other hand, the small arboreal animal leaping from branch to branch of its forest home would be in difficulty if it were forced to locate the next branch by sniffing it out, or by cocking a sharp ear and listening for it.

However, even for a creature whose sensory abilities were primarily those of a terrestrial mammal, the trees did offer an ecological niche relatively free from predators, and it required only one development to utilize them. This was the development of prehensile appendages — grasping hands and feet. From the fossil record of the earliest Cenozoic Primates we can see that they possessed the elongated snout of animals with a well-developed sense of smell. This is still reflected in most of the living Prosimians where the snout is capped by the naked and moist rhinarium which indicates olfactory acuity. Furthermore, the living Prosimians have sensory whiskers on the sides of the snout, the eyes have not rotated forward to give them the well-developed binocular vision of the higher Primates and, in some, the ears can be moved to help localize sound. Using the living Prosimians as a guide, and comparing their skeletal structure to that preserved for the earliest Primates, we are certain that the Paleocene representatives possessed sensory equipment rather like that of a modern lemur. By noting further that they lived in forested areas, we can infer that they possessed the grasping ability that has characterized Primates ever since. For this we have no direct evidence since no hand or foot bones have been discovered — not too surprising when the chances against fossilization and discovery of such small and delicate pieces of anatomy are overwhelming. We do, however, have arm and leg bones consistent with the assumption that their possessors were climbing creatures rather than terrestrial running animals, and it is reasonable to suppose that prehensile appendages had been developed.

PROLIFERATION

While this assumption is generally held and certainly cogent since the entire subsequent adaptive radiation of the Order Primates is based on it, it is apparent that the earliest Primates were not so restricted to the arboreal ecological niche as is true for most of their descendants up to the appearance of humans. There was a proliferation of Eocene Prosimians that attained a wide distribution for a brief duration and lived the life of small scurrying, scampering animals in bush and grasslands. Many of these showed dental modifications toward the increase in gnawing ability. This perhaps accounts for the worldwide distribution of Primates by the Middle Eocene by which time relatively similar Prosimians had spread throughout the tropics of the entire world connected by the grass and brush land of the more temperate zones. In the latter part of the Eocene and continuing into the Oligocene, the adaptive radiation of the rodents rather changes this picture. With more effective gnawing teeth, with the ability to withstand greater temperature fluctuations, and above all with the ability to produce little rodents in greater quantities in a shorter length of time, it was not long before the grassland ecological niche was the property of the rodents alone.

We do not know the crucial factor but certainly the difference in rates of reproduction must have been important. An arboreal animal with eight or ten offspring is rather restricted in its movements, and, with this background, Primates characteristically have a greatly restricted number of offspring per pregnancy — generally only one for the higher Primates. With the parental care concentrated on only one or two youngsters, the chances that any given individual may live to maturity are greatly increased, but in the competition for space in the Eocene grasslands, little Primates apparently were not produced at the same rate as little rodents.

PLESIADAPIS

Among the various scraps of evidence for Primates early in the Age of Mammals, one of the most completely represented is the creature called *Plesiadapis*. The reconstruction, from fragments of Paleocene age in Colorado and in France, shows that the creature had been a relatively unspecialized quadruped. Unlike subsequent Primates, however, the only preserved toes were equipped with claws rather than the flattened nail we usually (although not always) expect to find. The jaws and teeth display an interesting convergence toward the condition we usually associate with rodents. The incisors are enlarged and angled forward, and they are set off by a considerable gap from the cheek teeth behind. These are peculiarities not found in the later fossil Primates that constitute the links between the present and the past, and this is usually taken to indicate that *Plesiadapis* played no role in subsequent Primate evolution.

It is interesting to note that while Primates were not successful in challenging rodents for the small-mammal grassland ecological niche, the rodents on their part were not able to dislodge the Primates from their arboreal habitats. Rodents have made successful incursions into the arboreal ecological niche (squirrels for example) only in those parts of the world where native Primates are rare or nonexistent.

NOTHARCTUS

It is apparent that during the second epoch of the Cenozoic, the Eocene, the known Primates were still at the Prosimian Grade of organization. Of the Eocene Primate family Adapidae, the European genus *Adapis* is regarded very tentatively as a possible ancestor for the modern lemurs and lorises. Another member of this family, *Notharctus*, first identified in the Eocene deposits in Wyoming, does not display the limiting specializations of *Adapis*. It possessed a generalized skeleton suitable for quadrupedal arboreal climbing, but lacking the elongated tarsal bones of the modern leaping Prosimians such as the tarsiers and galagos. The snout has not been reduced to the extent it has in most more recent Primates, although it is apparent that some of the earlier reconstructions of *Notharctus* erroneously gave it a longer muzzle than it actually possessed. Interpretations come, and interpretations go, and sometimes they come back again. For some time after *Notharctus* was discovered more than a century ago, it was regarded as a general model for the ancestors of the higher Primates. With subsequent reconstructions and the discovery of other Eocene Primates, this view came to be regarded as unlikely, but now, at least in the opinion of some Primate paleontologists, *Notharctus* can, once again, be regarded as a tentative model for the form ancestral to both the New and the Old World monkeys as well as the anthropoid apes and humans.

DIET

As we have mentioned, when Primates first became tree dwellers, they brought with them the sensory equipment of terrestrial mammals. We can guess that they also brought with them the dietary preferences of their terrestrial relatives. It is interesting in this regard to note that the closest relatives of the early Primates were members of the order Insectivora, and, from the structure of the teeth of the first Primates, it would appear that an insectivorous diet was the general adaptation. To this day, Prosimians such as lorises, galagos, and tarsiers make insects an important if not an exclusive part of their diet. Other Prosimians concentrate to an increasing extent on the kind of frugivorous strategy predominant among the higher Primates. This leads us to suspect that the dietary shift from insect-eating to fruit-eating was the key to full-scale exploitation of the arboreal ecological niche and occurred long ago among the early Prosimians as they

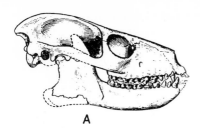
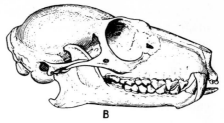

Figure 50. (A) The Eocene lemuriforme (*Notharctus*) from the Bridger Basin, Wyoming. (B) A modern lemur for comparison. (Both redrawn after W. K. Gregory.)

gave rise to the Monkey Grade. Some have argued that it was the early insect-eating proclivities of the ancestral Prosimians that developed the grasping and manipulative capabilities later put to use for locomotor purposes as they expanded in the arboreal world into which they moved. However, the big parrots who compete with monkeys for the resources of the rain-forest canopy show manipulative capabilities fully the equivalent of the most adept of the nonhuman Primates, and no insect-manipulating background can be suggested.

While surprising numbers of different Eocene Prosimians have been found, their relations to each other, to their predecessors, and to their followers are not conclusive. This is a problem frequently encountered in trying to interpret the fossil record, and its solution requires either an extraordinarily complete sequence of fossils such as is known for the development of the horse, or some other clearly interpretable phenomenon such as the unbroken line of the human cultural adaptive mechanism which, as the archeological record reveals, ties together the otherwise diverse and isolated human fossils of the Pleistocene. Pre-Pleistocene Primates left no cultural remains, and there are not enough of them to indicate clear evolutionary lines, so our discussion is forced to focus on the general emergence of the various Grades of Primate adaptation.

The Monkey Grade

Today the dominant Primates in the arboreal ecological niche throughout the tropics of the entire world are various kinds of monkeys. This simple observation takes on added interest when it is realized that the Primates of the Old and New Worlds have been separated since the Eocene, some fifty million years ago. This separation occurred before the Monkey Grade had been attained in either hemisphere. Further, the monkeys of each area developed from different

Prosimians, which makes the independent attainment of a similarly advanced grade of development a classic case of evolutionary parallelism.

VISION VS. OLFACTION

The most evident difference that distinguishes the Monkey Grade from the Prosimian Grade is the conversion of the primitive mammalian dependence on the olfactory means of orientation into one primarily dependent on vision, along with an accompanying increase in brain size. This can be simply stated as a change from a smell brain to a sight brain with attendant cerebral increase.

The advantages to a tree-living creature are obvious, and a whole series of anatomical adjustments accompanies this basic change. Full binocular stereoscopic vision is attained as the eye sockets swivel around toward the front. Not only are the visual parts of the brain developed at the expense of the olfactory parts, but the forward swivelling of the orbits (the eye sockets) greatly reduces the part of the face that can be devoted to the development of the nose. With the reduction in the importance of the sense of smell, and with it the development of the nose, the whole snout becomes shortened. This, along with the increase in brain size, is what contributes to the appeal monkeys have to the human imagination since it makes them look more human than any other animal, and, in our anthropocentric way, we tend to regard a human appearance as being, by definition, appealing.

The increase in brain size also requires some comment. Monkeys exceed the Prosimians in the relative size of their brains, but even the Prosimians are clearly distinguishable from the other early Cenozoic mammals by their relative cranial enlargement. Most likely this can be related to the conditions attendant upon an arboreal existence. Locomotion through the tree tops requires the continual making of choices — certainly to a much greater degree than would be the case for a terrestrial quadruped where there is virtual certainty that there will always be ground wherever one's feet are moved. In a tree, however, there is more space than support, and, in addition, locomotor decisions have to be made in three dimensions rather than in only two. Obviously an expanded choice-making mechanism, i.e., brain, is of relatively greater importance to an arboreal animal than it would be to an average terrestrial quadruped.

In the Monkey Grade also, molars had expanded to display the kind of broad crushing crown that indicates the adaptation to a frugivorous diet that evidently allowed the first full scale utilization of the arboreal ecological niche. Later dental changes occur as particular dietary specializations develop, but some form of the generalized

The Fossil Record

crushing molar is now present among all the higher Primates including humans.

EARLIEST MONKEYS

Fossils from a number of places in the Old World show that the
Monkey Grade had been reached by the Miocene, and there are indications that this must have been attained during the Oligocene. The
first fossil monkey recognized was a specimen from the upper Miocene of northern India. This was followed by relatively complete
remains of an early Pliocene monkey in Greece in 1840, and, in the
years that followed a slow trickle of finds attributable to the Monkey
Grade has accumulated. These are scattered over an area ranging
from Europe on the north to Africa in the south and extending as far
east as Japan. Most of these are Pliocene and Pleistocene in date but a
few are Miocene, as are some of the very few fossil monkeys from
South America. Evidently the Monkey Grade had been reached independently in both the Old and New Worlds by the Miocene.

However, the best evidence we have for the development of Primates at what we would call the Monkey Grade of organization has
come from the Old World; specifically, it has come from the Oligocene deposits in the Fayum depression in Egypt some fifty miles
south of Cairo and twenty miles west of the Nile. Today the Fayum is
dominated by the dry winds of the neighboring Sahara, but in the
Oligocene it was an area of lush tropical forest bordering swamps
and river deltas. Since the beginning of the twentieth century paleontologists have been excavating with phenomenal success, at
least as far as the recovery of fossil Primates is concerned. Much of
the recent work, including reassessments of what was done early in
the century, has been accomplished by the Yale paleontologist Elwyn Simons.

Professor Simons has demonstrated that the genus *Parapithecus*,
named during the first decade of the century and known from jaws
and teeth only, was not the aberrant and questionable Primate it was
once thought to be. Its previously dubious status was the result of a
mistaken reconstruction. Now it would appear that *Parapithecus*
is a good candidate for the ancestor of the Old World monkeys, although not an ancestor of apes or humans since those ancestors are
also to be found in the Oligocene of the Fayum.

One such specimen has been given the name *Aeolopithecus* after
Aeolus, the Greek god of winds. It was the action of the desert wind
that uncovered the first specimen to be recognized. Because of the
shape of the jaws and teeth, Professor Simons suggests that this genus just might represent the ancestors of the modern gibbons.

The most important and exciting of Simons' discoveries, however,

Figure 51. Lateral view of the skull of *Aegypto-pithecus* from the Oligocene of the Fayum of Egypt. (Courtesy of E. L. Simons, Yale Peabody Museum.)

is the creature he has called *Aegyptopithecus zeuxis*. The fragments assigned to this species include a facial skeleton with the front half of the skull, a reconstructable mandible, teeth, tail bones, foot and limb fragments, and one relatively complete arm bone. These finds, starting in 1966, have been given an absolute age of about 28 million years, placing them in the latter part of the Oligocene. The teeth definitely foreshadow the development of ape and human teeth rather than those of Old World monkeys. The form of the brain, however, is long and low and lacks the frontal lobe development of modern anthropoid apes. But although the olfactory bulbs project forward beyond the level of the frontal lobes, they are smaller and there is relatively more visual cortex than is true for most Prosimians. These observations, based on recent detailed studies, nicely confirm Professor Simons' initial judgment that he had discovered "the skull of a monkey equipped with the teeth of an ape." Adding further to this assessment has been a still more recent study of the limb bones which concludes that *Aegyptopithecus* had been a robust arboreal climber that moved in the manner of a modern howler monkey (although the study makes it clear there is no evidence that the tail had been prehensile).

Judging from the specimens in the Oligocene deposits at the Fayum in Egypt, and from scraps of primates elsewhere, it would seem that the Monkey Grade of organization had already been achieved. Certainly the main stream of Primate evolution would appear to have passed beyond the Prosimian level. And although *Aegyptopithecus* certainly appears to be ancestral to subsequent apes (and humans), it would be judged to be, from brain to body to palpable tail, a proper monkey.

The Fossil Record

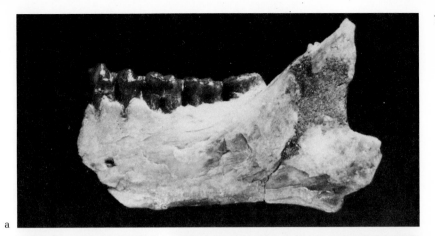

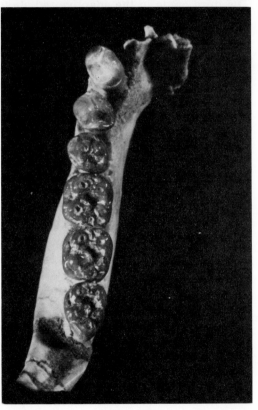

Figure 52. *Propliopithecus haeckli*, from the Egyptian Fayum, probably from the Oligocene. Three views: (a) Left lateral view of the mandible and teeth; (b) Occlusal view of the teeth of the same left side; (c) Occlusal view of the right side (reversed print). (Courtesy of Eric Delson.)

Pre-Pleistocene Primates

The find in 1908 in the Egyptian Fayum of a broken mandible, which was named *Propliopithecus haeckli,* has presented something of a puzzle. Probably of Oligocene age, the teeth present some remarkably anthropomorphous traits. The incisors were not recovered, but the remaining teeth were. The canines are relatively small and vertically implanted, the premolars are same sized, the molars are low crowned and increase in size from first to last. Simons has suggested that *Propliopithecus* may be ancestral to *Aegyptopithecus zeuxis* and fits fairly well into the model of a generalized dryopithecine. It is as good a working hypothesis as any.

The Ape Grade

The third grade in the adaptive radiation of the Primates, like the first and the fourth, is distinguished by a change in the characteristic means of locomotion. When a modern ape moves from one place to another in the trees, it does so by going hand-over-hand, hanging beneath the branches from which its weight is supported. This means of progression is called brachiation (arm-swinging), and as a primary means of locomotion, is used by the apes alone. Prosimians and monkeys, in contrast, are tree-going quadrupeds, scampering along the tops of branches and actually jumping from one to another.

Just as the grasping-manipulating development of the Prosimians and the expanded sight brain of the monkeys were important preadaptations without which the later Human Grade could not have arisen, so the development of brachiation in the anthropoid ape was an important step in the direction of the upright posture that ultimately freed human hands from any involvement in locomotion. The role played by brachiation in directing an organism toward a habitually vertical position is obvious—it is rather hard to hang horizontally—and if it can be assumed that humanity's precursors developed by way of the Ape Grade, then the extensive similarities between the chest, shoulder, and arm structure of humans and the modern great apes would be explained as would be the initial adaptation to erect posture on the part of the early human precursors.

Locomotion

Early in this century, some students of primate anatomy proposed an alternative explanation for the development of habitual upright posture, and a form of this explanation has been recently revived. This is now being called the "vertical clinging and leaping" hypothesis, and it advanced the view that the upright posture of both the ape and human lines was foreshadowed by the assumed mode of locomotion of their Eocene Prosimian forebears. Actually this interpretation

The Fossil Record

owes more to the extent to which its adherents are impressed by the **169** vertical posture of modern tarsiers and galagos than it does to the skimpy fossil record. Early developments of this view were influenced by a reluctance to see the human line coming from something resembling, in a structural sense, an anthropoid ape, so an attempt was made to offer a reason for the development of human erect posture by suggesting a very early and independent attainment of the vertical body position. But the evidence for vertical clinging and leaping in the Eocene is tenuous at best, and certainly *Aegyptopithecus* in the Oligocene was an orthodox arboreal quadruped. In our judgment, then, the detailed similarities between the human and anthropoid ape wrist, elbow, and shoulder joints is best regarded as a reflection of a common brachiating heritage, and this alone is sufficient to account for the generally upright carriage of the body.

Brachiation as a mode of arboreal progression allows for two possibilities that are not initially obvious. For a brachiator of average monkey-like size, it extends the area that can be used for locomotor purposes. Staying within the same kind of supporting framework commonly used by monkeys, it also allows for a considerable increase in body size without appreciably affecting locomotor efficiency.

These two possibilities result from the fact that an arboreal quadruped needs relatively more stable support for its normal mode of locomotion. As an effective support for running and jumping, a monkey needs relatively unyielding branches. When the support is flexible, the problem of maintaining balance on top is increasingly difficult, and jumping becomes quite impossible. As Dr. Virginia Avis has pointed out, this is no problem for a creature that habitually hangs from branches. Small brachiators, then, can utilize parts of the trees normally avoided by monkeys, and, in the more stable parts of the arboreal environment, brachiators can become very much larger without the attendant loss of locomotor efficiency — hence the orang.

This may also be related to the re-invasion of a terrestrial ecological niche such as that exhibited by the gorilla and partially by the chimpanzee. A creature that has successfully become large in an arboreal environment will have fewer natural enemies on the ground simply because of its size, and there will be less reason to avoid the ground as compared with the gibbon in the wild. It might even be possible to speculate that this may have had something to do with the return to the ground by the Pre-Pleistocene forerunners of humans, but we lack the fossil evidence to support such a supposition.

Against the theory that humans had a brachiating ancestor, it has been argued that humanity's more generalized hands and arms could not have developed from something like the comparable members of such an animal as a chimpanzee without reversing the evolutionary process. At bottom, this objection seems to be another manifestation of the difficulty some have had in facing the possibility that humans descended from something less human-like than themselves. This notion found equivocal support in the view formerly held that evolution was irreversible.

To counter these objections, the old idea of the irreversibility of evolution has been largely abandoned with the increase in understanding of the evolutionary process. To be sure, the *exact* reacquisition of a former stage of development is so unlikely as to be impossible, but a reversal of selective pressures or their suspension can result in reversals of adaptations or their reduction. The human pectoral appendage is not the exact replica of a former evolutionary stage, but it *is* just what one would expect of a limb that had formerly been adapted to brachiation, but which, as a result of the cessation of its function as a suspensory organ, had undergone reduction by means of the probable mutation effect. Finally one need not postulate that the human ancestor underwent such an extreme brachiating adaptation as that seen in the modern anthropoid apes, where it has continued for several million years after it had been abandoned by humans.

In sum, we feel that the extensive anatomical similarities between the upper parts of modern humans and modern apes indicate a community of descent of greater degree than that existing between any other two Grades in the Primate adaptive radiation. As a preadaptation to terrestrial bipedalism, it seems most likely that the precursors of humanity developed through the third or Ape Grade of Primate development.

While these statements all seem reasonable enough, there is an embarrassing lack of direct fossil evidence in their support — not that the fossils support any other view, but the problem is simply a lack of fossils. The deficiency is not total, since there are some tantalizing fragments, but interpretation is difficult, and it is not possible to say exactly when the brachiating grade was effectively attained.

PLIOPITHECUS ET AL.

An assessment of what we have in the form of better preserved fragments will convey some idea of the nature of the problem. Within five years of the death of Cuvier, his follower Lartet unearthed a small incomplete mandible in southern France, which was recognized as a possible precursor to the modern gibbons. This was named *Pliopithecus*, and subsequent finds in Europe and East Africa show that it must have been widespread in the Old World throughout the Miocene. In the patterns evident in the crowns of the teeth, *Pliopithecus* showed that it was more closely allied to the modern anthropoid apes than to the Old World monkeys and in fact

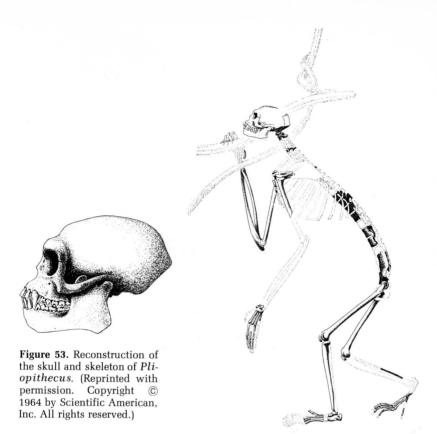

Figure 53. Reconstruction of the skull and skeleton of *Pliopithecus*. (Reprinted with permission. Copyright © 1964 by Scientific American, Inc. All rights reserved.)

the smallish low-crowned molars and saber-like canines foreshadow the form of those teeth in the modern hylobatids to a remarkable extent. Even more suggestive is the presence of long straight-shafted arm bones clearly indicating the development of suspensory feeding and locomotor behavior. This is developed to an even greater extent in *Pliopithecus*' African relative and contemporary *Limnopithecus*, where the arms are actually somewhat longer than the legs. Upwardly directed shoulder joints and the curved finger bones of the suspensory hand-hook further confirm the suspicion that the *Pliopithecus-Limnopithecus* group was adapted to a brachiating mode of progression and constitutes a good candidate for the ancestor of the modern gibbon-siamang group. The one drawback to this view is the fact that the bones at the bottom of the spinal column clearly indicate that *Pliopithecus* possessed a tail, quite unlike the modern gibbons. This, however, does nothing to disqualify its candidacy for ancestral status. *Aegyptopithecus* evidently had a tail also, but it is accepted by most students as the ancestor to the tail-less anthropoid ape and human lines of later times.

Figure 54. *Dryopithecus.* Reconstruction from portion of a mandible (darker color) of a representative of the genus thought to have given rise to the great apes and hominids. Of Miocene age. (Courtesy of the American Museum of Natural History.)

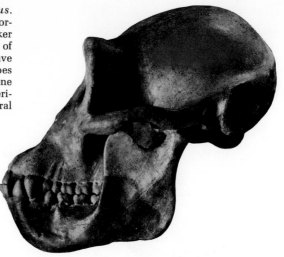

DRYOPITHECUS

In 1856, Lartet described another fossil ape from southern France, *Dryopithecus* (Fig. 54). Except for the fact that the incisors were smaller, the teeth were remarkably like those of a modern chimpanzee, and the pattern on the crowns of the lower molars was identical with those found on many well-developed modern human molars. While this was a very interesting, indeed, almost dramatic resemblance, such a finding did not greatly assist in solving the dilemma that remains with us today concerning the placement of the third adaptation of the Primates, since, however ape-like the teeth of *Dryopithecus*, the evidence of its postcranial skeleton showed that in this instance the attributes of suspensory locomotion were not developed to anything like the degree present in *Pliopithecus.* There are arguments among the experts concerning whether it was a "semi-brachiator" or a palmigrade quadruped with most considering quadrupedalism of some type to be its most characteristic form of locomotion, but in spite of these disagreements, majority opinion now recognizes the *Dryopithecus* group to include the ancestors of the modern great apes and possibly humans.

The original find in France, however, was only a jaw with its teeth, and it was not until nearly a century later that we could say anything about its postcranial skeleton and hence its mode of locomotion. During that period of time, many more specimens of jaws and teeth were recovered both from various places in Europe and importantly from extensive materials from the Siwalik Hills on the border between Pakistan and India. And starting in the 1920s similar material began to be discovered in various places in East Africa. This culminated, in a sense, with the find in the mid-1940s by Mary Leakey, wife of the late L. S. B. Leakey, of a complete set of jaws and teeth, facial skeleton, and front of the skull, and a series of limb bones of what was at first called *"Proconsul africanus."* The Leakeys, concentrating more on field work than comparative study, tended to give each specimen discovered a new formal taxonomic name regardless of whether or not it could be included with a previously described species. This tendency is by no means confined to the Leakeys, but it has resulted in a vast proliferation of names for what comparative study can show to be essentially the same thing. In the mid-1960s in an extensive review of the Miocene primate remains, Elwyn Simons and his Yale colleague D. R. Pilbeam greatly simplified the welter of different names. As a result, the specimens called *"Sivapithecus"* in India and *"Proconsul"* in Africa are now all recognized as belonging to the group that priority determines we should call *Dryopithecus.*

This is not to minimize the efforts of those who have discovered the specimens. Quite to the contrary, as a result of their years of work we can now recognize the Dryopithecines as a geographically widespread group represented by a series of related forms distributed from Europe east to India and south through East Africa during the Lower Miocene. While pieces of the postcranial skeleton have been found isolated elsewhere, it is the work of the Leakeys that allows us to reconstruct the general body plan of the genus *Dryopithecus.* Not only that, their discoveries show that there certainly were two species of *Dryopithecus* (and some would say three) living at the same time in East Africa. The large one, *Dryopithecus major,* is a good candidate for the ancestor of the modern gorilla, and the small one, *Dryopithecus africanus,* can serve either as a human or chimpanzee ancestor (or both).

The disagreement on whether there are two or three species of *Dryopithecus* in East Africa raises an issue that we shall have occasion to discuss later when we deal with the earliest hominids. The Leakeys recognized a third species of what they called *"Proconsul"* but which, if valid, would now be called *Dryopithecus nyanzae,* The problem is that there is no sharp boundary between *D. africanus* and *D. nyanzae,* and the student gets the distinct feeling that one is simply a larger version of the other. And when one looks at the modern anthropoid apes that are their likely descendants, one can see that the male is considerably larger than the female. The suspicion then crosses one's mind that what the Leakeys recognized as specific differences may in fact be nothing more than male/female differences in the same form. In spite of the relative abundance of the *Dryopithecus* discoveries in East Africa and elsewhere, we still do not have enough material to establish the normal within-population range of variation at any one time. As a result, we can propose the question of sexual dimorphism versus separate species as possi-

Figure 55. *Dryopithecus africanus,* formerly "Proconsul africanus," from the Miocene of Rusinga Island, Kenya. (Courtesy of the late Dr. L. S. B. Leakey.)

ble ways of accounting for the same set of facts, but we are not in a position to solve it.

While there can be no doubt that the late Miocene saw Primates, especially *Dryopithecus* and other similar forms, which may well have been ancestral to living apes and perhaps humans, it is equally clear that the brachiating adaptation had not developed to the same extent in all of them. *Pliopithecus* clearly was adapted to brachiation, but just as clearly *Dryopithecus* had not yet developed the limb structures found in its evident descendants. The form of their teeth could only indicate phylogenetic relationship, but it is ironic that, while the teeth are recognizable as ape teeth, their possessors had not yet reached the Ape Grade of development as we have considered it here. Pressing the argument we have developed here, then, it would appear that the gibbon line had attained its state of apehood before the line that led to gorilla, chimpanzee, and humans. While early workers, in their enthusiasm, felt that the presence of

The Fossil Record

the characteristic pattern in the molar teeth indicated that their Oligocene and Miocene discoveries were ancient apes, it is now clear
that, if brachiation is a distinguishing criterion, the Dryopithecines
had not yet passed out of the Monkey Grade. Phylogenetically they
are more closely allied to the later apes than they are to what remains
at the Monkey Grade today, but functionally they were still within
the second Primate adaptation.

OREOPITHECUS

If we do not have direct evidence that the great ape and human
ancestor was a brachiator, it is clear that at least one other group of
Primates had achieved the Ape Grade by the latter part of the Miocene. In this case, a careful examination of the teeth shows that it
could not have been in the anthropoid ape or ultimately in the
human line of development.

   This form, *Oreopithecus*, has been known since 1872 from
jaws and teeth, and the exact classification has been a continuing
source of minor dispute, but in 1959 an entire skeleton was dis-

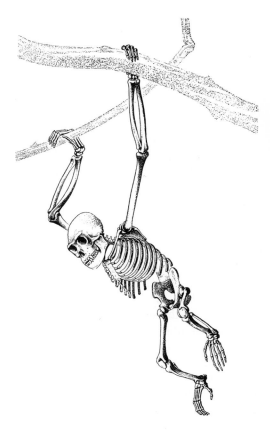

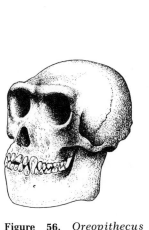

Figure 56. *Oreopithecus
bambolii.* Reconstruction of
skull and skeleton of apelike
primate from the late Miocene
of Tuscany, Italy. (Reprinted
with permission. Copyright
© by Scientific American,
Inc. All rights reserved.)

Pre-Pleistocene Primates

covered in a coal mine near the west coast of Italy, and the minor dispute has expanded to a major professional row. The postcranial skeleton shows that it was a brachiator, whereas the teeth show that it was not a pongid. Dentally it resembles the Cercopithecoidea to a greater extent than any of the other members of the Hominoidea, and it has recently been granted the status of a separate family, Oreopithecidae.

Faced with a Primate that had reached the Ape Grade but was not in the line of development of the modern apes, our explanation is that there is no reason why more than one family of Primates could not have made such an adaptation. The Monkey Grade was reached at about the same time by the Ceboidea in the New World, the Cercopithecoidea, and the Hominoidea (later to become apes and humans) in the Old World. Furthermore the spider monkey today in the jungles of South America is the only monkey in the world that characteristically uses brachiation as an alternate mode of progression, and, were it not for its prehensile tail, would come close to being an example of the Ape Grade among the New World monkeys. With such a background, it is not impossible that members of more than one family made the adaptation to brachiation at about the same time that the ancestors of the modern great apes were also beginning to take advantage of that facet of the arboreal ecological niche. Evidently *Oreopithecus* was not successful in this venture for it is not represented by descendants.

While we have confined our attention, in this survey of Pre-Pleistocene Primates, to those for which there is enough skeletal material for us to make some assessment of their way of life, we shall conclude our discussion with two genera for which we have only jaws and teeth. In spite of the inadequate nature of the material insofar as a full scale assessment of their adaptive strategies is concerned, we include them in our discussion because of the various claims advanced on behalf of one or the other possible ancestors to later true hominids.

Gigantopithecus

The first of these groups is the genus *Gigantopithecus* of which there are two species. And of these, the first to be named, *Gigantopithecus blacki,* was found by a most extraordinary method. In the late nineteenth century, an enterprising German naturalist discovered and capitalized on the fact that for centuries the Chinese have collected fossils for medicinal purposes. According to Chinese folk belief, they are dragon bones imbued with curative powers. When pulverized and ingested, they were thought to be good for ills ranging from infertility to cancer depending on the type used. Since the beginning of recorded history the Chinese apothecary business has been mining fossil beds catering to the ills of a large and growing population. The naturalist K. A. Haberer discovered that if he presented the correct prescription at a Chinese drug store, he could buy fossils without having to excavate them himself. In 1935, G. H. R. von Koenigswald used this technique on a visit to Hong Kong and was rewarded with an enormous molar tooth of distinctly hominoid form. This he christened *Gigantopithecus blacki* in memory of the late Davidson Black. This was during the period when von Koenigswald was making his discoveries in Java and going periodically to Peking to check with Weidenreich, Black's successor at the Peking Union Medical College.

In the early to middle 1950s a few more teeth were similarly found in apothecary shops and the warehouses from which their stocks were supplied. Since the ascendancy of Chairman Mao, these were under government control, and, although the old trade could not be eradicated, the ultimate sources could be checked by trained paleontologists under government auspices. This was done and the result was the discovery of three relatively well-preserved mandibles in 1956, 1957, and 1958 plus over a thousand teeth from Pleistocene deposits in the southern Chinese Province of Kwangsi. The mandibles, particularly the huge *Gigantopithecus* III mandible of 1958, display a massiveness and bulk unequalled in the spectrum of primate variation either before or since. Finally during the 1968 Yale expedition to north India, Elwyn Simons purchased another specimen that had come from the wall of a house in Bilaspur, Himachal Pradesh. This specimen is not quite so massive as the Chinese ones, and in spite of questions concerning its proper provenience, it may be a good deal older (late Miocene to early Pliocene?). Accordingly, Simons has assigned it to a new species: *Gigantopithecus bilaspurensis*. Even this smaller specimen, however, represented a creature of considerable bulk.

The molar teeth of *Gigantopithecus* display the arrangement of cusps and fissures found in *Dryopithecus* and present in subsequent apes and humans, so paleontologists and anthropologists have been aware, ever since von Koenigswald's original find, that there was some sort of phylogenetic connection with the Primates most closely related to the human line. In the absence of any other parts of the creature that might serve as guidance or control, the imagination of the interpreters has tended to run riot. The usually astute Weidenreich postulated that humanity had descended from a race of prehistoric giants, from *Gigantopithecus* to "*Meganthropus*" down to the normal-sized pithecanthropines. Even the usually hard-headed Simons has portrayed it in super-gorilloid form and guessed that it weighed around 600 pounds and reached up to nine feet high when standing erect. Others have pictured it as a twelve-foot tall hunter, striding the hills of southern China and carrying off the old and young of game animals to caves in the limestone cliffs where the bones now are found. And in Russia, W. Tschernezky has suggested that the bones of *Gigantopithecus* represent the ancestors of the Yeti, the Abominable Snowman of Himalayan legend.

To be sure, tooth size and jaw massiveness are approached by some of the large specimens of the earliest true hominids, the australopithecines. Although the Chinese group occurs too late in time to have been the general hominid ancestor—the most recent assessment puts it on the border of the early and Middle Pleistocene—this does not mean that the earlier representative from northern India could not have been ancestral to the later australopithecines. It is possible that the Indian group, *G. bilaspurensis*, shows the large end of the range of variation of the general Indian genus *Dryopithecus*, and it in fact seems likely that the ancestors of modern apes and humans as well as the Chinese *Gigantopithecus* are to be found in that genus. For the moment, however, we simply do not have enough evidence to form the basis for a reasonable guess, and we just do not know what manner of creature *Gigantopithecus* really was. Because of their bulk, the Chinese ones at least were unlikely to have been arboreal. Tooth wear suggests a rough vegetable diet, but we know precisely nothing of how *Gigantopithecus* moved or survived the threat of predation. Was it a running quadruped that survived by speed of foot? Was it a ponderous browser of rhinoceros-like build and large enough to be immune from predation when adult? Was it a weapon-wielding biped? The last suggestion seems unlikely, but with the limited evidence we possess to date, we are simply forced to admit that we do not know.

RAMAPITHECUS

The last inadequately based genus we shall consider is based on specimens originally included with the Siwalik (India-Pakistan) Dryopithecines. Mandibular material was identified in 1910 as *Dryopithecus punjabicus*. Later, in the mid-1930s, upper teeth and a maxilla were named *Ramapithecus brevirostris*. Subsequently the describer, G. E. Lewis, indicated that *Ramapithecus* was ancestral to the earliest hominid, *Australopithecus* (of which much more later), and to *Homo*. It is because the majority of anthropologists and paleontologists now accept Lewis' judgment that we include a consideration of *Ramapithecus* in this section. Then in the 1960s when Simons was re-examining the Dryopithecine material, he recognized that the jaw of *D. punjabicus* really belonged to the maxilla of *R. brevirostris*. Since the composite individual clearly did not belong with the Dryopithecines, the genus name *Dryopithecus* could not be used. The genus name *Ramapithecus* then is its appropriate designation. But the first specific name applied to a proper specimen of that genus is the name given to the mandible in 1910; *punjabicus* clearly has priority over *brevirostris*. Hence the correct name for the taxon, or at least for the first demonstrable representative, is *Ramapithecus punjabicus*.

Scraps of material attributed to *Ramapithecus*, in addition to the late Miocene of the Silwaliks, have been identified, tentatively, in China and Europe, and, most importantly, East Africa. Again, in the latter instance, we are indebted to the indefatigable labors of the late L. S. B. Leakey. And again, as was his custom, Leakey gave it his own designation. This specimen, discovered in 1960 at Fort Ternan in Kenya, he called *"Kenyapithecus" wickeri*. It may in fact be a separate species from the Siwalik finds, so we are not justified in throwing out his specific designation, but there are few who doubt that it properly belongs in the genus *Ramapithecus*.

Judging from the teeth alone, since that is really all we have to deal with, *Ramapithecus* was the closest thing to a true hominid of all the specimens we have considered so far. The canines are relatively small for an ape, although given the frequent instance of substantial male/female differences in canine development among the Primates, it is just possible that a male *Ramapithecus* has not yet been identified and the whole taxon is based on female specimens only. The molars have relatively low and rounded cusps and are relatively broad compared to the somewhat elongated molars of *Dryopithecus*. But beyond that, the various claims for the significance of the gradient of wear from the first to the third molars, the thickness of molar enamel, wear between the teeth, and the presumed vertical emplacement of the incisors (presumably indicating a vertical and un-snoutlike face) do not seem to be as distinct or important as some have claimed.

In fact, *Ramapithecus*, known only from a few specimens of teeth and jaws, is hard to distinguish from small worn specimens of *Dryopithecus*. Even so, it makes a good candidate for the ancestors of the later human line and provides a Middle to late Miocene link in the chain from *Aegyptopithecus* in the Oligocene, *Dryopithecus* in the early Miocene, and the true hominid *Australopithecus* in the Pliocene and early Pleistocene.

The fact that it can constitute a logical ancestor to later true hominids, that is, creatures dependent on culture for survival, has led some otherwise cautious scholars to make evidently inflated claims for its capabilities. Thus, there are those who have claimed, after a perusal of the scraps of jaw and teeth, that *Ramapithecus* was a weapon-wielding terrestrial biped; in fact a true hominid, ten million years or more before there is the first trace of evidence for the existence of tools in the archeological record. This, however, is simply reading too much into the evidence. No skull has been found and

180 no limb bones have been identified. In truth, we cannot tell whether *Ramapithecus* was arboreal or terrestrial, whether it was an erect-bodied brachiator, a biped or a quadruped, and we cannot even say whether it is legitimately distinguishable from *Dryopithecus*. All that we can really say about the taxon is that, from the patterns on the crowns of the molar teeth in the specimens attributed to it, it is most probably related to the Dryopithecines of the earlier Miocene and to the true hominids of the subsequent Pliocene and Pleistocene; and from the size of the specimens, it was about the bulk of a small chimpanzee. But even the latter conclusion must be regarded as tentative since, as we shall see in later chapters, teeth are not good indicators of body bulk. For example, the earliest hominids in the Pliocene were about the bulk of modern human beings, but their molar teeth were fully as large as those of a big modern gorilla. The material attributed to *Ramapithecus*, then, allows us to say that there is evidence for a link between the *Dryopithecus* group of the early Miocene and later true hominids, but it does not really allow us to say anything more.

As may be judged from what has been said above, the evidence for the third development in the adaptive radiation of the Primates is more inferential than direct. Somewhere within the middle of the Miocene, brachiation must have developed among the Hominoidea, the ancestors of the modern Pongidae and Hominidae. The living apes of today and the chest, shoulder, and arm structure of humans back to the beginning of the Pleistocene indicate that this must have occurred, but we are uncomfortably lacking in direct evidence. The development of the fourth or Human Grade in Primate evolution is, of course, the primary concern of this work and will be treated at somewhat greater length in a subsequent chapter.

Suggested Readings

CLARK, W. E. LE GROS. *The Antecedents of Man*. 3rd ed. Quadrangle Books, Chicago, 1971.
An introduction to the evolution of Primates.

PILBEAM, D. *The Ascent of Man: An Introduction to Human Evolution.* Macmillan, New York, 1972
The avowed coverage of this work, human evolution, is only introduced near the end, but prior to that Pilbeam presents an interesting summary of the evolution of the Pre-Pleistocene Primates.

SIMONS, E. L. *Primate Evolution: An Introduction to Man's Place in Nature*. Macmillan, New York, 1972.
The most detailed treatment available of the primate fossil record.

SZALAY, R. S. (editor). *Approaches to Primate Paleobiology.* **181**
Karger, Basel, 1975.

A collection of recent and authoritative contributions, that displays the rapid advances recently made in the study of primate paleontology.

History of
the Discovery of
the Fossils

Evidence of Prehistoric Humans

The impact Charles Darwin made on the world, and indeed on the whole course of development of natural science, was tremendous. However, as we have noted in the first chapter, the world was not wholly unprepared for Darwin. Even the most conservative scientists at the time (and earlier, as exemplified by Cuvier) were grudgingly admitting that changes of some sort had occurred in the past. Articles and books had been appearing regularly during the decades preceding publication of *"The Origin,"* presenting, albeit piecemeal, the ideas Darwin was to assemble into a single epoch-making volume.

Although interest in phenomena that might have a bearing on the question of the possibility of evolution was lively and enlarging, serious consideration of such matters was limited to a small segment of the reading public. Where it was a question of evidence for the prehistoric existence of humanity itself, there were few who were even willing to grant it a hearing. During the 1840s, the first clear-cut proof was collected that established the existence of humans in a prehistoric age.

M. Boucher de Perthes, a customs inspector at Abbéville in northwest France and the son of a distinguished botanist, had been an enthusiastic amateur archeologist for some years. In the late 1830s he propounded his views on the archeological antiquity of humans at a meeting of the Société d'Emulation at Abbéville, and in 1839 before the Institut at Paris, describing quantities of shaped flints he had discovered in the gravels deposited by the Somme river in ages past. In 1847 he put his views into print, though they were not actually published till 1849. These flints, Boucher recognized, could only have been shaped by human agency, and, since they occurred in deposits with animals now long extinct, he believed that they indicated the prehistoric existence of humans in northern France. They were the tools of prehistoric humans.

This, however, was France, and the intellectual tone in the natural sciences, especially those concerned with prehistoric events, had been set by the late Georges Cuvier. "L'homme fossile n' éxiste pas." If this were true, then it was clear that M. de Perthes must be deluded. This seemed so self-evident to the official representatives of French science that they denounced his conclusions without examining the finds on which they were based. This is not quite the complete story of the reception of Boucher de Perthes in his own country since one of his countrymen, M. Rigollot, was sufficiently aroused to visit Boucher's sites in an effort to discredit his claims. The evidence, however, was so convincing that, far from continuing in his attempts to discredit de Perthes, Rigollot became an ardent convert and proceeded to conduct his own investigations nearby. In 1855 Rigollot published an historic communication, *Mémoir sur des instruments en silex trouvés à St. Acheul prés d'Amiens.*

By and large, however, scientists continued to turn a deaf ear to accounts of prehistoric humanity. It was not until 1859, the year after Darwin and Wallace had read their papers at the meeting of the Linnaean Society, foreshadowing the appearance of the *Origin*, that a committee of British savants, Charles Lyell, Joseph Prestwich, John Evans, Hugh Falconer, and William Flower, visited Abbéville to satisfy their curiosity at first hand. One of them, Hugh Falconer, had visited Abbéville the year before and been convinced of Boucher's claims. Boucher de Perthes conducted them to the terraces of the Somme Valley where they witnessed the uncovering of stone tools in prehistoric strata that had clearly remained undisturbed since the time of deposition. Indeed, the first to discover a flint implement in situ was Arthur, the younger son of John Evans. Now thoroughly convinced, the committee returned to England and presented its findings before the Royal Society. Later on, in the autumn of the same year (24 November 1859), Darwin's epoch-making "essay," as he called it, appeared *On the Origin of Species By Means of Natural Selection or the Preservation of Favoured Races in the Struggle for Life*. Humanity's thinking concerning

Figure 57. Jacques Boucher de
Crévecoeur de Perthes
(1788 – 1868). Father of prehistoric archeology.

the antiquity of the life on earth and the forces shaping its development has never been the same since.

Stone artifacts, unlike fossil organic remains, are imperishable,
with the fortunate result that quantities of them have been found.
With the interest aroused by the events of 1859, a great deal of new
archeological evidence was uncovered and the skepticism with
which such discoveries were formerly greeted was now replaced by
a growing enthusiasm. There still remain many unsolved problems
in archeology, but this is simply a reflection of the healthy state of
affairs of contemporary research and by no means the residue of the
earlier disrepute that attached to claims made for human antiquity.

It has been otherwise with the actual remains of prehistoric humans themselves. Bones and teeth, the most durable parts of the
human body, are much more fragile than stone artifacts and far less
likely to be preserved, in addition to which, humans have been decidedly rare animals for the most of their existence on earth. The
result is that relatively little human fossil material has come to light,
especially from those earlier periods when humans less closely resembled their modern descendants. With human fossil material so
rare, it is not surprising that many prehistoric human fragmentary
remains have been interpreted in the atmosphere of the intellectual
climate prevailing at the time of discovery. In many cases, some residue of these former interpretations still remains.

The Fossil Record

Figure 58. Abbévillian tools. *a*. Lava hand-axe, Bed II, Olduvai Gorge, Tanzania. *b*. Quartzite hand-axe, raised beach, Morocco. *After Neuville and Ruhlmann*. *c*. Hand-axe, derived, Chelles-sur-Marne. *After Breuil*. *d*. Hand-axe, 150 ft. terrace of Thames, near Caversham, Berks. *By courtesy of Oxford University Museum*. (From K. P. Oakley, *Man the Tool-Maker*. Courtesy of the British Museum, Natural History.)

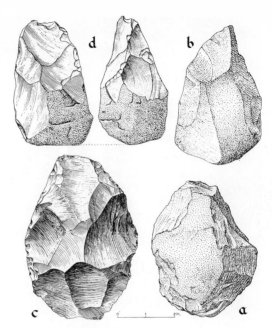

The Gibraltar Skull

Two representatives of a stage in human evolution earlier than that of modern humans had already been found by the time Darwin changed the orientation of the intellectual world. The earliest find of such a fossil occurred in a quarry on the north face of the Rock of Gibraltar in 1848. This was during the years when Boucher de Perthes was experiencing the frustration of having his work ignored by his contemporaries, and the same indifference befell the Gibraltar skull.

The Gibraltar skull was sent to England in 1862 where, following a brief appearance at the 1864 meetings of the British Association, it was turned over to the Museum of the Royal College of Surgeons in London in 1868. At that time, Hugh Falconer, the paleontologist who in 1858, and again in 1859, did most to help the cause of Boucher, referred to it as " . . . a very low type of humanity — very low and savage and of extreme antiquity — but still man. . . ." Falconer was fully alive to the fact that here was a new form of human and proposed the name *Homo calpicus,* after the ancient name for Gibraltar. Little further notice was taken of the Gibraltar find until the turn of the century. By the time it finally attracted the attention it deserved, the exact location and deposit in which it had been discovered could no longer be determined. This, together with the fact that

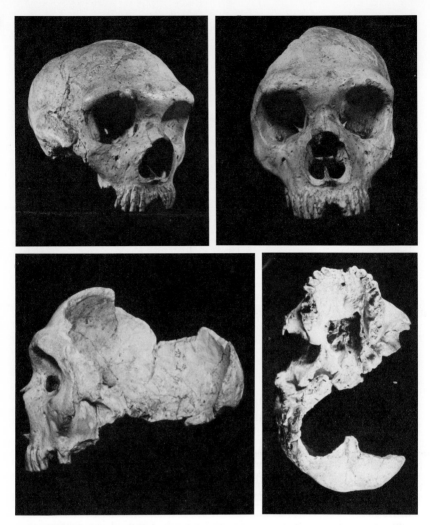

Figure 59. The Gibraltar skull.

there is no record of any archeological associations, means there is no way of determining its actual antiquity.

The Gibraltar skull, a face and part of a cranial vault, minus the jaw and all of the postcranial skeleton, is recognized as belonging to an earlier stage of human evolution. We are forced to make this judgment on the unsatisfactory basis of anatomical features alone and this implies familiarity with trends in human evolution that could not have been available to mid-nineteenth-century students. It is not too surprising, then, that Gibraltar received so little notice even in a world alive to the implications of Darwin's *Origin*.

More dramatic and more important was the finding in 1856 of fossil human remains in a little German valley that has given its name to a whole stage of human evolution—Neanderthal. With the growth of archeological and paleontological knowledge in the preceding decade and with the first published description of the gorilla in 1847, general interest in the possibility of human evolution was much keener in 1856 than at any previous time. It is a great pity that the remains could not have waited a few more years to be found, for had they been discovered after the publication of the *Origin*, their reception would almost certainly have been more sympathetic. It is useless, however, to speculate, and we can only be grateful to the Industrial Revolution for the material comforts it has given us, for the revolution in scientific thinking it has supported, and for the fact that in the constructions it has engendered, roads, bridges, buildings, a great many pieces of evidence relating to the human past have turned up (although unknown numbers have been destroyed) that would otherwise have remained buried.

The small stream, the Düssel, flows from Elberfeld to Düsseldorf where it joins the Rhine just north of one of the most famous wine-producing regions in the world. Just east of Düsseldorf the stream passes through a narrow valley named after the seventeenth century organist and poet Joachim Neumann. This gentle scholar had used a pen name, Neander, which was a translation of his own name (new man) into Greek, and the Düsseldorf townsfolk named the valley Neanderthal in his honor. The steep sides of the valley, however, were formed of Devonian limestone and with the industrial expansion and the attendant building boom in the nineteenth century, the quiet charm of Neumann's beloved valley fell prey to the commercial value of limestone.

In August 1856, workmen at a quarry in the Neander valley were cleaning out a cave locally known as the Feldhofer Grotto. In the course of their work they came across some old bones and, not realizing their significance, threw them out. These were brought to the attention of Johann Carl Fuhlrott, a teacher at the Realschule in Elberfeld who had been collecting geological and paleontological specimens from the area for many years. Fuhlrott immediately recognized their importance, and, realizing that a proper professional appraisal was beyond his competence, communicated with his friend Hermann Schaaffhausen, Professor of Anatomy at the University of Bonn.

Schaaffhausen and Fuhlrott exhibited the discovery at the meetings of a number of scientific societies where they discussed the implications and presented their interpretations. The remains included thigh bones, some arm bones, fragments of ribs, clavicle, scap-

Figure 60. The Neanderthal skull-cap, from the Neander Valley, near Düsseldorf, Germany. (Courtesy of the American Museum of Natural History.)

ula, and pelvis and a complete skull cap, although unfortunately this latter lacked the basal parts and face. Fuhlrott's investigations showed that the skeleton had most probably been complete, indicating that it had been a deliberate burial. In spite of his efforts it proved impossible to associate the skeletal material with any layer of earth. No artifacts and no associated fauna could be found, and therefore the Neanderthal remains were fated to become the subject of argument and controversy continuing well into the twentieth century. Some of the repercussions of that controversy are still being felt today.

Although they had no inkling of the vast vistas of time that twentieth century science was to open up for human evolution, both Schaaffhausen and Fuhlrott felt that the Neanderthal relics represented a form of humanity more ancient than the human of today. They felt that the thickness of the low skull vault, the heaviness of the bony brows over the eye sockets, and the curved heavy thigh bones were simply the normal attributes of earlier forms of humans. When these characteristics were compared with those of the newly described gorilla, it was recognized that the Neanderthal man had a hint of the gorilloid in some of his features. It was but a short step for the popular mind to invest the "cave man" with many other supposedly gorilloid traits. Thus, he was said to have long "ape-like" arms, although we know today that, if anything, the Neanderthal arm was short in relation to stature and body bulk. He was fancied to be stooped in posture although there was no evidence to support this figment of the imagination, and it has recently been thoroughly discredited. Finally, Neanderthal behavior was pictured as being bestial and ferocious—again on the assumed model of the gorilla. In this

The Fossil Record

instance, not only was there no evidence to support such a claim for the Neanderthal, but it involved the matter of being grossly unfair to the gorilla! The popular imagination would change that peaceful vegetarian into an embodiment of the principles of ruthless competition applauded by the economists and social theorists associated with the industrial developments of the eighteenth and early nineteenth centuries in Europe.

Such was the interpretation placed on the Neanderthal find even by the minority of people who *did* believe that it was a genuine representative of a former stage in human evolution. More than just residues of this libel remain today in casual conversation, in the standard newspaper cartoon portrayal, in numerous popular books on science, and even in professional circles where it should have long since disappeared.

If such was the treatment accorded the find by people inclined to believe that this really *was* a fossil human, then one could expect even less charitable behavior from those who were not prepared to admit that the modern human had evolved from anything less than the modern human. Opinion ranged from one extreme to the other. To some, the Neanderthaler was to be regarded as merely a crude specimen of modern humanity — extreme perhaps, but still a modern

Figure 61. Rudolf Virchow (1821–1902). German pathologist, physical anthropologist, statesman, and publicist. (Courtesy of the New York Academy of Medicine.)

human. One eminent anatomist referred to it as an "old Dutchman." Rudolf Virchow declared it to be pathological; another authority, Pruner Bey, thought it was the skull of a powerfully built Celt, "somewhat resembling the skull of a modern Irishman with low mental organization." Another authority believed it to have been an idiot, and another suggested that it may have been ". . . one of those wild men, half-crazed, half-idiotic, cruel and strong . . ." who occasionally lurk at the outskirts of civilization and often come to a violent end.

One of the most imaginative appraisals was delivered by the anatomist Mayer, a colleague of Schaaffhausen's at Bonn. The Neanderthaler's left elbow had apparently been broken early in life, and this, claimed Mayer, along with the pain caused by the rickets the individual was said to have suffered since childhood, had caused him to pucker his brow in a permanent frown that was eventually ossified in the skull's heavy brow ridge. Mayer continued with his free-wheeling deductions by pointing to the bowed femora (thigh bones). These, he claimed, were the result of having spent long years in the saddle. He also believed that the skull had a Mongolian appearance, although in fact it would be hard to find a skull bearing less resemblance to the Neanderthaler than the skull of a typical modern Mongolian. It is rather like comparing a coffin to a billiard ball. Putting these fuzzy ideas together, he emerged with the unique conclusion that the Neanderthal skeleton had belonged to a rickety Mongolian Cossack, a residue of the Russian forces that had chased Napoleon back to France in 1814!

It need scarcely be said that few scientists since have shared Mayer's view. However, this piece of history does serve to illustrate the extent and nature of the controversy stirred up by the discovery in the Neanderthal. While there was no lack of interest in the remains, clearly no fully considered appraisal of these undatable relics could be made on the basis of existing evidence alone. It is interesting to note that in the book Darwin eventually did write devoted specifically to human evolution, *The Descent of Man*, published more than fifteen years (1871) after Neanderthal became known, only very brief and cautious reference is made to the Neanderthal remains. With one exception the soundest students generally adopted a wait-and-see attitude.

The one exception was the eminent German physician, pathologist, anthropologist, and politician Rudolf Virchow (1821–1902). Virchow's influence during the late nineteenth century was enormous, his impact in the scientific, social, and also political worlds being analogous to that of Cuvier a half century previously. Perhaps it is unfair to compare him with Cuvier since that immediately implies that his scientific contributions merely balance his scientific obstructions, which in Virchow's case is something of an injustice.

The Fossil Record

His contributions to medical and anthropological research are of permanent value, and the value of his insistence on accumulating documented proofs before accepting likely theories far outweighs the slight inhibiting effect such an attitude has upon the initial formulation of said theories — in most instances.

It so happened that, in the field of fossil humanity, the likely theories arose long before there was adequate evidence with which to test them. Neither the Gibraltar nor the Neanderthal finds could serve as evidence for human antiquity since their ages were completely unknown. Virchow, then, was in the position of casting legitimate scientific doubt on what we now know to be perfectly genuine human fossils. He did, however, go beyond the bounds of proper scientific caution in the case of the Neanderthal skeleton and attempted to explain all its anatomical peculiarities by viewing them as pathological. Since Virchow was the founder of cellular pathology and accepted as the world's leading authority on the subject, no one dared contradict him.

The Cro-Magnon Remains

T. H. Huxley's cautious dismissal of the Neanderthal find as merely an extreme variant of the modern type of human was shared by most other contemporary anatomists. An exception was William King, Professor of Anatomy at Queen's College, Galway, Ireland. King classified the Neanderthal find on the basis of the skull as a new species of human, *Homo neanderthalensis* — a classification generally recognized as valid. But in the 1860s the most reasonable position to take seemed that of Huxley. Furthermore, as a result of the excavations of a rising generation of archeologists stimulated by the reception of Boucher de Perthes' work, the increasing discoveries of fossil humans, which were generally recognized and accepted as such in the 1860s, were not markedly different in form from modern humans. In 1868 descriptions were published of the human skeletal remains from the famous rock shelter of Cro-Magnon in the town of Les Eyzies in southwestern France. The Cro-Magnon remains were associated with Paleolithic (old stone) tools and with remains of extinct animals, and, although there was some debate about the significance of the fact that they represented burials, most authorities accepted these finds as clear evidence of the antiquity of humanity.

More finds of a similar nature were to be made in the years that followed, but, for the moment, we shall consider the impact made by the discovery of the Cro-Magnon remains. As with so many of the crucial finds, discovery was purely accidental, coming as a result of work connected with putting a railroad line through Les Eyzies. There could be no question of fraud, and, because of the great inter-

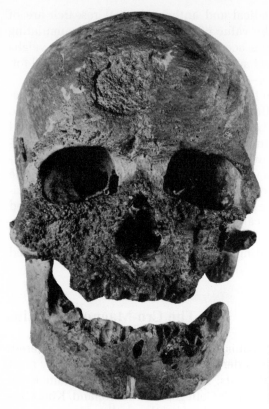

Figure 62. Cro-Magnon skull from Cro-Magnon, Les Eyzies, Dordogne, France. (Courtesy of the Musée de l'Homme, Paris.)

est surrounding such matters, the work was carried out under the closest public scrutiny and supervised by people with archeological training. The fragmentary remains of five skeletons were uncovered, which were clearly contemporary with the extinct fauna and very probably the manufacturers of the Paleolithic cultural debris.

Paviland and Engis

After the authenticity of Cro-Magnon had been established, some scientists recalled that similar finds had been made in earlier years. In the University Museum at Oxford lay the bones of a headless skeleton found in a cave at Paviland on the coast of southern Wales in 1823 where it had been recovered with the bones of mammoths, woolly rhinoceros, reindeer, cave bear, hyena, and other animals long since gone from the British Isles. Paleolithic tools were found as well, but, because of the climate of opinion at the time of discovery, no claim had been made for the antiquity of the human remains. Similarly in Belgium, P. C. Schmerling had excavated the cave of

Engis in the province of Liège in 1829 and discovered human bones **193** associated with stone tools and extinct animals. Although he had clearly stated that the human remains must date from the time of the extinct animals, he was not taken seriously. Following the revolution in thinking that came with the acceptance of Boucher de Perthes, the publication of Darwin's *Origin*, and the discovery at Cro-Magnon, the importance of these earlier finds was eventually recognized. The "Red Lady" of Paviland turned out to be a man not markedly different from the Cro-Magnon remains, and the Engis finds apparently included cultural and skeletal materials belonging to similar as well as even earlier populations. Fossil humans were accepted.

Now that fossil humans had been discovered and found to be not markedly different from the inhabitants of modern Europe, it seemed to many that this confirmed Virchow's appraisal of the Neanderthal skeleton, which clearly did not look like any modern human. What was not realized was that there are all sorts and degrees of antiquity. Even the best practicing archeologists were lumping strata belonging to fifty thousand years into single "ages" without any real awareness of the immense amounts of time involved, while individuals unconnected with the actual process of prehistoric research simply had no inkling of the antiquity of life on earth and of the various already-discovered fossil humans.

Catastrophism

Part of the problem stemmed from the fact that much of the cultural and osteological evidence for human antiquity emanated from continental Europe. This meant that those doing the interpreting had been brought up and educated in an atmosphere dominated by the catastrophism of Cuvier. They had been trained in the view that the animals of the modern world, including humans, dated from the last of a series of deluges—the Biblical flood or "diluvium." The extinct animals found in cave deposits and river terraces were regarded as having been drowned by the flood, hence they were called "diluvial," a term that survives in German learned publications to this day. It was in reference to the possibility of human existence with a "diluvial" or "antediluvial" fauna that Cuvier made his pronouncement that fossil humans did not exist. To the discoverers of the cultural and physical remains of undeniable fossil humans, the fact that their discoveries were all "diluvial" implied that they all belonged to the same time level.

Research that was to correct this confusion was already in process. As a consequence of the great expansion of prehistoric research at this time, geologists and paleontologists became aware that the conditions of life just prior to the supposed deluge must have been decidedly colder than at present, since the "diluvial" animals were of notably arctic species — reindeer, musk-ox, arctic fox, lemming, and the like. In addition, many topographic features could best be explained by the action of ancient glaciers. Before long, geological chronologies based on the supposed flood made way for those based on an "Ice Age." At first this was not much better than the flood theories, since it appeared that all fossil humans and cultures dated from Ice Age times and were therefore contemporaries. A really sound basis for judging the relative placement of human fossils in the estimated million years or so of their existence did not begin to assume a substantial form until well into the twentieth century, when it slowly became evident that humans have lived through four major ice advances (in the northern hemisphere) and innumerable minor oscillations.

Neanderthal and Modern Humans

This knowledge belonged to the future, however, and during the late 1850s and 1860s, when the controversy over the interpretation of the Neanderthal skeleton was at its height, judgment had to be delivered in terms of the information available at that time. Two sets of facts dictated the form of this judgment:

1. All known fossil humans came from the Ice Age and were not markedly different from modern humans.
2. The Neanderthal remains, while of unknown date, were clearly different from modern humans and the differences had been declared to be due to pathology by the greatest living pathologist and one of the founders of German anthropology.

Although the grounds for interpretation have shifted many times since that period as information has accumulated, the conclusions reached during the decade following discovery are largely the same as those held by the great majority of anthropologists today. Neanderthal is *not* regarded as a representative of a former stage of evolution and is *not* regarded as a precursor of modern humans.

While this is the view of the majority of modern anthropologists, although the genuine antiquity of the population to which the Neanderthaler belonged is unquestioned, it is *not* the view presented in this book. It seems clear to us that the Neanderthaler *did* belong to one of a series of populations that do represent a former stage in human evolution and did evolve into modern man and woman. We should mention that this idea is far from being original with us since it has had highly respected proponents of nearly half a century (Gustav Schwalbe, 1844 – 1916; Aleš Hrdlička, 1869 – 1943; Franz Weidenreich, 1873 – 1948) although, besides ourselves, it finds few outspoken defenders at the present time. The reasons for the common interpretation of the significance of the Neanderthal remains have been set out above. As our survey of the history of the discovery of fossil humans proceeds, we shall see how the new material that came to light with the passing years was used to support the basic tenets of the judgment of the 1860s and 1870s, and we shall set forth the reasons for our own interpretation.

During the 1870s and early 1880s, skeletal remains of more than a dozen fossil humans were discovered in Europe. None of these resembled the Neanderthal skeleton and seemed to offer support to the legitimately skeptical views of Virchow and to the beliefs of the great number of continental students who did not want to accept evolutionary ideas — especially when applied to humans. During this time also, bits and pieces of what we now know to be Neanderthal-like skeletal remains were found. It happened that these fragments were all mandibles (lower jaws) or pieces of mandibles, and since the original Neanderthal find had been lacking a mandible, there was no basis for making a comparison. Only a couple of these finds can be given a relative age. They are rather robust fragments, but not really complete enough to call much attention to them. One of them, the La Naulette mandible, found in 1866 with an extinct fauna in a large cave not far from Dinant in the Belgian province of Namur, consisted of about three-quarters of the tooth-bearing part, but all the teeth were missing. Despite this, the heaviness of the jaw and the size of the tooth sockets impressed many and somehow the rumor got under way that it was "primitive" and even had projecting "ape-like" canine teeth, which, of course, was ridiculous since it did not have any teeth at all. One other datable jaw, found in the Moravian (Czechoslovakian) cave of Šipka in 1880, proved to be a juvenile mandibular fragment, as could be seen from the unerupted state of some of the teeth. It is a rugged piece of jaw nevertheless, but it had the misfortune to get into the hands of Virchow who promptly labeled it — as one might have expected — pathological.

Nevertheless, the ferment of evolutionary thinking had been at work during these years and many people were now alert to recognize the faintest traces of "primitive" characteristics in excavated fossil remains. The proponents of a theory of human evolution were anxious to find "primitive" features that would support their theoretical position, and the opponents of evolutionary views were equally sensitive to anything "primitive" so that they could be ready with their denials. As a result, the few fragmentary pieces of nonmodern human fossils to turn up were recognized, at least for their anatomical peculiarities, as soon as they were found.

History of the Discovery of the Fossils

During these years also, especially as a result of the growing field of prehistoric research in France, cultural subdivisions of the assumed Ice Age were made, and it was gradually realized that an Ice Age date was no assurance that different fossil humans were anywhere near each other in time. Then in 1886, just thirty years after the discovery in the Neanderthal, two Neanderthal-like skeletons were discovered in a known archeological deposit at the mouth of a cave in the district of Spy (pronounced Spee) in the Belgian province of Namur. The bones were associated with flint tools of an industry called Mousterian, after the site of Le Moustier not far from Cro-Magnon in southern France where they had first been recognized. Because of this it was now realized that the Spy remains must be older than the Cro-Magnon remains associated with the subsequent Aurignacian tool-making tradition.

The two Spy skeletons were represented by two skulls, fragments of both faces and jaws, teeth, arm bones from both individuals, and leg bones from both skeletons. The postcranial fragments, while yielding more information than those of Neanderthal, evidently belonged to individuals of the same sort as the Neanderthaler. The skulls, more complete than the Neanderthal skull cap, are most interesting and illustrate the truth of Virchow's observation that one fossil

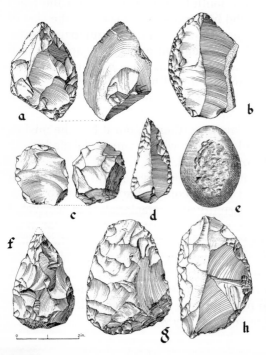

Figure 63. Mousterian tools. *a, b.* Side-scrapers (racloirs), *c,* disc-core, and *d,* point, from rock-shelter at Le Moustier near Peyzac (Dordogne). *e.* Small anvil or hammerstone (pebble of ferruginous grit), Gibraltar caves. *f.* Handaxe from Le Moustier. *g.* Hand-axe (chert), and *h.* oval flake-tool (flint), from Kent's Cavern, Torquay. *a-d.* Typical Mousterian; *f.* Mousterian of Acheulian tradition; *g. h.* of Acheulo-Levalloisian tradition. (From K. P. Oakley, *Man the Tool-Maker.* Courtesy of the British Museum, Natural History.)

does not make a population. One skull has the low vault and heavy **197** brow ridge noted in the Neanderthaler, while the other skull, belonging to the robust male, has a much higher vault and a brow ridge intermediate in form between the heavy Neanderthal brow and the ridge of a particularly heavy browed skull of a modern human. Yet they are obviously morphologically related and they were certainly from the same time layer.

The Spy finds should have taught prehistorians that, individuals being what they are, whenever more than one member of a population is discovered, one should expect to find differences illustrating the normal range of morphological variation. Furthermore, Spy No. 2 should have indicated that there is no unbridgeable gap between members of Mousterian and members of more recent populations. Both these points have been overlooked and the fact that they have been so has caused no end of trouble from that day to this.

The resemblance the Spy remains had to the earlier Neanderthal discovery was noted soon after they had been found. In 1893 the American paleontologist E. D. Cope proposed that they be called by the species name *Homo neanderthalensis*, which the Irish anatomist William King had given in 1864 to the skeleton from the

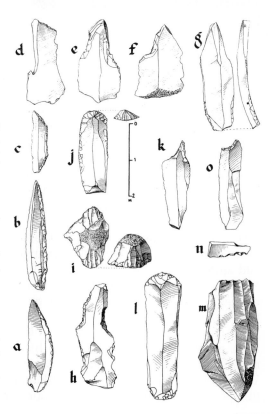

Figure 64. Upper Paleolithic flint tools. *a.* Chatelperronian knife-point, Châtelperron (Allier). *b.* Gravettian knife-point. Laussel (Dordogne). *c.* Trapezoid blade, Creswellian, Kent's Cavern, Torquay. *d.* Perigordian (Gravettian) graver or *burin*, Laugerie Haute (Dordogne). *e.* Aurignacian nosed graver (*burin busqué*), Ffynnon Bueno, Vale of Clwyd. *f.* Aurignacian *burin busqué*, Cro-Magnon, Les Eyzies (Dordogne). *g.* Magdalenian graver (burin bec-de-flûte), La Madeleine rock-shelter, Tursac (Dordogne). *h.* Strangulated blade, or double "spokeshave," Aurignacian. (From K. P. Oakley, *Man the Tool-Maker*. Courtesy of the British Museum, Natural History.)

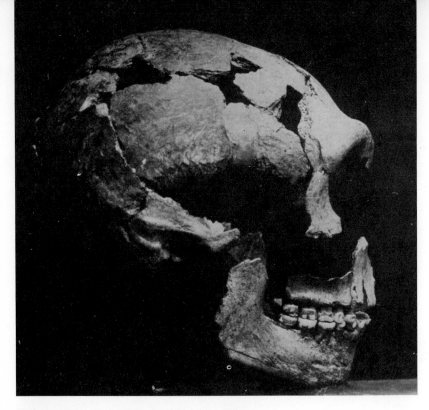

Figure 65. One of the Spy skulls from the Bec-aux-Roches near Namur, Belgium.

Feldhofer Grotto in the Neander Valley. Ever since, fossil humans of similar anatomical features have been called by English-speaking scholars "Neanderthal men," "Neanderthalers," or "Neanderthals." In 1897, a German anatomist proposed the specific name *Homo primigenius*, which has enjoyed wide popularity in Germany ever since. Not to be outdone, the French have used the name *Homo mousteriensis* after the French site Le Moustier where the tools of the Neanderthalers were first recognized. This usage was strengthened by the find in 1908 of a complete Neanderthal skeleton at Le Moustier.

Despite these various attempts at labeling, there is general agreement among even the most conservative of zoologists, anatomists, and anthropologists of the English-speaking world that the differences between Neanderthals and modern humans are not great enough to warrant separate specific designation. Both are included within *Homo sapiens*.

Two things conspired to limit the influence of the Spy discoveries. First, anything with a Neanderthal-like morphology tended to be regarded as abnormal or peculiar because of the position held by Virchow. Admittedly the cry of "pathological" began to grow a little thin as a total explanation for nonmodern morphology, as find after

find was made in early strata, but such was the immense influence of **199**
Virchow as a champion of the scientific method, as the founder of
cellular pathology, and as a social and political leader that the true
significance of the Spy remains was not appreciated till well into the
twentieth century. Virchow's influence is felt today in the writings
of modern anthropologists who make the vague claim that the Neanderthals were too "extreme," "specialized," or "aberrant" to have
served as the ancestors of subsequent humans.

The second consideration that served to keep the Spy remains
from occupying the center of the stage was the discovery during the
early nineties of a representative of a far earlier stage in human evolution. Even the most ardent defenders of the antiquity and prior
evolutionary status of the known Neanderthalers granted that they
were fully human and that there was a far greater gap between Neanderthal and nonhuman than between Neanderthal and modern
humans.

"The Missing Link" Myth

Despite the cautions of Darwin that the nonhuman Primate that preceded the human stage of evolution probably looked nothing like an
ape of today, the popular and even the scientific world looked with
fascination at the living Primates, picking the most human-like as a
model for the precursors of humans. The flamboyant German evolutionist Ernst Haeckel predicted that an intermediate form must exist
somewhere in the fossil record that stood on the borderline between
ape and human, and he even went so far as to give it a name—
Pithecanthropus alalus, or "ape-man without speech." These
speculations, criticized by Virchow as being without factual basis,
were the source of talk about the mythical "missing link" that survives even today in twentieth century folklore.

HOMO ERECTUS (PITHECANTHROPUS ERECTUS)

Beginning in 1890, some fossil fragments came to light in Java that
appeared to correspond to the popular conception of the "missing
link," and these soon became the center of a lively controversy. The
circumstances surrounding the finds seem so unlikely that it is
worth recounting them here. This is one of the very few cases where
a competent and scientifically trained individual deliberately set out
to find a human fossil. The fact that he actually found what he was
looking for constitutes one of the most remarkable stories in the history of human paleontology. In one of the only other instances in
which an explorer set forth to find the origins of humanity he returned with a clutch of dinosaur eggs, but even that is no less im-

History of the Discovery of the Fossils

probable than was the finding of the remains of that rarest of all fossils, the human itself.

The discoverer of this "missing link" was a young Dutch physician, anatomist, and former student of Haeckel, Eugene Dubois who had been greatly stirred by the evolutionary ferment in German and British scientific circles. Darwin, writing in *The Descent of Man* (1871), had noted that humans, being hairless animals, probably arose in the tropics, and that the most likely place to look for early human fossils should be Africa where there is a wide variety of non-human Primates, including the two apes, gorilla and chimpanzee, that show the greatest structural and behavioral similarities to modern man. Discoveries within the last few decades have fully substantiated Darwin's prediction and so it may seem a little peculiar to us that Dubois went to Java to make his find, although there actually were a number of good theoretical and practical reasons for doing so. In the first place, Indonesia is in the tropics and it is the home of a wide variety of nonhuman Primates including the two remaining members of the Superfamily Hominoidea found outside of Africa, the orang and the gibbon. Furthermore, Haeckel, whose writings had much influenced Dubois, had stressed those parts of the anatomy of the gibbon that bore a particular resemblance to human characteristics. Reasoning that the circumstances that gave rise to human-like characteristics in a nonhuman might also have influenced the development of a related line that eventually did become human, Dubois' choice of a southeast Asian field for research can be seen to have intellectual justification. The final reason, however, was a purely practical one. After years of rivalry with England in the acquisition of as much as possible of the African colonial grab-bag, Holland had finally lost out. This meant that even had Dubois wanted to search for fossil humans in Africa, he would have had to finance his research himself in territories under foreign control—not very tempting circumstances for a young scientist without much money. In Indonesia, however, the Dutch still had a booming colonial empire, and, with his medical training, Dubois had no trouble getting himself assigned there as a health officer in the colonial armed forces.

In 1887, his first assignment was in Sumatra where he spent some time searching cave deposits and where he became familiar with the published works on Indonesian paleontology, which dated back a considerable time before his arrival. This plus the interesting prehistoric material that had been sent to him from Java, convinced him that Java was a more likely place in which to pursue his search. He succeeded in getting himself transferred in 1889, and from 1890 until 1895 he was supported in his paleontological researches by the colonial government. The result was that the government gained information concerning geological deposits of potential economic val-

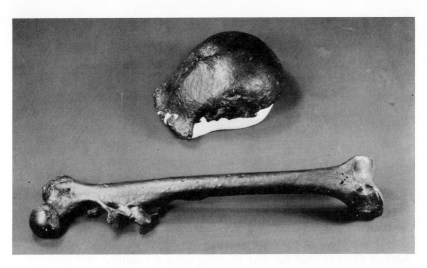

Figure 66. Skull-cap and femur of Dubois' original "Pithecanthropus erectus." (Courtesy of the American Museum of Natural History.)

ue to mining interests and science acquired its first "ape-man."

The first find came late in 1890 and was a small fragment of a jaw that Dubois recognized later as being definitely human but with even less chin than the La Naulette and Šipka mandibles. Then late in 1891, at the village of Trinil on the banks of the Solo river in central Java, he made the discovery that made him famous. In September, he found an upper right third molar of what he at first believed was a chimpanzee, and a month later he found what was to become one of the most celebrated skull caps ever discovered. In August 1892, he found a complete femur approximately forty feet from the place where the skull cap had been found. Another molar, an upper left second, was found a short distance away. All of these finds were at first attributed by Dubois to an extinct creature he labeled *Anthropopithecus erectus*, or erect-walking man-ape, which he believed to be an extinct species of chimpanzee.

The results of his findings were originally published in an obscure mining journal, but since their significance became increasingly evident to him, he published a pamphlet in 1894, which had wide circulation and was the cause of heated controversy in the intellectual centers of Europe. He recorded in detail measurements he had made on the skull and compared them with those published by other investigators on the skulls of chimpanzees. His gross skull measurements are recorded in Table 2, together with his estimate of cranial capacity, while the chimpanzee measurements are averages calculated from the figures he quotes. As he realized, the gross measurements of his find greatly exceeded those of the chimpanzee

History of the Discovery of the Fossils

Skull length	185 mm	135 mm
Skull breadth	130 mm	95 mm
Cranial capacity	1000 cc	400 cc

and fell within the lower limits of the range of variation of modern humanity. Cranial capacity, which various authorities have since estimated to be between 900 and 1000 cubic centimeters, was more than double that of an average chimpanzee and, as we now know, a third again as large as the largest recorded gorilla, yet markedly smaller than the approximately 1400 cc average for modern humans. To be sure, modern humans do exist with skulls of 1000 cc or less and some of these have been persons of recognized genius, but the small size of the Java skull *plus* the heavy brow ridge projecting some 2 cm beyond the forward extension of the brain cavity clearly showed Dubois that he was dealing with a creature that possessed more morphological resemblances to the great apes than do any humans living today.

He noted that while the skull approached that of humans in size, in some ways it resembled that of a chimpanzee or of a gibbon. His solution was to create a new genus for his find indicating that it was to be a transitional form which leaned toward the human side. Hence, he called it *Pithecanthropus erectus*, the erect-walking ape-man, which he believed to be the precursor of modern humanity itself.

From the vantage point of more than half a century of added experience and a much greater number of human fossils, we are able to see that while Dubois went somewhat too far in creating such a special category for his fossil, in the light of the state of knowledge at the time of discovery, one cannot but sympathize with him. Today, most anthropologists interested in fossil humans prefer to include Java man, or Pithecanthropus as many still call him, in a nontechnical sense, in the genus *Homo*. Some anthropologists have gone so far as to see no specific differences between the Java finds and *Homo sapiens*, but we prefer a designation suggested in 1950 by Ernst Mayr that has been gaining increasing support, that is, *Homo erectus*.

In 1895, Dubois returned to Holland, carrying his fossils with him. In Holland he demonstrated them before several groups of the most eminent anthropologists, anatomists, and zoologists in the world. Interest was intense and virtually all the scientists involved published their opinions almost simultaneously. It was immediately obvious that opinion was very far from unanimous. One group of savants felt that the remains were clearly human, although of a crude sort, another group of the less eminent, chiefly noted for the fact that they were headed by the renowned Virchow, claimed they were not human at all, and a third group led by Dubois himself was of the opinion that they were intermediate, which was perhaps the wisest stand to have taken in view of the meager amount of evidence available at the time.

Virchow took the extreme position that the Pithecanthropus remains belonged to an extinct species of giant gibbon, although as time went on fewer and fewer authorities were inclined to agree with him. He was, however, greatly interested in the finds, which he regarded as extremely important, and he invited Dubois to Berlin to lecture on his discoveries, which may not be without significance in explaining Dubois' final views on the fossils.

For the next few years arguments and opinions multiplied, ranging all the way from regarding Pithecanthropus as a human to viewing him as an idiot, a freak, an ape, a transitional form, or an illusion. Dubois, originally at the center of the controversy, gradually withdrew into silence and for the next two decades made almost no contribution to the subject. During this withdrawal, he also withdrew the controversial bones from public view; in fact, he pried up the boards of his dining room floor and buried the boxes of fossils in the earth beneath, apparently under the impression that the world was intent on stealing them. This may be contrasted with the relaxed behavior of Dubois when he had just returned from Java and was so eager to discuss and demonstrate his finds that he carried them from place to place in a satchel. This satchel and its precious contents were almost lost when Dubois left them in a Paris restaurant when he and the professor whom he was visiting became so engrossed in their conversation that they walked away without them.

While Dubois' secretive behavior, contrasting as it did with his earlier open enthusiasm, has occasionally been taken as an inexplicable personal aberration, one must remember that the years of his silence coincide with the time of rising political tensions that culminated in the First World War. To many concerned observers, it seemed obvious that Germany and France were going to engage in open hostilities, and among those to whom it seemed most obvious were the Dutch since, located as they were between the threatening antagonists, they thought that their country stood a fair chance of being overrun. In fact, Holland was not invaded until the Second World War.

The bones were not to be seen again until 1923, when, quite inexplicably, Dubois allowed the American anthropologist Aleš Hrdlička and a number of other scientists to see and handle them. Dubois had just published on two other fossil skulls in his collection from Java, but which did not belong to the Pithecanthropus (*Homo erectus*) stage, being of apparently more recent origin but nevertheless remarkable in their own right. These were the two Wadjak skulls, which, along with other material, show that, prior to the Malay invasions, Indonesia had been inhabited by people who looked more like Australian aborigines than modern Indonesians. Curiously, Dubois waited until the 1920s to reveal that there were four more fossil thigh bones from the area where his *erectus* material had been discovered.

Dubois' final judgment, published in *Man* in January 1937, was clear and unequivocal, *"Pithecanthropus* was not a man, but a gigantic genus allied to the Gibbons, superior to its near relatives on account of its exceedingly large brain volume, and distinguished at the same time by its erect attitude." This view, Dubois went on to say, confirmed the opinion of Marcellin Boule who, in his *Les Hommes Fossiles*, published in 1921, considered that *Pithecanthropus* "may have been a large species either of the genus *Gibbon*, or rather of a closely allied genus related to the same group."

Dubois delivered himself of his last word on the subject in a communication to a meeting of the Netherlands Royal Academy of Sciences on 30 November 1940, and published in its *Proceedings* in the same year. In that communication, Dubois protested against statements that had been made to the effect that he had changed his mind concerning the evolutionary status of *Pithecanthropus erectus* "from an originally hominide view to a surprisingly, new Hylobates-one." To the contrary, Dubois cited evidence from his earliest to his latest publications in order to show that he had always been of one mind, that from the beginning he had held the view that *Pithecanthropus* was not a hominid but a form closely allied to the living gibbons, but distinct from them, "a descendant of less specialized (less long-armed) ancestors of the Gibbons (*Prohylobates*), a descendant that had assumed the erect posture." He had never felt, he said, "at liberty to regard 'Java Man' as a real, be it ever so primitive, man."

As if to cap the whole discussion, Dubois declared, "Man did not come into being in the Darwinian way, by gradual transformations required by the outer world power, but by inner world, autonomous power."

In this final interpretation of the evolutionary status of *Pithecanthropus* Dubois almost reverted to the views of Virchow who had died more than twenty years earlier, firm in the conviction that none of the fossils yet discovered provided any evidence for the course of human evolution. Virchow's opposition to evolutionary ideas was due in part to his opposition to the chief proponent of evolution in Germany, Ernst Haeckel. The clash between Virchow and Haeckel, however, was less over the basic idea of organic evolution than it was over social and political issues. Virchow was an ardent proponent of liberal democracy, and, in his long and distinguished political career, he served as one of the chief voices opposing the policies of Germany's "Iron Chancellor," Otto von Bismarck, architect of German nationalist expansion and one of the driving forces behind the events that led to the First and Second World Wars. Haeckel, on the other hand, was more than a mere German imitation of Darwin. He united a revised form of evolutionary philosophy with a kind of mystical faith in the innate superiority of the German "Volk" and was a passionate supporter of Bismarck and his policies, even going so far as to invite Bismarck to visit the University of Jena where he conferred upon him the honorary degree of "Doctor of Phylogeny," the first and last time that curious accolade has been bestowed on anyone.

In any event, these were among the social and political tensions that greeted Dubois when he returned to Europe at the end of the nineteenth century. There he found that his former mentor, Haeckel, had renounced Christianity and attempted to substitute his own evolutionary and mystical "Monism" as the true faith. Haeckel was no minor crank. His Monist League numbered its adherents in the thousands on the eve of the First World War, and after the war became transformed into the rising phenomenon of the Nazi movement. Evidently this course of events was more than Dubois, a good Catholic, could accept, and it is not surprising to see that his intellectual loyalties, devoted to Haeckel in his youth, underwent a complete switch, finding a more congenial kinship with Haeckel's principal opponent, Virchow, in his later years. That interpretations of the Java fossils became a casualty in this conflict is one of the generally forgotten ironies in the course of recent European intellectual history. Despite the discovery of more Pithecanthropus material from Java during the 1930s and quite extensive remains from a related form of fossil human in China, Dubois maintained his altered views until his death in 1940 — alone in a scientific world that had at last come to accept his discoveries as truly representative of an early but fully human stage in the evolution of humanity.

Schwalbe and Neanderthal Man

As the furor over Java man began to subside during the first decade of the twentieth century — partially at least because no one was allowed to see the original fossils and expeditions to Java failed to produce any more — the spotlight of public attention was focused on fossil finds of a more familiar sort, Neanderthals. In the breathing spell between the excitement over the Java finds and the discovery of the new Neanderthals, one eminent anatomist, Gustav Schwalbe (1844–1916) of Strasbourg, synthesized the knowledge of fossil humans that had been collected so far. In his publications, he proposed two possible schemes for human evolution which arranged the known fossils in relation to each other (see Figure 68). Schwalbe placed Java man, Neanderthal man, and modern man in their respec-

Figure 67. Gustave Schwalbe (1844–1917). German anatomist and physical anthropologist.

tive time periods and drew lines indicating their possible lines of relationship. He postulated that a Pithecanthropus stage was the direct ancestor of both modern humans and the Neanderthals, but that the Neanderthals had separated from the main line of evolution well back in time, proceeded on their separate way for a while, and eventually had become extinct. In Figure 68b he postulated a direct line of evolution from a Pithecanthropus stage through a Neanderthal phase to humans as we know them today. This latter scheme, in its simplicity, he regarded as the most likely picture of what had actually occurred.

Now, some seventy years later, it is our belief that Schwalbe's appraisal was correct, as we shall attempt to demonstrate in Chapter 9. But since most anthropologists now use some modification of Figure 68a we shall have to explain how this situation came about. Part of this can to some extent be appreciated from the discussion of the manner in which Neanderthal man came to be regarded as "peculiar" or somehow not normal even before he was sufficiently well

The Fossil Record

Figure 68. Two possible courses of human evolution suggested by Schwalbe.

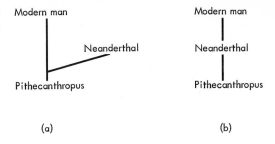

(a)   (b)

known for such a judgment to have an adequate basis. The remainder can be understood from the subsequent history of fossil discovery.

Further Neanderthal Discoveries

For two decades following the turn of the century, scarcely a year elapsed without another fragment of fossil human being discovered

Figure 69. The Krapina C skull, probably female. One of the Neanderthals from late in the third interglacial of Croatia, Jugoslavija.

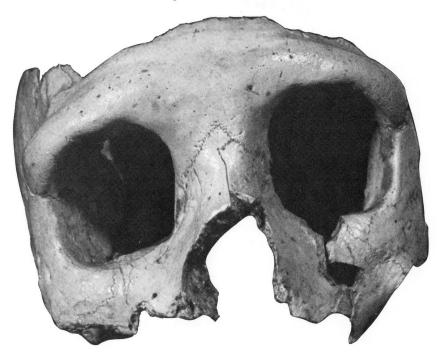

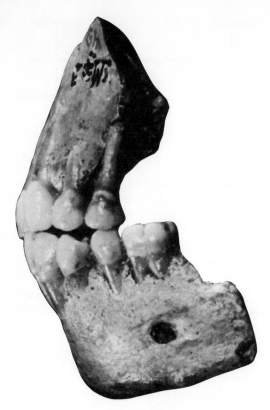

Figure 70. A maxillary and mandibular fragment from Krapina in Croatia, Jugoslavija, showing the degree of jaw and tooth development at the front of the dental arch in a European Neanderthal population late in the last interglacial.

in Europe. Between 1899 and 1905 fragments of fourteen or perhaps fifteen individuals of Neanderthal morphology were discovered at Krapina in Croatia, now one of the republics of Jugoslavia. All ages from birth to adulthood were represented, but because the pieces were so badly broken and because the describer was a relatively unknown professor of paleontology at Zagreb, capital of Croatia, the Krapina remains have suffered from the same fate that overtook the Spy discoveries. Despite excellent descriptive monographs, both finds have received far less attention than they deserved. In some respects, the Spy remains showed fewer differences from recent humans than has often been assumed to be "typical" for Neanderthals, and the Krapina remains amply confirm these tendencies. It transpires that every prehistoric site yielding the bones of more than one individual of a population also produces anatomical variations that many earlier authorities found hard to account for. It is now recognized that individual variability is no exclusive prerogative of modern humans and is really what one should expect when evidence appears in quantity.

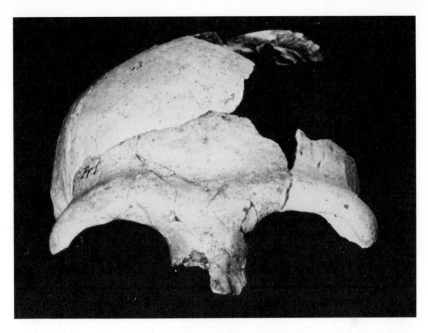

Figure 71. Frontal view of the Krapina E skull from Krapina in Croatia, Jugoslavija.

Heidelberg Man

Although the range of variation of the Krapina population was well documented in the publication of Croatian professor Gorjanović-Kramberger in 1906 — the year Schwalbe's extensive attempt to synthesize existing knowledge concerning the evidence for human evolution ranging from Pithecanthropus, Neanderthal, Gibraltar, and Spy to modern humans — these excellent works had relatively little influence on the reading public, whether learned or lay. One cause for the neglect of these worthy efforts was the discovery in 1907 of the famous Heidelberg mandible by workmen in the Grafenrain sand pit at the little village of Mauer, just 10 kilometers southeast of the university town of Heidelberg in western Germany. Mauer is situated on a stream called the Elsenz, which is a tributary of the Neckar River. The Neckar in turn, like the Düssel, is a tributary of the Rhine, which it joins at Mannheim after flowing through Heidelberg just south of the area that produces Germany's famous vintage wines. Commercial operations at the Grafenrain pit had been yielding Pleistocene animal fossils for thirty years and Professor Otto Schoetensack of Heidelberg had been keeping watch on the fossils coming from Mauer with the patient hope that eventually a human

History of the Discovery of the Fossils

Figure 72. Lateral view of the Krapina E skull.

fossil might turn up. His patience was rewarded on 21 October 1907, when the owner of the pits informed him of the anticipated discovery. Schoetensack immediately commenced his study of the mandible and the clear stratigraphic circumstances surrounding the find and shortly (1908) produced an admirable and detailed monograph on his findings.

Two outstanding sets of facts guarantee the permanent position of the Mauer jaw, or *Homo heidelbergensis* as Schoetensack tried to

Figure 73. The Heidelberg jaw, found at Mauer, Germany. (Courtesy of the American Museum of Natural History.)

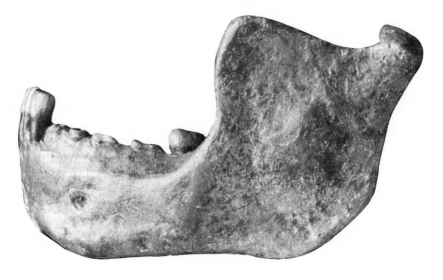

The Fossil Record

christen it, among the most important human fossils ever discovered. Most striking is the enormous size of the jaw. As a heavy, bony, chinless mandible it far exceeded the known Neanderthal jaws (La Naulette, Spy, Krapina) although its teeth were remarkably similar to the latter. The molars, in fact, are not distinguishable from those of a robust big-toothed modern human, although the incisors, in spite of being heavily worn, were apparently beyond the upper limits of the modern range of variation, although decidedly human in form. The canine teeth did not project above the chewing surface and it was quite clear from the morphology of the dentition as a whole that the jaw belonged to an early form of human.

The second important set of facts involves the dating. The stratigraphic sequence in the Mauer sand pits was well known from the quantities of fossil animals discovered. Among these animals were a straight-tusked elephant and a browsing rhinoceros, an extinct form of horse, a giant beaver, a hippopotamus, a saber-toothed tiger, and others, indicating an antiquity far greater than the last (fourth) glacial stage to which the Neanderthals belonged. Schoetensack believed that his find belonged to the warm period between the first glacial stages of the Pleistocene chronology, which the geologists Penck and Brückner were at that time working out. Other authorities revised his estimate to place Heidelberg man between the second and third glacial stages, while today, as a result of detailed reappraisal by Clark Howell of the University of California, Berkeley, the

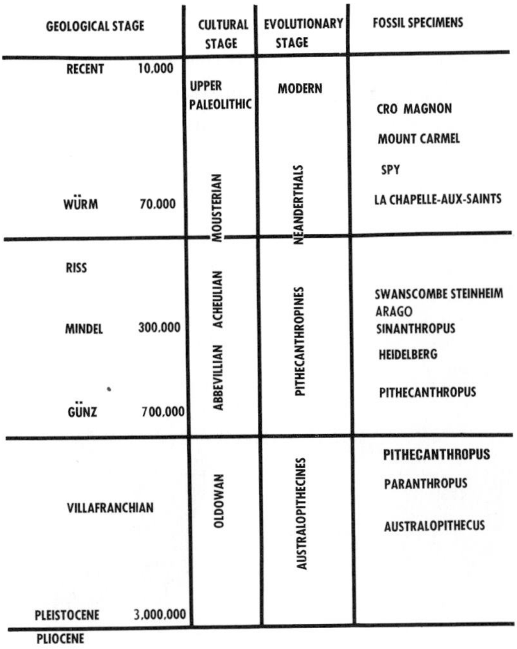

GEOLOGICAL STAGE		CULTURAL STAGE	EVOLUTIONARY STAGE	FOSSIL SPECIMENS
RECENT	10.000	UPPER PALEOLITHIC	MODERN	CRO MAGNON
				MOUNT CARMEL
				SPY
WÜRM	70.000	MOUSTERIAN	NEANDERTHALS	LA CHAPELLE-AUX-SAINTS
RISS				SWANSCOMBE STEINHEIM
		ACHEULIAN	PITHECANTHROPINES	ARAGO
MINDEL	300.000			SINANTHROPUS
		ABBEVILLIAN		HEIDELBERG
GÜNZ	700.000			PITHECANTHROPUS
				PITHECANTHROPUS
VILLAFRANCHIAN		OLDOWAN	AUSTRALOPITHECINES	PARANTHROPUS
				AUSTRALOPITHECUS
PLEISTOCENE	3,000.000			
PLIOCENE				

Figure 74. The Pleistocene. The glacial periods, cultural stages, and fossil specimens.

History of the Discovery of the Fossils

212 date has been fixed as a climatic amelioration (interstadial) *within* the latter part of the second glacial stage (see Figure 74). Despite the slight uncertainty of the exact date, the early estimates were quite close and there could be no doubt that the Heidelberg jaw was by far the oldest human fossil to have been discovered in western Europe, a circumstance that remains true to this day. The date and the morphology of the mandible make Heidelberg man a probable contemporary of Pithecanthropus. This we recognize by placing him in the same precise taxonomic category, *Homo erectus*. Crude, rolled stone tools were subsequently found in the same level at the Grafenrain pit. These are widely distributed elsewhere in Europe and allow us to postulate that wherever they occur, they demonstrate the area was once occupied by Heidelberg-like forms of humans.

Nationalisms and Irresponsible Diggers

The interest and excitement surrounding the discovery of the Heidelberg jaw were intense. Now that the twentieth century was well under way and a greatly extended antiquity for human ancestry was being documented and appreciated, national scientific prestige was, in some circles, being measured by the number of striking sites yielding the remains of early man. Kudos went with the oldest finds. Germany, with its Neanderthal and now with its Heidelberg man, enjoyed the highest prestige.

England, grasping at straws, claimed great antiquity for a number of fragments, the most important being the Galley Hill skeleton discovered in 1888 on a terrace of the Thames in Kent, southeast England. Such was the desire for pre-eminence in the field of prehistory that one Englishman was even led to forge a fossil discovery—the famous Piltdown fraud—but the further significance of these events will be considered in due course.

Figure 75. The Heidelberg jaw, compared with the jaw of a chimpanzee and that of a modern man. (Courtesy of the American Museum of Natural History.)

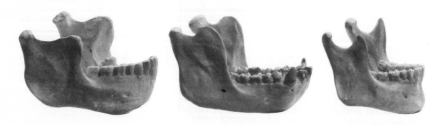

Germany's period of pre-eminence was short lived, for in 1908 the scene shifted to France where a decade was ushered in which assured France of first rank status in the realm of human fossil discoveries. Two complete Neanderthal skeletons were discovered in southern France, and the years that followed saw several more complete and a quantity of fragmentary Neanderthals brought to light. On 7 March 1908, Otto Hauser, a Swiss "dealer" in antiquities, uncovered the complete skeleton of a Neanderthal youth in a rock shelter at Le Moustier — the village of the Vézère river in southern France that had given its name to a whole stage of human cultural evolution, the Mousterian.

Several unfortunate coincidences have combined to prevent the Le Moustier skeleton from receiving the attention it deserved. First of all, Hauser was a difficult and unpopular personality who had acquired a deservedly unsavory reputation for systematically looting prehistoric sites and selling the proceeds to foreign museums at inflated prices. The scientific world, and particularly the French whose sites he was plundering, were understandably unsympathetic to his efforts to be accepted as a prehistorian. Since Hauser was well aware that proof of any genuine find he should happen to make would have to be iron clad, he made certain that several groups of persons witnessed the discovery of the Le Moustier skeleton. After the initial discovery, which had been made by his field foreman, Hauser ordered the find buried. A month later he uncovered it again in the presence of several French officials who were then required to sign a statement testifying to its authenticity. It was then reburied to be "discovered" once more in the presence of a group of Germans in June. Once more Hauser had the skeleton buried, and the performance was repeated for some Americans in July. Excavation was finally carried out on 10 August 1908, in the presence of several eminent German scholars (Figure 76). Significantly, the skeleton was finally sold to the Museum für Völkerkunde in Berlin in 1910 for what amounted to a small fortune.

Unrest continued to plague the skeleton of the Le Moustier youth, since it was the subject of four reconstructions during the next fifteen years. The first two were by Hermann Klaatsch, the anthropologist from Breslau. Klaatsch unfortunately died before a detailed report could be written (actually, he died from the lingering effects of the malaria he had contracted some years earlier while visiting the Java site where the first *erectus* find had been made), and, since the reconstructions he had made were still regarded as unsatisfactory, a third attempt was made by the preparator at the Berlin Museum. This effort was made with plaster of Paris, colored to match the bones, and the shading was so skillful that no one could tell what

History of the Discovery of the Fossils

Figure 76. An Otto Hauser visiting party. Excursion to the Vézére Valley, Laugerie-Basse site, on the farther bank of the Vézére opposite Cro-Magnon. Left to right, Drs. Haake (holding shovel), Wirtz, Hahne, Kossina, Mrs. Paul Virchow and her husband, Drs. Klaatsch and von den Steinen, Counselor Rehlen, von Baelz. (Courtesy of the American Museum of Natural History.)

was reconstruction and what was actual fossil without actually cutting into it. This resulted in the loss of many of the important small fragments and details when the fourth reconstruction was made by Hans Weinert, the anthropologist at the University of Kiel. Weinert's descriptive monograph was finally published in 1925, more than seventeen years after the find had been made and more than a dozen years after the publication of the exhaustive description of the La Chapelle-aux-Saints skeleton discovered in the same year as Le Moustier. For the few individuals who were still interested in the features shown by Le Moustier after this long and difficult history, the differences in form between it and the La Chapelle skeleton — which has served as a "type specimen" from that day to this — were attributed to the youth and immaturity of the Le Moustier remains. The fact, however, is that at age sixteen, the Le Moustier youth had relatively little growing left to do, and that in those few remaining years, interrupted by his early death, he could never have acquired the formidable supraorbital torus or brow ridge so markedly developed in the remains from Neanderthal, La Chapelle-aux-Saints and one — not both — of the Spy skeletons.

The Fossil Record

Figure 77. The Le Moustier skull. (Courtesy of the Musée de l'Homme, Paris.)

215

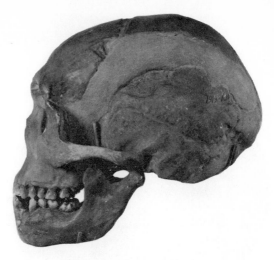

Because of this variety of circumstances the differences between Le Moustier and the assumed "typical" Neanderthaler have been generally ignored. As a further and final distressing development in the troubled career of the Le Moustier Neanderthaler, the Museum was the unfortunate target of a bomb during the Second World War and, for more than twenty years, it was assumed that the Le Moustier skeleton had been blown to bits. In fact, it had been taken from the exhibit hall before the bombing and removed to a place of safe storage. From there, it was taken, along with a collection of other valuables, to Russia by the victorious forces after the war. Eventually somewhat the worse for wear and in pieces it was recognized and returned to East Germany where it is now undergoing yet a fifth reconstruction. The acquisition of trophies is a universal attribute of victorious armies, whether Russian or otherwise, and we should note that the Heidelberg mandible was for a time the property of souvenir-hunting American soldiers. It too, when returned, was somewhat damaged.

THE COMBE CAPELLE SKELETON

Another important human fossil in the Berlin museum was less fortunate. This too had been discovered by Hauser on 26 August 1909, just a year after Le Moustier and in the same (Dordogne) region of southern France. This was the Combe Capelle skeleton, which possessed some of the features one would expect of a population intermediate in form between Neanderthal and Modern. Furthermore, the skeleton represents a burial from a time and cultural level somewhere on what has been regarded as the borderline between the Mousterian and the Upper Paleolithic. The skeleton was a burial,

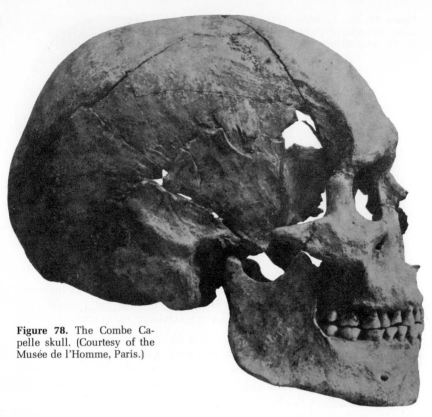

Figure 78. The Combe Capelle skull. (Courtesy of the Musée de l'Homme, Paris.)

however, and so it is impossible to be precise about the level from which it was buried. In addition, because of Hauser's pick-and-shovel digging "technique," no one can be quite sure of what the various surrounding layers contained. The indications of cultural transition may be genuine or they may be the result of the actual mixing of what had been distinct layers. We shall never know. In any event, that second World War bomb destroyed one of the most important skeletons in European prehistory.

THE LA CHAPELLE-AUX-SAINTS SKELETON

To return to the year 1908, in which the Le Moustier skeleton was discovered, success crowned the three years of archeological effort by a small group of French priests, the brothers A. and J. Bouyssonie and their colleague L. Bardon. On 3 August, just a week before Hauser finally exhumed Le Moustier, they discovered a complete human skeleton in a Mousterian cultural layer in a small cave at La Chapelle-aux-Saints. Morphologically their find exhibited all the characteristics found in the original Neanderthal, and furthermore it was

The Fossil Record

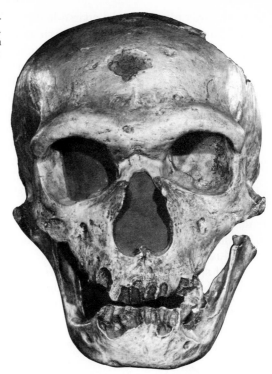

Figure 79. La Chapelle-aux-Saints skull. From a cast. (Courtesy of the American Museum of Natural History.)

far more complete. Disregarding the fact that all but two of the teeth had been missing for years before death, this was the first Neanderthal to be discovered with the whole brain case, including a complete face.

The excavators immediately informed their friend l'Abbé Henri Breuil of their good fortune, and Breuil (1877–1961), well on his way to becoming the most renowned archeologist in the world, gave them what appeared to be the best of advice. He urged them to turn their find over to the famous paleontologist Marcellin Boule for proper study. Boule (1861–1942), a professor at the National Museum of Natural History in Paris, who later founded the Institute of Human Paleontology, was one of the outstanding natural scientists of his day, and, on the face of it, he would seem to have been the obvious man to undertake the description. He immediately got to work and his exhaustive results were soon published in three weighty installments appearing in 1911, 1912, and 1913.

THE CARICATURE OF NEANDERTHAL MAN

As a result of this imposing publication, the cartoon image of Neanderthal man was foisted upon an all-too-receptive world. Neander-

History of the Discovery of the Fossils

thal man was pictured as a coarse-featured brute with a brain that, though large, was qualitatively inferior to the brain of modern humans. He was endowed with a heavy, lumbering body that could not quite maintain an erect posture. Together with this it was claimed that he characteristically walked on the outer edge of his foot since his big toe was supposed to diverge widely from the axis of the other toes in a way that was semi-prehensile. Furthermore, he was pictured as proceeding in a permanent slouch, unable to straighten his knees and restricted by the fact that his backbone formed a single arch, lacking the convexities that allow modern humans to stand erectly. As a final touch, Boule claimed that the shape of the spines of the neck vertebrae and the backward slope to the foramen magnum indicated that the heavy head was slung forward in a gorilloid manner. All these features were recounted with frequent references to modern apes and monkeys and the aggregate picture was of an individual that scarcely looked human.

Recent studies have shown that *all* of these traits which Boule attributed to his La Chapelle Neanderthal are without substance in fact. Of all these characteristics, only perhaps the one claiming coarse facial features may have any validity to it and even this is

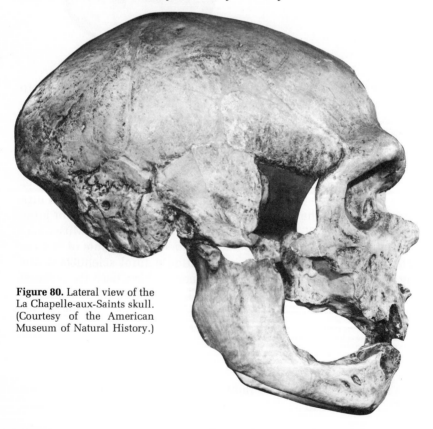

Figure 80. Lateral view of the La Chapelle-aux-Saints skull. (Courtesy of the American Museum of Natural History.)

The Fossil Record

highly questionable, since facial expression is determined by the soft parts that have no representation in the skeleton. That there might be some slight justification in suspecting coarse features in a Neanderthal is suggested by the fact that the one area of anatomy where Neanderthals clearly differ from modern humans is in the face. The Neanderthal face was large, and, if one counts largeness as "coarseness," then it must have been coarse. This, however, is a value judgment and not really subject to measurement, and we shall simply note that the Neanderthal face and everything related to it was large – jaws, teeth, eye and nose openings, and brow ridges.

It is legitimate to ask why Boule painted such a biased portrait. Of course, it is impossible to answer such a question with absolute certainty but a number of things suggest themselves. Boule was a paleontologist and had acquired his training in Toulouse and Paris during the 1880s. Paleontology had been founded in France by Georges Cuvier during the first third of the nineteenth century and virtually all of France's paleontologists in the nineteenth century had been rigorously grounded in Cuvier's ideas. Boule's thinking, then, was thoroughly conditioned by the ideas of catastrophism and was at bottom opposed to an evolutionary point of view.

By the twentieth century one could no longer deny, as Cuvier had done, the existence of fossil humans, but one could claim that the fossils discovered were not the ancestors of subsequent forms of humans if they looked noticeably different from them. Boule, then, denied that either Pithecanthropus or Neanderthal were precursors of modern humans. He allowed that they might be considered primitive cousins – extinct side lines – but not in the direct line of human evolution. With the overemphasis of the nonmodern features of the La Chapelle-aux-Saints skeleton it became a much less likely candidate for the forefather of the succeeding Upper Paleolithic forms. The fully modern features of the Cro-Magnon were also overemphasized to demonstrate the gap between the Mousterian and Upper Paleolithic populations. This was easy enough to do since the Cro-Magnon male was without teeth and possessed a somewhat eroded face, which allowed rather a broad latitude in reconstruction.

The supposed sudden break between the Mousterian culture and the Upper Paleolithic tools that overlie it in the same European sites was also stressed. To Boule and to many European archeologists, this meant that the Upper Paleolithic had developed elsewhere – somewhere outside Europe, perhaps in "The East" – and swept in as an invasion. This, of course, was simply the kind of thinking represented in the theory of catastrophism and was here reapplied to explain the sequence of fossil humans and their cultures as an alternative to an evolutionary explanation. Clearly Boule and his followers have done their best to discredit evolutionary explanations where they have been applied to humanity's prehistory, and the accident of

History of the Discovery of the Fossils

historical events during the first two decades of the twentieth century has allowed this antievolutionary view to persist in many quarters right up to the present time.

Boule's influential position and extensive, if biased, publications on the well-preserved La Chapelle-aux-Saints skeleton gave great weight to the views of hominid catastrophism he advocated. Apparent support for his position was given, not only by the ill-fated Le Moustier find, but by the fact that the next few years produced more well-preserved Neanderthal skeletal material from nearby parts of southern France. In 1909 and 1910 undoubted Neanderthal skeletons were found at the site of La Ferrassie not far from Le Moustier and Cro-Magnon and more juvenile fragments were to follow in 1912. In addition, the site of La Quina not far away yielded a Neanderthal skeleton in 1911 and many more fragments in the immediately succeeding years. The La Quina skeleton was the subject of sound descriptive publications by the discoverer, Henri Martin, but these did not appear for another decade and contained no interpretations or comparisons, and it was generally assumed that this simply supported Boule's well-known assertions. The La Ferrassie material was turned over to Boule himself for description, but, either because he was so busy with the La Chapelle-aux-Saints material or because a careful consideration of the variation indicated by the two adult skeletons from La Ferrassie would have contradicted the views for which he stood, he never published anything on them. A basic description of the La Ferrassie material in fact was not available until after 1970. A full appraisal of the French Neanderthals found between 1908 and 1912 will show that the picture of the curious and

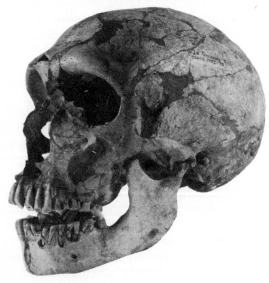

Figure 81. The La Ferrassie I skull. (Courtesy of the Musée de l'Homme, Paris.)

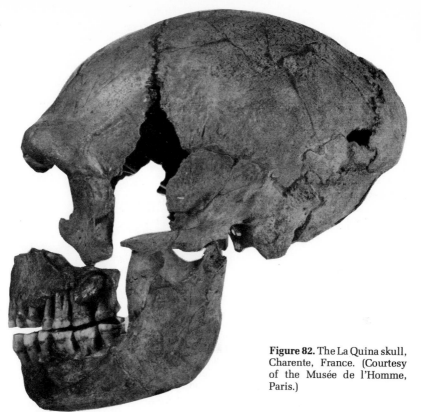

Figure 82. The La Quina skull, Charente, France. (Courtesy of the Musée de l'Homme, Paris.)

supposedly uniform "type" created by Boule primarily on the basis of the La Chapelle skeleton represented a distortion of his type specimen and cannot in any way be supported by the evidence from its contemporaries.

One final event served to solidify the antievolutionary views of French paleontology as represented by Marcellin Boule, namely, the First World War. Boule's only systematic critical opposition came from German anthropologists. German intellectual prestige suffered a severe blow as a result of the war, and then with the rise of the Nazi regime, most of the independent scientists interested in the various aspects of the science of humanity (anthropology) were effectively silenced. The effect of two disastrous wars and an intervening era of vicious intellectual repression can be seen in the fact that little survives of pre-World War I German anthropological thinking. As far as paleoanthropology is concerned, most modern German students avowedly trace the source of their thinking back to the position of Marcellin Boule, especially as it was expounded in the monograph on La Chapelle-aux-Saints and in Boule's compendious volume, *Les Hommes Fossiles (Fossil Men)*, which appeared, respectively, immediately before and just after the First World War.

History of the Discovery of the Fossils

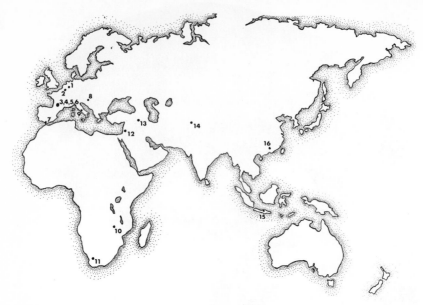

Figure 83. Location of sites where major Neander-thal discoveries have been made. 1. Neanderthal. 2. Spy. 3. La Chapelle-aux-Saints. 4. Le Moustier. 5. La Ferrassie. 6. La Quina. 7. Gibraltar. 8. Krapina. 9. Saccopastore. 10. Broken Hill (Rhodesian Man). 11. Saldanha. 12. Mount Carmel. 13. Shanidar. 14. Teshik Tash. 15. Solo. 16. Ma-Pa. (Drawing by Mary L. Brace and Richard V. Humphrey.)

A brief history of the discovery of the major fossil finds, such as this, must necessarily omit many minor and fragmentary ones as well as some major and relatively important ones. During the last several decades finds have been made in such quantity that there is not space enough to describe the circumstances surrounding the discovery of each one. We shall, therefore, limit our concern to the treatment of those major discoveries that have important implications in the construction of a coherent scheme for understanding human evolution.

The Piltdown Forgery

With all the excitement revolving around the Neanderthal discoveries and interpretations in France, one Englishman apparently resolved that England, too, could have its fossil human and he proceeded literally to create it—both the fossil and the excitement. This is the story of one of the most elaborate and successful scientific hoaxes ever perpetrated, and, while there is no need to discuss fraudulent

Figure 84. Reconstruction of the faked Piltdown skull.

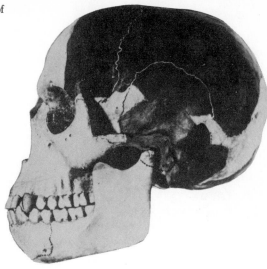

material in any detail, it is introduced here since it seriously clouded issues and colored the thinking of serious students for nearly half a century afterward.

In 1911, a Sussex solicitor and amateur prehistorian, Charles Dawson, claimed to have found a fragment of a fossilized human skull in a gravel pit at Piltdown in southern England. This he took to Dr. (later Sir) Arthur Smith Woodward of the British Museum (Natural History) who was greatly excited by the discovery. During the next year Dawson and Smith Woodward worked over the deposits in the gravel pit and discovered some more fragments, presumably of the same skull, as well as pieces of a variety of extinct animals which purportedly demonstrated the great age of the deposit. A few more finds were made during the next three years, apparently confirming the 1911 and 1912 discoveries.

The remarkable thing about the supposed Piltdown man is that it coupled a brain case of essentially modern form — steep smooth-browed forehead — with an entirely ape-like jaw, undeveloped chin, and with a projecting canine. After a few years of discussion, British anatomical authorities resolved their differences and agreed that the form of the skull was not different from that of modern humans, and that the form of the jaw was not different from that of a modern anthropoid ape, which latter is not surprising since eventually it was demonstrated that that is precisely what it was.

While many non-British scientists balked at accepting such a bizarre association of apparently incompatible pieces, all doubts concerning the accuracy of the reconstruction were removed in a demonstration of anatomical virtuosity by Professor (later Sir) Arthur

History of the Discovery of the Fossils

Figure 85. The Piltdown Committee. Personalities concerned with the Piltdown "discovery": *back row:* Mr. F. O. Barlow, maker of the casts; Professor G. Elliot Smith, anatomist; Mr. C. Dawson, the "discoverer"; Dr. A. S. Woodward, zoologist; *front row:* Dr. A. S. Underwood, teeth expert; Professor Arthur Keith, anatomist; Mr. W. P. Pycraft, zoologist; Sir Ray Lankester, zoologist. The portrait on the wall is of Charles Darwin. (From the painting by John Cooke, R. A., exhibited at the Royal Academy in 1915. Courtesy of the Geological Society of London. Photo British Museum, Natural History.

Keith of the Royal College of Surgeons in London, who for the next forty years was looked up to as the most distinguished and respected of British physical anthropologists. Critics of Keith's reconstruction of Piltdown challenged him to a test and he willingly complied. They took a skull of known shape and size from the collections, broke it into fragments resembling those of the Piltdown skull, and asked Keith to reconstruct the original. With astonishing skill, Keith came within 20 cc of the true cranial capacity. Considering that the original measured capacity was in the neighborhood of 1400 cc, an error of only 20 cc can be regarded as totally insignificant. The result was an enormous boost to Keith's prestige and the removal of all doubts concerning the accuracy of the Piltdown restoration.

While many anthropologists continued to doubt the association of skull and jaw in a single individual, the fact that no other anthropoid

ape fragments had been found in early Ice Age strata in England
tended to increase the apparent probability that the Piltdown pieces
belonged together. With the prestige and authority of such eminent
scientists standing behind the discoveries, it never occurred to anyone — even the most critical scientists — that the finds might be forgeries and that they might not be genuinely ancient, although in retrospect it is clear that the published accounts of the actual findings
were anything but satisfactory. To prove such great antiquity for a
human fossil, especially one that so profoundly affected all interpretations of the course of human evolution, much more accurate documentation should have been demanded than the "Several years ago I
was walking along. . . ." sort of account which was offered. More
than one amateur archeologist who was acquainted with Dawson
and had examined his artifacts was convinced that they were fraudulent, but nothing to that effect was put into print.

Apparently the desire to believe in Piltdown was great enough to
overcome any doubts. Among other things, it demonstrated to the
satisfaction of the English that humanity had its origins on British
soil; furthermore this most ancient human had the smooth and
lofty brow of modern *Homo sapiens*, and this was taken as proof
that the heavy-browed Neanderthals of continental Europe and the
small-brained and bestial fossil from Java were not the direct
ancestors of modern humans. Interesting evidence for unsuccessful
parallel evolutionary developments perhaps, but it was generally
felt that Boule was correct in regarding them as having become
extinct without issue. Thus, by chance, the concepts of hominid
catastrophism became established among the very people who were
raised in an atmosphere of Darwinian evolution, and, as we shall
see, the curious historical twist has continued to influence interpretations of the most recently discovered and most ancient hominids.

THE GALLEY HILL SKELETON

The evidence that Piltdown presumably offered for the great antiquity of the modern form of braincase was regarded as reinforced by the
claimed antiquity of another skeleton that had been discovered in a
gravel pit at Galley Hill on the banks of the Thames in 1888. The
skull and skeleton were well preserved and relatively complete, unlike the highly fragmentary Piltdown remains, and were perfectly
modern in form, although allegedly possessing some hints of the
"primitive." The date was claimed to be mid-Pleistocene but the
documentation again was more in the form of verbal assertion than
demonstrable fact. Nevertheless, Galley Hill was accepted by British
scientists as further evidence for the remote antiquity of modern
forms of humans. They did, however, admit that certain doubts

could be entertained concerning the precise dating of their finds, which only produced further intensified efforts to discover unquestionable evidence of ancient *sapiens*.

The solution of the problems surrounding both Galley Hill and Piltdown came about as a result of a combination of events. Research by Kenneth P. Oakley of the British Museum (Natural History), in the late 1940s, led him to reinvestigate some of the late nineteenth century attempts to determine how old things were by various forms of chemical analysis. Specifically it was shown that the amount of fluorine contained in bone increases in proportion to the time the bone has remained buried in the ground. It also depends on the amount of fluorine present in the particular area where the bone in question is buried. Hence, high fluorine content for a bone from one area does not necessarily mean that it is older than a fragment with less fluorine from another area. On the other hand, high fluorine content for a particular piece of bone *does* mean that it is older than another fragment from the same area but with a lower F content.

In 1948 Ashley Montagu made a thorough study of the Galley Hill remains, the results of which convinced him that none of the alleged "primitive" traits that were supposed to characterize it were in fact present. The skull was that of a modern human in every way, shape, and form. Meeting Oakley shortly afterward, Montagu communicated his findings to him. A study of the Galley Hill site had brought Oakley to the same conclusion. Subsequent fluorine analysis of the Galley Hill bones confirmed the suspicion that the skeleton could not be of Middle Pleistocene age. This supported the view of those who had long pointed to the fact that the discovery of a complete and well-preserved human skeleton was exceedingly unlikely to have occurred *in situ* in a deposit completely devoid of the fossil remains of other animals. The downward percolation of carbonic acid-laden waters through the gravels was so pronounced at the site that all bones would have been decalcified in much less time than the age attributed to this skeleton. Additional evidence indicated an artificial burial and a Post-Pleistocene age.

Oakley next applied the fluorine test to the Piltdown fragments, and his preliminary conclusion was that they were more recent than the early Pleistocene or late Pliocene dates originally claimed, but he still did not suggest anything irregular. Examining the Piltdown "remains" in 1948, Ashley Montagu came to the conclusion that the mandible was that of an ape and morphologically could not possibly belong with the rest of the skull.

PILTDOWN CASHIERED

The suspicion that the whole thing might be a fake was first seriously entertained in 1953 by J. S. Weiner of Oxford University.

Among other things it was known that Charles Dawson had treated the fragments he claimed to have found in 1911 with potassium bichromate according to the widespread nineteenth century belief that this hardened fragile bones. When Dawson showed the fragments to Smith Woodward at the British Museum in 1912, the latter commented that such a procedure was worthless, yet, later that same year when the mandible was found by Dawson in the presence of Smith Woodward, it was already stained with potassium bichromate and it clearly must have been a "plant."

There were other discrepancies that reinforced Dr. Weiner's suspicions and led him to institute a thorough reappraisal of the Piltdown remains with the collaboration of Oakley and Sir Wilfrid E. Le Gros Clark of Oxford. Microscopic examination showed that the separate canine tooth had been ground down artificially so that it would not seem so large as to be unquestionably anthropoid. To produce a color appropriate for an iron oxide stain, the tooth was given a coat of paint. New drillings to get larger samples for chemical analysis produced the expected powder from the skull, but from the jaw came tiny white shavings of fresh bone accompanied by an odor like that of "burning horn." Only recent bone gives off such a burnt horn odor, fossil bone does not. Obviously this was not a fossil.

Exhaustive analysis showed that the skull fragments came from a recent human being and the jaw was that of a recent female orangutan. Furthermore the Pleistocene mammalian remains discovered at the same time were shown to have come from other parts of the world far removed from England, and the crude stone and bone tools were likewise shown to be forgeries.

Weiner, Le Gros Clark, and Oakley made their sensational findings known to the world late in 1953 ending a hoax that had perplexed the anthropological world for more than forty years. The whole story was published in 1955 by J. S. Weiner in a fascinating book entitled *The Piltdown Forgery*, which reads like a detective story, which in fact it is.

There remains only to identify the forger. Only two people who had figured prominently in the history of the Piltdown discovery remained alive in 1953. One was the French Jesuit and eminent paleontologist Père Teilhard de Chardin, who had actually found the canine in 1913, but who was relatively dissociated from the wrangles over Piltdown interpretations. The other was Sir Arthur Keith who had played a prominent role in the establishment of the Piltdown remains as an authentic fossil. Sir Arthur's whole approach to human evolution—as was that of his numerous followers—was colored by the attempt to explain the existence of such a bizarre combination of traits at such an early time level. Teilhard could only register baffled astonishment without any suspicion of who had perpetrated the fraud or what the motivation had been. But Sir Arthur Keith, when queried by a former student (Ashley Montagu) for a possible explanation of the forger's motivation, replied (19 September, 1954), "If you knew the wonderful fame won by Schoetensack in 1907 by the discovery of the Heidelberg jaw you would realize the fame waiting for the discoverer of the skull of that early date." It was as simple as that: the forger sought to win fame by his forgery.

Sir Arthur Smith Woodward had passed on many years previously, but the evidence of the years of fruitless toil that he had expended in the hope of discovering more material relating to Piltdown clearly declares his innocence. There remains only Charles Dawson who had died in 1916 before the issues surrounding Piltdown had fully gained momentum. Circumstantial evidence all points to Dawson as the forger, but Weiner is careful to make it clear that this does not constitute proof, and that we may never be certain of the forger's real identity or of all the reasons for his conduct.

Whoever the forger may have been, and wherever his shadow may now be wandering, he may well reflect

> With jawbone of an ass great Samson slew
> A lion; but my deed his feat surpasses.
> For forty years, and with a jawbone, too,
> I made our scientific lions asses!

The Discovery of the Australopithecines

Following the important Neanderthal finds of the first two decades of this century and the beginnings of the excitement over Piltdown, the scene of actual discovery was due to shift away from Europe. The first hint of what was to come was announced from South Africa in 1924 in the form of a small fossilized skull found during quarrying operations at Tuang, Bechuanaland. This was given to a young professor of anatomy at the University of Witwatersrand Medical School in Johannesburg. Raymond A. Dart studied it for several months and then, early in 1925, published a relatively complete preliminary description in the British scientific weekly *Nature*. In this he noted that despite the juvenile age of his fossil — equivalent to that of a six year old child in the human growth cycle — it appeared to be closer to the human line of development than any other living or fossil ape. His cautious conclusion was that this little fossil was an advanced ape, and he christened it *Australopithecus africanus* (southern ape of Africa).

Dart's conservative description of the find and statement of his conclusions stirred up a storm in British scientific circles, which continues to reverberate to the present day. The most distinguished and influential men in anatomy and anthropology, some of whom had been Dart's former teachers, read his paper before it was printed and then wrote disparaging comments that were published just after

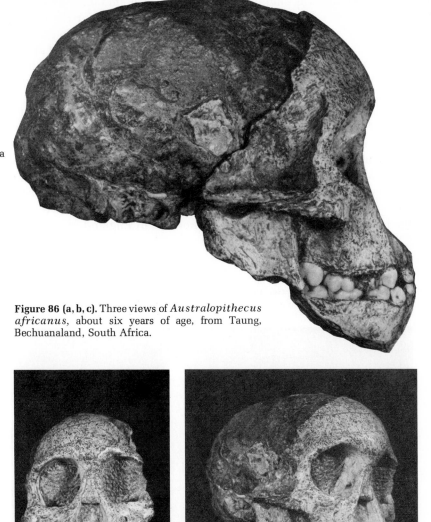

Figure 86 (a, b, c). Three views of *Australopithecus africanus*, about six years of age, from Taung, Bechuanaland, South Africa.

the article itself appeared. Dart, of course, had not seen these comments and was given no chance to discuss or reply to them. Criticism continued, becoming increasingly harsh. The impression thus created was that Dart was rash and hasty in publishing without the assistance of some established "authority"—and so soon after discovery.

History of the Discovery of the Fossils

Furthermore, it was claimed that he had exaggerated the human-like features of his fossil, and finally he was ridiculed for displaying his ignorance of the classics in his "barbarous" combination of Latin- and Greek-based terms in the word *Australopithecus*. Of all the criticisms leveled against his work, only this last has any truth to it, and, since it is totally irrelevant to the appreciation of the significance of *Australopithecus*, it should be ignored.

Time and further discoveries have shown that not only were Dart's critics badly in error, as they had previously been about the Piltdown remains, but that Dart's own interpretation was a conservative underestimate of the status of the population to which *Australopithecus* belonged. In retrospect, it seems as though the source of the criticism could be attributed to a mixture of stuffiness and jealousy. Apparently the feeling existed that Dart should properly have turned the fossil over to the established authorities in England for descrip-

Figure 87. Professor Raymond Dart developing a block of breccia containing an australopithecine skull, a baboon skull, and two lower jaw fragments. (Courtesy of Professor Raymond Dart.)

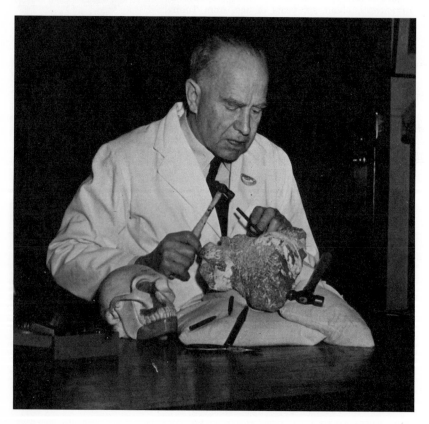

The Fossil Record

tion and eventual publication, and there was evident annoyance that he had gone ahead on his own.

The prestige of his critics was such that an unbiased appraisal of his account could not be given, and it was more than ten years before further finds from South Africa reopened the issue and raised the possibility that Dart might have been right. Meanwhile, however, the spotlight had turned to other parts of the world, and in a sense the discoveries of the late 1920s and 1930s further reinforced the feeling that Dart had been ill advised when he had intimated the possibility that *Australopithecus* might have been remotely ancestral to later fully human forms.

As a holdover from the economic and political practices of the nineteenth century, European influence continued to be directly felt in many parts of the world until the Second World War, while much of the budding nationalism and antiwestern sentiment prevalent in the world today can be traced to this, it is also true that scientific advances occurred which would otherwise have been long delayed. In the search for exploitable mineral deposits, the colonially orient-ed governments employed trained geologists, and inevitably they made discoveries of general scientific significance as well as per-forming their commercial functions. We have seen how such activi-

Figure 88. Australopithecine sites. 1. Tuang. 2. Sterk-fontein. 3. Swartkrans. 4. Kromdrai. 5. Makapansgat. 6. Olduvai Gorge. 7. East Rudolf. 8. Omo. 9. Afar Depression.

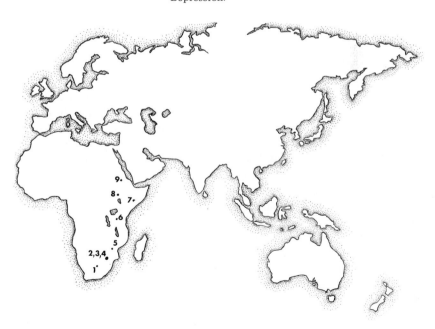

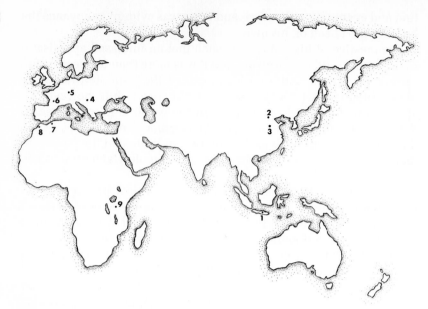

Figure 89. Location of Pithecanthropine sites. 1. Pithecanthropus (Java). 2. Choukoutien. 3. Lantian. 4. Vertesszöllös. 5. Heidelberg. 6. Arago. 7. Ternefine. 8. Rabat. 9. Olduvai Gorge.

ties led to the discovery of Pithecanthropus in Java, and it has been mentioned that *Australopithecus* in Southern Africa was discovered in the same way.

The Discovery of Peking Man

During the early 1920s European-trained geologists were active in China, and as a consequence of their efforts evidence began to accumulate pointing to the existence of prehistoric humans in the town of Choukoutien somewhat less than thirty miles southwest of Peiping (formerly Peking) in northern China. The first traces of the presence of humans were in the form of quartz fragments in the fill of what had formerly been large limestone caves. Quartz could only get into such a place by human agency, and before long the presence of humans was revealed by the discovery of a small number of human teeth. In 1927, on the basis of the study of a single tooth, Davidson Black (1884–1934), the Canadian born anatomist at the Peking Union Medical College, announced to a skeptical world that Choukoutien contained a new genus and species of fossil human, "*Sinanthropus pekinensis*."

Modern experts in taxonomy deplore the tendency that formerly

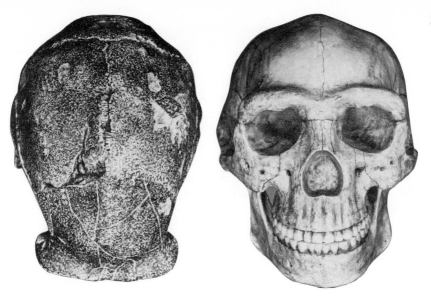

Figure 90. Skull-cap and reconstruction of "Sinanthropus pekinensis," *Homo erectus* from Choukoutien, China. Reconstruction by Franz Weidenreich. (Courtesy of the American Museum of Natural History.)

resulted in each new discovery being given a new taxonomic designation, but despite the fact that from the vantage point of our greater perspective, Black appears to have been overly enthusiastic in creating new names, nevertheless his appreciation of the significance of the fragments discovered led to a systematic investigation of the sites of Choukoutien and the recovery of one of the largest and most important collections of early human fossils ever made. Excavations in 1928 yielded skull and jaw fragments, and during the last day of the excavating season in December 1929, W. C. Pei, the paleontologist in charge of the excavation, himself found a complete skull minus only the face. This fully vindicated the predictions made by Black and served to usher in the 1930s on an appropriately dramatic note, for this decade was to uncover a greater variety of remains from more corners of the world illustrating all the various phases of human evolution than had been discovered during any other comparable period of time. In fact, not until the late 1960s and subsequently has a given period produced such a rash of discoveries.

Operations at Choukoutien during the next ten years produced abundant remains of a population at the same stage of evolution as Pithecanthropus. Furthermore, stone tools and the remains of hearths and butchered and roasted animals amply confirmed the first opinion of Dubois offered as long ago as the mid-1890s. Ironical-

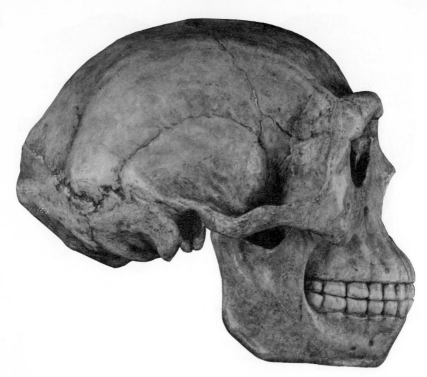

Figure 91. Lateral view of reconstruction of *Homo erectus* from Choukoutien, China. Reconstruction by Franz Weidenreich. (Courtesy of the American Museum of Natural History.)

ly, now that the world was finally convinced by the finds of Peking man that Dubois had been right, the only dissenting voice to be heard was that of the aging Dubois himself who refused to recognize any relationship between the Chinese fossils, which he regarded as fully human, and his precious Pithecanthropus, which he alone, like Virchow so many years before, claimed to be a giant gibbon.

The excavations in China were momentarily halted in 1934 by the untimely death of Black. At first it seemed as though this might present a serious hindrance to the work at Choukoutien, but the almost calamitous effect of the death of Black was alleviated by the appointment of the redoubtable Franz Weidenreich (1873–1948) to fill his position (see Figure 96). Weidenreich, a former student of Gustav Schwalbe before the turn of the century, together with his late teacher, was one of the very few scientists to defend a view of human evolution which in overall grasp is substantially similar to that being presented in the present volume. After a stormy but successful two-phased academic career (the phases being before and after the First World War) and another career in politics, Weidenreich was forced to become an exile from Hitler's Germany, and at a time in life when

The Fossil Record

Figure 92. *Homo erectus* site at Choukoutien, China. (Courtesy of the American Museum of Natural History.)

most people are beginning to think of retirement he began the work that was to make him one of the immortals of biological anthropology. He continued his predecessor's work, and, although his life was again to be changed by war, he produced a series of outstanding monographs in the best tradition of German thoroughness. As a result, Peking man constitutes one of the best known of the early characters in the story of human evolution.

Among the various lands in which significant fossils were found during the 1930s the greatest variety came from Java. As the decade wore on, older and older fossils were discovered, so that by the time the war in the Pacific put a halt to research, remnants of two distinct stages in human evolution had been accumulated.

THE SOLO SKULLS

The first finds were made in the years 1931–1932 at Ngandong on the banks of the Solo River, immediately downstream from Trinil,

History of the Discovery of the Fossils

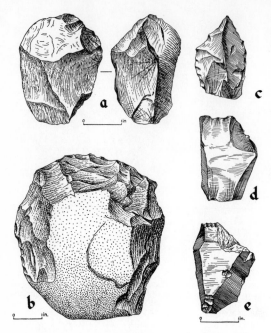

Figure 93. Stone tools of Peking Man (*Homo erectus*). *a.* Quartz chopper-tool. *b.* Boulder of green-stone flaked into chopper form. *c.* Pointed flake of quartz. *d.* Bi-polar flake of quartz. *e.* Bi-pyramidal crystal of quartz utilized as tool. After Pei and Black. (From K. P. Oakley, *Man the Tool-Maker.* Courtesy of the British Museum, Natural History.)

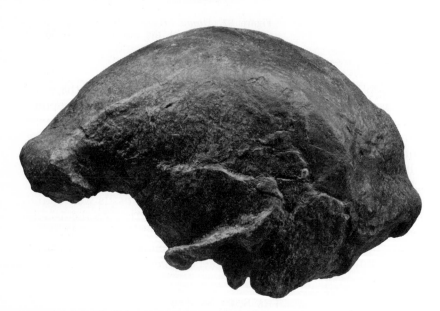

Figure 94. Solo Skull V, typical of all the Solo skulls, from Ngandong, Java. (Courtesy of the American Museum of Natural History.)

The Fossil Record

where Dubois had opened up the study of Javanese prehistory. All told, eleven Solo skulls were unearthed—each minus the skull base and the facial skeleton, facts which have been taken to indicate that their owners were probably victims of cannibalism, a view that has been strongly doubted by Dr. Teuku Jacob, the Indonesian anthropologist. The important thing to note, however, is that in age and morphological development the Solo humans are the far eastern equivalent of the Neanderthals of Europe. It has been claimed that in some respects they show affinities to the pithecanthropines, and Weidenreich has noted that this is just what one would expect if they were the Upper Pleistocene descendants of this early Pleistocene stage.

More Pithecanthropines

In the mid-1930s, the Dutch paleontologist G. H. R. von Koenigswald, who had participated in the discovery of the Solo remains, exploited a number of successful methods of obtaining fossil material.

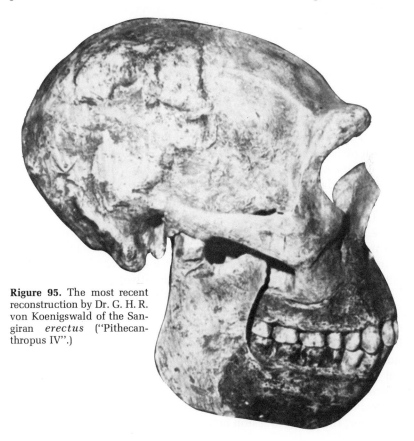

Rigure 95. The most recent reconstruction by Dr. G. H. R. von Koenigswald of the Sangiran *erectus* ("Pithecanthropus IV".)

In addition to his own collecting efforts, he trained Javanese villagers to spot fossils that might be discovered after the rains. He paid a flat price per fragment, a practice that almost led to his undoing in 1937. At Sangiran just upstream from Trinil in Central Java, his collectors had come across a skull in the same layer in which Dubois' 1891 find had occurred. His assistants, being practical minded, proceeded to multiply the number of pieces he had to pay for by the simple expedient of breaking the skull into some forty small fragments. They were all accounted for, however, and, since the breaks were clean and fresh, it was a simple matter to fit the pieces together. The resulting skull was so similar to Dubois' original Pithecanthropus that Weidenreich remarked that they "resemble each other as much as do two eggs." Furthermore von Koenigswald's skull was somewhat more complete and supported the Peking finds in providing additional confirmation of the correctness of Dubois' original judgment claiming the ancient and primitive human status for Pithecanthropus.

The Javanese fossils mentioned so far have all come from beds containing the so-called "Trinil fauna" indicating a Middle Pleistocene age. Von Koenigswald's efforts, however, also turned up fossil human material from beds containing the "Djetis fauna" and therefore belonging to an earlier part of the Pleistocene. In 1936 a fairly complete skull minus face was discovered at Modjokerto which apparently belonged to an infant scarcely a year old. Had it lived to maturity it probably would have developed into an adult of the Pithecanthropus variety, although this is mostly speculation, and it is evident that an infant fossil cannot tell us a great deal about the characteristics of the population to which it belonged. In 1939, however, von Koenigswald unearthed the back of the skull and part of the face of an adult from the Djetis stratum at Sangiran. Although this could still be regarded as a pithecanthropine, it featured the thickest, heaviest skull bones and the most robust teeth of any such fossil hitherto found.

The final treasure that this period in human paleontology was to produce from Java was found by von Koenigswald in 1941 in the Djetis layers of the same Sangiran area that had yielded the 1937 and 1939 Pithecanthropus skulls. This was a relatively small fragment of lower jaw, and from the form of the teeth there could be no doubt that it was human. What, however, makes it remarkable, is its enormous size. It is so large that it makes the massive dental apparatus of the 1939 Pithecanthropus look almost delicate by comparison. Because of the great thickness of the mandible, von Koenigswald felt that this was not just another pithecanthropine, and he christened it *"Meganthropus palaeojavanicus."* Another similar mandible was found in the same area of Java in 1952, which some have taken as support for the impression created by the earlier discovery. From

a

Figure 96 (a). Franz Weidenreich (1873–1948) and Dr. G. H. von Koenigswald examining a Solo skull. (Courtesy of the American Museum of Natural History.) **(b).** Reconstruction of the Sangiran *Homo erectus modjokertensis* ("Pithecanthropus IV") by Franz Weidenreich.

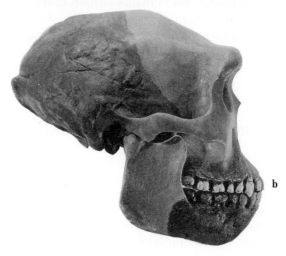

b

History of the Discovery of the Fossils

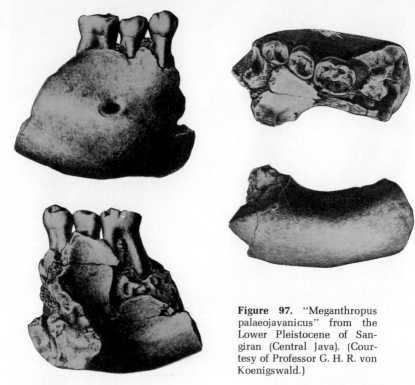

Figure 97. "Meganthropus palaeojavanicus" from the Lower Pleistocene of Sangiran (Central Java). (Courtesy of Professor G. H. R. von Koenigswald.)

the evidence available so far, however, the arguments in favor of creating yet another category of hominid are not compelling. Although the dating is not certain since the relationship between the radiometrically dated strata and the actual location of the jaw fragments is unclear, there are many who feel that the "*Meganthropus*" material is nearer two than one million years old. Those who have favored a great antiquity for the specimens have tentatively regarded it as a Far Eastern equivalent to the australopithecines of Africa. So far, however, neither the measurements nor the dates available can sustain such a view without argument, a matter to which we shall return in the next chapter.

Late Pleistocene Hominids from Omo

In 1967 Richard Leakey discovered the skeletal remains of three hominids from the lower levels of the Kibish formation in the Omo region of Ethiopia. By means of the thorium/proactinium method Butzer has dated these deposits as in the vicinity of 100,000 years of age. Radiocarbon dating of Omo I fragments of bone showed that they were completely dead, thus indicating an age in excess of

Figure 98 (a). Omo II, from the Omo region of Ethiopia. (b). Omo II and I, posterior view. (Courtesy of M. H. Day.)

40,000–60,000 years. Skulls I and II are shown in Figs. 98a, and b. What is fascinating about these skulls is that they are so modern looking. As Michael Day has pointed out, Omo II shows many features resembling those of the Solo skulls and, to a lesser extent, the Broken Hill ("Rhodesian Man") skull, the Vértesszöllös occipital, and the Kanjera skulls described by Louis Leakey in 1933. In its general robustness and markings it even resembles *Homo erectus*, but in its complete absence of prominent brow ridges and in its general configuration it closely resembles *Homo sapiens*. This is even more strikingly seen in the contemporary Omo I, which is virtually modern in every respect and, as Day says, may be reasonably compared with the Skhūl skulls from the Middle East.

If these findings are eventually sustained—at the present time there is some debate concerning dating—it may well be that we shall have to revise our ideas relating to the time of appearance of modern-looking types of humans.

Mount Carmel

While all those remarkable finds were being made in the Orient, the Middle East was not lagging far behind. Isolated material of importance had been found before the decade under consideration, but this was simply a prelude to what was to come. The real prize came as a result of the efforts of a joint expedition by the American School of Prehistoric Research and the British School of Archaeology in Jerusalem. Little more than a mile from the Mediterranean shore some fifteen miles south of Haifa in Palestine, the expedition excavated the contents of two caves on the western slopes of Mount Carmel. There in the years 1931 and 1932 the fossil remains of more than a dozen individuals were found, ranging from a few teeth to complete skeletons—all associated with stone tools belonging to a Middle Eastern version of the Mousterian, the industry of Neanderthal man in Europe.

In the cave of Mugharet et-Tabūn (Cave of the Oven) there was found the complete skeleton of a woman who was morphologically identical to the Neanderthals of Europe, which was not too surprising, but in the cave of Mugharet es Skhūl (Cave of the Kids), ten skeletons were found showing every possible combination of the features of Neanderthal with those of modern humans. The anthropological arguments that the Mount Carmel finds stirred up continue unabated to the present day and revolve chiefly about two problems.

First, the dating of Mount Carmel has been a source of controversy from the outset, but in a sense the solution to this problem preferred by many authors has been largely influenced by their perception of the second problem that involves assumptions concerning the course of human evolution. Most practicing students of human paleontology were operating under the belief that the Neanderthals suddenly became extinct during the fourth and last glaciation, being replaced by humans of modern form who had evolved elsewhere and whose ancestry, as indicated by Galley Hill and Piltdown, extended far

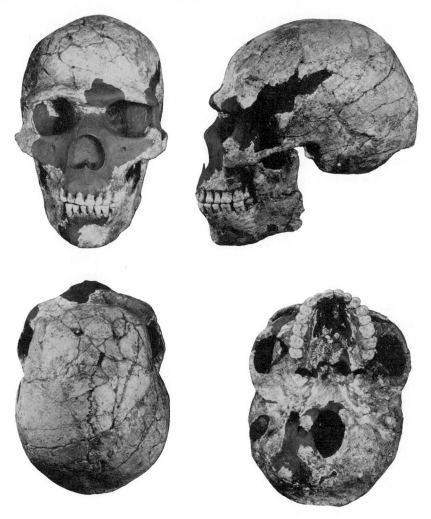

Figure 99. Four views of Skhūl V. (Courtesy of the late Professor Charles Snow and the Peabody Museum, Harvard University.)

back into the early Pleistocene. Here, however, in the very area where ancient *sapiens* was postulated to be most ancient, there was this curious melange of modern and Neanderthal traits at Skhūl, and a frankly Neanderthal skeleton from Tabūn.

Clearly the age of the strata was not early Pleistocene, and the efforts to make the remains seem as old as possible could do no more than claim a third interglacial date. At least this was earlier than the fourth glacial placement of the European Neanderthals and the proponents of hominid catastrophism thus received some consolation, although this was not the sort of evidence for early moderns which they had hoped to find. One solution to the puzzle was suggested which still left the door open for the as yet unfound ancient modern who was assumed to exist — still farther east perhaps? — and that was to regard the Mount Carmel remains as evidence for the hybridization of a local Neanderthal group, represented by the Tabūn female, and a population of the undiscovered *sapiens*.

The problem was dumped squarely in the lap of Sir Arthur Keith who was primarily responsible for the description and interpretation of the Mount Carmel remains. The uncertainties of the situation were the cause of a good deal of mental agonizing on the part of Keith, but he finally came up with the tentative suggestion that the Mount Carmel fossils presented a picture of a population in the throes of evolutionary change, which presumably accounted for the amount of variability present. Precisely why an unusual rate of evolution should be going on here in the Middle East Keith did not even venture to guess, and why the Neanderthals of Europe presumably lagged behind was not a question that appeared to concern anyone.

Some authorities offered an alternative solution to the Mount Carmel population by pointing out that Tabūn and Skhūl were actually different in age and hence not really part of the same population. Tabūn had to be regarded as Neanderthal in any case, but Skhūl could then be treated as the long sought for *sapiens*, a little crude and "primitive" perhaps, but still "pure." While it was conceded that Tabūn and Skhūl may be of separate ages, most experts could not evade the realization that Skhūl was clearly neanderthaloid, i.e., morphologically half way between Neanderthal and *sapiens*. Then of course the plaguing problem of the third interglacial date would arise again, and there seemed no way to decide whether this was actually a picture of evolution in process or simply a case of hybridization.

Since the evolutionists could think of no particular reason why the observed changes should occur, and the would-be hybridizers could only produce a representative of one of the supposed parent populations, it seemed like a stalemate. Recently, however, the problem has been greatly simplified by the growing realization that the Skhūl remains occurred not in the third interglacial before the European Neanderthals, but only about thirty-five thousand years ago and hence substantially later than the Neanderthals. Not only are they half way between Neanderthal and modern in form, but they are also half way between in time. Tabūn (dated at possibly more than 60,000 B.P.) would then be a contemporary of the European Neanderthals, which, on the basis of form alone, is just what one would expect. Mount Carmel, then, does present a picture of the evolution of modern humans out of Neanderthal precursors just as Schwalbe predicted more than a half-century ago, and as we shall see in Chap-

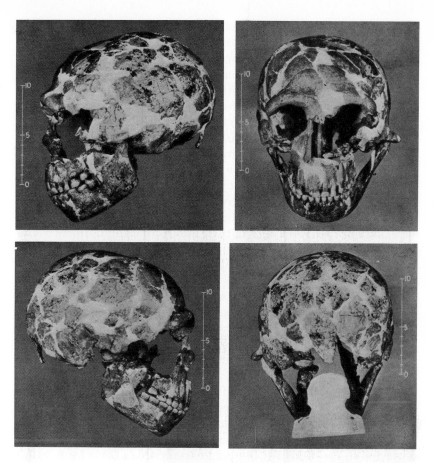

Figure 100. Four views of the Tabūn skull. (Courtesy of the Oxford University Press.)

ters 9 and 10, we now think we can understand the reason why it occurred and why it should have happened at exactly this time.

The Swanscombe Skull

While the Far Eastern finds were providing confirmation for the late nineteenth century views of Dubois and his followers, and Palestine was proving to be a troublesome thorn in the side of the hominid catastrophists, England finally acquired its only really ancient fossil human. This was found in 1935 at Swanscombe on the lower Thames in a gravel pit whose strata are composed of sediments laid down in the latter part of the second interglacial. Abundant evidence for the presence of prehistoric humans had been accumulating for many years in the form of the Acheulean hand axes of the Lower Paleolithic but it was only after years of vigilance on the part of a London dentist, A. T. Marston, that a human occipital bone (the back and bottom of the skull) was discovered in 1935. Marston continued his interest and early the next year a left parietal bone (top and side) was found which articulated with the previously discovered occipital. This meant that the whole rear half of the skull could be reconstructed. It is interesting to note that by virtue of continued diligent search the right parietal was discovered in 1955, just twenty years after the other pieces, and confirmed the reconstruction.

Naturally, interest was intense, and, as a result, every conceivable method has been employed to check the reliability of the apparent Middle Pleistocene age of the Swanscombe skull. There can be no question that the skull is genuine, but from this point on certainty ends. Perhaps partly because of their intellectual commitment to the existence of modern forms of humans in the early Pleistocene, such as the now-discredited Galley Hill and Piltdown forms, British writers have been disposed to view Swanscombe as modern. This of course has been most difficult to argue since, during the latter part of the Pleistocene, human evolutionary changes have largely occurred in the region of the face, and the face of Swanscombe was totally lacking.

Nevertheless, the analysts have done the best they could with what they had. They have discovered every possible measurement wherein Swanscombe did not differ from modern humans, and they played down the one obvious dimension where Swanscombe clearly exceeds more than 90 per cent of modern humans. Furthermore a recent reappraisal by T. D. Stewart has shown that they have totally neglected to mention that the paramastoid area is of a form found

Figure 101 (a and b). The Swanscombe skull, top and back views. (Courtesy of the British Museum, Natural History.)

a   b

all. And finally, an Italian anthropologist, the late Sergio Sergi, has convincingly demonstrated that the curvature profile of the back corners of the skull is just the same as that in the classic Neanderthals and quite different from that of modern humans. It certainly seems that the claim that Swanscombe constitutes clear evidence for the existence of modern humans in the second interglacial has yet to be substantiated, for it may yet be shown that the earliest Englishman was an early Neanderthal.

The Steinheim Skull

An accurate appraisal of Swanscombe is especially important because it is one of the very few pieces of evidence for the shape of mankind between Heidelberg and the pithecanthropines and the Neanderthals of the fourth glaciation. Two years before the discovery of Swanscombe, in strata of approximately the same age, a more complete skull was uncovered in a gravel pit at Steinheim, not far from Marbach, the birthplace of the German poet Schiller. The Steinheim skull had been partially crushed and warped by its long interment, but the frontal part of the skull is present and all but the incisor-bearing part of the face is preserved. As in the case of Swanscombe, the attempt was made to demonstrate that here, too, was ancient *sapiens*, but again this was primarily based on the nondiagnostic parts of the back of the skull and, because of the degree of deformation, proves relatively little. The heavy, projecting brow ridge or supraorbital torus, however, while not quite up to that of a pithecanthropine, clearly exceeds that of all the known Neanderthals of the fourth glaciation, as one would expect in a population

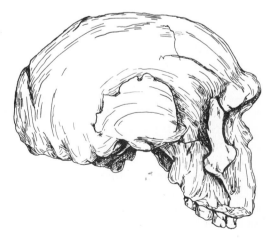

Figure 102. The Steinheim skull. (Drawing by Mary L. Brace.)

halfway in time between the pithecanthropines and the Neanderthals.

Steinheim and Swanscombe, discovered within two years of each other during the mid-thirties, are the only pieces of fossil evidence that fit in that blank part of the record between the pithecanthropines and the Neanderthals. While they do not constitute evidence for the evolution of the pithecanthropines into the Neanderthals, neither do they provide support for the presence of an elusive Middle Pleistocene population of "yet-to-be-discovered" *sapiens*.

By and large, the anthropological world regarded the finds made in the 1930s as valuable confirmation of the views that had become accepted on much less extensive evidence earlier in this century. Pithecanthropus supported by Sinanthropus was considered the crudest possible form of human, Neanderthal was perceived as a gross and clumsy caricature, and *sapiens* was assumed to be of an antiquity that extended back to the beginning of the Pleistocene and was believed to have blossomed, unaccountably, late in the Pleistocene while engaged in the business of exterminating his primitive cousins.

To be sure the Mount Carmel problems had not been solved to the satisfaction of all concerned, von Koenigswald's Meganthropus and some finds of isolated teeth of enormous size had not been satisfactorily explained, and, most vexing of all, really solid evidence for ancient *sapiens* continued to elude discovery despite the confidence that this would be rectified by further exploration. However the most disquieting development from the point of view of anthropological orthodoxy came once again from South Africa.

More Australopithecines

Just when it seemed as though the accumulation of newly found fossil material coming from all over the Old World was effacing all memory of the brief stir caused by Dart's *Australopithecus*, the activities of the indomitable Robert Broom (1866–1951) resulted in the discovery of another australopithecine. This time no one could claim that the hominid features were a product of its relative youth because this time the skull was that of an adult. It had been blasted out of the face of a lime works quarry at Sterkfontein in the Transvaal area of South Africa, west of Johannesburg.

Broom, born in Scotland, had been an internationally famous paleontologist since the turn of the century. He supported his field work by practicing medicine in his spare time, or, if one prefers, he was a practicing physician who devoted his spare time to paleontology. Perhaps the first is the better way of considering it since the real interest of his life was fossil hunting, an interest that has contributed

Figure 103. Sts 5 "Mrs. Ples," "Plesianthropus transvaalensis" from Sterkfontein with the mandible SK 23 from Swartkrans, which would be a remarkably good fit had the skull retained its teeth. **(a).** Left lateral view. **(b).** Frontal view. **(c).** Right lateral view. **(d).** Three-quarter view.

History of the Discovery of the Fossils

250 to the enrichment of all humankind. Broom's discoveries in the Karoo beds of South Africa have done much toward clarifying the story of the origin of mammals two hundred million years ago, and he was regarded as one of the world's leading authorities on fossil mammal-like reptiles. As was true for Franz Weidenreich, Robert Broom was in his sixties when he became involved in discoveries of importance to the construction of a picture of human evolution. Like Weiden-

Figure 104. Stone tools from Sterkfontein and Makapansgat. (Courtesy of Professor Raymond Dart.)

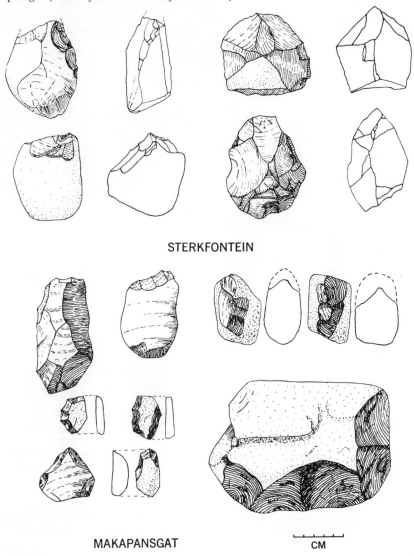

STERKFONTEIN

MAKAPANSGAT   CM

The Fossil Record

immense output during the course of his fifteen years in paleoanthropology. He also followed the practice of giving each new find a
different official name, but this was later simplified as we shall
subsequently have occasion to observe.

PLESIANTHROPUS

The Sterkfontein find of 1936 was christened *"Plesianthropus
transvaalensis"* by Broom. Brain size evidently was within the
upper limits of the anthropoid ape range of variation and the molar
teeth were of fully gorilloid dimensions, but the teeth at the front of
the dental arch were small, and the canine tooth did not project beyond the level of the incisors. Finally the spinal cord entered the bottom instead of the back of the skull, and the upright carriage of the
head thus indicated was strong evidence that *"Plesianthropus"*
(almost man) was an erect-walking biped, and therefore must have
led a very different sort of life from that of any known nonhuman
primate. This received confirmation from the fragment of femur
(thigh bone) found at the same time.

Some years before, a piece of local publicity had advertised "Come
to Sterkfontein and find the missing link." While Broom had not
been attracted to the spot by this froward publicity, there was a
growing suspicion that he might have fulfilled the prophecy. At least
it was now much less easy to ignore the South African "man-apes"
as they began to be called, although there was still no suspicion even
on the part of their most enthusiastic proponents that they might
actually be very primitive humans. After all it had only been a few
years since the Peking discoveries had convinced a skeptical world
that the pithecanthropines were human and regarded as standing on
the lowermost rung of the human ladder. The australopithecines,
with cranial capacities little more than half those of the pithecanthropines, seemed much too bestial to warrant even the most incipient claim to the status of humanity. Anthropological opinion was
summed up by the American anthropologist Earnest Hooton, a devoted follower of Keith's, in the following limerick:

> Cried an angry she-ape from Transvaal
> Though old Doctor Broom had the gall
> To christen me Plesi-
> anthropus, it's easy
> To see I'm not human at all.

It must be remembered that the general view was that more advanced types of humans existed in the earliest Pleistocene, which, if
true, would have meant that the australopithecines were their contemporaries and could at most have been only crude cousins,

History of the Discovery of the Fossils

Figure 105. SK 46 "Paranthropus crassidens," from Swartkrans, South Africa.

doomed to eventual extinction. While this was hominid catastrophism again and could only be contradicted by inferences concerning the adaptations of the australopithecines based on an analysis of the significance of certain anatomical traits, direct evidence for an informed appraisal was not to come for more than a decade.

PARANTHROPUS

Two years later Broom's vigilance led to the recognition of another australopithecine at the Kromdraai farm, some two miles away from Sterkfontein. The molar teeth were larger even than those from Sterkfontein and Broom felt justified in creating yet another genus and species, *"Paranthropus robustus."* Time has shown that this new name in its full taxonomic sense is not justified.

The thirties were coming to a close, and the pursuit of fossil humans, however fascinating and however significant for the understanding of the manner in which humanity has reached its present estate, was destined to be suspended for a while. The best illustration of the difficulties that beset paleoanthropology can be gained by tracing the fate of the Sinanthropus remains.

Loss of the Peking Fossils

Because of political instability in China, working conditions had been somewhat precarious from the beginning. Choukoutien was sometimes isolated from Peking for weeks at a time by roving bands of "soldiers." Late in the 1930s, the Japanese moved into northern China and the future for paleontological research became increasingly uncertain. Working conditions became even more difficult, and finally, in 1941, Weidenreich was persuaded to take refuge in the

American Museum of Natural History in New York. He brought with him an excellent set of casts, his notes, photographs, and drawings, which enabled him to complete his masterly works on Sinanthropus, but he left the originals in China where they properly belonged as the property of the Geological Survey of China.

Late in 1941, however, W. H. Wong, the director of the Geological Survey, became convinced with good reason that the originals were not safe in China, and, should they remain there much longer, were likely to become Japanese souvenirs. As conditions grew more tense and the American Embassy in Peking prepared to withdraw, Wong arranged to have the Sinanthropus fossils taken along in the hope that they would eventually reach the safety of the American Museum of Natural History. They were packed together with secret documents in the personal luggage of the colonel in charge of the American Marine detachment from the Embassy. Fossils and Marines left Peking by train headed for Chin Wang Tao, the port of embarkation, but by the kind of coincidence that only fate can arrange, they reached the coast on 7 December 1941, just as the bombs on Pearl Harbor ushered in a general state of war in the Pacific.

The Marines spent the war in a concentration camp, the liner on which they were to have sailed was sunk by an American submarine, some of the luggage from the captured train was seen in the possession of the Japanese, but no trace has ever been found of the priceless human fossils. Many theories have been offered to explain their disappearance, but the fact remains that they are gone and no one has any idea what became of them. In their brief resurrection after half a million years in the earth, the Sinanthropus population made a substantial contribution to the understanding we are beginning to have concerning our own evolution, and having thus assured their place in our memories they have passed into what we can only hope is a temporary physical oblivion.

So ended the 1930s, having produced a variety of types of human fossil with enough evidence for geographic distribution to provide us with the basis for an appreciation of the spread of hominid occupation during each of the major stages in human evolution. To be sure, the preconceptions of the majority of scientists prevented them from perceiving this, and it is only possible to make such a statement in retrospect. To those actually concerned with making sense of the fossil record, the thirties seemed to have raised more problems than they had solved.

Problems

As the fossil evidence accumulated, two problems became increasingly pressing. First, and most practically important, was the placement of each in the correct time relationship with the others. Fluorine analysis and allied techniques introduced in the late 1940s served to establish such gross relative differences within localized areas. The use of Carbon 14 further helped to sort out the ages of finds within given stratigraphic sequences and, in addition, enabled the comparison of widely separated areas, since it made possible the establishment of the exact absolute age (up to approximately fifty thousand years) of the objects so dated. Yet further vistas of antiquity have been opened up by the refinement of the Potassium-Argon technique, now being used to give some idea of the placement of the earliest Pleistocene strata.

The second of the problems mentioned above was the growing need to make some sort of evolutionary sense out of the remains discovered. Adequate interpretations could not be offered until some definite picture of the relative stratigraphic ages involved was established. However, it still should have been possible to consider the kind of adaptation made by these early populations from the anatomical features exhibited by the fossil remains that resulted in the development of their characteristic appearance. With respect to interpretations of the australopithecines, it might be argued that there simply was not enough anatomical evidence to consider. In retrospect we can see that there was. This, however, will be the concern of our next chapter.

Australopithecines Again

The postwar period, ranging from the late 1940s to the present, has seen the gradual accumulation of evidence for the characteristics and distribution of the various stages of hominid evolution, with the most spectacular finds again coming from Africa and associated with the australopithecine group. After the war, Broom resumed operations literally with a bang. Although 80 years of age, he was as dynamic as ever, as may be gathered from his use of dynamite in excavating. Petty bureaucracy, in the form of the new Historical Monuments Commission, temporarily prevented Broom from continuing with his irruptive approach. The technical objection offered was that dynamite might destroy valuable evidence for stratigraphy. Not only was this an insult to Broom, but it was also a declaration of ignorance on the part of the officials on the Commission. One scarcely needs Broom's more than fifty years of experience in geology and paleontology to realize that one cannot excavate anything from solid rock by the use of the approved whisk broom and trowel, let alone discover anything relating to stratigraphy. By now, however, Broom, with quantities of new australopithecines from Sterkfontein, was an international figure in the public mind as well as to the rarified little

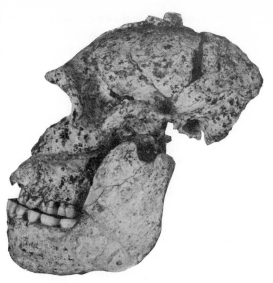

Figure 106. SK 46 with the mandible SK 23, both from Swartkrans but from different individuals. (Courtesy of the Museum of Anthropology, University of Michigan.)

fraternity of vertebrate paleontologists, and he was able to gain the support of an official who outranked the Historical Monuments Commission, namely the Prime Minister of the Union of South Africa. Field Marshal Jan Christian Smuts personally saw to it that Broom could continue unhampered.

Broom's efforts were promptly rewarded with the most important addition to the hominid fossil record since the discovery of "Dart's child," the original *Australopithecus*, almost a quarter century before. In the summer of 1947 Broom recovered a complete half pelvis of his Plesianthropus at Sterkfontein. Of all the pieces of human anatomy, nothing is more distinctive than the pelvis. The dentition is no less distinctive, and it had been recognized for some time that the australopithecine dentition was far closer in form to being fully human than it was to resembling the dentition of an ape. Now, in addition, the first australopithecine pelvis had been discovered and it was radically different from that of a nonhuman primate, and in most important respects practically indistinguishable from that of a human being. Here without question was the pelvis of an erect-walking biped — an organism that was thoroughly terrestrial and had ceased to be a tree climber in the very remote past.

Some skeptics still refused to accept the growing evidence for the hominid status of the australopithecines, claiming that the pelvic and other postcranial fragments were the long-sought remains of modern humans, which simply happened to occur in the same strata as the australopithecine skulls. During the coming years when a quantity of stone tools began to be recovered from deposits of the same time levels containing australopithecine remains, the cry of

History of the Discovery of the Fossils

"ancient moderns" was raised again, and it was suggested that it was not the australopithecines who were responsible for these signs of intelligent activity, but rather that some as yet undiscovered true human had been their author and had furthermore been hunting the australopithecines themselves. A modification of this view still enjoys some popularity.

"AUSTRALOPITHECUS PROMETHEUS"

The year 1947, marking the resumption of australopithecine discoveries, also saw the return of Dart to an active concern with paleoanthropology. In the dump of an abandoned limeworks at Makapansgat, two hundred miles northeast of the Sterkfontein area, his assistants found hominid fossil material for which he promptly created yet another species. He recognized that it belonged to the same genus as his 1924 skull, but because of the traces of carbon in the layers he assumed that fire was the cause, and he therefore credited his new australopithecine with the control of fire. Hence *Australopithecus "prometheus,"* in honor of the fire bringer of Greek mythology. It transpired, however, that the amount of carbon present was so minute that it was in all likelihood only the residue of the organic constituent of the bones and was quite unrelated to any fire, whether deliberate or accidental. Also, in 1947, Sir Arthur Keith, long the most outspoken skeptic on the importance of the australopithecines, publicly acknowledged that he regarded the views he had previously held as being in error and graciously credited Dart with having been correct from the outset. But 1947 was simply the beginning. In 1948 Broom initiated work at another site, Swartkrans, about a mile from Sterkfontein, where, not to be outdone by Dart, he, too, found what he claimed was another species of the genus he had first identified at Kromdraai. This new find he christened *"Paranthropus crassidens."* The reader should not be discouraged by the proliferation of genera and species of australopithecines. A greatly simplified picture will be presented in the next chapter.

Dart, by now, was just getting up steam. In 1948 Makapansgat produced pelvic fragments that, like the Sterkfontein and later Swartkrans pelves, were thoroughly human. Now that he had lived to see his anatomical judgment of the australopithecines vindicated, he embarked on another and more tenuous path—he determined to prove that the australopithecines were toolmakers, hence culture-bearing creatures, and therefore true, if primitive, human beings.

Makapansgat has yielded an enormous accumulation of battered and fragmentary animal bones belonging to animals of the latter part of the Lower Pleistocene ranging from saber-toothed tigers down to hares and turtles, although the vast majority (over 90 per cent) were

Figure 107. SK 48. A crushed skull from South Africa.

from antelope of more than a dozen kinds. While Dart and others considered these finds to constitute clear evidence for the activities of a successful hunter, a careful analysis of the structure of the caves where they were found shows that these were not habitation sites. Rather these caves were sink holes into which the animals of the savanna occasionally tumbled. The crushing and battering evident on many of the bones was simply the result of repeated episodes of cave roof collapse and stratum consolidation and cannot be regarded as evidence for deliberate manipulation.

"TELANTHROPUS CAPENSIS"

In 1949 and again in 1950, during excavations at Swartkrans, where *"Paranthropus crassidens"* had been discovered, there was found a complete jaw and other fragments of the dental apparatus of an individual whose teeth were more like those of a pithecanthropine than an australopithecine. J. T. Robinson, Broom's assistant and successor and the discoverer of the new fragments, created yet another genus and species, *"Telanthropus capensis,"* which he now regards as identical with the pithecanthropines. He also assumes that the population represented was a contemporary of the Paranthropus material, but with the poor control over the relative (and

History of the Discovery of the Fossils

even the absolute) dating, this would seem to be a risky supposition to make, particularly in view of the complexity it introduces into interpretations of the australopithecine material.

If Paranthropus was contemporary with a pithecanthropine population, then we are faced with the difficulty of having to explain in terms of population isolation and differential selective pressures how they ever came to diverge in their evolutionary history. Robinson makes such an attempt, and this we shall consider later. At the moment, suffice it to say that this seems to us to be another application of the catastrophist view that we reject in principle.

Neanderthal Man in the Far and Near East

Before completing our discussion of the fossil finds that concern australopithecines and Africa, we shall digress for a moment and mention some material that has been slightly overshadowed by the voluminous, spectacular, and extremely early finds south of the Sahara. In the Far East, the Chinese resumed work at Choukoutien in 1949 and a scattering of finds has resulted, adding to the Sinanthropus material. More important was the find, some distance north of Canton in southern China, of a skull cap including most of the right eye socket of what appears to be a genuine Neanderthal. This discovery at Ma-pa in 1958 marks the first appearance of a Neanderthal on the soil of continental eastern Asia, and, except for some teeth, this is the only fossil to fill the gap between the earlier Sinanthropus material and historic China.

Had it not been for the wealth of material coming out of Africa, the most spectacular finds to follow the war would have been the skeletal material excavated by Ralph Solecki of Columbia University at

Figure 108. The Ma-pa skull. Frontal and right lateral views. (After Woo, *Vertebrata Palasiatica* 3, No. 4, Plate I, 1959.)

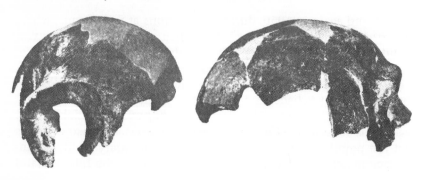

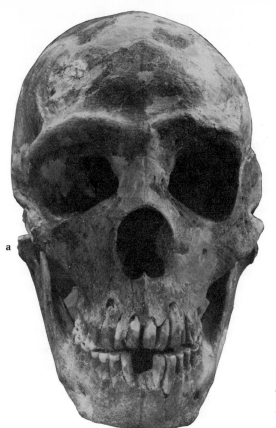

a

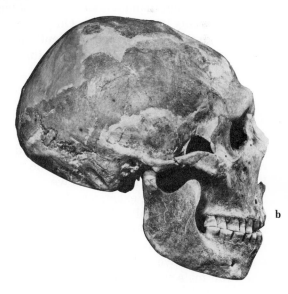

b

Figure 109 (a and b). Skull of Shanidar I. Frontal and lateral views. (Courtesy of the Iraq Museum, Baghdad.)

History of the Discovery of the Fossils

Shanidar cave in the Zagros Mountains of northern Iraq. Despite the various hardships that inevitably beset the archeologist who digs in the various corners of the world—like running out of money at the crucial moment, or getting caught in local revolutions—Solecki has been digging intermittently at Shanidar cave since 1951. The first skeleton was found in 1953, and although an infant, it already showed signs that it would have grown up to be a Neanderthal. Since then there has been ample proof of this supposition. To date Solecki has discovered more than half a dozen skeletons, some badly crushed and incomplete, but all of full classic Neanderthal form.

Perhaps the most important aspect of Solecki's work is the light it throws on the sequence of human evolutionary stages in the Middle East. If, as was once claimed, southwestern Asia was the cradle of the development of the elusive modern *sapiens* form, then one should expect some sign of it in the upper parts of the Pleistocene. Mount Carmel, when it was believed to be third interglacial, was taken to be a possibility of such an occurrence. But as has been seen, Skhūl is estimated as being around 35,000 B.C. and coincident with the climatic amelioration between the two maxima of the last glacial stage. Tabūn then would be at least five thousand years older, and the distinct possibility is opened up that the population of which the Tabūn female was a member could be ancestral to the Skhūl population. Shanidar does not prove that such a development must have occurred, but it does prove that the Tabūn female was not a lone out-of-place Neanderthal. A C14 determination shows that the Neanderthals of northern Iraq lived about fifty thousand years ago with the temporal extent of their occupation from perhaps a few thousand years more recent than that date back to somewhere in the neighborhood of seventy thousand years. Only a fraction of the Shanidar cave has been excavated, and we confidently look forward to the discovery of many more Neanderthals from this the richest site of its time period.

The Amud Skeleton

Other sites, both old and new, have yielded their secrets to persistent research efforts, but we do not have the space to mention them all. We would be remiss, however, if we did not call attention to one of the most outstanding examples of careful research and elegant presentation of the results. During the early 1960s, a Japanese team under the direction of Hisashi Suzuki of the university of Tokyo carried out a meticulous excavation at Amud Cave in the Galilee Mountains just northwest of Lake Tiberias (the Sea of Galilee) in Israel. The adult male skeleton excavated during the 1961 field season displays a set of characteristics intermediate between the full Neanderthals of Shanidar and the "primitive modern" appearance of the material from Skhūl at Mount Carmel. The date appears to be about halfway between Shanidar and Skhūl as well, and the stone tools represent a transition from the Mousterian to a local form of the Upper Paleolithic. In every respect, then, Amud provides evidence for the course by which modern form developed from a Neanderthal predecessor.

Louis Leakey and Olduvai Gorge

The final series of discoveries that we shall cover in this survey are those that have been made in various parts of East Africa during the sixties and seventies. These finds and the work that continues there as we write these lines can be regarded as the result of the initiative and persistence of the British archeologist, the late L. S. B. Leakey (1903–1972). Leakey was another one of that rare and astonishing breed of dedicated men who devoted a lifetime to a subject that has demanded tedious and frequently thankless labor without offering much prospect of worldly reward. He had been working at the systematic study of East African prehistory since the mid-1920s, and since 1931 he had been periodically making expeditions to a site rich in archeological remains as well as the fossilized bones of Pleistocene mammals. This site is Olduvai Gorge in northern Tanzania where Leakey had uncovered one of the most important archeological sequences ever found, involving the transition from the crudest recognizable chipped stone tool (Figure 110) to the classic "handaxe" (Figure 111) of the kind which Boucher de Perthes a century ago used to advance his claims for the prehistoric existence of humans.

Figure 110. Oldowan pebble-tools (lava), Bed I, Olduvai Gorge, Tanzania, East Africa. (From K. P. Oakley, *Man the Tool-Maker*. Courtesy of the British Museum, Natural History.)

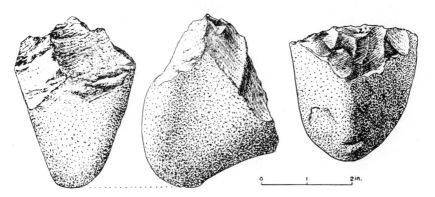

History of the Discovery of the Fossils

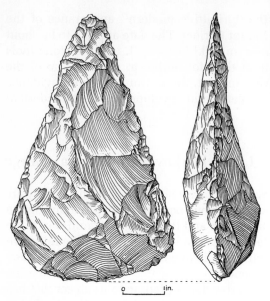

Figure 111. Acheulian hand-axe associated with the Swanscombe skull. (From K. P. Oakley, *Man the Tool-Maker.* Courtesy of the British Museum, Natural History.)

This discovery alone would have assured Leakey a permanent place among the most eminent contributors to our knowledge of human origins, since this clearly demonstrated that the oldest evidence of human culture comes from Africa. One of the generally stated reasons for the relegation of the australopithecines to a nonhuman status had been the fact that no stone tools had been found in the deposits that yielded the bones of the australopithecines themselves, although crude pebble tools did exist in the river valley deposits that were contemporaneous with the cave breccias containing the fossils. Then in 1957, a few unmistakable stone tools were found at Sterkfontein. While this somewhat shook the formerly confident claims concerning the cultureless state of the australopithecines, it was now claimed that the layer that contained them must necessarily be later in time. Swartkrans also had yielded tools, but little note had been taken of them until the Leakeys had produced ample evidence for their distribution and antiquity by their years of labor at Olduvai Gorge on the edge of the Serengeti Plain in Tanzania.

"ZINJANTHROPUS BOISEI"

The Leakeys not only found the most primitive of tools, they then proceeded to find remains of the "man" who had made them. On 17 July 1959 at Olduvai Gorge, Mary Leakey found a fragmentary but reconstructable skull in the midst of a working floor of early stone tools where, by the quantity of waste flakes, it was evident that the tools had been in process of manufacture. The skull, apparently, be-

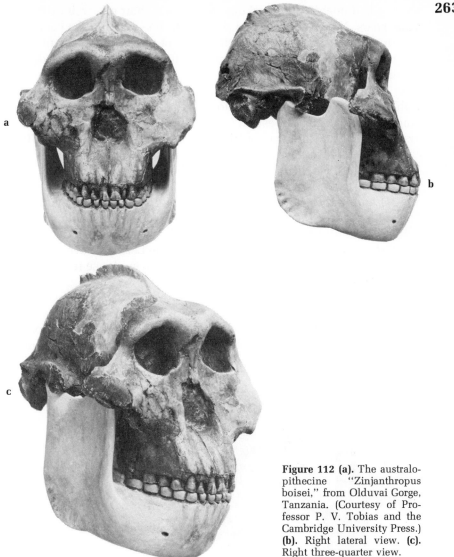

Figure 112 (a). The australopithecine "Zinjanthropus boisei," from Olduvai Gorge, Tanzania. (Courtesy of Professor P. V. Tobias and the Cambridge University Press.) **(b).** Right lateral view. **(c).** Right three-quarter view.

longed to one of the manufacturers. When Leakey himself first looked at the skull, he was aware of the implications depending on a correct diagnosis of the stage of hominid evolution to which it should be assigned, but there was no problem in making this judgment. There could be no doubt that this was an australopithecine. To be sure, he followed the lamentable practice of African paleoanthropologists in assigning it a new generic and specific name, *"Zinjanthropus boisei."* "Zinj" is the old Arabic word for East Africa, and *"boisei"* was in honor of Charles Boise whose financial backing had enabled the Leakeys to maintain their research over so many years. Nevertheless, the discovery of the skull and the context within which it was found constitute one of the most important—if not *the* most important—single contribution to the understanding of human origins ever made.

As a result of the work of the Leakeys, we now know that our highly touted "Western Civilization" actually had its remote beginnings in Africa. This "Western Civilization" is an outgrowth of the first farming Neolithic way of life in eastern Europe and the Middle East, which in turn developed out of the hunting and gathering way of life of their Paleolithic precursors in the same regions. The Paleolithic itself extends far back into the Pleistocene, where we see its earliest and crudest form expressed in eastern and southern Africa. This must mean that human physical origins are traceable to the same place. Culture without a creator is, of course, an impossibility, and the creator by definition is human. As the Leakeys have shown, this human at the earliest stages of the tangible evidence for culture was an australopithecine.

The deserved recognition that came to the Leakeys as a result of the Zinjanthropus discovery brought with it a vast increase in the amount of financial backing for renewed excavations at Olduvai Gorge. One of the severest problems that had beset Leakey's operations over the years had been transporting supplies over the non-

Figure 113. "Zinjanthropus." Palate and teeth, compared with those of a modern man below. (Des Bartlett, Armand Denis Productions.)

The Fossil Record

Figure 114. Olduvai Gorge from the south rim.

Figure 115. Olduvai Gorge Site FLK I, where "Zinj"
was found in 1959.

existent roads. The nearest water, for instance, was thirty-five miles away, and survival itself required more than a minimum of precautions since such not insignificant inhabitants of the area as poisonous snakes, leopards, rhinoceroses, and lions regarded the place as their home. With the additional financial backing, the Leakeys were able to enlarge the extent of operations considerably, and during the following year it was possible for them to accomplish more than twice the work they had done in the preceding thirty.

The expanded activities paid off, and late in 1960 they discovered more australopithecine remains from an even earlier level in Olduvai Gorge. While the bones of Zinjanthropus had belonged to an individual of approximately eighteen years of age, this new find was that of an early adolescent. Although immature, the bones of the left foot provided confirmation, in addition to the evidence offered by the pelves of the South African australopithecines, for the erect bipedal mode of locomotion of these early hominids.

As if this were not enough, the final dramatic find of the season, made 2 December 1960, provided solid confirmation for the view that the australopithecines were the ancestors of the pithecanthropines, for in Bed II, a level substantially younger than the Zinjanthropus level of Bed I, they discovered a fully pithecanthropine skull (Figure 120) in association with evidence for a culture that had evolved without break from the pebble tools of Bed I.

The crowning touch to the work of the Leakeys was added when some perspective was given to the age of Zinjanthropus as a result of a Potassium-Argon determination. On the basis of former estimates of an age bordering on one million years for the extent of the Pleistocene, they had estimated that Zinjanthropus must be in the neighborhood of six hundred thousand years old, which would have made him roughly a contemporary of Pithecanthropus in Java. The date that the Potassium-Argon determination indicates for their find is three times that figure, being a million seven hundred and fifty thousand years.

With the publication of the date for the "Zinj" skull, an entirely new era in the study of human evolution was inaugurated. No longer could the australopithecines be passed off as too recent in time to have given rise to the pithecanthropines. In fact the new dates, initially from Olduvai Gorge, but confirmed and extended elsewhere in East Africa, have provided ample time for the slow development of human form. Before these dates were available, some evolutionary biologists had felt that the evolution of humans in the Pleistocene must have been much more rapid than that usually encountered in other mammalian groups. A number of efforts were made to rationalize this presumed "quantum" evolution, but the new dates again have made such intellectual acrobatics unnecessary.

Ironically, once the Leakeys had provided the evidence that al-

Figure 116. Dr. L. S. B. Leakey measuring "Zinjanthropus." Under his right hand is the skull of a chimpanzee. (Courtesy of the National Geographic Society.)

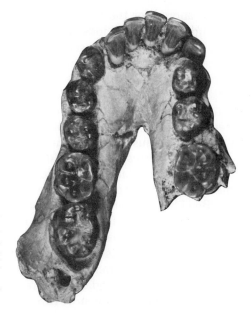

Figure 117. OH 7, the adolescent mandible that has been offered as the type specimen for "Homo habilis," the supposed "true man" from Bed I at Olduvai Gorge, Tanzania. In fact it is a good representative of *Australopithecus*.

History of the Discovery of the Fossils

lowed us to give serious consideration to the possibility that the australopithecines were the ancestors of later stages of human evolution, the most prominent opponents of such an interpretation were none other than the Leakeys themselves. After Leakey's first enthusiastic claim than his "Zinj" was the maker of the Oldowan tools, which continue into the Middle Pleistocene where they change gradually into more advanced tool traditions, he reverted to the views that have proven to be so hardy in spite of the evidence (or its lack). Specifically, he returned to the idea that "Zinj" was really a crude, specialized, and aberrant form incapable of cultural sophistication, and that the tools had really been made by a form of "true man" for which there was, as yet, only the scrappiest kind of evidence. "Zinj," then, may have been a victim of this more advanced hominid. If the argument sounds remarkably like the old attempt to deny the Neanderthals a place in the line of human evolution, one should not be too surprised. Leakey received his formal training at Cambridge at a time when Piltdown was generally accepted as a representative of a modern form existing at a very ancient time level, although even during its heyday its claims were not always regarded as fully convincing. Yet the conviction of the existence of an ancient modern never wavered and was one of the driving forces behind the years of Leakey's field work.

The Quest for Early "True Man"

So despite the world-wide acclaim earned by the "Zinj" discovery, Dr. Leakey labored for the last ten years of his life in a continuing effort to find his ancient modern. These efforts resulted in the discovery of many more early fossils, several of which he offered as possible candidates for "true man," but on closer examination, each has turned out to be something else. He even created a name for this creature, "*Homo habilis*," or skillful man, but of the pieces said to belong in this category, the more recent ones fit nicely within the documented range of the pithecanthropines and the older ones within the range of the australopithecines. But whatever the reasons behind his quest, the result was the discovery of a great quantity of early Pleistocene and late Pliocene fossils. Bed II of Olduvai Gorge contains a couple of specimens that can be regarded as *Homo erectus*, Bed I has yielded a varied assortment of australopithecines, and the widening search for other early hominid sites in East Africa has produced a rich harvest.

Late in his life when his constitution could no longer keep pace with the fierce drive to which he subjected it, other researchers took up the quest. Prominent, and in fact pre-eminent among these, has been his son, Richard Leakey, now Director of the National Museum

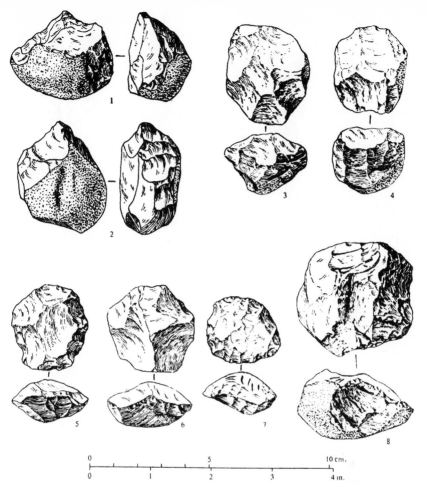

Figure 118. Light-duty choppers and discoids from Lower Bed I, Site DK at Olduvai Gorge. Choppers (1) and (2) and discoids (3), (4), and (8) are made from lava; discoids (5), (6), and (7) are of quartz. (Courtesy of Dr. M. D. Leakey and the Cambridge University Press.)

of Kenya (formerly the Coryndon Museum). Near the eastern shore of Lake Rudolf in the nothern part of Kenya, Richard Leakey has discovered a series of fossil-bearing localities, and he and his colleagues have been gathering a yearly crop of early hominid material. Richard, like his father before him, evidently possesses a generous amount of what a generation of field workers referred to as "Leakey's luck," the gift of finding key specimens in areas hitherto unproduc-

History of the Discovery of the Fossils

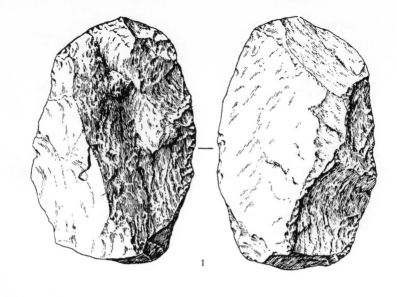

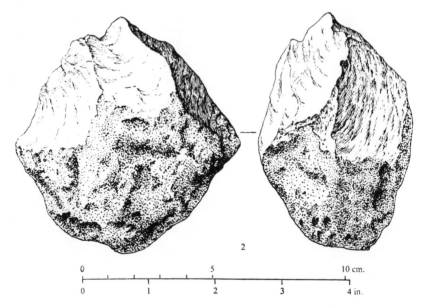

0   5   10 cm.
0   1   2   3   4 in.

Figure 119. Two heavy-duty scrapers from the "Zin-janthropus" Level, at Olduvai Gorge. 1. Double-edged quartz side-scraper. 2. Side-scraper made of lava. Site FLK. (Courtesy of Dr. M. D. Leakey and the Cambridge University Press.)

The Fossil Record

tive or unexamined. But like his father, Richard is driven by the faith that "true man" of some kind must have existed at an early time. This phenomenon is not the would-be *"Homo habilis"* of his father, but some other as yet unspecified representative of the genus *Homo*. So far, however, the most substantial claimant, skull "1470," is indistinguishable from a large-brained australopithecine.

The faith in this ancient phantom is infectious. Late in 1974, a joint French and American field expedition in the Afar triangle of Ethiopia discovered its own candidate. Others have been tentatively identified in the Omo valley of southern Ethiopia, and still others have been claimed elsewhere. There are, however, so many unresolved questions concerning dating in every one of these cases that we can come to no other conclusions in the critical matter of age except to put all these specimens in "the suspense account."

But this should not blind us to the possibility that more than one kind of hominid may have existed at the same time in the Pliocene or early Pleistocene. The situation is rather like that of the little boy who cried wolf. When there really was a wolf, no one believed him. Leakey began advancing his claims for very early "true man" back in the early 1930s and, by the time of his death in 1972, had repeated his claim for at least half a dozen different finds at various times, all of which eventually have been recognized as something else. The same tradition is being perpetuated, albeit with greater caution, by

Figure 120. OH 9, *Homo erectus*, from Bed II at Olduvai Gorge. (Courtesy of the National Geographic Society.)

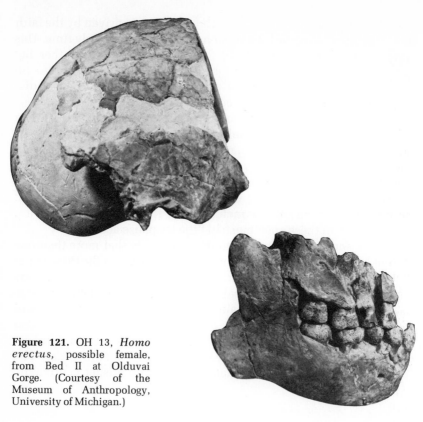

Figure 121. OH 13, *Homo erectus*, possible female, from Bed II at Olduvai Gorge. (Courtesy of the Museum of Anthropology, University of Michigan.)

his son Richard Leakey. And he may have something. Although it almost certainly is not the long-sought "true man" of relatively modern form, the evidence at hand suggests that there may well have been more than one kind of hominid, and that only one of them gave rise to the later stages of human evolution. This will be discussed in greater detail in Chapter 9.

Suggested Readings

Andersson, J. G. *Children of the Yellow Earth*. Kegan Paul, London, 1934, reprinted by the M. I. T. Press, Cambridge, 1973.
   Studies in prehistoric China, containing the account of Andersson's discovery of quartz in the cave at Choukoutien which led to the discovery of Sinanthropus.

Bishop, W. W., and J. D. Clark (editors). *Background to Evolution in Africa*. University of Chicago Press, Chicago, 1971.
   An invaluable survey of the paleontological, stratigraphical, and archeo-

logical findings and problems relating to man's evolution in Africa, by
leading authorities from many lands.

BRACE, C. L. The fate of the "classic" Neanderthals: a consideration
of hominid catastrophism, *Current Anthropology*, vol. 5, 1964,
pp. 3–43.
  A re-examination of thinking on the Neanderthal question.

———, P. E. MAHLER, AND R. B. ROSEN. Tooth measurements and
the rejection of the taxon *"Homo habilis," Yearbook of Physical
Anthropology*, vol. 16, 1973, pp. 50–68.
  A review of some of the claims for early moderns.

BROOM, R. *Finding the Missing Link.* London, 1950.
  Broom's own account of his australopithecine discoveries.

DANIEL, G. *A Hundred Years of Archaeology.* Duckworth, London, 1950.
  Giving an account of the most important archeological discoveries since
  1840.

DART, R. *Adventures with the Missing Link.* Harper & Row, New
York, 1959.
  Dart's own account of his steadfast and illuminating work on the australo-
  pithecines.

DAY, M. H. *Guide to Fossil Man.* World Publishing Co., Cleveland
& New York, 1966.
  A valuable handbook of human paleontology, providing the basic information for each of the sites which have yielded the bulk of significant
  hominid fossils.

HOWELL, F. C., AND F. BOURLIERE. (editors). *African Ecology and
Human Evolution.* Viking Fund Publications in Anthropology No.
36, 1963.
  A major reference work on African prehistory, covering a wide variety of
  topics.

HRDLIČKA, A. *The Skeletal Remains of Early Man.* Smithsonian
Miscellaneous Collections, vol. 83, 1930.
  A fundamental work, and up to the date of publication the best of its kind.

KEITH, A. *The Antiquity of Man.* 2 vols. Williams & Norgate, London, 1929.
  Invaluable for the history and detail of the subject.

KOENIGSWALD, G. H. R. VON. *Meeting Prehistoric Man.* Thames &
Hudson, London, 1956.

274 ———. *The Evolution of Man.* 2nd ed. University of Michigan Press, Ann Arbor, Michigan, 1976.
> Two books, giving firsthand descriptions of the discovery of a number of fossil hominids.

LEAKEY, M. D. *Olduvai Gorge: Excavations in Beds I and II. 1960–1963.* Cambridge University Press, London & New York, 1971.
> The fundamental report on the archeologic findings in the lowermost beds in Olduvai Gorge.

LEAKEY, L. S. B. Finding the earliest man, *National Geographic,* vol. 118, 1960, pp. 420–35.
> A beautifully illustrated account of the discovery of *Australopithecus boisei* (Zinjanthropus).

———. Exploring 1,750,000 years into man's past, *National Geographic,* vol. 120, 1961, pp. 564–89.
> A description of additional finds including the first Olduvai pithecanthropine.

LEAKEY, R. E. F. Skull 1470, *National Geographic,* vol. 143, 1973, pp. 818–29.
> The discovery of a large australopithecine east of Lake Rudolf considered by Richard Leakey to be an early "true man."

McCOWN, T. D., AND A. KEITH. *The Stone Age of Mount Carmel: The Fossil Human Remains from the Levalloiso-Mousterian.* The Clarendon Press, Oxford, 1939.
> The classic description of the Skhūl and Tabūn finds.

OAKLEY, K. P., AND ASHLEY MONTAGU. A reconsideration of the Galley Hill skeleton. *Bulletin of the British Museum (Natural History),* vol. 1, 1949, pp. 27–46.
> The demotion of Galley Hill man.

PHENICE, T. W. *Hominid Fossils: An Illustrated Key.* W. G. Brown, Dubuque, Iowa, 1972.
> A straightforward presentation of human fossil finds, especially valuable because they are presented in alphabetical order.

POIRIER, F. E. *Fossil Man: An Evolutionary Journey.* C. V. Mosby, St. Louis, 1973.
> A cautious presentation of the traditional view of human evolution.

TOBIAS, P. V. *Olduvai Gorge 1951–1961,* vol. 2, *The Cranium*

of Australopithecus: Zinjanthropus boisei. Cambridge University
Press, London & New York, 1967
   The definitive analysis and description.

WEIDENREICH, F. *Apes, Giants, and Man.* University of Chicago
Press, Chicago, 1946.
————. *Anthropological Papers of Franz Weidenreich
1939–1948.* (Edited S. L. Washburn and D. Wolffson), The Viking
Fund, New York, 1950.
   Two books containing Weidenreich's always interesting views on the evo-
   lution of man.

WEINER, J. S. *The Piltdown Forgery.* Oxford University Press,
London and New York, 1955.
   The most fascinating of anthropological "whodunits" by the leading de-
   tective who uncovered the fraud.

WOLPOFF, M. H. *Metric Trends in Hominid Dental Evolution.*
Case Western Reserve Studies in Anthropology, No. 2, Cleveland,
1971.
   The most complete review of hominid dental information available.

————. The evidence for two australopithecine lineages in South
Africa, *Yearbook of Physical Anthropology,* vol. 17, 1974, pp.
113–139.
   A critical reappraisal of the view that assumes more than one lineage of
   early hominids.

The Stages of Human Evolution

Relationships

While a recounting of the history of the discovery of the major human fossil finds helps us to understand their importance as well as the genetic position assigned to them, it does not automatically produce a clear sequential picture of the crucial developments that have occurred in human evolution. Only by arranging the various fossils according to their relative geological ages can such a picture be constructed, and full understanding can be reached only when it is accompanied by a discussion of the major observable differences between the phases considered. Finally, the differences noted must correlate with major changes in selective factors of sufficient importance to have been able to produce such effects.

Before we apply these principles to the human fossil record, we should state the basis of our claim that the known fossils are most realistically placed in a linear evolutionary relationship. It has been argued, particularly by modern French paleoanthropologists, that the vast majority of the fossil plants and animals discovered to date represent lines that became extinct without descendants. These authorities have attempted to apply the same line of reasoning to hominid fossils, claiming that australopithecines, pithecanthropines, and Neanderthals were too specialized to evolve further and therefore eventually died without progeny. This, however, is an argument by analogy and fails to appreciate the real nature of human adaptation.

In spite of the vague claims for the "specialized" nature of various human fossils, the only discernible specialization that humanity has ever developed is culture, and this is only indirectly reflected by skeletal anatomy. Furthermore, as humanity's primary adaptative mechanism, it has done far more to prevent than to cause its extinction (thus far). None of the earlier forms of humanity could have existed without the adaptation of culture, and it is significant to note that the evidence for human cultural traditions commences in the early Pleistocene and continues without break right up to the present time with subsequent traditions being clearly derived from earlier ones by cultural evolution: from the Oldowan to the hydrogen bomb without a break. Since the various hominid fossils can be associated with successive stages in the relatively more complete archeological record, it would be absurd to deny that these fossils represented previous stages in the evolution of modern humans. Finally, if culture can be correctly regarded as humanity's principal adaptation, then major changes in this adaptation should be paralleled by major changes in the anatomy of the fossil humans, and it is our intention to consider the cause and effect relationship between such correlated changes as we discuss the stages of human evolution.

The possibility has been advanced by some anthropologists that more than one primate developed culture as an adaptive mechanism in the early Pleistocene. These developments presumably occurred independently, and it has been suggested that the various australopithecines and pithecanthropines represent these separate lines as contemporaries occupying different ecological niches. We shall discuss this view further in our consideration of the australopithecines. At the moment, however, we should mention the two major objections that contradict such an interpretation.

The first objection is a theoretical one. Culture as a major means of adaptation is unique in the world of living organisms, and for all important purposes can be considered an ecological niche in itself — the cultural ecological niche. There is an evolutionary principle based on the logic of efficiency which states that, in the long run, no two organisms can occupy the same ecological niche. In the end, one will out-compete the other and retain sole possession of the niche in question. Applied to the primates, this should mean that no two forms could occupy the cultural ecological niche for any length of time. This objection has been countered with the claim that the various supposedly contemporary australopithecines and pithecanthropines were in the process of being eliminated in the competition for survival in the cultural ecological niche, but this raises the final and, we believe, conclusive objection.

All the evidence for the existence of culture, from the present day back to the early Pleistocene, appears to stem ultimately from a single tradition, and any claim that different kinds of primates simultaneously invented the same cultural adaptation puts a strain not only on our credulity, but also on the laws of probability. In addition, it adds unnecessary complexity to a situation that can be much more simply explained by a straightforward evolutionary approach.

We will hedge slightly, however, and recognize the possibility that before the development of the tangible evidence (i.e., stone tools) of continuing cultural traditions, there may have been more than one early creature that made tentative advances toward cultural dependence. Since there is now fossil evidence for the existence of hominids a million and more years before the first stone tools are recognizable, we cannot deny that a number of such tentative beginnings may have occurred. But the evidence is ambiguous, and although we shall mention some of the possibilities as we proceed, we shall organize our discussion into a series of sequential stages.

The Four Stages of Human Evolution

To begin with, we recognize four stages or phases in human evolution: Australopithecine, Pithecanthropine, Neanderthal, and Modern. In reality these merely represent arbitrary stages in what is in fact a continuum. The main justification for focusing our attention on these four phases of development is the simple fact that we have more fossil evidence for these four phases than for the periods in between. It seems highly probable that, as more material becomes available in the future, our scheme will have to be modified by the addition of stages or by the modification of some of the stages we posit. Basically our scheme is that of Gustav Schwalbe, with the addition of an australopithecine phase at the bottom. It is already apparent that there may be complications within the australopithecine stage, and further discoveries may cloud things still more. For the time being, recognizing that our stages are arbitrary matters of convenience, we shall adhere to the four here discussed.

THE AUSTRALOPITHECINE STAGE

Bipedalism. No complete australopithecine is preserved although some hundreds of fragments have been collected and recognized. From these we can construct a fair picture of what the australopithecines looked like. That they were all bipedal is clearly evidenced by the form of the pelvis. The broad and expanded crest of the ilium indicates that the trunk muscles were so situated they could serve as adjustors that continually act to maintain the center of gravity in the trunk over the center of support in the legs and feet. The form of the upper pelvis is related to the body balancing, which

Figure 122. Map of the principal sites of fossil australopithecines and humans in East Africa. (Courtesy National Geographic Society.)

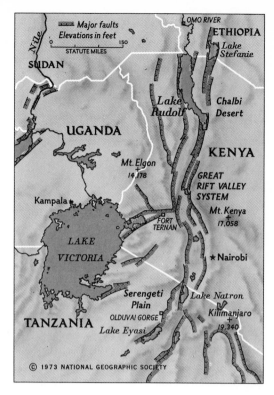

is so obviously important for a biped, and therefore the position of the pelvis differs little from that of modern humans. Earlier workers felt that the australopithecines were less efficient bipeds than more recent hominids. To be sure, there are some minor differences in pelvic anatomy: the neck of the femur in australopithecines was longer, the femoral head smaller, and the blade of the ilium flared outward more strongly. However, recent biomechanical analysis has shown that, if anything, this meant that they were slightly *more* efficient bipeds than more recent hominids. The greater flare of the iliac blade and the longer femoral neck give a greater mechanical advantage to the two muscles, gluteus medius and minimus, which fix the trunk upright over the leg when the latter, in midstride, is the sole source of support. Because such an arrangement requires less muscular effort than that in the more modern configuration, less pressure is exerted on the femoral head, which does not require quite such a large bearing surface. In its functional aspects, however, it is apparent that the australopithecine gait was indistinguishable from that of recent humans. One might ask why recent forms have not preserved the slightly greater efficiency of the australopithecine configuration, and the suggested answer has to do with another aspect of pelvic function, the preservation of an adequate birth passage for a large-brained

The Stages of Human Evolution

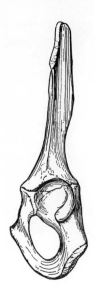
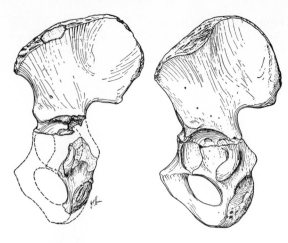

Figure 123. Left lateral views of innominate bones in chimpanzee (left), *Australopithecus "prometheus"* (center), and Bushman (right). Male adolescents taken from dioptographic tracings of the assembled pelvis. (Courtesy of Professor Raymond Dart and the *American Journal of Physical Anthropology*.)

infant. If australopithecine hip width was effectively the same as in later hominids, but the neck of the femur heading in toward the hip sockets was longer, evidently those joint sockets were closer to the midline and the diameter of the birth canal was somewhat restricted. With selective pressures favoring the birth of larger brained infants increasing as time went on, it has been suggested that the increase in the size of the birth canal was accomplished by moving the hip joints outward. This in turn was done by a shortening of the femoral neck, leaving the outer diameter of the hips from side to side exactly the same. Apparently a total widening of the hips would have brought the line of weight transmission far enough from the center of gravity so that locomotor efficiency would have decreased. Apparently the modern condition requiring slightly more muscular contraction to maintain erect posture is preferable to the potential waddle that would occur with still wider hips.

A word on the adaptive significance of hominid bipedalism. If bipedalism were simply a means of locomotion and nothing more, there would never have been any advantage inherent in this development. As anyone who has ever tried to catch a frightened house cat is well aware, *Homo sapiens* pound for pound is one of the slowest and clumsiest of all terrestrial mammals. Evidently if humans cannot outrun even the smallest of carnivores, their chances of relying on speed of foot to evade pursuit by a dangerous animal are lamentably small.

Nor is bipedalism any more efficient for hominid predatory activi-

Figure 124. Reconstructed pelvis and femur of South African australopithecine. The pelvis is level and the foot lies beneath the midline D. The line of action of the abductor muscles is indicated as line A. The line of action of body weight is indicated as line C. The joint reaction force (line B) must then pass through both the weight-bearing point of the hip joint and the interaction of lines C and A. A force triangle can then be constructed (left of main figure) and the joint reaction force calculated in units of body weight. When the ground reaction force and the surface area of the femoral head are considered, the results show that the australopithecine hip-joint pressures were only half those of modern humans. This results from the longer femoral neck, greater lateral flare and smaller stature of the australopithecines. (Courtesy of C. Owen Lovejoy and the *Yearbook of Physical Anthropology*, 1973.)

Figure 125. Schematic representation of pelvic evolution during Pleistocene (anterior view). While maximum pelvic breadth is unchanged, the interacetabular distance increases with encephalization. This increases the torque developed about the hip by body weight in stance phase and decreases the lever arm of the abductors. As a result, the diameter of the femoral head must be larger in *Homo sapiens* than in *Australopithecus* to keep femoral head pressures within physiological limits. These changes also necessitate greater iliac robusticity in *Homo sapiens* as the total abductor force will be greater. (Courtesy of C. Owen Lovejoy and the *Yearbook of Physical Anthropology*, 1973.)

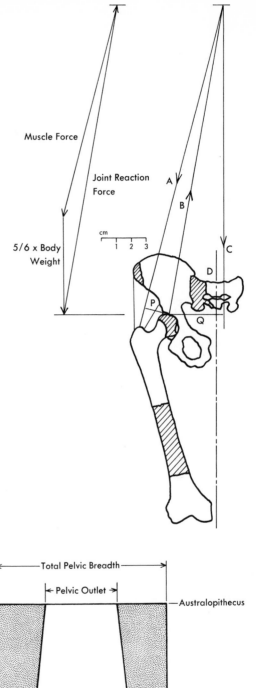

The Stages of Human Evolution

282   ties. A human cannot even catch the smallest cottontail rabbit, let alone run down an antelope in a flat race. In fact it is not certain that a human in full sprint can outrun a bipedally running chimpanzee or gorilla, and these primates are habitual quadrupeds which only occasionally use bipedalism as an alternate mode of progression. It seems probable, then, that speed of progression is not something which has ever had much significance for hominid survival.

Human Status.   If any mammal had to rely on uncompensated bipedalism for its survival, it would quickly become extinct. In the hominid case, however, bipedalism is not uncompensated. The big advantage of a bipedal mode of progression is that it frees the hands from any involvement in locomotor duties. An organism with freed hands can not only manufacture tools, but also carry tools and other objects with it as a substitute for anatomical inadequacy. The regular manufacture of tools and the reliance on them as a primary means of survival immediately implies the existence of a complexity of learned behavior and traditions, which we recognize under the name of culture. Even without any further evidence then, anatomical indications for bipedalism should lead us to suspect that culture was the primary means of adaptation, and since we define "human" as the organism whose primary means of adaptation is culture, then our biped must by definition be human, however primitive. On these grounds alone, we should recognize the australopithecines as human beings, but we must be careful not to overstress their humanity solely on this basis. Early interpreters were so vehement in denying that the australopithecines could tell us anything about the genesis of the human condition that there has been some temptation to stress their human resemblances simply to counteract such views. But now that the fact of australopithecine significance is unquestioned, several recent students have commented that were we to encounter such a group today, we would probably consider it more ape-like than human. In any case, the generic designation *Australopithecus* is here retained in recognition of their difference from the subsequent genus *Homo.*

Brain Size.   Human status was denied to the first australopithecines discovered largely because anatomists had preconceived notions as to what size a brain should be before it could deserve the designation of human. The human minimum was established by Sir Arthur Keith at 750 cc. This he called "the Cerebral Rubicon." The earliest australopithecines discovered all had cranial capacities below 700 cc. Furthermore, Pithecanthropus was already firmly entrenched as the most primitive of possible humans, at least as far as the generality of anthropological thinking was concerned. Then the pelvic fragments were found, and, when *"Paranthropus crassi-*

The Fossil Record

dens" was discovered, Broom claimed a cranial capacity of over 900 **283**
cc. While this may have been a little too enthusiastic, australopithecine discoveries in East Africa by L. S. B. Leakey and his son Richard
have shown that some individuals had brains that were well above
the minimum set by Keith and thus within the very lowermost part
of the normal range of variation of modern humans. Since normal
functioning can accompany such great differences in brain size in
modern humans (approximately 800 cc to over 2000 cc), no great
weight can be placed on brain size as a criterion for determining the
humanity or subhumanity of fossil primates.

Much has been made of the fact that the majority of australopithecine cranial capacities fall at or below 650 cc. This is the approximate upper limit of the range of variation of the living anthropoid
apes, although it should be noted that such a capacity is only attained by the largest of adult male gorillas who generally weigh in
the neighborhood of a quarter ton or more; the australopithecines
ranged from approximately sixty pounds to a little more than twice
that weight. Per unit body size, therefore, the australopithecines
were much brainier creatures than are the modern apes, although the
curve of their body-brain proportion is substantially below that of
modern humans.

The fact that Schultz has described an adult male gorilla skull
with a cranial capacity of 750 cc puts Keith's "Cerebral Rubicon"
completely out of business. In addition, it shows that brain size is no
indication of mental capacity, and at the same time suggests the kind
of variability in brain size that almost certainly characterized the
australopithecines.

Attempts have also been made to magnify the importance of the
sagittal crest that appears in the larger australopithecines, recalling
the condition commonly found in adult male gorillas and orangs,
even though the crests are less developed than they are in these pongids. The assumption has been that the sagittal crest is a specifically
pongid character of great genetic and taxonomic importance, which
indicates close relationship to the nonhuman primates, but this ignores the real nature of the crest and its significance. The crest is the
result of the extension of the temporal muscle, the muscle that closes
the jaw, beyond the limits of its usual attachment on the skull to the
midline on top. There further expansion is limited by the meeting of
the right and left temporal muscles, which now have nowhere to go
but up. If the chewing apparatus grows to such a size that yet larger
muscles are required, muscle then piles up on both sides of the skull,
and the septum between the two muscles at the midline ossifies into
a bony crest that is as high as the muscle mass is thick. The crest,
then, is simply a reflection of the proportion of cranial to facial size.
A primate with a large face and a small brain case will have a crest,
but if the brain case becomes large then there will be sufficient area

on it to provide for adequate muscle attachment without the necessity of the muscle to overspread the whole skull and meet at the midline on top. The sagittal crest should be regarded as a manifestation of functional morphology and not as a feature of much taxonomic significance.

Taxonomic Interpretations. Controversies concerning the interpretation of australopithecine brain size and sagittal crest significance have been generally resolved by most anthropologists. Disagreement, however, remains concerning taxonomic interpretations and relationships. At this point it should be said that as material has accumulated it has become increasingly apparent that existing theories of Linnaean taxonomy are quite inadequate to deal with the complexities presented by the early Pleistocene hominids. Although something more than a postprandial occupation, speculation is at the present time rife in the area of paleoanthropology. Bearing this in mind, we shall use our appraisal of the most dependable of morphological traits, the dentition, to indicate our preferred solution to the problems involved. In what follows we set out interpretations of the australopithecine material made by several students of the subject.

In accordance with the policy of proliferating taxonomic categories, pursued by Broom and softened by Dart, all the South African early Pleistocene hominids have been placed in a separate formal subfamily, Australopithecinae, under the assumption that they were not true humans. J. T. Robinson, for some years Broom's successor in the Transvaal Museum, Pretoria, and now at the University of Wisconsin, has simplified some of the welter of conflicting names by reducing the number of genera to two, *Australopithecus* and *"Paranthropus."*

Subsequently Robinson reintroduced a degree of complexity by removing the specimens he previously called *Australopithecus* and transferring them to the genus *Homo*, while retaining *"Paranthropus"* as before. This would leave the group known as australopithecines without any specimens that could be described as being genus *Australopithecus.*

It is possible to argue several different points of view. The first is the *single lineage interpretation.* Under the single species view it is argued that there is not enough difference between the various australopithecine specimens found to date to justify separation at the generic level, and in fact that there is not yet enough justification to warrant the designation of more than one species. It is further argued that there is no justification for granting them status as a separate subfamily, the Australopithecinae. The authors of the present work have backed off from the view they advocated in the earlier edition of this book in which the australopithecines were all lumped into the genus *Homo.*

The Fossil Record

A number of students of the australopithecines take the view that the presence of robust and gracile forms constitutes good or at least reasonable evidence that at some time in their development the australopithecines split into two lineages. This view has been challenged on the ground that investigation of the small samples involved reveals an extensive overlap in the range of variation of most of the traits exhibited by the two samples, and that it would therefore be more reasonable to suppose that these South African australopithecines represent but a single lineage. This, we feel, represents something of an overreaction to claims by Dart's critics that the australopithecines were of no significance to the study of the hominids proper.

Hominids, indeed, the australopithecines are, and quite properly belong within the family Hominidae, but they differ sufficiently from more recent hominids to warrant recognition at the generic level. Since it is maintained that they can be encompassed within a single species, a return is suggested to the usage established by Raymond Dart in 1925 and the recognition of the known specimens formally as *Australopithecus africanus*. The species designation is less convincing than that of the genus, and this raises problems of interpretation that have contributed to the arguments between the scientists who are currently studying the material available.

When the first australopithecine discoveries swelled to include fragments of several dozen individuals, it appeared to most students of the material that two distinct types were represented. Informally these came to be called the gracile type, early recognized by Robinson as belonging in genus *Australopithecus*, and the robust type, which he placed in genus *"Paranthropus."* Furthermore, it appeared as though the two types came from different sites and truly represented different populations. Before East Africa started yielding its specimens, the gracile specimens were principally thought of as being represented by the discoveries at Sterkfontein and Makapan, whereas the robust specimens were thought of as occurring at Kromdraai and Swartkrans, all in the Transvaal region of South Africa.

According to what has become the conventional wisdom of the field, the most striking difference between the gracile and the robust australopithecines was gross size. It was estimated that the forms included as graciles weighed in the neighborhood of sixty pounds, whereas the robusts were more than twice that in bulk. Next, a sagittal crest was observed on the robust specimens but not on the gracile ones, resulting in a more advanced appearance for the latter. Likewise, it was claimed that the robust pelvis had a long ape-like ischium as opposed to the short, more modern condition in the graciles. Finally, major differences in the dentition were claimed. The front teeth of the graciles were said to be relatively and absolutely

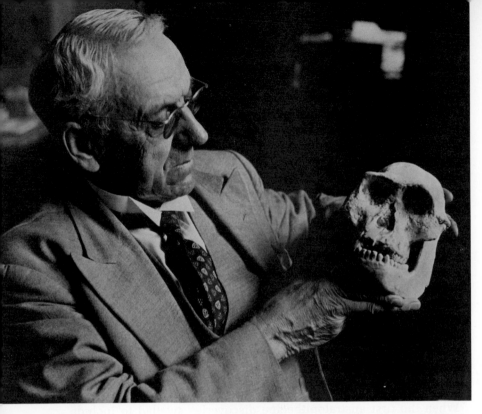

Figure 126. Robert Broom (1866–1951), South African paleontologist with a cast of "Plesianthropus." (Courtesy of the American Museum of Natural History.)

larger than those of the robusts, whereas the molars and premolars of the robusts were said to be substantially larger in size. Robinson offered this as evidence that there was a major dietary difference between the two forms, with the robusts being specialized vegetarians. The larger canines of the graciles he felt indicated a more carnivorous adaptation. In stressing the supposed pongid features of skull and pelvis for the robust forms and contrasting these with the more hominid features of the gracile forms, Robinson has built his case for regarding the former as an aberrant side group that eventually became extinct while the latter went on to evolve into subsequent human forms in the Middle Pleistocene.

This view was originally based entirely on the material found in South Africa, and, given some minor modifications, remains the interpretation of most of the serious students in the field. There were, however, two serious flaws in the initial development of this interpretation, and, in fact, it cannot be substantiated by the South African finds alone. The East African material may yet show that some form of this interpretation has merit, but we shall discuss that possibility later.

Skimpiness of the Evidence. One of the serious flaws in the standard interpretation is due to a problem that perennially plagues the would-be interpreter of the hominid fossil record, and that is the extremely skimpy nature of the evidence. Although fragments of some hundreds of individuals are now known from South Africa, there is no single complete skeleton from any site. The body-size estimates were made on the basis of the application of standard formulas used for that purpose for modern *Homo sapiens* and presuppose measurements from complete leg and/or arm bones. But there are no complete australopithecine arm or leg bones in South Africa, and the body-size figures must be regarded as crude estimates at best. Nor is there a single complete and undistorted pelvis. In fact, the supposedly elongated ischium said to characterize the robust

Figure 127. Profile of mean mandibular tooth cross-section areas in mm² for robust and gracile Transvaal australopithecines. Robust specimens are from Swartkrans and gracile specimens are from Sterkfontein.

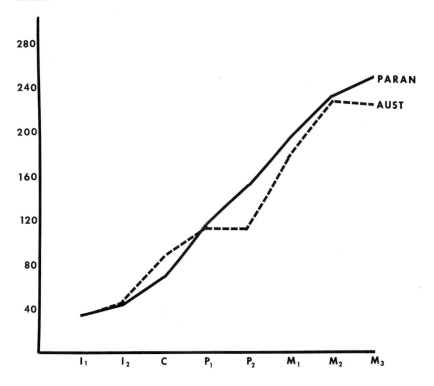

specimens is based on a single badly distorted and incomplete specimen from Swartkrans.

Alleged Differences in Teeth Size. The impression of pronounced differences between supposedly large-molar, small incisor robusts and the small-molar, large-incisor graciles was based on an analysis of selected specimens rather than all of the available evidence. If all the known australopithecine teeth from South Africa and those identified as gracile are compared with those identified as robust, less average difference in size is found, tooth by tooth, than that which distinguishes modern Chinese from Australian aborigines. Not only that, the difference in tooth size of Australians from northern Queensland and those in the Murray Valley in southern Australia is also greater than the difference between the robust and gracile australopithecines. Evidently the dental difference between the supposed two forms of australopithecines would not even be sufficient to warrant the recognition of racial difference if one uses modern human populations as a standard. On the basis of the dentition, where more evidence is available than for any other part of the skeleton, there are insufficient grounds for making a distinction between graciles and robusts at least as far as the South African evidence is concerned.

The Skulls. Finally, the extensive arguments concerning the form of the skull of the supposed two forms were almost entirely re-

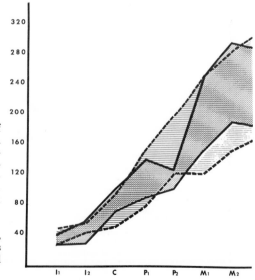

Figure 128. The range of variation of cross-section areas in mm² for the mandibular dentitions of the transvaal australopithecines showing the nearly complete overlap of gracile and robust forms. The gracile (Sterkfontein and Makapan) range is indicated by crosshatching, and the robust (Swartkrans and Kromdraai) is indicated by horizontal shading.

stricted to one toothless gracile skull and two badly crushed robust
ones. The gracile one lacked a sagittal crest, and both robusts had
one, but fragments from Swartkrans suggest that some skulls were
just as smooth and rounded as the gracile specimen from Sterkfontein, and incomplete fragments from the supposed gracile sites of
Sterkfontein and Makapan give clear indications that at least some
individuals did have sagittal crests. It would appear that both robust
and gracile cranial forms occurred at all the South African sites, but
since only one skull was taken to represent the supposedly gracile
sites, and two to represent the robust sites, the perception of average
difference was conditioned more by the luck of the draw than the
average contents of the sites themselves.

Sexual Dimorphism. The relatively complete skulls do present
marked differences in appearance, however, and if these did characterize the differences between the individuals at the various sites
there would indeed be grounds for making some kind of distinction.
This raises the question of the other serious flaw in the approach
used by earlier students of the early hominid fossil evidence. This
flaw was the expectation that the early hominids should show the
same kind of within-group range of variation as exhibited by modern
humans. And why not, one might well ask? The answer is to be found
in the great differences between the nature of the selective pressures
operative on the earliest hominids and those more recently at
work. Although there can be no doubt that the australopithecines
depended on culture in the form of tools and their by-products,
these were of a much less effective nature than those of later manufacture. With implements of a rudimentary sort, one may speculate that the survival problems confronting an australopithecine
group were far more like those confronting a nonhuman terrestrial primate than those facing the skilled tool makers and fire-using
Middle Pleistocene hunters and their more recent descendants.
If the australopithecine way of life was closer to that of the terrestrial nonhuman primates than has previously been stressed,
then we should expect that this would be reflected in the nature
of their anatomical variation. Specifically, the terrestrial nonhuman primates show an average degree of male: female difference—sexual dimorphism—quite beyond that normally encountered in modern human populations. Male gorillas, for example, are
literally twice the bulk of female gorillas, and the same degree of difference is to be found in the widely distributed baboon category.
Evidently the maintenance of group integrity in the face of threatened encroachment by other similar groups and in the face of potential predators gave an advantage to those groups in which there were
individuals who were well capable of fulfilling those defensive

roles. Because of the involvement of females with periodic pregnancy and infant care, inevitably the defensive role devolved upon the male. At the earliest stages of cultural development, then, we should expect that sexual dimorphism among the hominids was not unlike that characteristic of the existing non-culture-dependent terrestrial primates. It is conjectured that since basic defense even at that stage was accomplished by implements or "weapons" and not teeth, we would not expect to find the kind of male: female difference in canine size evident in baboons and gorillas, but it would be no surprise to discover that males were twice the size and robustness of females.

Perhaps, then, the widely held supposition that there were two kinds of australopithecine was created first of all by the expectation that their within-group range of variation should approximate that of modern *Homo sapiens* and second by the use of only one or two specimens to typify whole populations. After all, if males are really twice the size of females and only one individual is taken as representative of the group, one has a fifty-fifty chance of assuming that the average group member is well above the mean of both sexes taken together and an equal chance of greatly underestimating the proper mean size. This, it is argued, is what has happened with australopithecine interpretations. So when we take the best preserved, most frequently found, and most easily measured traits, namely the teeth, it can be shown that group differences between australopithecines from the South African sites are unimportant and the degree of overlap is nearly complete. On the other hand, within a given site one would expect that the range of variation would be large. This may be seen in Figure 129, which portrays a large and a small mandible from Swartkrans where, in the general view, only robust australopithecines were to be found. The difference between mandibles Sk. 12 and S. 74 is greater than can be found in any known modern human population. Such a degree of difference *can* be matched, however, in a modern gorilla population.

Gorillas too show a substantial sexual dimorphism in the development of the sagittal crest. This too is simply an accompaniment of the great difference in body size. Large and small members of the same animal group show their largeness and smallness in different degrees in different structures. For example, among human beings, a pygmy who is very much reduced in body size is also slightly reduced in brain size, but the cerebral reduction is less pronounced than the reduction of the body. There are still the same number of fingers and toes and various essential organs, which the brain has to administer. In a very large person conversely, arms and legs and face increase relatively more than does brain size. If we regard the major bodily difference between individual australopithecines as primari-

Figure 129. Two mandibles from Swartkrans, Sk 74 (above) and Sk 12 (below), showing the size difference between large and small australopithecine specimens from a single site.

ly one of size, then expectably the limbs and face should be larger in proportion than the brain. According to expectation Paranthropus with more than twice the bulk of Australopithecus has a cranial capacity that runs, at most, only one third larger. This means that the musculature needed to operate a chewing mechanism that has increased in proportion to body size does not have an equivalently enlarged brain case on which to attach. Not surprisingly, then, the temporal muscles enclose the skull and actually meet at the top where a small sagittal crest forms for their attachment.

Dating and Distribution. Two problems remain to be discussed concerning the australopithecines: their dating and their distribution. Of these, the more difficult is that of the dating. One of the primary sources of the difficulty is that no two authorities can agree on the age that should be allotted to the Pleistocene. Estimates by the experts have ranged all the way from a few hundred thousand years up to two million, and even the two laboratories that have computed absolute dates by using the Potassium-Argon technique have differed by nearly 100 per cent in their age determinations for the strata of Olduvai Gorge. In the past, many authorities have used for convenience the rough approximation of one million years for the Pleistocene with the feeling that at least this was in the right order of magnitude even if it were not exact. Now, however, it seems increasingly apparent that the Pleistocene was considerably older, some saying three million years in extent, and others pushing it back to five million years where it threatens to absorb all of what was once regarded as the Pliocene.

While arguments concerning the absolute age of the various parts of the Pleistocene continue, more vexing are the questions concerning their relative ages. It is true that absolute age determination could tell without question which fossil is older than which, yet this is not possible at the present time and those problems of relative dating remain unsolved. Even if absolute ages can never be precisely established for the Early and Middle Pleistocene, an understanding of the relative ages of the various fossils is crucial.

It is sometimes stated that the australopithecines could not have been the actual ancestors of the pithecanthropines if both forms co-existed. But this is a dubious argument, for it is quite possible for the unmodified descendants of ancestral forms to live into the same period as other descendants that have undergone more or less considerable evolutionary change. Today we have some evidence suggesting the contemporaneity of australopithecines and pithecanthropines in the Koobi Fora area of Lake Rudolf south of Ileret in Kenya, as well as from other sites dating between 1.4 and 1.7 million years. And, of course, we have dates for australopithecines much older than those. Finally, an important fact that needs to be underscored is that the brains of the large-brained australopithecines virtually fall within the range of those of the small-brained pithecanthropines. We therefore see no difficulty in viewing the australopithecines as ancestral to the pithecanthropines.

The adult cranium KNM-ER 3733 found *in situ*, in September 1975, in the Upper Member of the Koobi Fora Formation east of Lake Rudolf (now Lake Turkana) is an undoubted example of *Homo erectus*. A large proportion of the facial bones and teeth have been preserved, and the relatively complete skull vault yields an estimated cranial capacity of between 800–900 cc. In 1969 from the same Upper Member of the Koobi Fora Formation there had already been recovered, and described in 1971, a robust australopithecine skull, KNM-ER 406, with a cranial capacity of 510 cc. As Richard Leakey and Alan Walker have shown, these discoveries conclusively demonstrate that before members of our own genus came to be the sole hominid representatives, there was a period when both *Australopithecus* and *Homo* existed at the same time.

"Zinjanthropus" and "Homo habilis." Until the 1960s, the dating of the australopithecines was the subject of considerable and unresolved argument. The South African deposits where the original finds were made were the results of accumulations in sink holes in limestone country. Stratigraphy and relationships were extremely difficult to determine, and, in the absence of any interleaved volcan-

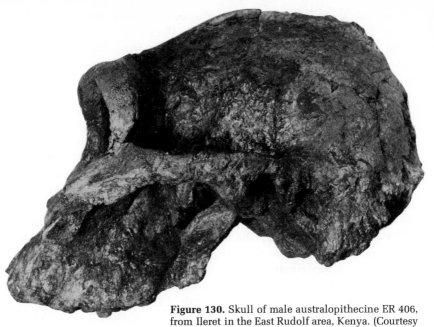

Figure 130. Skull of male australopithecine ER 406, from Ileret in the East Rudolf area, Kenya. (Courtesy of Richard E. Leakey.)

Figure 131. Frontal view of probable male skull of australopithecine ER 406 from Ileret in the East Rudolf area, Kenya. (Courtesy of Richard E. Leakey.)

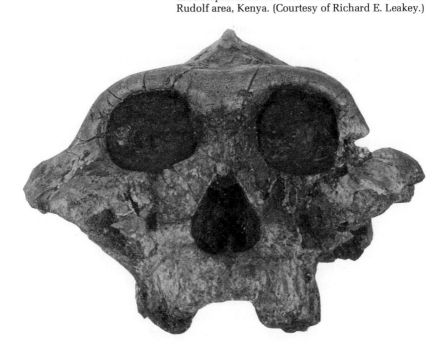

The Stages of Human Evolution

ic material, there is no way that an absolute age determination can be made. Then in 1959, the Leakeys made the first of what was to become a veritable magnificence of discoveries from East Africa, and our whole conception of the early Pleistocene, its fauna and its dating, has been radically changed as a result. The Leakeys' first australopithecine was found in Olduvai Gorge, a canyon on the southeast edge of the Serengeti Plain in Tanzania, and consists of most of the skull and upper jaw (with teeth) of a robust, probably male, australopithecine. They promptly and prematurely designated it *"Zinjanthropus boisei"* and privately referred to it as "dear boy." Best of all, it was in stratigraphic relation to an overlying volcanic tuff that could be dated by the Potassium-Argon technique, and the date, 1.75 million years, is more than twice as old as that of the Trinil layers containing the pithecanthropines of Java. The "Zinj" discovery of 1959 was made in Bed I, the lowermost stratum at Olduvai Gorge; then, late in 1960, their continuing efforts were rewarded by a skull from Bed II, approximately the same age as the Trinil finds. After an initial attempt to claim that it represented the long-sought "true man," they recognized the fact that they had found an African pithecanthropine. The discoveries at Olduvai Gorge, then, have given us the first clear-cut evidence that the australopithecines were not only older than the pithecanthropines but older by a long enough span so that they could serve as logical ancestors to the first accepted members of the genus *Homo*.

Throughout the 1960s, Bed I of Olduvai Gorge continued to produce crude stone tools and the remains of extinct animals and australopithecines. One australopithecine mandible, also found late in 1960, was offered as evidence for the existence of their long-wished-for "true man," for which the taxon *"Homo habilis"* was created. Other specimens from Olduvai Gorge have also been added to this presumed category, although they can all be comfortably included in previously named and well-documented groups. In fact, all the Bed I specimens called *"habilis"* cannot be distinguished from *Australopithecus*, and the Bed II material cannot be distinguished from *erectus*.

So much material has now been found that it is in fact easier to refer to the specimens by their numbers rather than by the nicknames that have been given to them. "Zinj," for instance, is Olduvai Hominid number five, or OH 5. The supposed type specimen for *"habilis,"* also sometimes called the "pre-Zinj juvenile," is OH 7; the *erectus* skull from Bed II, sometimes called "Chellean Man," is OH 9. Another Bed II skull with jaws and teeth, "Cinderella," or OH 13, has been referred to *"habilis,"* although, statistically, the teeth cannot be distinguished from *erectus*. In 1963, a skull washed out of the side of Maiko Gully in a rainstorm and was trampled on by a herd of Masai cattle before it was recognized. Later work showed

some of the teeth *in situ* in upper Bed I. This specimen, called **295**
"poor George," or OH 16, was also referred to *"habilis,"* although
later statistical work has shown that the teeth cannot be distinguished from *Australopithecus.* In fact, it would seem that Olduvai "George" was a female australopithecine. In their efforts to
demonstrate the existence of their "true man," the Leakeys have tak-
en all the more delicately constructed material and lumped it into a
single category. This, we feel, is one of the consequences of failing to
recognize the great average degree of sexual dimorphism among the
australopithecines and, as we shall see later, among the pithecanthropines of the middle Pleistocene.

More Australopithecine Finds. The Olduvai finds have
served to focus our attention on East Africa, and this has been richly
rewarded by discoveries at a great many sites in several different
localities. A massive australopithecine mandible and dentition was
found at Peninj near Lake Natron in Kenya and is dated at about 1.6
million years; a heavy australopithecine skull was found at Cheso-
wanja near Lake Baringo in Kenya and is dated at about 1.4 million
years; a quantity of tools, extinct mammal remains, and scraps of
hominid jaws and teeth have been discovered in datable deposits in
the Omo Valley in southern Ethiopia at the northern end of Lake
Rudolf; extensive hominid, faunal, and archeological finds have been
made at many sites on the eastern shore of Lake Rudolf from 20 to
60 miles south of Omo in northern Kenya; mammalian and australopithecine (erroneously, we believe, announced as "true man") material has been discovered at Laetolil, 25 miles south of Olduvai in
Tanzania; and now exciting new hominid and faunal material has
been found north of Addis Ababa in the Afar region of Ethiopia.

Of all these new discoveries, the most exciting and portentous
have come from the East Rudolf area of Kenya and the Afar Depression area of Ethiopia. As a result of the indefatigable efforts of Richard Leakey beginning in the latter part of the 1960s, more than a
hundred hominid-yielding sites have been located in the East Rudolf
area, and more will surely be found in the future. The range of visible variation in the discovered material is impressive. Some of it is
extraordinarily robust, being large of tooth, and equipped with sagittal crests and heavy muscle markings. Other specimens are smaller
and more gracile of form, and the argument has once again been
raised that these represent "true man" as opposed to *Australopithecus*, to which all the more robust material is generally referred.
Although many are now willing to recognize that there was a great
deal of sexual dimorphism within the australopithecine spectrum, it
is still a matter of doubt whether a single species can encompass the
whole observed range. By 1971, for example, Richard Leakey sug-

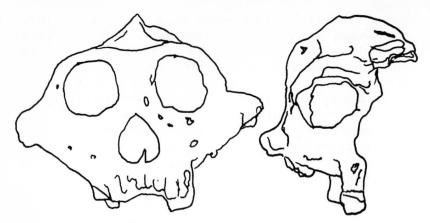

Figure 132. Male and female australopithecines from Ileret in the East Rudolf area (ER 406 on the left and ER 732 on the right) showing what is now being suggested as an example of australopithecine sexual dimorphism. Drawn with the aid of a camera lucida from photographs of the casts in the Peabody Museum of Archaeology and Ethnology, Harvard University.

gested that two relatively complete skulls from Ileret, in the East Rudolf area, represented male and female of a robust australopithecine. These we depict in Figure 132. Yet this form was still thought to be different at the generic level from Olduvai Hominid 24, "Twiggy," found in 1968. To be sure, OH 24 was crushed absolutely flat

Figure 133. A claimed "Homo habilis" skull from Olduvai Gorge (Olduvai Hominid 24 on the left) compared with a female australopithecine from Ileret in the East Rudolf (ER 732 on the right.)

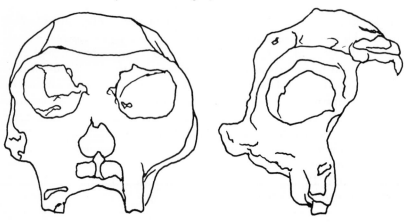

The Fossil Record

when discovered, being no thicker than the palm of a human hand, but the reconstruction seems reasonable, and as we can see in Figure 133, there is far less difference in size and morphology between this particular example of *"Homo"* and the accepted female *Australopithecus* (ER 732) than there is between the latter and its male counterpart (ER 406).

Skull ER 1470. In the summer of 1972, in between Ileret and Koobi Fora in the East Rudolf area, another true *"Homo"* was discovered, this being the much publicized ER 1470 skull. The skull itself is relatively complete. It is rounded of contour and just slightly over 750 cc in cranial capacity. This is at the upper end of the expected range of *Australopithecus* and near the bottom for *Homo*. The rounded contours have led some to welcome this as the long-sought "true man," but we should recall that crest-less *Australopithecus* skulls are also rounded of contour and relatively lacking in heavy brow ridges. The contour of ER 1470, in fact, is remarkably similar to that of Broom's "Mrs. Ples," Sts 5 from Sterkfontein, although the skull is distinctly larger. The giveaway is in the preserved facial skeleton. Although there were no teeth found with it, the roots of the molars indicate that the molar crowns must have been at least the size of those belonging to "Zinj" (OH 5), an accepted robust australopithecine. With a contour like the best-preserved australopithecine skull from South Africa and teeth like the first major find from Olduvai Gorge, it is hard to avoid the conclusion that ER 1470 is a large-brained australopithecine from East Rudolf. However, the endocast of ER 1470 exhibits a broad development of the frontal lobes, which has not been seen in other australopithecines, so that in spite of some of their cranial characteristics it may well be that the large-brained australopithecines, as represented by ER 1470 in particular, represent forms that very closely approach if they do not belong in the genus *Homo*. Since the australopithecines made tools with which to make other tools, a fact that suggests some form of speech, each of these traits—the tool making and the dependence on tools as well as the speech—constitutes a criterion of human status. Together they make a strong case for the human status of the australopithecines. At this level of classificatory analysis it is not so much what the creature looked like, but what it probably behaved like that is of importance. Morphological traits should not be permitted to outweigh functional, i.e., behavioral traits. The desirable thing is to make good use of both by balancing and evaluating one in relation to the other. When this is done with the morphological and behavioral traits of the australopithecines, it is difficult to avoid the conclusion that they represent the transition if not the earliest representatives—at least in their larger brained forms—of the genus *Homo*.

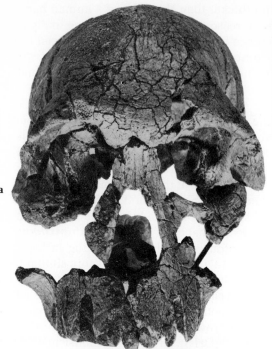

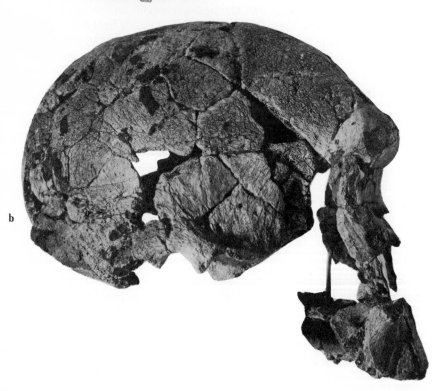

Figure 134 (a). Frontral view of Skull 1470 from East Rudolf, Kenya. (Courtesy of Richard E. Leakey.) (b). Lateral view of Skull 1470 from East Rudolf, Kenya. (Courtesy of Richard E. Leakey.) This view gives a truer picture of the form of the frontal region than does the view from the front.

The Fossil Record

Stratigraphically the specimen comes from below a volcanic layer, the KBS tuff, which was originally dated at 2.6 million years. There were tools at this level, and the first feeling was that this represented a new antiquity for the first occurrence both of tools and of the claimed "true man." However, the paleontologists working at Omo in Ethiopia, only fifty miles to the north, were getting a similar fauna in a well-dated context that was between 1.8 and 2.3 million years old, somewhat younger than the claimed date for East Rudolf. Recently it has been recognized that, although there was nothing wrong with the Potassium-Argon determination of the ER 1470 site date, it did not necessarily prove that the deposit beneath it was older. Some of the volcanic material did indeed erupt 2.6 or more million years ago, but at a later date this older volcanic tuff was subject to erosion and redeposited along with much younger sediments. This instance simply serves to illustrate just one of the many problems that beset attempts to unscramble the events of the remote past, and how necessary it is for all kinds of evidence to be taken into account and apparent discrepancies discussed, investigated, and reconciled before conclusions can be accepted. In many cases, absolute date determinations have served to put the fossil record in its proper perspective, as they did at Olduvai Gorge. In this case, it was an appraisal of the fossils that forced a re-examination of the geology and what it was that the date really signified.

In spite of the differences in age it may be that ER 1470 was contemporary with "Zinj" (OH 5), "Twiggy" (OH 24), and the lowermost deposits of Olduvai Gorge and that it represents the large-brained end of the australopithecine range of variation.

This picture is not as easy to sustain for the other less complete material from the East Rudolf area. One reads repeated claims that this or that leg bone indicates the presence of *"Homo"* rather than an australopithecine, but the leg bones and feet of *Homo* and *Australopithecus* are identical through most of their range of variation. Simply because the bones of the lower extremities look like *Homo* does not constitute sufficient reason to declare that it cannot be an australopithecine. Where cranial and dental fragments are concerned, however, there may be some basis for the claim that the material represents more than one kind of creature. We must remind ourselves, as well as our readers, that even though the century-old claim for the contemporaneity of "true man" with this or that more primitive hominid has always proved to be erroneous in the past, the possibility cannot be discounted. Just as the little boy finally did encounter a genuine wolf after many a false alarm, there might really be more than one kind of hominid in the strata of the East Rudolf area. In order to demonstrate this, however, many problems must

The Stages of Human Evolution

be overcome. Not the least of these is the problem of dating. Are the specimens for which contemporaneity is being claimed really contemporaneous? Even where the sequence is relatively secure, real differences in age of half a million years cannot be corrected for simply because of the built-in uncertainty of measuring ages in millions of years on the basis of quantities of radioactive materials at the microgram level. Then too, strata with actual differences on the order of half a million years in age can be superimposed on each other and it may be impossible to tell whether a given fossil at the interface belongs to the upper or lower member. Finally the actual differences between specimens that are offered as evidence for the existence of more than one creature must be examined in terms of the range of variation of the most appropriate modern reference species. As we have noted, there is reason to believe that the modern human range of variation is inadequate for determining the kind of variation we might encounter in an early hominid with a degree of sexual dimorphism comparable to that of a gorilla or a baboon. At that, the modern human range of variation is rarely given full consideration.

Where the East Rudolf material is concerned, we do not know whether the different specimens are really contemporary or hundreds of thousands of years apart in date; whether they were living the same kind of life or were the product of different ecological adaptations; and whether or not they differ more from each other than members of a single population in which a high degree of sexual dimorphism is the normal condition. Of these various problems, those related to dating are the most difficult to solve. More field work will help, but because of difficulties with techniques and the nature of natural deposits, a measure of uncertainty will always remain. The problems relating to the significance of anatomical differences are easier to handle, but even here the material is often incomplete and badly preserved (although new discoveries from more field work can help here also) and there remains the problem of whether the comparisons are really being made between individuals that lived within half a million years of the same time.

"Lucy" from Afar. Before leaving our consideration of the important new East African hominids of the Pliocene and early Pleistocene, we should make mention of the remarkable discovery made by Donald C. Johanson of the joint French-American expedition in the Afar Depression area of Ethiopia late in 1974. There in one of the hottest, driest, and most desert areas of Africa, a series of important fossil primates have been discovered. Among these is the skeleton of a late Pliocene or early Pleistocene (depending on where the boundary is set) hominid that is significant for several reasons.

For one thing, it is older than the East Rudolf discoveries. Although only one Potassium-Argon determination has been done so far, its age of approximately three million years makes it one of the very earliest hominids found to date. Not only is it very early, but it is also remarkably complete. In addition to skull fragments, jaws, and teeth, there are ribs, vertebrae, hand and foot bones, and arm and leg bones as well. Although the popular press has again raised the familiar cry of ancient "true man," there can be no doubt that it is an early australopithecine. Furthermore, it is far more complete than any other such find. Up to the date of the present publication only preliminary reports are available, but a number of significant features are already apparent. First, it is clear that the creature was quite small, being somewhere between three and three-and-one-half feet tall, but an erect-walking biped nonetheless. With relatively large molars and an ape-sized brain, but bipedal and lacking projecting canines, its australopithecine status cannot be questioned. The creature was called "Lucy" because its small size suggested a female, although an examination of the pelvis, the best means of determining the sex of a skeleton, did not permit an unequivocal verdict. The pelvis has been cleaned, however, and Lucy's sexual status can now be confirmed.

Ever since human evolution has been accepted as a fact, and the discovery of hominid fossils has been taken as documentation for this fact, there has been an expectation that the earlier stages of the fossil evidence should show a convergence with the pongid form from which the human line is thought to have diverged. Such expectations, however, have only been given substance in slow and piecemeal fashion. For instance, in spite of the efforts to portray the stance of Neanderthals as semi-erect, and of apocryphal accounts of projecting canine teeth and opposable great toes, it is now clear that Neanderthals do not differ enough from modern humans to warrant assignment to a separate species. Posture was fully erect; teeth, though large, are within the modern range of variation; and the postcranial skeleton, although robust, functioned exactly as it does in modern humans. Back through the pithecanthropines and the australopithecines, molar teeth get larger and brain size gets smaller, both reaching anthropoid ape levels with the Australopithecine stage, but other pongid convergences have been difficult to impossible to demonstrate.

Two aspects of Lucy's form suggest that these long-frustrated expectations were not on the wrong track. An examination of the postcranial skeleton reveals that Lucy, like all later hominids, was well adapted to an erect, bipedal mode of locomotion, but that the arms were uncommonly long in proportion to total body size. They are not longer than the legs, but they do approach them in length. While

The Stages of Human Evolution

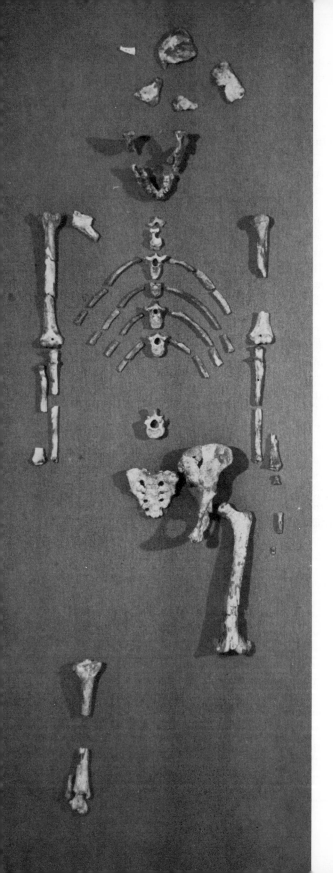

Figure 135. Skeletal remains of "Lucy," a Late Pliocene or Early Pleistocene Austral-opithecine from the Afar Depression Area, Ethiopia. (Photo by David Brill, (c) National Geographic Society.)

there is no suggestion that they functioned in a fashion unlike that of more recent hominid arms, the suspicion immediately comes to mind that Lucy was closer to a past in which the arms played a role in locomotion rather more fully than in any other fossil hominid for which we have the requisite preserved pieces.

Second, the lower first premolar (the tooth right behind the lower canine) shows a front-to-back elongation, which also points toward an ancestry in which that tooth played a special role. In all other known hominids, the premolars are simply crushing teeth used for essentially the same kinds of things as molars. In creatures with enlarged canine teeth, on the other hand, the lower first premolar tends to be elongated front to rear with the crown elevated into the form of a knife-like cutting edge. As the jaw is closed, this forward-sloping ridge slides up on the inside of the projecting upper canine, the two functioning as the blades on a pair of shears. A premolar of this form is called a sectorial, or cutting, premolar. Even when no canines are present in a fossil mandibular fragment, the presence of a sectorial lower first premolar indicates that the canines were enlarged to project above the dental occlusal surface, and the conclusion that most would accept is that the possessor could not have been a hominid. But if the general ancestral condition did feature pongid-like projecting canines (a condition questioned by a few doubters), we should expect to find some hint of it either in the canines or the lower first premolars of the earliest hominids. To be sure, a couple of isolated australopithecine canines from Sterkfontein and one from Swartkrans in South Africa do hint at the possibility that a large canine had been the ancestral condition, but these are isolated and undatable finds. In Lucy, the teeth are implanted within the jaw of a relatively complete and datable early australopithecine, and the lower first premolar is suggestively elongate—not sectorial, but definitely a bit drawn out.

Although Lucy has elicited much contemporary public attention, there are many other interesting specimens that Johanson and his colleagues have discovered as a result of their work in the Afar Depression of Ethiopia. In some of these, the observer can detect a somewhat unhominid-like enlargement at the front end of the jaw, evidently related to expanded dimensions of incisors and canines. Whatever the verdict, the evidence from the Afar Depression suggests that we are closer to the time of the pongid-hominid split than indicated by any previous discovery.

Tools, Culture, and the Australopithecines. So far, we have concentrated principally on australopithecine anatomy and its indications, and now, using both this and other sources of information, we shall try to say something about the general way of life of the australopithecines. Despite a premature enthusiasm for the idea that hominid hunting activities were adopted during the australopithecine stage, the discoveries made since 1960 have not given it much support. We suspect that the predilection for such a view as well as the ease with which the public accepted the imagery evoked by "killer-ape" types of catch phrases is due in no small part to the common assumptions in the background of Western Civilization regarding the innate depravity of humanity—a kind of secularized belief in the doctrine of original sin.

It must be inferred from the evidence that organisms so anatomically ill-equipped as the australopithecines necessarily had sufficient ability to exchange ideas so that they could plan future activities in which different group members performed specific functions, i.e., they must have had some sort of language, however crude. The tangible evidence for australopithecine culture, largely as a result of the work of the Leakeys, is today much fuller than it ever was. The evidence of the artifacts supports the view that the australopithecines must have had some form of language, for in addition to the unifacial and bifacial choppers known as "pebble tools" by far the larger number of their artifacts were clearly made for a variety of specialized purposes.

The tools from the lowermost bed (Bed I) are made from chert and tuff and comprise some five different types of choppers, several kinds of polyhedrons, discoids and spheroids of various sizes, and light duty scrapers, as well as a variety of heavy duty tools (Figs. 118 and 119). It was at this level also that the remains were found of a loosely piled circle of stones suggestive of an artificial structure. This, however, is regarded by some authorities who have seen it as nothing more than an erosion feature. No primate fossil remains have been found at the lowest level of Bed I, but the tools indicate use in cutting, pounding, and scraping, and in the butchering of small animals.

Similar tools have been found by Richard Leakey at Lake Rudolf in Northern Kenya with a radiogenic argon date of less than 2 million years, and also by Clark Howell in the Ethiopian part of the Omo Valley. The age of the finds at Omo is thought to be in the vicinity of 2 million years. In both instances the associated remains of australopithecines were found.

Mary Leakey suggests that the presence of spheroids in Beds I and II at Olduvai may indicate their employment as the essential parts of bolas, a hunting implement still in use in many parts of the world to bring down birds in flight and running animals by entangling their legs in the ropes from which the spheroids are swung.

The existence of an array of tools in early Pleistocene strata from the coast of North Africa to the Cape proves that some creature was relying on culture in the broader sense as its primary means of survival. We would argue that such a creature warrants the designation hominid rather than pongid, but whether one should go so far as to call it "human," or not, remains an open question.

The australopithecine tools we have described belong to a cultural tradition called Oldowan, after the clear developmental sequence described by the Leakeys during their forty years of work in Olduvai Gorge. If, as we have argued, the australopithecines culture enabled them to survive, then the Oldowan tools, including hammerstones and anvil stones, i.e., tools with which to make tools, constituting the only evidence for the existence of culture in the early Pleistocene, must be the products of australopithecine manufacture. Consequently, the distribution of tools of Oldowan type must coincide with the distribution of australopithecines. Furthermore, if humans are to be defined as the creatures who make tools with which to make other tools on the use of which they are dependent for their continued survival, then the australopithecines would have to be considered human. It is a question, however, whether such a definition of humanity adequately defines and distinguishes it. Finally, we should perhaps take notice of the fact that definitions can be meaningful only at the end of an inquiry rather than at the beginning or in the middle, and we are far from certain that we have even yet reached so much as the middle of our inquiry into the origins and distinctive characteristics of humankind. The very earliest australopithecines are not accompanied by any recognizable tools at all, but since it is difficult to imagine how they were able to survive without them, the suggestion has frequently been tendered that they were making tools with perishable materials. Among the nonagricultural peoples of the present and the recent historical past, the most basic and universal tool is the simple wooden digging stick. Add to this the observation by one anthropologist that savanna baboons could effectively double their food-getting activities by the use of a digging stick, and we suspect that this may well have been the key that allowed the early australopithecines to compete successfully with baboons for the resources of the Pliocene and early Pleistocene savannas. Not only is a digging stick useful in gathering starchy tubers, roots, and bulbs, but turned the other way, it can be used as a crude but effective predator deterrent. If a baboon is actually forced to use its formidable canine teeth for defensive purposes, it must literally come to grips with the would-be predator, a decidedly uncomfortable position in which to be if same is a hungry leopard. The wielder of four or five feet of pointed stick, on the other hand, can produce its deterrent effect at a slight remove. That too may be decidedly uncomfortable, but one could argue that those creatures who did their defending even from the slight distance of a few feet would have a fitness $(\overline{W})$ that was somewhat greater than those whose de-

Figure 136. Pebble-tool distribution through the tropics of the world. (Drawing by Mary L. Brace and Richard V. Humphrey.)

fensive activities brought them literally cheek by jowl with their enemies. This also may have given the early australopithecines a competitive edge in vying for a place among the savanna-dwelling creatures of the Pliocene and early Pleistocene. This may be the reason why australopithecine canines are already reduced to the level of the incisors long before the appearance of the first stone tools.

The earliest Oldowan tools (Figure 110) were apparently restricted to Africa in the Lower Pleistocene. As can be seen in the map of Oldowan tool distribution (Figure 136), eventually Oldowan tools came to be found throughout the tropics of the Old World including India, Southeast Asia, out into Indonesia, and also up into the temperate latitudes of China and Europe, the latter being in the form called Clactonian after its early recognition at Clacton-on-Sea in England. Recent evidence suggests, however, that the northern and eastern extensions of pebble tools may have an antiquity that is little better than half that of the earliest African finds. As of now, an African origin seems likely.

The Fossil Record

Hunting and Scavenging. While our sweep entirely encompasses the tropics of the Old World, it is not to be assumed that the archeological remains are particularly abundant or that the human populations represented were ever particularly dense. The evidence, especially the fortunate Zinjanthropus find, indicates that the hunting part of human foraging activities was primarily concerned with immature animals. Apparently techniques had not yet been developed whereby regular and successful hunting of the abundant numbers of Pleistocene mammals could be practiced. Possibly the most explicit demonstration of this to date has been the discovery by Richard Leakey in the East Rudolf area of a quantity of pebble tools and flakes surrounding the remains of an extinct hippopotamus. Some have interpreted this as evidence for big-game hunting, but there is reason to believe that this only represented scavenging. For one thing, half the hippopotamus skeleton has been preserved nearly intact down to the toe bones. Evidently the hominids who wielded the butchering tools left one whole side of the creature undisturbed. Geologists, paleontologists, and archeologists have all participated in determining the circumstances related to the burial and fossilization of the ancient and now-extinct hippopotamus. During its life, the area to the east of Lake Rudolf was better watered than it is now. Meandering rivers with tree-lined banks flowed through the savanna land and joined the lake. A hippopotamus in one of those rivers died of unknown causes, presumably natural, and floated downstream until it grounded in the delta. As it lay on its side in the shallows, it became embedded in the silt of the river bottom. A group of itinerant australopithecines chanced on it, manufactured a quantity of tools, and set about butchering the exposed portion. They left the part that was beneath the mud, and it was this that eventually became fossilized, to be excavated more than a million years later by Richard Leakey and his assistants, the remote descendants of those who had made the butchering tools in the first place.

From this and other less dramatic finds, it is known that the australopithecines were scavengers, and there is no positive evidence that they hunted anything more formidable than turtles, lizards, rodents, and the newborn or young of larger mammals. Scavenging, however, is not effective in providing the principal subsistence for anything larger than a vulture. Even the supposedly cowardly hyena is primarily adapted to active hunting. Most of their hunting is done at night, however, which is why it was not discovered until very recently. It is suspected, then, that the australopithecines were primarily dependent on the gathering of plant foods—roots, shoots, nuts, berries, and greenery—which they ate without benefit of cookery or further preparation. The occasional addition of small game or scavenged food added variety to their diet, but was relatively unimpor-

The Stages of Human Evolution

tant from a nutritional point of view. As a portent of things to come, however, such activities are significant indeed.

Australopithecines and Pithecanthropines. In general our claim for the evolutionary relationship between the australopithecines and the pithecanthropines is supported wherever there is any clear-cut evidence. There are some loose ends, however, which cannot all be successfully resolved. Specifically, von Koenigswald's 1939 "Pithecanthropus" skull came from the Djetis beds underlying the Trinil layers, in which he later found the fragments of two lower jaws he christened Meganthropus." If, as some have claimed, this represents a Javanese australopithecine, it is possible that pithecanthropines and australopithecines might have been contemporaries. Recently a Potassium-Argon date of nearly two million years has been published for the Djetis beds, but this does not mean that the whole deposit of some hundreds of feet in thickness is the same age. Many tens or even hundreds of thousands of years may separate different Djetis fossils, and until a more precise demonstration of their exact position is available, we can draw no conclusions. As for what can be determined from their form, there is not enough of the so-called "Meganthropus" material on which to base an adequate conclusion. Statistical analysis of "Meganthropus" tooth measurements would result in the teeth being classified as *erectus*. If they are *erectus*, however, they are above average in size and, in fact, within the australopithecine range of variation. We feel that this simply is not enough evidence for the existence of australopithecines outside of Africa, and, since this is all the evidence available so far, we close the case for the moment with the old verdict of "not proven."

We should repeat that we have presented a picture of australopithecine development and its significance for subsequent human evolution that is not generally accepted at the present time. Not that it is generally believed to be wrong, although there are those who would so argue, but many authorities claim with some reason that the evidence is not at present sufficient to warrant taking any position. However, we believe that the evidence, the logic, and the internal consistency of such an evolutionary view constitute powerful enough arguments to warrant our stand, and that it is the presentation of an alternative view that would require the support of a great deal more than the now available evidence would allow.

The Pithecanthropine Stage

The complexities and uncertainties that beset our consideration of the australopithecines necessarily made our presentation relatively long. Although many questions still remain unsolved concerning the

no necessity for such lengthy treatment.

The greatest number of pithecanthropines so far discovered has come from the Far East. Not only has this large number come from eastern Asia, but the first discovery of a pithecanthropine was made by Dubois beginning in 1890. The confirmation provided by the Choukoutien finds in the late 1920s and in the 1930s led many people to believe that Haeckel had been more or less correct and that Asia was the original "cradle of mankind." The subsequent finds of skeletal material as well as archeological remains in Africa have changed all this, and it is now recognized that the early and abundant discoveries in Asia were the result of great if somewhat misleading good fortune.

Brain Size. Anatomically there are two major differences between the later australopithecines and the pithecanthropines. First, the pithecanthropines possess significantly larger brain cavities without being different in body size. While larger brains do not necessarily imply greater intelligence for their possessors, when large differences in cranial capacity exist between otherwise similar groups one does begin to suspect that mental differences exist as well. With few exceptions australopithecine cranial capacity lies below 700 cc, whereas that of the pithecanthropines is higher. In fact, the pithecanthropines fall within the lower 300 cc of the range of variation for modern humans. The other major difference appears in the teeth and face. In most respects, the pithecanthropine teeth fall within the upper limits of the modern range of variation. The molars, while large by modern standards, show a marked degree of reduction when compared with those of the australopithecines.

While the remainder of the body is represented by incomplete and highly fragmentary remains, the indications are that below the neck the pithecanthropines were not particularly distinctive, but one look at the face and head is sufficient to tell even the most untutored observer that more changes will have to occur before the form we know as modern human is to be attained. The major morphological developments that occurred during the Middle and Upper Pleistocene have been in the head and particularly the face.

The reader will recall that the selective pressures operating on humans have been progressively changed by cultural adaptations, and, with this in mind, one should expect the anatomical differences between the australopithecines and the pithecanthropines to be related to cultural developments. However crude a measure brain size is for determining intelligence — and it does not work at all when the differences are no greater than those between various living peoples — the great changes visible in the human fossil record show that there was a distinct selective advantage to the possession of increased brain size. Since the primary human adaptive mechanism is the behavioral and technological complex we call culture, it is reasonable to suppose that increases in brain size indicate increases in cultural capacities, and since we presume this to have increased human chances for survival, it is to be expected that these two changes should have occurred between the australopithecine and pithecanthropine stages.

The Use of Fire. The differences of face and head are obvious, but at first glance the cultural differences do not seem correlatedly as great. The chipped pebbles and flakes are scarcely distinguishable from those of Bed I in Olduvai Gorge, but it should be remembered that tools are only a small fraction of the totality of culture, and stone fragments were probably only a fraction of the tools used. We can assume that the nonmaterial part of culture underwent a significant expansion before the Pithecanthropine stage. While this is an inferential assumption, it is not entirely guesswork since there is tangible evidence for the presence of one very significant cultural item that had not been present before — fire.

The earliest evidence for the human use of fire comes from Choukoutien where the numerous hominid fossil fragments of what was originally called *"Sinanthropus"* were found. Fire implies more than might at first be supposed. The hearths at Choukoutien indicate that it was a campsite that was re-used repeatedly over a long period of time. Re-use of a campsite is not a behavioral characteristic of humanity's closest nonhuman relatives and implies that the ability to communicate the concepts of time and place must have been characteristic of pithecanthropine culture. One of the big advantages to an agreed-upon campsite, as pointed out by Irven DeVore, is that the amount of food collected by a gathering and hunting group can be greatly increased since the band can then split up for the day, search in different places, and meet to share their food later on. We can infer that the consistent use of a campsite indicates the existence of a division of labor.

Because of the nature of human reproductive physiology, it is inevitable that the simplest division of labor will be by sex. Women, charged with the care of children, cannot be expected to be as effective in the pursuit of game animals as men. In gathering and hunting cultures from the Pithecanthropine stage right up to the present day, women have devoted their subsistence efforts to the collection of vegetable foods and whatever small animals can be caught with the hands, while men have directed their activities toward the capture of larger game. The competitive advantages conferred by even such a rudimentary division of labor as this must have been an important factor in the successful survival of human groups from at least the early Middle Pleistocene onward. Although it is impossible to identify direct evidence for the sexual division of labor itself, the existence of re-utilized hearths at Choukoutien can be taken as *indirect* evidence for it. It is probable that this aspect of culture became of importance during the Australopithecine stage, but, lacking indications for campsites, this simply remains an educated guess.

The control of fire confers several distinct survival benefits on the possessors, and in addition provides evidence of the increasing complexity of the cultural survival instrumentality. Fire can serve as a source of protection from large predators. Because of the heavy dependence on a visual means of perceiving the world that humanity has inherited from its arboreal primate ancestry, human beings have always been relatively helpless at night. Fire, in addition to providing illumination by which humans can operate, is a substantial deterrent to the depredations of large carnivores.

The protective benefits the control of fire afforded early humans resulted in a somewhat unexpected consequence. Fire permitted the possessors to occupy caves and rock shelters in safety, whereas, prior to this time, such areas would have acted more like traps than shelters. To the modern prehistorian this is an enormous help since it means that the number of places where one is likely to discover the remains of Paleolithic populations can immediately be narrowed down. This may in part constitute the reason why remains of the Pithecanthropine and later stages of human evolution are so much better known than those of the earlier stages. Furthermore, fire has the effect of enlarging the day by providing the light that the setting sun removes. The effect of this is manifold for, among other things, it increases the opportunities for leisurely social exchange and discussion, thus contributing to the development of consciousness, social organization, and cohesion.

Fire also can be used to alter the nature of what is eaten. Cooking breaks down the fibers of protein and converts the starches and carbohydrates of vegetable foods to more readily digestible form. The result is a marked reduction in the amount of compulsory chewing and a consequent lessening in the need for the enormous molars so characteristic of the australopithecines. We suspect that this may well be related to the fact that molar size by the Pithecanthropine stage had undergone a substantial reduction.

The final benefit the control of fire conferred on its possessors was the freedom to extend their range of habitation into areas normally too cold to permit unprotected humans to survive. Humans possess all the physiological characteristics of thoroughly tropical mammals, but, as a result of their increasing ability to manipulate their immediate environment, they have been able to move out of the tropics and take advantage of the extensive living areas of the temperate zones and even the arctic. Fire, while it may not at first have been of great importance, must nevertheless have provided enough artificial

312 warmth to allow the pithecanthropines to extend their range into slightly colder climates. Even without a change in population density, more human beings must have been surviving in the world than ever before.

While the first pithecanthropine hearths recognized were at Choukoutien, recent excavations in Spain, Hungary, and southern France have shown that fire was part of the cultural repertoire of the early Middle Pleistocene hominids wherever their campsites have been found.

Hunting and Hairlessness. At this juncture we should like to indulge in a bit of interpretation that borders on sheer speculation. There is a corollary that might be added to Washburn's observation that the development of the hominid pelvis indicates the adaptive advantage inherent in covering long distances bipedally with the expenditure of relatively little effort. It is true that a foraging animal can increase its food supply by extending its range, but there is another facet to hominid bipedalism that is often overlooked. Slow though they are, human bipeds do run down fleet and nimble quadrupeds by the simple though tedious method of continuing to plod after the animal until it drops from exhaustion. This method of hunting was utilized right into the present century by members of the few gathering and hunting populations that still inhabited a plains environment, for instance, the aborigines of the Australian bush, the Bushmen of the Kalahari desert in Africa, and the Indians in the American Great Basin. This rather exhausting but effective means of hunting depends on two factors. First, a large herbivorous quadruped has to spend a considerable portion of its time ingesting sufficient quantities of its fibrous and bulky food in order to get enough nourishment to survive. If it is kept constantly on the move for a day or two, even if it doesn't have to move very fast, it begins to run out of fuel.

More important, however, is the fact that large furry quadrupeds are less well provided with heat-dissipating mechanisms than are humans with their hairless skin richly endowed with sweat glands. Humans, as is true for the majority of primates, inherit excellent visual powers from their remote arboreal ancestors, but their ability to see is drastically curtailed as the intensity of illumination decreases. Unlike the great majority of terrestrial mammals, the vision of humans is quite poor in the dark, and, since their arboreal ancestry confers on them an indifferent sense of hearing and a very poor sense of smell, it is evident that human activities are primarily confined to the daylight hours when their vision is effective. Of all the major predators in the world, humans alone function exclusively in broad daylight.

Until the advent of humans as a serious menace, the large game

The Fossil Record

quadrupeds had less to fear from predators during the heat of mid-day than at any other time. Hunting canines tend to perform their activities during the latter part of the afternoon, while the big cats operate during dusk and early evening. Humans, however, with their bare and sweaty skin can effectively dissipate the heat generated by metabolic activity. To this day, the Kalahari Bushmen pursue and capture large antelope during the heat of the day. However uncomfortable such activites may be for humans, they are even more difficult for a bulky fur-covered quadruped, which must either seek shade or face heat exhaustion.

Although no proof can be offered for our inference, we suspect that the clear evidence for extensive big-game hunting, which we begin to see in the Middle Pleistocene, was accompanied by the loss of the hairy coat. Whether due to the advantage this gave to a diurnal hunter or simply to the fact that it merely increased the amount of activity, and hence range of operations, of a simple collector, human hairlessness allows for a relatively greater concentration of subsistence efforts during the heat of the noonday sun.

A hairless biped on the tropical savanna is subjected to selection from another quarter, however, — the sun itself. In modern humanity, relatively slightly pigmented people exposed to repeated and prolonged doses of unimpeded sunshine are prone to develop skin cancer. The damaging agent is ultraviolet radiation of solar origin. The human skin pigment, melanin, prevents the penetration of ultraviolet rays beyond the middle layers of the epidermis, and the records of tropical hospitals show no instances of solar-induced skin cancer among highly pigmented patients. It is no accident, then, that hairless tropical mammals all have high concentrations of melanin in their skins. Hairlessness evidently was evolved as a means of eliminating a metabolically generated heat load. In the cases of the elephant, rhinoceros, and hippopotamus, just the amount of muscular effort necessary to move a creature of such bulk engenders the burning of a quantity of calories, and one can readily appreciate the advantages of being able to dissipate the heat so generated via a hairless and sweaty skin. The subsequent adjustment to the problems of exposure to ultraviolet radiation is visible in the greatly increased amount of epidermal melanin, as compared with the relatively depigmented skin found beneath the normal hairy coat. In human beings, it was not so much the great bulk that led to the loss of the regular mammalian fur coat as it was the fact that the focus of human subsistence activities occurs during the hours of broad daylight. In the tropics where human form was originally shaped, this time of day coincides with the period of maximum heat. It seems reasonable to suggest that the hairless skin richly endowed with sweat glands that the unclad human presents to the world was developed as an adaptation that allowed body heat to be controlled where intense and prolonged activities took place during the hottest parts of the tropical day.

Although we cannot prove it, we suspect that the hunting adaptation, abundantly documented in the archeological record, which had emerged as the hominid way of life by the Pithecanthropine stage was crucial to the development of those biological and behavioral manifestations that we regard as being particularly human. We do not really know whether the australopithecines were fur covered or not, but since we have no good reason to assume that they were not, probability favors the assumption that they were. Our inference concerning the loss of the standard mammalian pelt coupled with the demonstration that brain size had doubled, bringing it up to the bottom of the modern range of variation, and molar size had reduced, bringing *it* to within the top of the modern range, leads us to suspect that the pithecanthropines would strike us as being distinctly human if a bit on the "primitive" side, whereas the australopithecines before them would seem distincly ape-like, if a bit on the advanced side. This is the basis of our taxonomic distinction wherein we recognize the pithecanthropines as the first member of our own genus, albeit specifically distinct, as *Homo erectus*, while we retain Dart's original designation for their predecessors, *Australopithecus africanus*.

Hunting and Brain Size. Hunting, particularly for so anatomically ill-equipped a creature as a hominid, can be directly linked to a number of biological and behavioral developments. Most obvious and probably most important was the great increase in brain size. The abilities to learn from the past, plan for the future, and communicate one's ideas are at a premium for a creature who, alone and unarmed, is unable either to out-sprint or out-fight its potential prey. The striking enlargement of the brain, which coincides with the emergence of the pithecanthropines in the Middle Pleistocene, surely indicates a great increase in the capacity for learned behavior, which, in its developed form, is so characteristically human.

Hunting and Diet. Hunting, particularly the pursuit of large and dangerous game, also involves prolonged activity for which the reward is often delayed as much as a period of days. Not only does this have a profound effect on the characteristic mode of hominid as opposed to pongid behavior, but it has had its impact on the human digestive physiology. As we noted in our chapter on primate behavior, the typical primate eating pattern is that of the more-or-less uninterrupted snack, followed by a similar output of day-long defecation. We suspect that this pattern was basically altered by the adoption of systematic hunting at the beginning of the Middle Pleistocene. The alteration was profound, but in some respects it

was not absolute. As the fast-food industry has discovered, the be- **315**
havioral pattern of the nonstop nibble can be reactivated without
much difficulty, and a generation of affluent Americans has come to
expect that instant gratification is nothing more than its due.
Other aspects of our primate heritage appear to have been altered
permanently. Although we would deny that there is anything so
specific as the urge to kill or an instinct to wage war, there can be no
doubt that various kinds of aggressive behavior can be learned with
astonishing ease. If we view this alteration of the basic primate pattern with some suspicion, we can register a bit more enthusiasm for
the fact that our Middle Pleistocene hunting heritage has apparently
permanently and irrevocably modified the typical primate style of
defecation.

Hunting and Bone Thickness.   Hunting with crude weapons
evidently had another consequence visible in the skeletal anatomy.
This was a reinforcement of both the skull and the long bones to
counteract the possibilities of trauma. The walls of the cranial vault
reach their maximum thickness among the pithecanthropines. This
fact has been recognized ever since Dubois' finds in the 1890s, but it
has often been regarded as a demonstration of the "primitive" or
ape-like approximation of the pithecanthropines. The great apes,
however, in spite of heavy brow ridges and robust muscle attachments, actually have rather thin bone in those portions of the skull
that serve only to encase the underlying brain. The same is also true
for the australopithecines. By the Middle Pleistocene, however, the
average thickness of the cranial vault has increased several times.
Subsequent changes have involved thinning and lightening the skull
bones and other parts of the skeleton, but we shall reserve our consideration of this for treatment of the emergence of modern form.
The postcranial bones of the pithecanthropines also display an increase in robustness. The cavity in the middle of the long bones is
relatively small and the walls of the shafts are relatively thick.
Knees, elbows, wrists, and ankles are broad and sturdy, and we can
suspect that they were in less danger of strain or damage to the ligaments than is true in most cases today.

   It does not take much effort to realize the advantage that such manifestations of muscular development and skeletal reinforcement
would have for a hunting hominid at a relatively crude stage of cultural development. Propulsive aids such as the spear thrower or even
the bow were unknown, and a hand-thrown, wooden-tipped spear
would constitute little more than an annoyance and certainly no
danger to an animal with the bulk of a rhinoceros or even a buffalo.
And yet such creatures as elephants, rhinoceros, horses, and giant
prehistoric cattle were regularly hunted. Some may have been driv-
en over cliffs and there is evidence that some were driven into

swamps where they became mired, but there is no indication that pits or traps were used. Again we have no direct evidence, but by analogy with recent African elephant hunters, it is possible to suggest that the principal lethal activity of the Middle Pleistocene hunter was the thrust of a hand-held spear into the bowels of a creature that had been approached by stealth. When correctly done, the thrust is made and the hunter jumps aside behind a bush or tree unperceived by his prey. The wounded beast may take several days to succumb and is tracked at a discreet distance until it does. This technique of hunting, as one can easily imagine, is not without its risks, to put it mildly. Even if the hunter has managed to get within spear-thrusting distance unperceived, the prey can hardly be expected to endure a stab in its vitals without a twitch, and the twitch of a ton or so of wounded bison can have literally traumatic consequences to the man at the other end of the spear. Bumps and bruises are the least of these consequences. Torn knee ligaments, a broken leg, or a cracked skull on a hunting expedition, if not immediately fatal, could easily spell the end of a hunting career and, eventually if not sooner, the life of the hunter. This constituted the operation of strong selective force in favor of just the kind of skeletal robustness that we observe among Middle Pleistocene hominids. And on the bones preserved for our examination, the evidence for healed injury occurs with a frequency unmatched in recent human samples.

Sexual Dimorphism. The reader will recall that the australopithecine ancestors of the pithecanthropines displayed a degree of sexual dimorphism that rivaled that of the nonhuman terrestrial primates. The question now arises, what happened to that dimorphism during the transformation from *Australopithecus* to *Homo erectus*? From the evidence available to us, it would appear that the degree of male/female difference decreased somewhat, although not to the level typical in modern *Homo sapiens.* At the Australopithecine stage, male body size was maintained by the selective forces inherent in the role of defender and maintainer of group integrity. In the Middle Pleistocene, the role of big-game hunting served to maintain male size and robustness. The reduction in dimorphism, then, was produced by an evident increase in female body size. This, we can surmise, was the result of the selective forces related to bearing a large-brained infant and carrying and caring for it for a prolonged period of time.

We cannot know, of course, just how long it took for a pithecanthropine to attain maturity, but we can suspect that the doubling of brain size in contrast to its australopithecine ancestor was a direct indication of the increased importance played by learned behavior in their way of life. Along with this, it seems only reasonable to expect that there was a prolongation of the period of immaturity during which learning takes place. This, in turn, can be expected to have prolonged the period of necessary maternal care and protection. With hunting activities taking males away from the camp for extended stretches of time, such maternal protection would have placed a greater burden on female physical capabilities than had been true in the previous Australopithecine stage where adult males were generally present in the group at all times. Five feet and one hundred plus pounds of aroused maternal protectiveness of her young will deter all but the largest of carnivores, whereas a three-and-one half foot tall, fifty pound counterpart would have more than a little trouble with jackals, civets, wild dogs, and some of the small to medium members of the cat family.

At the pithecanthropine site where the greatest quantity of material has been found, Choukoutien in China, there is a marked difference between the large and the small individuals. The original describer, Franz Weidenreich, felt that the difference was too large to be accounted for by invoking sexual dimorphism, and he speculated that the small specimens might represent a race of pithecanthropine dwarfs. Unlike the assessments of the australopthecines where many observers have felt that the differences between robust and gracile forms were so large that they could not be encompassed within the same species or even genus, Weidenreich did recognize that they belonged to the same species. As with the majority of the interpreters of the australopithecines, however, he was still viewing the pithecanthropines with the expectation that male/female differences should be of the same magnitude as those existing in modern humans. But if we realize that the modern model may not be appropriate for interpreting Middle Pleistocene conditions and keep in mind the circumstances concerning hunting as opposed to child care, then we might just expect to find a degree of sexual dimorphism among the pithecanthropines that was *greater* than that visible in moderns but *less* than that of the australopithecines. Weidenreich's pithecanthropine dwarfs then can be regarded as the female end of the range of variation. From the very few other instances in which there are more than one individual from a single site, it is also evident that the difference between specimens can be more pronounced than what one would normally expect to find when randomly choosing a similar number of individuals from a modern human population. At the cave of Arago in the French Pyrenees, the two pithecanthropine mandibles discovered in 1969 and 1970 by Henry and Marie-Antoinette de Lumley differed to such a degree in size and robustness that they postulated not only that they were of opposite sexes but that the average difference between the sexes was greater then than it is now. And at Olduvai Gorge, the two best preserved specimens from the Middle Pleistocene layer (Bed II), OH 9 and OH 13, differ in size to such an extent that many are not willing

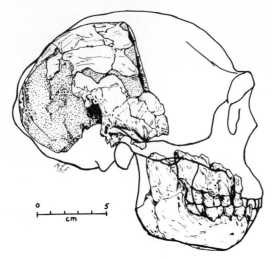

Figure 137. The outline of Weidenreich's reconstruction of a female *Homo erectus* superimposed (and drawn to the same scale) on Olduvai Hominid 13. (Drawn by Mary L. Brace.)

to consider them members of the same taxon. Olduvai hominid 9 ("Chellean Man") is generally accepted as a robust and probably male pithecanthropine, but there are doubts about the status of OH 13 ("Cinderella"). The jaws and teeth of OH 13 are typically *erectus* in size and development, but the skull is small and rounded. Admittedly the skull vault fragments of OH 13 are so fragmentary that any reconstruction must be suspect. Furthermore, there are unresolved problems concerning the precise stratigraphic location and relative date of the specimen. But if OH 9 and OH 13 are contemporaries roughly speaking, then it is indeed possible to regard them as repre-

Figure 138. The *Homo erectus* specimens from above the faunal break in Bed II of Olduvai Gorge, seen from the back. Olduvai Hominid 13, a presumed female, is on the left and Olduvai Hominid 9, a presumed male, is on the right.

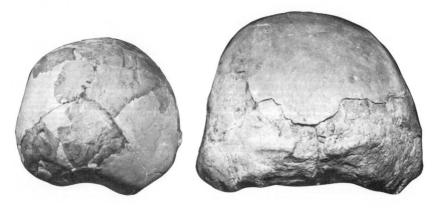

The Fossil Record

sentatives of male and female pithecanthropines, respectively. Taking a side view of OH 13, drawn from a photograph, and superimposing on it the outline of a female pithecanthropine from Choukoutien, which Weidenreich reconstructed from the most complete skull available, the correspondence of chin, jaw contour, teeth, ear, and back of skull is remarkable indeed. The top of the skull of OH 13 is lower, but one can certainly find that degree of variation within the same sex in virtually any hominid population. It is this lower vault that has led some to feel that OH 13 is really an australopithecine, and, in view of the very incomplete nature of the specimen and the questions concerning the date, we are not in a position to make a conclusive determination. If it is Middle Pleistocene, then the probability is good that it is a pithecanthropine. Given that "if," the contrast in size and robustness between OH 13 and OH 9, seen from the rear in Figure 138, would be a dramatic indicator of the degree of sexual dimorphism present in *Homo erectus.*

Age and Relationships of Pithecanthropines. Two aspects of the Pithecanthropine stage remain to be discussed — its dating and distribution. As is so often the case for the earlier stages of human evolution, the general picture appears reasonable, but the amount of specific evidence that can be mustered is uncomfortably small. While the dispute in learned circles continues as to whether the earliest pithecanthropines belong to the late Lower Pleistocene (Late Villafranchian) or the early Middle Pleistocene, it is generally recognized that the pithecanthropines go back at least to a time that would correspond to the second glaciation of the Alpine sequence.

The earliest skeletal remains assignable to the Pithecanthropine stage came from Java in the form of the infant Modjokerto skull of 1936 and the robust but fragmentary pieces of skull and face of 1939 at Sangiran — both discovered as a result of the efforts of von Koenigswald. As we have indicated, there remains some doubt as to exactly how old these fragments are, with von Koenigswald regarding them as late Villafranchian (Lower Pleistocene), and other authorities regarding them as early Middle Pleistocene, perhaps of an age equivalent to the early Mindel (second) glaciation of the Alpine sequence. While some authorities have tried to claim that the early pithecanthropines were contemporaries of the late australopithecines, it is evident that the exact dating of both has not been settled. Even their relative dating is unclear. While both "Meganthropus" and early pithecanthropines occur in the same (Djetis) layer in central Java, the layer in some places is over a thousand feet thick and must represent accumulation over a considerable period of time — tens, maybe even hundreds of thousands of years. Thus, the recent date of nearly two million years must be regarded as only one point in what could be a relatively long period of time.

At present it seems most reasonable and in consonance with the evidence to offer the tentative suggestion that the australopithecines evolved into the pithecanthropines at the end of the Villafranchian. Certainly full-fledged pithecanthropines exist by the beginning of the Middle Pleistocene, but the exact placement in time of these two stages will have to await refinements in absolute dating techniques and the accumulation of much more evidence correlating the local stratigraphic sequences with those in other parts of the world for which the relative dating has been well worked out.

It is clear, however, that by the time equivalent to the second glaciation of the Alpine sequence, the pithecanthropines had spread throughout the tropics of the Old World. Dubois' original finds as well as those by von Koenigswald from the Trinil layers in Java all belong to this time level. The "Sinanthropus" finds at Choukoutien may actually be a little more recent since there is a possibility that they belong to the earlier part of the long warm interval between the second and the third glaciations. This fits the anatomical evidence since the Choukoutien men had slightly larger brain cases and slightly smaller teeth than the Java finds, so it is possible on both anatomical and geological grounds to regard them as a later version of the Pithecanthropine stage.

With Java and Peking giving evidence of the existence of early Middle Pleistocene pithecanthropines in the Far East, we turn now to their westernmost representatives.

The Heidelberg Jaw. At the northwestern extreme of the area inhabited by humans during the early Middle Pleisocene, the only skeletal fragment discovered up to the time of the first edition of this book was the famous Heidelberg mandible of 1907. With so little to go on, any judgment as to whether or not Heidelberg is a pithecanthropine is bound to be tentative. While morphologists have argued long and inconclusively over the nuances of chin formation etc., we believe that the measurements tell the tale. As Table 3 shows, the measurements of the teeth that are least subject to modification by wear, that is the width or buccal-lingual diameters, are almost the same for the Heidelberg mandible as the average measurements that Weidenreich discovered from the extensive Choukoutien material. Since a definitive placement within the Pithecanthropine stage requires an appraisal of both face and brain, obviously we cannot be certain that Heidelberg, minus its brain case, was a pithecanthropine, but the teeth are the right size, the dating is the same, and the evidence for culture in the same stratum of the sand pit where the mandible was found and elsewhere in western Europe at that time are just what one would expect, so we feel fairly confident in assigning the Heidelberg jaw to the Pithecanthropine stage as its most northwesterly representative.

Table 3   **321**

Sinanthropus and Heidelberg Mandibular
Buccal–Lingual Tooth Measurements

	I_1	I_2	C	PM_1	PM_2	M_1	M_2	M_3
Heidelberg	7.1	7.8	9.0	9.0	9.2	11.2	12.0	10.9
Sinanthropus	6.4	7.0	9.2	9.9	9.8	11.8	12.2	11.2

Other Pithecanthropines in Europe. Subsequent discoveries in the late 1960s and early 1970s have provided us with more evidence for the appearance of *Homo erectus* in Europe. The find of early Middle Pleistocene tools, a couple of teeth, and a piece of the back end of a human skull at Vertesszöllös in Hungary was initially taken as a candidate for an ancient modern, but subsequent reanalysis has shown that the skull fragment fits in with the kind of form we would expect to find for that part of the skull among the pithecanthropines of the Far East. This suggests that their European contemporaries were similar in skull as well as jaw form.

Then in 1969, 1970, and 1971 Henry and Marie-Antoinette de Lumley of the Laboratory of Prehistory at the University of Marseilles made discoveries in the French Pyrenees that further confirmed the pithecanthropine nature of the makers of the Middle Pleistocene tools known from so many sites in Europe and else-

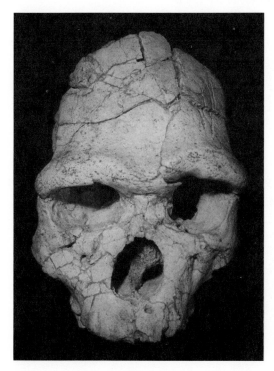

Figure 139. *Homo erectus* from the cave at Tautavel in the French Pyrenees. (Courtesy of Professor and Mrs. Henry de Lumley and the Museum of Anthropology, University of Michigan.)

The Stages of Human Evolution

where. The de Lumleys have excavated a number of sites on the Riviera and in the eastern Pyrenees, both Middle and Upper Pleistocene in date, and have provided us with valuable information on the way of life of the *erectus* hunters and their Neanderthal descendants. From our point of view, their most exciting discoveries to date have come from the cave of Arago near Tautavel in the eastern Pyrenees in a district famous for its sweet golden wines. A small *erectus* mandible in 1969; a large one in 1970; and the upper teeth, face, and forehead of a skull in 1971 have given us an excellent idea of what a European pithecanthropine looked like face on. In fact, until 1969, no complete *erectus* face had been known from any site. The discovery in that year of a complete skull base with attached face at Sangiran in Java provided the first unbroken picture of a pithecanthropine facial skeleton, while the Arago discovery of 1971 and the ER 3733 find east of Lake Rudolf (Turkana) are so similar that we do not feel uneasy in using these three finds to suggest that facial form was roughly the same at the beginning of the early Middle Pleistocene from the eastern to the western and the northern to the southern extreme of the area of human habitation.

As far as the north to south distribution is concerned, various

Figure 140. Mandible of Ternefine Man, "Atlanthropus mauritanicus III." (Courtesy of the late Dr. C. Arambourg.)

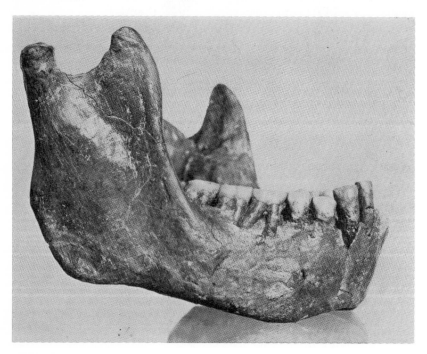

pieces of evidence have been found in the area between Europe and the middle of Africa, but these are tantalizingly incomplete and difficult to evaluate. At Ternifine in Algeria the French paleontologist Arambourg was responsible for the discovery of three mandibles and the parietal bone of a human skull in 1954 and 1955. These were associated with crude stone tools including Abbevillian-type hand axes and with what has been considered to be an early Middle Pleistocene fauna. Ternifine, then, is roughly contemporary with Heidelberg, Vertesszöllös, Arago, and the Far Eastern pithecanthropines, but since the parietal belonged to an immature individual, and in any event represents only a part of the skull, it is not possible to determine with any confidence what the skull looked like. The jaws and teeth fall within the range of variation indicated by the Asiatic finds, and our tentative assumption is that the skulls must likewise have been similar.

Finally Louis Leakey's discovery in 1960 of a complete skull cap, OH 9, in Bed II of Olduvai provided the first positive confirmation of the existence of pithecanthropines in Africa in association with Middle Pleistocene strata and a hand-axe tool-making tradition which itself is directly derived from the Oldowan tool tradition associated with the australopithecines. Although Heidelberg and Ternifine are jaws without skulls, and Olduvai Bed II (1960) is a skull without a jaw, the time designations are the same, as are the evidences for associated cultures where these are present, and we regard them all as belonging to the same Pithecanthropine stage of human evolution. The dating and associations of the possible female *erectus*, OH 13, found in Bed II of Olduvai Gorge in 1963 remains a problem.

The Spread of the Pithecanthropines. The view that the pithecanthropines arose at one point and then spread throughout the range indicated by their maximum extent is now widely held, and most agree that this spread represents an expansion into a previously unutilized ecological niche, that of the midday predator. The northern extent of this spread was limited by the basically tropical physiology of this new kind of hunter, and it was not until later cultural adaptations in the forms of dwellings and clothing interposed a barrier between the environment and the human skin that this physiological limitation could be transcended. Just when the first *erectus* spread out of Africa took place and when the cultural adaptation to colder climates began are questions that cannot yet be answered. Butchering tools and the evidence for human hunting activities go back more than a million years in Africa and perhaps almost as far in Java, which may mean that the initial *erectus* spread was confined to the tropics of the Old World. Contacts between adjacent bands of pithecanthropines ensured the rapid spread of cultural innovations that had particular survival value throughout the pithecanthropine world within the space of, at most, a few thousand years. Since cultural adaptation accounts for the most marked change in the operation of selective forces, the big changes in the forces affecting human survival took place roughly simultaneously, as far as evolutionary time is concerned. Genetic responses to these simultaneous alterations in selective factors would necessarily have been similar or identical since any differing responses would have been selected against. Furthermore, the intermittent but repeated contact of adjacent groups would have ensured the exchange of significant genetic material throughout the inhabited world providing the basis for Weidenreich's view that, at any one time level, there has only been one species of human during the course of hominid evolution.

In the temperate portions of the Old World, the evidence for pithecanthropine presence is only one half to one third as old as it is in the tropics. We suspect that this northern presence, whether in China or Europe, was made possible by cultural developments that

Figure 141. Bifaces in quartzite associated with Ternifine Man. (Courtesy of the late Dr. C. Arambourg.)

The Fossil Record

are not preserved in the hard remains of the archeological evidence.
Stones may be imperishable, but skin cloaks and bark or brush shelters vanish without a trace. But if we assume that it is cultural developments that allow a northerly penetration, then we must grant that these represent steps in the alteration of the selective forces affecting human survival, which, if extended upward in time, lead without break to the next stage in human evolution.

The next full stage in our scheme is the Neanderthal stage, and while there is relatively extensive evidence for its appearance and date, this does not occur until very near the onset of the last (fourth) glaciation less than 100,000 years ago, which means that there is a long gap for which we have relatively little evidence in the form of actual human fossils. There are a few fossils, and, most important, they can properly be placed in the evolutionary continuum because of the existence of an unbroken and increasingly rich archeological record. In Europe and Africa, at least, cultural evolution proceeds from the Pithecanthropine to the Neanderthal stage without break, and what skeletal evidence exists can most conveniently be interpreted as confirming the transition between these two stages.

From North Africa and southern France there are a number of finds that belong to the latter part of the Middle Pleistocene, but these are mainly jaws and teeth. Since there was no important change in jaw and tooth size or shape between the Pithecanthropine and Neanderthal stages, these scattered finds are no help. The Steinheim skull of 1933 and the Swanscombe skull of 1935–1936–1955 furnish the only picture we have of what the human head looked like at the end of the second interglacial, and, as has been already noted in Chapter 8, these constitute the focus of a continuing controversy — Steinheim because it was distorted and Swanscombe because it lacked the frontal and facial portion, and because as possibly females in populations where male/female differences were more pronounced than in modern populations, their rounded and gracile contours differed less from the typical modern form than would males from the same groups. These sources of uncertainty have led different authorities to interpret them according to their own view of human evolution, and since some authorities have believed that a modern form of human may have existed much earlier than is generally considered possible, the doubtful, distorted, or missing parts are generally regarded as modern unless proven otherwise. However, examination of the original reports and available evidence does not contradict our expectation that the only cranial material available stands morphologically half way between the pithecanthropines and the Neanderthals in both size and form.

"Rhodesian Man." Illustrating this last point rather nicely are two well-preserved skulls, which have often been thought of as be-

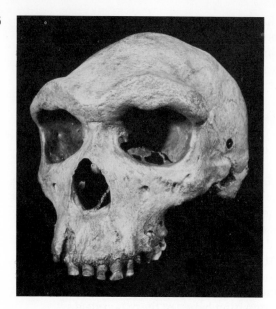

Figure 142. The "Rhodesian skull," an African Neanderthal from Kabwe (formerly Broken Hill) in Zambia (formerly Northern Rhodesia).

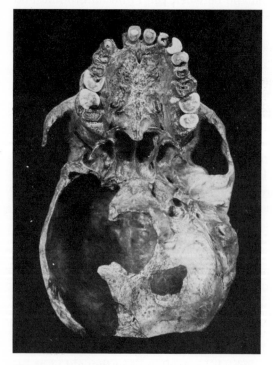

Figure 143. The "Rhodesian skull." Basilar view showing among other things, the form of the palate and the badly decayed teeth.

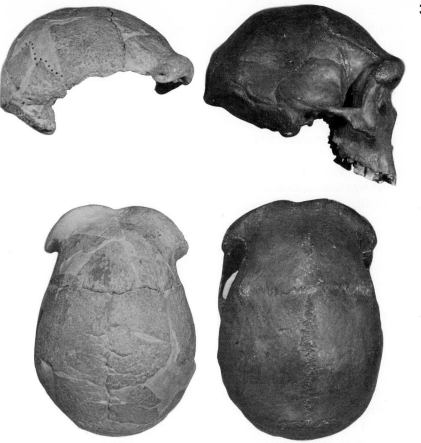

Figure 144. The Saldhana skull (left) compared with cast of the "Rhodesian skull" (right). (Courtesy of Professor Ronald Singer.)

ing encompassed within the Neanderthal range of variation. The first of these to be discovered was found in a fissure at a mine in Kabwe (then Broken Hill), some seventy-five miles south of Lusaka, Malawi (then Northern Rhodesia) in 1921. This skull, frequently referred to as "Rhodesian Man," was thought to be late Pleistocene, about forty thousand years old, and considered somewhat uncritically by many (including one of us: C.L.B.) to be an African version of the Neander-thals. To be sure, the cranial capacity, at somewhat below 1300 cc, was small for a Neanderthal of similar robustness, and the brow ridges, neck muscle attachments, and size of the palate and face were rather exuberantly developed. Peripheral to our main concern, but interesting nevertheless, is the fact that the Rhodesian dentition shows extensive evidence of tooth decay and dental abscesses — the first human specimen known to do so. This is an exceptional instance, however, since tooth decay did not become an important human ill until the enormous increase in the use of processed carbohydrates within the last thousand and especially the last two hundred years.

Recently, a reappraisal of the fauna and the artifacts associated with the Rhodesian skull has pushed it back into the end of the Middle Pleistocene about 125,000 years ago. The top of a skull of identical form had been found in 1953 at Elandsfontein near Hopefield, Saldanha Bay, in South Africa, The context including artifacts and fauna was more satisfactory than the Rhodesian discovery and serves to confirm the recent reassessment of the latter.

Petralona. The other well-preserved specimen illustrating the approximation of the late pithecanthropines to the early Neanderthals is the skull found in a cave at Petralona in northern Greece in the late 1950s. With a capacity of just over 1200 cc, huge brow ridges, neck muscle attachments, palate and face, it bears a remarkable resemblance to the Rhodesian skull. Those who have studied it have remarked on the mixture of Neanderthal and *erectus* traits and anguished over the category to which it should belong.

In either case, to worry about the category is to miss the point. Categories are created by people for their own convenience and should not be allowed to achieve a reality of their own; to insist on putting specimens in one or another category would be to obscure the fact that the course of human evolution has been smooth and continuous. We should in fact expect to find a gradual transition late in the Pithecanthropine stage to what, for convenience sake only, we shall call the Neanderthal stage. As far as we are concerned, the important thing about the Rhodesian and the Petralona skulls is not whether they belong in this or that category, but the very fact that we cannot categorize them at all — that they illustrate the kind of transition we should expect to find at what appears to be precisely the point at which we should expect to find it.

Fontéchevade. There is one other find prior to those properly associated with the Neanderthal stage which should be mentioned in our survey since so much attention has been devoted to it. This includes the skull cap and the part forehead and eye socket fragment discovered in 1947 at Fontéchevade in the southwestern part of France. Fontéchevade is referred to here, not because it is particularly important, but because of the interpretation that has been attached to it. Most authorities now regard it as the long-sought representative of pre-Neanderthal "sapiens," modern in form and lacking the primitive brow ridges. It is instructive to note, however, that the author of this interpretation is Professor Vallois of Paris who was much influenced by the teachings of his former mentor Marcellin Boule, whose position he inherited following Boule's death. Since Boule's thinking was implicitly opposed to evolutionary interpretations, it is no surprise that Vallois finds the concept of hominid catastrophism not uncongenial.

A number of difficulties surrounds the attempts to interpret the Fontéchevade remains. First, the human skeletal material was not all found *in situ*, but part was actually discovered in the shade of the laboratory where blocks of the site had been brought for more leisurely study. Unfortunately, no sample section of the site was left unexcavated as a demonstration of what the stratigraphy had been, and, as a consequence, a cloud of doubt will always hang over the age of the Fontéchevade human remains, although most authorities agree that they probably belong in the early part of the last interglacial.

The biggest stumbling block to interpretation, however, lies in the fragmentary nature of the skeletal remains themselves. The brain box represented by Fontéchevade II was soft and crumbly when found and there was no assurance that it was undistorted. Fontéchevade I, the fronto-orbito-nasal fragment was not distorted. In spite of Vallois' best efforts with this refractory material the character of Fontéchevade remains ambiguous. The calotte is too fragmentary to make any safe conclusions possible about its probable status. The fronto-orbito-nasal fragment while sapiens-like is again too full of problems for any firm conclusion to be based on it. In a recent metrical analysis of the cranium R. S. Corruccini finds that in its measurements Fontéchevade falls clearly into the Neanderthal and not the modern group, the shape of the calotte suggesting special affinity with the slightly earlier pre-Neanderthal Steinheim. Careful consideration of the evidence assembled in Vallois' monograph leads one to the cautious conclusion that there is not enough material from Fontéchevade of known sex, age, form, and date to warrant an appraisal of evolutionary stage. Certainly it is questionable whether it offers any support for Vallois' claims of ancient *sapiens* and hence Neanderthal extinction, i.e., hominid catastrophism.

THE NEANDERTHAL STAGE

Neanderthal man has gone farther toward capturing the imagination of the general public than has any other fossil with the possible exception of the original "Pithecanthropus," which was hailed as the "missing link." While it is true that many misconceptions are attached to this image—the hairy, slouching, cave man clad in loin cloth, club in hand, anachronistically contemplating a dinosaur—the dim awareness exists that the precursors of modern humans were physically distinguishable from humans of today and do provide direct evidence that humans have evolved much as other organisms have.

Despite the fact that both experts and laypeople have recognized the importance of the Neanderthals, few have attempted to define precisely what it is that constitutes a Neanderthal. The definition we use has been proposed by one of us (C.L.B.) and is as follows:

> Neanderthal man is the man of the Mousterian culture prior to the reduction in form and dimensions of the Middle Pleistocene face.

This recognizes the fact that the only area in which the Neanderthals differ significantly from modern humans is in the face. While most of the individual measurements can be equalled in single members of modern populations, taken together it would be most remarkable to find them in a living human. Certainly the difference between the Neanderthals as a population and the various modern populations is most striking in the facial dimensions. From the neck down, the Neanderthal skeleton is scarcely distinguishable from that of a modern human, although there is a slight tendency for the joints and muscle attachments to be a little more robust. Certainly the bent-knee gait and semi-erect posture with which the hominid catastrophists have tried to invest the Neanderthals was largely a product of their own wishful thinking. On the contrary, the Neanderthals stood just as erectly as we do today and were never forced to shuffle along, unable to straighten their knees.

When Boule made his study of the famous skeleton from La Chapelle-aux-Saints, he discovered that the cranial capacity was in excess of 1600 cc, which is approximately 150 cc larger than the average for modern male Europeans. However, since he was so firmly convinced that this large-brained man must have been a primitive and inferior individual, he tried to claim that the organization of the brain was inferior to that of modern humans. Boule's claims are without support, for even if one could infer anything whatever concerning the complexity and relative proportions of the various parts of the brain from the impressions on the inner surface of the skull — which one cannot — the range of variation within which perfectly normal and even extraordinary mental ability can occur is so large that no such judgment is possible on skulls differing so little from modern ones as did those of the known Neanderthals. On anatomical grounds there is no reason to regard Neanderthal mental capacity as having been different from that of modern humans. The evidence indicates that the human brain reached its present state of development by the Neanderthal stage at least one hundred thousand and perhaps as much as two hundred thousand years ago and has changed in no significant respect since that time. With a brain and a postcranial skeleton that were functionally indistinguishable from those of modern humans, we recognize the Neanderthals as generically and specifically the same as ourselves, *Homo sapiens*. We could tentatively grant them the status of subspecific distinction, namely *Homo sapiens neanderthalensis*, but this would gain us little and the issue is not important.

Brain Size, Intelligence, and Survival. It has seemed puzzling to some that the increase in brain size, which was undoubtedly related to an increase in information storage capacity and problem-solving ability, should suddenly have ceased. The puzzlement has been due to the assumption that, if brain size and intelligence are indeed related, then further increases should have been of even greater benefit to the possessors. The answer, while not of a kind that can be subjected to rigorous testing and proof, is nevertheless, cogent enough so that there would not seem to be much doubt of its truth. It derives from an appreciation of the nature and mode of operation of humanity's principal adaptive apparatus, which, as we have said, is not brain power *per se*, but culture.

One of the most important facets of culture is the role that it plays in the acquisition of information by the individual. With cultural traditions forged by the experience of preceding generations, the individual is not obliged to depend on his or her own wits and the accident of his or her own experience to acquire many of the essential facets of knowledge that improve the chances for suvival. As soon as language can be developed, the experience of an individual can be shared with other members of the group, and the learning of one is of benefit to all. This has an interesting consequence that is not often mentioned: with just enough intelligence to be able to master one's language and grasp the significance of the insights verbally transmitted from generation to generation, even a relatively unimaginative individual has almost as good a chance for survival as a genuine genius. In the evolutionary process, as soon as culture has achieved notable success as an adaptive mechanism, then, above a certain minimum, an excess of brains or intelligence does not greatly improve one's probability of reproducing and hence of passing such traits on to future generations.

The success of the cultural adaptive mechanism by the time of the Neanderthals is evident in the greatly increased number of Mousterian tools, indicating a significant increase in population density. It is also evident in the fact that humans could now successfully survive in numbers in what today is called the temperate zone, despite the lowering of the temperature signalling the onset of the last glaciation. Occupation of such an area meant access to the quantities of game animals that inhabited the periglacial parts of the Old World,

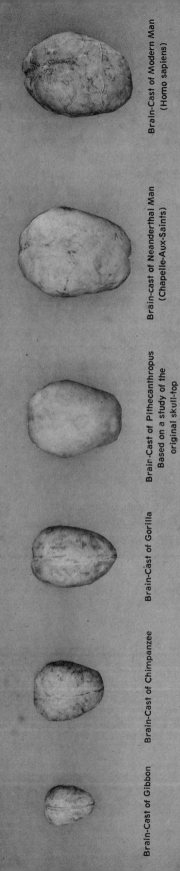

Brain-Cast of Gibbon

Brain-Cast of Chimpanzee

Brain-Cast of Gorilla

Brain-Cast of Pithecanthropus
Based on a study of the
original skull-top

Brain-cast of Neanderthal Man
(Chapelle-Aux-Saints)

Brain-Cast of Modern Man
(Homo sapiens)

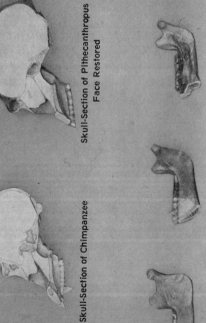

Skull-Section of Chimpanzee

Skull-Section of Pithecanthropus
Face Restored

Skull-Section of Neanderthal Man
(Chapelle-Aux-Saints)

Skull-Section of Cro-Magnon Man

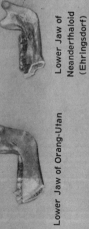

Lower Jaw of Chimpanzee

Lower Jaw of Orang-Utan

Lower Jaw of
Neanderthaloid
(Ehringsdorf)

Lower Jaw of
Heidelberg Man

Lower Jaw of
Neanderthal Man of
La Chapelle-Aux-Saints

Lower Jaw of
Cro-Magnon Man

Lower Jaw of
Modern White Man

Figure 145. Comparison of the brains, mid-sagittal section of the skulls, and inner aspects of mandibles of anthropoids and humans. (Courtesy of the American Museum of Natural History.)

333

but this was only made possible by the solution of certain problems that would normally have prevented a tropical animal like the human from being able to survive under such climatic conditions. Clothing and shelter must have been essential.

From the concentration of Mousterian tools in rock shelters and caves, we have pretty good evidence that shelter was being used. It is probable that the cave entrances were modified by brush and skin barriers; regular post-hole arrangements at Mousterian sites in southern Russia indicate the construction of more sophisticated housing, and certainly the abundance of hearths indicates that fire was being used as a source of heat. Evidence for the use of clothing is a little less direct, although it can be inferred and no one can doubt that the Neanderthals, with the full cerebral development of modern humans were bright enough not to face the raging blizzard clad only in the fur-lined G-string so foolishly depicted in cartoon caricatures. The great proliferation of stone scrapers in the Mousterian clearly indicates that considerable attention was paid to the preparation of skins. Furthermore, the remarkable rounded wear on the front teeth of the Neanderthal's themselves, as in the present-day Eskimo, suggest that it was at least partially the result of their use in the process of softening hides by chewing (see Figure 182).

Incisor Functions and Face Size. The mention of the wear evident on the Neanderthal incisors brings us to the reason for the difference in face size between the Neanderthals and moderns. Except for the part of the face immediately related to the housing for the respiratory passages, i.e., the nose, the major determiner of face size is the dentition and its supporting architecture. Big teeth with long roots mean a large face, and as can be seen in Figure 146, the forward portion of the late Neanderthal dental arch is substantially larger than even the very largest population average (Australian aborigines) for moderns. Because of the heavy use to which the front teeth were subjected, it is hard to secure figures for unworn teeth, but our use of the buccal-lingual (cheek-to-tongue-side) diameter should minimize this difficulty since this dimension reaches its maximum near the level of the gums.

It is interesting to note that although Neanderthal incisors are about the largest developed during human evolution, they were generally subjected to such heavy usage that they were worn down to the gums by early middle age. Such a heavy, rounding kind of incisor wear clearly indicates that the front teeth were used for something more

The Stages of Human Evolution

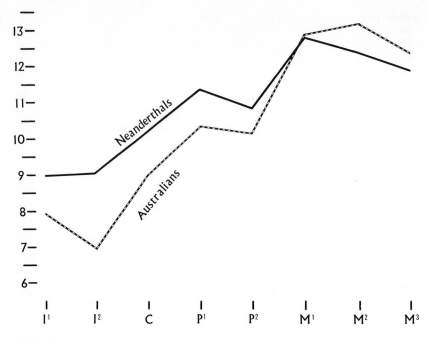

Figure 146. Measurements of teeth of Neanderthals and Australian aborigines.

than simply biting food. One of the keys to successful human survival has been the developing ability to manipulate the world to one's advantage, and it is apparent that into Mousterian times, the front teeth did heavy duty as manipulators — one might say they were the Lower and Middle Pleistocene equivalent of the Boy Scout knife. It seems likely that they were used to crack nuts, peel bark, squeeze, scrape, pry, and cut a variety of objects, and also to soften rawhide. Evidently the possession of large strong incisors was a necessity if Neanderthals were to live through their most productive years.

If the reason for the existence of large incisors at the onset of the last glaciation is obvious, then the reason for the transformation of the Neanderthal face into the face of modern humans should be equally easy to account for. One need only account for the suspension of the adaptive significance of the possession of large incisors, and by the process of the probable mutation effect, the accumulation of variation will result in their eventual reduction. Since the only real difference between Neanderthals and moderns lies in the size of the face, a simple reduction would be all that was required to effect the transformation. Analysis of the changes in human cultural adaptive mechanism, as seen in the archeological record, provides the necessary insight; one of the most obvious changes, beginning with the early Mousterian, is the proliferation of cutting and manipulat-

The Fossil Record

ing tools. The technological changes that mark the development of the Upper Paleolithic out of the Mousterian are particularly concerned with the increase in number and variety of cutting, gouging, chiselling, engraving, and scraping tools. As specific tools were made for the purpose of performing specific tasks in the developing Mousterian and more particularly in the derived Upper Paleolithic, there was a gradual reduction in the former extreme of incisor usage and a gradual suspension of the adaptive significance of the enormous Neanderthal front teeth. Now that they were free to vary, the accumulation of random mutations resulted in their inevitable reduction, hence the modern face.

Food, Function, and Molar Size. In Figure 146 we have compared Neanderthal teeth with those of Australian aborigines, but it is clear to many observers that the splendid strong aboriginal Australian teeth strike us as being distinctly less "modern" than the crooked, uneven, misshapen, rotten, or missing condition that we expect to encounter in most contemporary human populations. If Neanderthal teeth are compared with those of modern Europeans or Chinese, for example, the difference is almost as apparent at the back end of the dental arch as it is at the front. Evidently molars also have undergone a pronounced reduction during the last one hundred thousand years. While we have made a case for the manipulative function of the front teeth, the molars are unquestionably involved with the processing of food. The drop in molar size, then, should be related to some change in the need for their service as food grinders. In the absence of any other evidence, we could expect that some cultural development had probably taken over the functions formerly performed by the molars. Food grinding equipment, however, is not prominently a part of the Mousterian cultural repertoire, so we can suspect that whatever the nature of the food preparation technique that reduced the amount of compulsory chewing, it was not simply a mechanical process. Aside from pounding and grinding, the other major means of food preparation that reduces the previously necessary amount of chewing is the artificial application of heat: i.e., cooking. So far as we can determine, the Neanderthals did not have cooking containers. Pottery was not invented until ten thousand years ago at the very earliest, which is some thirty thousand years after the Neanderthals had evolved into what we are calling "modern" humans.

Hearths in the Mousterian are extensive, however, and we can guess that the fires were being used for cooking as well as for keeping warm. Many of these "hearths," as they are called, show depths in Mousterian stratigraphic sections of as much as two feet or more, and they often contain quantities of fire-blackened river stones or cobbles. It may very well be that the Neanderthals had developed a form of earth oven cookery, in which a fire was made on a pavement of stones at the bottom of a shallow pit, allowed to burn down, the food then placed among the heated stones, covered with skins or vegetation, and the whole heaped with earth and allowed to steam until done on the retained heat of the stones. This cooking technique was prominently used among the recent populations of Australia, New Guinea, and Oceania, where pottery was unknown or not used, and it is quite capable of reducing both plant and animal foods to a consistency that demands far less chewing than would otherwise be required. Although we cannot yet prove that this is what the Neanderthals were doing, it is clear that they were doing something that started the reduction in molar usage and size that continues at the present to the extent that many people now fail to develop their third molars, or "wisdom" teeth, at all.

Teeth, Face, and Nose. Although brain size in the Neanderthal stage had reached fully modern levels, and the postcranial skeleton functioned precisely the way it does in the Modern stage, there are details of head and body in which the Neanderthals on the average differ from moderns on the average. We have mentioned the large tooth crowns, and we have suggested that large teeth were the key to understanding the differences in face form between Neanderthals and moderns. Not only were the crowns large, but the supporting tooth roots were extraordinarily long also, and the long tooth roots were housed by a necessarily large midfacial skeleton. The growth dynamics required to produce a large tooth-supporting portion of the face also resulted in the production of a large nose, eye sockets, and overhanging brow ridges. As we shall see when we discuss the distribution of nasal form in modern human populations, there may have been a separate set of selective forces influencing the size of the nasal skeleton. In fact the supposedly large Neanderthal nose may not be just the consequence of growing a large tooth-supporting face, but may be related specifically to the problems engendered by breathing the cold air of a periglacial climate. If this is actually the case, then we should expect to see large noses only on those Neanderthals in the northern portions of their area of habitation. Unfortunately the only Neanderthals for which we have enough preserved material to discuss the phenomena of nose form happen to be just those that come from the northerly areas, and we simply do not know what nose form looked like where it was not so cold.

Neanderthal Morphology. The back end of the skull has also received its share of attention. Typical Neanderthal form was said to be characterized by what appeared to be the addition of a bony bun-like projection at the rear of the skull. This "bun-shaped occiput" was then said to be a "specialization," which was one of the specific distinctions between Neanderthal and modern forms. This development at the back of the skull, however, appears to be simply the accompaniment to the attachment of especially well-developed neck and back muscles and is largely restricted to male Neanderthals. Unfortunately a previous generation took a single Neanderthal skeleton, La Chapelle-aux-Saints, described by Boule before the First World War, to typify all Neanderthal form, and it so happens that this particular specimen had been an especially robust and muscular male.

There are aspects of the postcranial skeleton for which claims have been advanced for the existence of a marked difference between Neanderthal and modern forms, but as with the back end of the skull, these are principally related to manifestations of muscularity. Elbow, wrist, knee, and ankle joints tend to be larger than the modern average; the shafts and joints of the finger and hand bones are more robust than the modern average; the bones of the forearm curve to a marked extent for the encompassing and attachment of what would appear to be remarkably well-developed muscles; ribs are thick and stout to an extent not usually found in moderns where ribs generally are flat and ribbon-like; and muscle and ligamentous attachments of arms, legs, and trunk appear to be powerfully developed. All these features as well as some other more trivial ones are especially noticeable in male Neanderthals, and, unfortunately, early treatments took a single male skeleton to typify the group as a whole.

When all the Neanderthal material is assessed, one of the things that clearly emerge is that there was a more pronounced difference between male and female form than is true on the average for more recent human populations. This sexual dimorphism may not be quite so marked as it was in the preceding Pithecanthropine stage, but it evidently was clearly developed. The average male Neanderthal was a robust and powerful person who differed from the average modern male more by virtue of his greater muscularity than would be true if the comparison were between Neanderthal and modern females.

Dating and Distribution. Before leaving the Neanderthals, mention should be made of their dating and distribution. As a group, there is no doubt that they flourished from the end of the last interglacial, about one hundred thousand years ago, up to the beginning of a climatic amelioration between the early and late parts of the Würm glaciation some forty thousand years ago. Although this places the Neanderthals as a stage, it is hard to be more precise where individuals are concerned. First, the relative placement of the finer subdivisions of the Würm is a source of continuing disagreement among professional geologists and archeologists, and, second, the

The Stages of Human Evolution

338   Neanderthals had instituted the practice of burying their dead. While this assured us of the discovery of more complete skeletons and greater numbers of individuals, it also meant that the actual level of the bones within the ground did not correspond with the time at which the individual had lived. It should also be remembered that excavating techniques were not so refined when most of the significant Neanderthal skeletons were discovered, and many stratigraphic details that could now be determined were not observed or recorded and were lost with the removal of the contents of the sites. As a result of these two sources of uncertainty, it is not yet possible to discuss the trends of development that must have occurred during the sixty thousand years or more of the Neanderthal stage.

The distribution of the Neanderthals is a little easier to plot since there is abundant archeological evidence for the areal extent of the Mousterian tool-making tradition and other contemporary traditions of the same approximate level of technological complexity. The occasional occurrence of skeletal remains with this

Figure 147. Mousterian and derived cultures. Oblique hatching indicates the area of Mousterian concentration; vertical hatching indicates the distribution of other derived cultures.

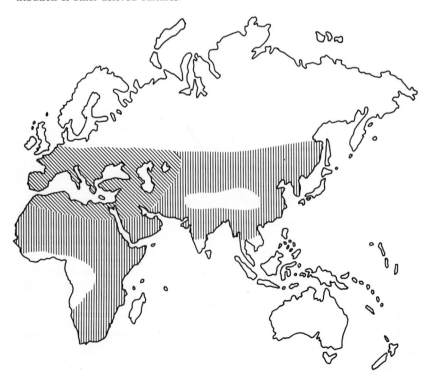

cultural spread completes the picture with Figure 147 showing the location of the most significant finds. It is evident that the entire inhabited portion of the Old World in the early Würm was peopled by groups at the Neanderthal stage of development. To be sure, some authors have tried to present a modified version of hominid catastrophism claiming that the early Neanderthals, represented by Skhūl and Krapina, appear more modern than the later ones represented by La Chapelle-aux-Saints, La Ferrassie, and others. These supposedly early Neanderthals then are presumed to have given rise to true moderns somewhere "in the East" who then swept into Europe and extinguished the late-surviving "classic" Neanderthals. This view assumes, however, that the supposedly early Neanderthals were more modern in form. When the actual date is associated with properly analyzed form, quite the reverse is the result. The earlier material is more robust on the average and has larger teeth than the more recent examples, although the sizes of our various samples are so small that we cannot provide statistical guarantees for our conclusions.

Krapina. A few examples will serve to illustrate our points. Except for the Solo specimens found in Java at the beginning of the 1930s — about which more later — the most ancient group of specimens assignable to the Neanderthal stage was discovered at Krapina in Jugoslavia at the beginning of the twentieth century. These specimens were thought to date from the end of the Third Interglacial, just before the Würm, and although there were a number of attempts to assign them to a more recent warm period within the Würm, recent studies have confirmed their pre-Würm status.

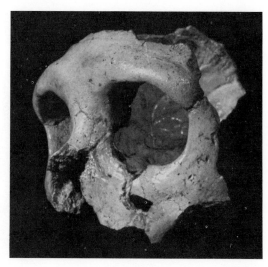

Figure 148. The Krapina C skull, from Croatia, Jugoslavija.

The Stages of Human Evolution

Not only are the Krapina finds equivalent in age to the oldest specimens found in Europe, there are more individuals represented than
in any other collection. Although at least fourteen and perhaps fifteen people contributed to the scraps discovered, the word scraps
describes the collection rather well. No complete skull and no complete long bone is preserved; cut marks made when the bone was
fresh are visible on some fragments; and some of the pieces are
charred. The three preserved nasal skeletons all show a peculiar de-
viation of the suture from the midline that could only be due to a
shared genetic anomaly, which, with other features, suggests that at
least several of the individuals represented belonged to a single local
breeding population. This population, it would appear, had met a
violent end. The indications are that they were killed and eaten by
members of another group.

Early studies remarked on the smooth and rounded form of some of
the skull pieces, the lack of muscle markings on some of the limb
bones, and the fact that reconstructed skull form showed heads that
were relatively broad in proportion to their length, a trait not normally to be found until one encounters modern populations within
the last five thousand years. As it turns out, this last "fact" is the result of faulty reconstruction, and the length/width proportions of the
Krapina skulls do not differ from those of Middle and Upper Pleistocene crania wherever else they are found. The hints of modern
form, then, are entirely due to the lack of robustness of *some* of the
bones in the collection. It was this that led, on the one hand, to the
idea that the remains of two populations, one modern and one Nean-

Figure 149. The Krapina D skull, from Croatia,
Jugoslavija.

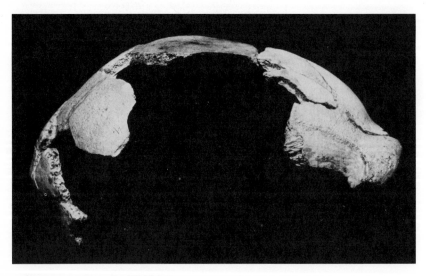

derthal, were mixed together at the site, and, on the other hand, to
the view that the amalgamated average form was less robust than the
full "classic" Neanderthal condition. ("Classic" form, one will recall, was based entirely on one extremely rugged male skeleton.)
What is represented, however, is a mixture of male and female bones
from a population where the difference is more marked than is typically true for modern humans and where the males were distinctly
more robust. Where male and female measurements are lumped together, as in an assessment of the loose teeth of which there are as
many at Krapina as among all the other Neanderthal sites put together, average robustness is distinctly greater than in any subsequent
population for which we have measurements.

Solo. There is one other site that has yielded material of possibly
similar date and quantity as Krapina. The specimens referred to were
found at Ngandong on the banks of the Solo River in Java in 1931,
and although more than a dozen individuals are represented, the
collection consists almost entirely of skulls and pieces of skulls
without jaws and teeth. The latter is most unfortunate, since it makes
the fragments preserved a bit hard to compare systematically with
anything else. But from what has been preserved, it would appear
that skull form ranges from something generally recognizable as
moderate Neanderthal to a degreee of ruggedness reminiscent of
erectus. Weidenreich, who wrote the descriptive monograph, recognized their *erectus* derivation and regarded them as a link between the pithecanthropines and the moderns. This, in effect, is very
close to what we mean by the Neanderthal stage and why we would
regard the Solo specimens as representatives of the Neanderthals in
Southeast Asia.

As we have mentioned, the Mousterian and its cultural relatives
are distributed from China to Morocco and from Europe to South
Africa. Here and there in this distribution are scraps of skeletal material, and wherever we can make an assessment, the observed form
fits what we would expect for Neanderthal appearance. A skull cap
with the upper face found at Mapa, Kwangtung Province, China, in
the late 1950s is a convincing Chinese Neanderthal. A complete cranium with its facial skeleton (but minus its teeth) plus another skull
cap found in the early 1960s at Jebel Ighoud (or Irhoud, depending on
how one transliterates the Arabic) near Marrakesh can be recognized
as a Moroccan Neanderthal. Mandibular and dental scraps from Dire
Dawa in Ethiopia and the Cave of the Hearths at Makapansgat in the
Transvaal of South Africa also can be included within the Neanderthal spectrum.

Middle East Neanderthals. The most extensive evidence we
possess, however, comes from the region extending from western

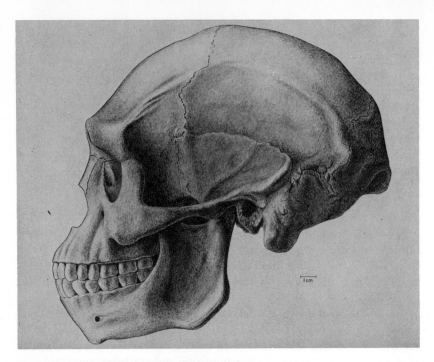

Figure 150. Reconstruction of the Skull of Solo Man by Franz Weidenreich. (Courtesy of the American Museum of Natural History.)

Europe through the Middle East. This is partially because archeologists have spent a lot more time digging in this area, but from the quantity of tools and the size of the sites, one could guess that Neanderthal population density was greater throughout this area than elsewhere in the Old World. In any case, our ideas about typical Neanderthal form, sexual dimorphism, and the decrease in robustness between the early and the late Neanderthals is largely based on specimens from this portion of the world.

In the Middle East, for example, relatively complete Neanderthal skeletons from the early Würm have been found at Shanidar Cave in northern Iraq, and at the cave of Tabūn on the slopes of Mount Carmel, just south of Tel Aviv in Israel. The most complete Shanidar specimen is large and rugged with heavy muscle markings and displays what is widely regarded as full "classic" Neanderthal form. The Tabūn skull, on the other hand, is small and rounded and lacks strong muscle markings, although the heavy face and teeth and the strongly developed brow ridge demonstrate its Neanderthal status beyond any doubt. In both skeletons, a well-preserved pelvis allows us to make an accurate assessment of sex, and, not surprisingly, the robust Shanidar specimen is male and the relatively gracile Tabūn

The Fossil Record

individual is female. A similar contrast in cranial form can be seen in early Neanderthal skulls from Italy: for instance, the rugged and probably male skull from Monte Circeo on the coast some eighty miles south of Rome, as opposed to the more rounded skull from a gravel pit at Saccopastore on the outskirts of Rome itself. Unlike the Middle Eastern specimens mentioned, there is no postcranial skeleton to confirm the estimate of sex in either case, but the cranial contrast is similar. Also displaying a similar degree of contrast are two specimens from the site of La Ferrassie in the Dordogne area of southern France. In this case, again, the preserved postcranial remains allow us to identify the large, rugged individual as male and the small, gracile individual as female. But in this case, also, the archeological evidence suggests that the skeletons are not quite so early and the male skull is not quite so robust. The tooth-bearing part of the face does not project quite so far beyond the support of the jaw, and the result is the appearance of an incipient chin, while the brow ridges above the eyes are not quite so heavy as in the earlier Neanderthals.

The only place where material has been found that is clearly more recent in date than the "classic" Neanderthals but older than the most ancient known moderns is in the Middle East again. This has sometimes been taken to indicate that modern form evolved in the Middle East, but such a judgment would be premature since no remains of comparable date have been found elsewhere. The most widely recognized of these were found at the rock shelter of Skhūl, like Tabūn, located on the slopes of Mount Carmel in Israel. The Skhūl skeletons are little more than half the age of the Neanderthal woman from Tabūn, being from a Mousterian level approximately 35,000 years ago. Tooth size is virtually identical to that of the aborigines from central Australia but noticeably smaller than that of the earlier Neanderthals. The supporting facial skeleton and attendant brow ridges are also smaller, and the evidence for muscularity on the male skeletons is less pronounced. Still, these features are developed to such an extent that they suggest a Neanderthal ancestry in much the same way that the Neanderthals proper lead one to expect the existence of pithecanthropine forbears. The obviously in-between status of the Skhūl skeletons has led some observers to call them "Neanderthaloid," that is, early moderns that hark back to but do not fully exemplify Neanderthal form.

If the Skhūl "Neanderthaloids" suggest the development of modern out of Neanderthal form 35,000 or more years ago, the discovery of the Amud skeleton in a cave just northwest of Lake Tiberias (the Sea of Galilee) represents a step toward the confirmation of this view. This was found as a result of the efforts of an excavation directed by Hisashi Suzuki of the University of Tokyo in 1961. The skeleton is that of a male found in a late Mousterian context and, like the Skhūl material, can be regarded as "Neanderthaloid" rather than ful-

The Stages of Human Evolution

344 ly Neanderthal. The dentition and accompanying midfacial skeleton is reduced when compared to full Neanderthal development, leaving an emergent chin below and a reduced but still prominent brow ridge above.

Variability. Before concluding the discussion of the Neanderthal stage, we must deal with the matter of possible regional variation. Students of modern human physical form have traditionally recognized bloc differences between human populations to which they have given racial designations. Furthermore, some have suggested a comparable degree of variation also characterized the populations of the previous stages of human evolution. For reasons we shall develop in a later chapter, we do not feel that racial categorization helps us understand the nature of variation in contemporary *Homo sapiens,* and if it does not help us understand the modern condition, certainly it cannot help us understand the prehistoric one. Although many of the differences between human populations have arisen because of the different selective forces imposed by different environments, at least as important is the fact that there have been different cultural solutions to the problems faced in different areas. For example, where manipulating tools and cooking techniques developed earliest, we should expect to see the greatest consequent dento-facial reduction. In our discussion of modern human form, we shall see that this is indeed the case. But when we try to look at the earlier stages of human evolution, we simply do not possess enough skeletal material for a given time level for each of the main provinces of the world to perform a similar kind of analysis.

There are some hints of such differences, however, and we can mention one that is both readily apparent and easy to interpret. This has to do with the relative lengths of the different segments of the limbs. A study of the first Neanderthals to be discovered, the Neanderthal skeleton itself, Spy in Belgium, La Chapelle-aux-Saints in France, and others, disclosed that in contrast to the ape-like form that many expected to discover in "primitive man," the limbs of the Neanderthals were comparatively short. Not only were they short, but this lack of length was particularly due to the shortness of the distal segments, the forearm and lower leg. At first this was thought to be a species or "racial" characteristic of the Neanderthals, but since it is not present in some Neanderthals but readily apparent in others, and since there appears to be a relatively simple climatic correlation, it makes better sense to regard this as an adaptation to the different selective forces present in the different parts of the world inhabited by the Neanderthals.

In modern human populations, the shortest distal segments of arms and legs, relatively speaking, belong to those people who have to contend with the coldest climates. This reaches its extreme in the aboriginal inhabitants of the Asian and American Arctic, the Siberians and Eskimos, respectively. Of all the parts of the body, the forearm and the lower leg are literally the "skinniest," that is there is more surface per unit volume than in any other major body segment. Since body heat is dissipated through the skin, the distal limb segments are the most effective radiators. As one might expect, those populations longest associated with very hot climates such as East Africa or northern Australia display the most elongate lower legs and arms while those longest associated with extremely cold climates have the shortest distal limb portions. In the tropics, dissipation of metabolically generated body heat is a positive adaptation, while in the arctic it is distinctly disadvantageous. In the latter case, a too-rapid cooling of the extremities can lead to frostbite, and frostbite, far from being a trivial annoyance, is a frequent cause of fatalities among Eskimos. The adaptive significance of short extremities for cold climate populations is readily apparent. It is no surprise, then, to discover that it is only among the most northerly of the known Neanderthal skeletons that particularly short distal limb segments are to be observed. It just so happens that the first Neanderthals to be discovered were at the very northern extreme of their area of habitation, and we can surmise that they were more affected by the stringencies of a glacial climate than those further south and east.

While we have direct anatomical evidence of regionally identifiable adaptive differences between Neanderthal populations where body proportions are concerned, there are many kinds of regional adaptive differences that cannot be determined from an analysis of skeletal remains. In modern populations, we can trace the association between environmentally related selective forces and the distribution of such features as hemoglobins, blood groups, skin color, and various aspects of metabolism to name just a few. If we cannot determine how such perishable aspects of prehistoric peoples may have varied by actual measurement, we can determine from the archeological record something of what they were doing to counter the environmental pressures they faced. When environmentally posed problems are regularly countered by cultural solutions, the strength of the selective forces formerly represented by those problems are of necessity altered. And alteration of selective forces will almost certainly be followed by modifications in those aspects of basic biology that constitute their adaptive response.

We can give one example of a biological change that can be deduced by pursuing an analysis of this kind. We know that humans, possessing the physiology of tropical mammals, cannot survive unaided in latitudes in which the temperature stays below freezing for any appreciable length of time. At present, people survive in otherwise inhospitable areas only because they make use of sources of heat, shelter, and clothing, which are not themselves a part of the

The Stages of Human Evolution

basic human biological heritage. We also know that the Neanderthals existed in some numbers close to the glaciers of Europe and the Middle East. Since their ability to survive was subject to the same basic biological limitations as ours, it is clear that they had developed some kind of control as far as heat, shelter, and clothing were concerned. Mousterian hearths have been found in quantity, and it is obvious that they could control fire. Post-hole arrays show that they knew the art of shelter manufacture. And surely the cartoon caricature of the classic cave man trudging barefoot through the glacial winter clad only in a fur-lined bikini bottom says more about our own notions of propriety than it does about the reason for Neanderthal hide-preparing activities. Although no Neanderthal clothing survives, one of the most common Mousterian stone tools was a "side-scraper" or "D-scraper", so-called because it is shaped like a large capital letter "D." No one doubts that this played an important role in hide preparation, and it is equally obvious that the skins so prepared were not simply for the purpose of ornament or personal modesty.

Pigmentation. Hence, although it may be speculative to claim that the Neanderthals wore fur clothing, it is not unwarranted guesswork. For the first time in the course of human evolution, then, a barrier was interposed between the human skin and the environment. At least some of the adaptive role played by the skin was therefore altered, and consequently we should expect to find a change occurring in the skin itself. In dealing with the outward appearance of the pithecanthropines, we suggested that the loss of the normal mammalian fur coat was accompanied by an increase in the amount of melanin in the skin, to the extent that the *Homo erectus* who emerged in the tropics of the Old World as the common ancestor of all later humans was pigmented to the degree we now (somewhat inaccurately) designate "black." Interposing clothing between the skin and the sun means that the significance of skin pigment was drastically reduced, particularly since the development of clothing enabled the Neanderthals to inhabit a portion of the world where damage by ultraviolet radiation was a great deal less in the first place. Our line of reasoning leads us to suggest that cultural developments preempted the role of melanin, particularly in the northern areas of habitation made possible by just those particular cultural features. We can further suggest that the probable mutation effect did its work proportional to the time that the significance of epidermal melanin had been superseded, and that the consequence was a progressive decrease in the amount of pigment in the skin.

The image of a blond Neanderthal again is somewhat at variance with our cherished stereotype. Neanderthals, after all, were the classic cave men and therefore "primitive" and "brutish." Since our cultural heritage has taught us that dark should be the color of the "primitive" and "brutish," there are some who are a trifle non-plussed at the idea of a pale-skinned blue-eyed cave man. But the maximum degree of depigmentation occurs in just those portions of the world where the archeological evidence indicates that clothing has been longest employed, and if, as we suggest, the inhabitants of northern and western Europe today are largely the descendants of the northern and western Neanderthals, it seems more than likely that the process by which their current pallid appearance was achieved goes right back to the beginning of the last or Würm glaciation.

Before the Neanderthal stage, the evidence for human cultural adaptation does not differ much in any major functional sense from one part of the inhabited world to another. This, in turn, leads us to suspect that the selective forces imposed on the human physique were also largely similar fom one place to another as was the appearance of the various human populations. There may have been some slight differences in the degree of pigmentation between the sunniest parts of the tropics and the cloudier parts of the inhabited temperate zone, but the difference probably did not begin to approach the differences in skin color apparent among the peoples of the world today. Other archeological evidence shows that the pithecanthropines were living much the same kind of gathering and hunting existence wherever they were to be found.

By the Neanderthal stage, however, major regional differences in cultural adaptation appear for the first time. At the current state of our archeological knowledge, these differences emerge as a result of the developments that first occurred in an area running from western Europe through the Middle East. At first, it seems clear that some sort of special cultural development was necessary simply so that people could survive in an area to which their physiological heritage constituted an inadequate adaptation. As the climate became more severe with the onset of the last glaciation, it was a matter of adapting in the cultural realm or ceasing to exist. And when the cultural adaptation was accomplished, the people found themselves living life under conditions that differed from those elsewhere in the world. These circumstances and their derivatives may well have been responsible for much of the physical and cultural differentiation between the populations of the world which can be observed today.

MODERN HUMANITY

We turn now to the Modern stage of human evolution, but we begin with something of a warning. Firstly, there is probably more visible variation between human populations today than has existed at any

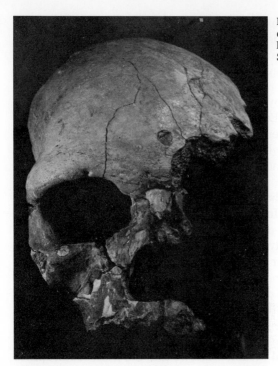

Figure 151. Florisbad, an early modern skull from Bloemfontein, Orange Free State, South Africa.

previous time. The reason for this is that with the development of increasingly different forms of cultural adaptation, the nature of the selective forces and the biological responses to them in different areas has come to display a diversity not previously possible. Finally, simply because we have labeled a given form modern in the sense that it can be encompassed within the observable range of variation of living human populations, we should not make the mistake of assuming that human evolution has come to a halt now that "we have arrived," so to speak. On the contrary, if anything, the pace of human evolution may well have accelerated during the last thirty thousand years. We suspect that much of what is called "racial" variation has developed or at least been intensified within that span.

The first datable appearance of humans of relatively modern form is in the latter part of the last warmish interstadial immediately prior to the final major intensification of the Würm glaciation. The first moderns are associated with the earliest true Upper Paleolithic toolmaking traditions, although there is increasing if scrappy and poorly published evidence to show that the beginning of what we would call modern form is to be seen late in the Mousterian. Unfortunately both the skeletal and the archeological evidence for the appearance of modern humans is somewhat sketchy. The earliest population

that has been called modern is that of Skhūl at Mount Carmel in   **349**
Palestine, but it is associated with a variety of the Mousterian and
most authorities recognize that the skeletal remains are "Neanderthaloid." Clearly Skhūl presents the best picture of a transitional
population. Unfortunately there is no good clearly datable population associated with the early Upper Paleolithic although there are
a number of hints.

Cro-Magnon.   The most famous Upper Paleolithic find is the so-
called Old Man of Cro-Magnon discovered in 1868 at Cro-Magnon in
the Commune of Tayac near Les Eyzies, southwestern France. The
fame of Cro-Magnon is largely due to the fact that this was the earliest *recognized* discovery of an undoubted fossil human, having
been made at a time when most paleontologists still accepted Cuvier's dictum that fossil humans did not exist. Natural scientists of
nineteenth-century France, while dominated by the ghost of Cuvier,
could not deny that a genuine fossil human had been uncovered,
but, with Darwinian evolution creating a disturbing intellectual fu-

Figure 152. Upper Paleolithic and derived cultures.
Oblique hatching indicates the area of Upper Paleolithic concentration; vertical hatching indicates the
distribution of other derived cultures.

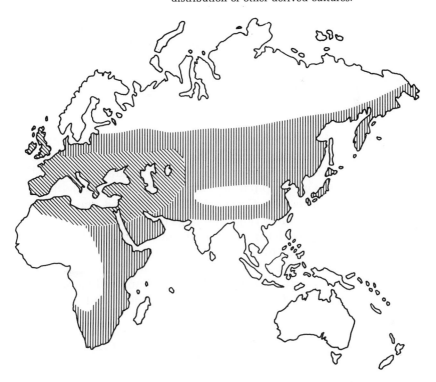

ror, at least they could claim that their human fossil was indistinguishable from humans of today, and therefore they could strongly imply that evolutionary ideas need not be applied to humanity.

While Cro-Magnon is indeed a genuine fossil human and does belong to the Upper Paleolithic, its exact significance is obscured by a number of factors. It was discovered accidentally by railway workmen, which would not be much of a guarantee of stratigraphic accuracy even today when the importance of precise dating technique is much more clearly realized. Then, too, the other skeletons with which it was found were part of a series of burials, and, even under the best of circumstances, burials are often difficult to date precisely. Aside from the uncertainty that surrounds the precise dating of Cro-Magnon, the exact morphological status is subject to a variety of interpretations. There can be no question that the individual was robust, male, and tall (5 ft 11 in.), but the assertions relating to the noble chin and lofty brow are perhaps overenthusiastic. Evidently Cro-Magnon man did not possess the heavy brow ridges of a Neanderthal nor did he possess the huge Middle Paleolithic dentition that occupied so much jaw space that the chin would be labeled "retreating," but here we run into some difficulty because Cro-Magnon had lost all his teeth. With the teeth lost before discovery, it is somewhat difficult to make an accurate reconstruction of the face. Furthermore, the whole middle part of the face has been etched and pitted by weathering, further adding to the difficulties of reconstruction (see Figure 62). This is not to say that Cro-Magnon was not a characteristic member of an Upper Paleolithic population and hence within the range of variation of modern humans, but it is intended to constitute a caution to those who would attempt to construct a rigid picture of what is assumed to be the earliest representative of humans of today.

Other Fossil Moderns. Other Upper Paleolithic skeletons have been discovered, although many of them were found before the turn of the century and are not accompanied by accurate stratigraphic documentation. One population discovered in the mid-1890s at Předmost, in what is now Czechoslovakia, included one specimen with a heavy enough brow ridge and large enough front teeth so that it could very well have been placed in the midst of the Skhūl population without disturbing even the most vigilant hominid catastrophist. Another early Upper Paleolithic population from Mladeč in Czechoslovakia is even more robust than Předmost with more than a hint of the bun-shaped occiput, heavy brow ridges, and powerfully developed dentition.

While this is the extreme of variation, with the rest of the individuals looking progressively more modern, it does indicate that Upper Paleolithic populations did overlap the range of variation of the

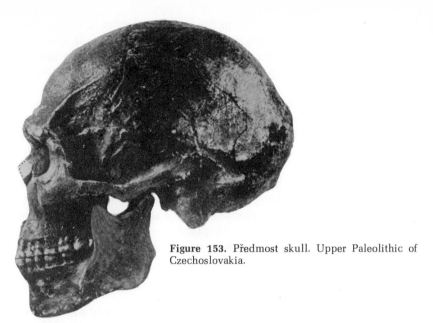

Figure 153. Předmost skull. Upper Paleolithic of Czechoslovakia.

neanderthaloids. This same generalization finds support in the skeletal material found in 1928 at Afalou-Bou-Rhummel, Algeria. Even the late Upper Paleolithic (Magdalenian) male skull from Obercassel, near Bonn on the Rhine, is characterized by a development of jaws and brow that is neanderthaloid, and the same thing can be said for a number of other skulls of probable Upper Paleolithic age, although the exact date of many is in doubt because of the fact that many are burials or were discovered accidentally or under other questionable circumstances.

One of these was the famous Combe Capelle skull of 1909 with a lower face of a neanderthaloid form. Unfortunately this was discovered by the pick and shovel technique that Hauser was using to loot the site, so that, even if the skull had not been blown to oblivion in the Second World War, the exact stratigraphy must remain in doubt. Another was the discovery in 1901 of the so-called Negroids, in one of the Grimaldi caves near Monaco on the Riviera. Two skeletons were discovered at this time: of an adult woman and an immature male. These are of interest since, more than sixty years ago, Boule claimed that these were of the same age as the "classic" Neanderthals despite the fact that an eminent archeologist associated with the discovery had pointed out that they were buried from an Upper Paleolithic level. Furthermore the form of the faces of the Grimaldi remains is subject to some doubt because of the liberties taken in reconstruction. Many authorities, on seeing the reconstruction of the immature male, regard it as an adolescent of fourteen or fifteen years,

352   but most people have overlooked the fact that the deciduous molars were still in place when the remains were discovered. It was only later, in the laboratory, that Boule removed the deciduous molars, elevated the unerupted permanent premolars to the level of the occlusal plane, and restored the entire face by sheer guesswork. The photograph taken before "restoration" shows that the face had been at least 25 per cent longer than it was when he had finished. It is evident that not only the dating, but also the form of the Grimaldi remains must remain in doubt—certainly there is no justification for calling them Negroid.

These remarks have been made to show that many problems still becloud attempts to portray the earliest appearance of modern morphology. What there is of reliable evidence shows that the transition from Neanderthal to modern took place gradually at the end of the Mousterian, continuing into the early Upper Paleolithic as a response to the changes in selective factors which have been outlined above.

Changes in Morphology.   It has been erroneously assumed by some that there have been virtually no changes in human morphology since the Upper Paleolithic. While no major changes have occurred nevertheless skeletal changes are evident. For example, there has been a slight but definite decrease in skeletal robustness, and in the associated structures for the attachment of muscles. There has been a pronounced decrease in the visceral parts of the face, markedly affecting the size of the jaws and teeth. This reduction has occurred to different degrees among the various peoples of the world, varying all the way from no reduction at all for the Australian aborigines, to marked decrease in size and in frequent failures of such teeth as third molars to erupt in peoples in the area from Central Europe over into the Middle East and in China and adjacent parts of the Far East.

The differences in the degree of reduction are directly related to the extent to which the various cultural traditions in question have suspended the adaptive advantage inherent in the possession of a large dentition, a matter to be discussed further in Chapter 12.

The final noticeable skeletal change that has occurred since the Upper Paleolithic has been the development of the overbite— again a change related to the dental part of the face. Most of the readers of this book will find that their lower incisors bite behind their upper incisors when mandible and maxilla meet in normal occlusion. This, however, has not been true for the majority of human beings during the course of human evolution. Until recently, the lower incisors met the upper ones edge to edge when the molar surfaces were approximated, and this edge-to-edge bite still is characteristic of the few food-gathering and hunting peoples remaining in the world.

The Development of the Overbite. The development of the
overbite has been an extremely recent phenomenon. Although we
tend to think of it as the natural condition for humans, in fact it did
not come to characterize the form of the human bite until within the
last two hundred years in Europe, and possibly somewhat more recently in Americans of European ancestry. In China, where general
gastronomic sophistication was achieved earlier than anywhere else
in the world, the overbite may have a correspondingly greater antiquity, but this suspicion will require further research before it can be
confirmed. To show how the initial loss of the edge-to-edge bite is
due to a change in use rather than to genetic alteration, reference
may be made to the case of the Alaskan Eskimo who has made the
change in one generation. Canned food, store-bought bread, and eating utensils have resulted in a radical change in eating and manipulating habits so that, whereas the oldsters all have edge-to-edge
occlusions, the younger generation is growing up with an overbite.
The same situation prevails in other parts of the world such as Australia, Polynesia, the Balkans, and elsewhere following the introduction of "refined" Chinese or European gustatory practices.

The seeds of the change were sown, literally, with the food-producing revolution some ten thousand years ago. Prior to this time,
human subsistence depended primarily on success in hunting
and gathering. Technological complexity was limited by the fact that
groups could not remain for long in any one place, which put rather
a restriction upon the total number of possessions an individual
could accumulate. Protein in the form of the products of the chase
formed a substantial part of the diet. Since protein requires a minimum of chewing or mixing with salivary enzymes, the main need is
to reduce it to bite-sized morsels, which can then be swallowed with
a minimum of further processing, In this connection it is interesting
to note that throughout the Paleolithic the molar teeth show relatively little wear in comparison to the frequently extreme degrees of
abrasion exhibited by the incisors. The standard way of producing
bite-sized pieces of meat, during the time span before the development of the overbite, was to take a chunk of meat in one hand, stuff it
part way into the mouth, clamp the incisors on it, and then saw it off
at the level of the lips with a knife or other cutting implement. The
same technique is still used among the hunting and gathering peoples
of the world, and a residue of it can still be seen in the rural parts of
Europe where coarse bread is still a major item of diet. Such a process encourages the edge-to-edge use of the incisors and the flat wear
of their occlusal surfaces.

The Food-Producing Revolution. With the coming of the
food-producing revolution, humans began to exert an increasing
amount of control over their future food supply, and the most reli-

able way in which this could be done was to plant and tend grains and vegetables. As the amount of protein in the diet decreased and the starch and carbohydrate content increased, the amount of chewing for the purpose of increasing the digestibility of the food became relatively greater. Unlike meat, starches and carbohydrates initiate the process of digestion in the mouth where through mixture with salivary enzymes commences their conversion into simple sugars that can then be handled by the stomach, and the intestines in which digestion actually takes place.

Chewing, however, is only one way in which the digestibility of foods can be improved. Others include chopping, grinding, and above all cooking. We have previously noted the evidence for the utilization of the earth oven, which, we have suggested, began to reduce the need for compulsory heavy-duty chewing back in the Mousterian. This, we suspect, led to the earliest appearance of what could be regarded as modern face form in the more northerly areas of human habitation. After the end of the Pleistocene, a further major refinement of food-processing technology occurred in just those areas where the food-producing revolution had its origins. This was the invention and utilization of pottery.

Food can be cooked in watertight containers even if they are not fireproof by the simple expedient of dropping in fire-heated rocks. This process, called stone boiling, works well enough for cooking of limited duration, but it does not really approach what one can do with pottery. After a day of simmering in a pot of water over a slow fire, even the toughest of foodstuffs will be reduced to mush, and the amount of actual chewing then required to make them digestible will be relatively slight. And if the teeth are not even up to a slight amount of chewing, further simmering with more water will produce a soup from which nourishment can be obtained by drinking, completely bypassing the use of the teeth. Pottery also allows the preparation of carbohydrates into a form that is not only drinkable but has mind-altering properties as well, namely alcohol. Philosophers and moralists may argue whether the result is a benefit as well as a pleasure, but the fact remains that it represents calories that can be ingested without the need of the dentition. A subsequent rapid reduction in tooth size could be predicted, and indeed, it is in just those areas of the world where the archeological record tells us that food-producing practices have been longest in existence that we encounter the smallest faces and teeth among modern human beings.

The food-producing revolution did not immediately result in the loss of the edge-to-edge bite since it took several thousand years before the full possibilities of the change in subsistence began to be realized. With a sedentary existence, the production of food surpluses, and the accumulation of tangible possessions that this made possible, invention and technological progress occurred at an ever increasing rate. The development of metallurgy culminating in the bronze and later iron ages finally gave people a tool-kit that effectively put teeth as manipulating tools out of business, and it is not surprising to observe the cessation of incisor wear and the gradual appearance of partial overbites making their appearance with the beginning of the bronze age.

The full scale development of the overbite, however, is evidently a completely nongenetic change and occurs only when new eating habits suspend the use of the front end of the dental arch. In Europe this is accomplished by the addition of the fork, and the etiquette concerning its use, to the utensils and habits related to normal eating. The fork became a standard item of tableware in Europe after the American Revolution. Following its introduction, food was no longer held with the teeth to be cut off at the lips with a knife. Instead, it was speared with the new gadget and sliced into chewable pieces down on the plate before being popped into the mouth. This represented a radical change in function for the front teeth and the consequences for their eruption and wear were the appearance of the overbite.

In the Orient, culinary practices have dictated that food be cut into bite-sized morsels even before cooking, so that when it appears at the table no further reduction in size is necessary and it can be conveyed to the mouth in satisfactory fashion by chopsticks. The consequences as far as the front teeth are concerned are precisely the same as are those that follow the introduction of the fork to the gastronomic repertoire of the West. The only difference is that chopsticks appeared in China more than three thousand years ago, and, although not immediately adopted for common use, there is reason to believe that the overbite was an Oriental phenomenon considerably earlier than it became a Western one.

In both areas, however, the antiquity of major reliance on pottery is about the same, and the people of both areas display the greatest degree of dental reduction visible in modern *Homo sapiens*. By contrast, aboriginal Australia had no pottery at all prior to the European conquest, and teeth remained as large as they were in Europe at the beginning of the Upper Paleolithic or the end of the Mousterian.

Decrease in Robustness and Muscularity. As the Modern stage has proceeded toward the present, there has been one other major change that has become visible but has rarely been discussed. There has been a marked decrease in robustness and muscularity, but it has not been equally true for all modern populations, and it represents more a male than a female phenomenon. As with post-pottery dental reduction, it would seem that robustness has undergone the most marked decline in those populations that have been associated longest with intensive agriculture, and, furthermore, it is just there that sexual dimorphism is now least evident. We suspect that the harnessing of sources of energy in addition to human muscles, whether water power, wind, or domestic animals, took an additional burden from the male physique, giving less robust men an equal chance to support a family. According to the standard argument we have previously developed, a reduction in average male robustness could then be predicted in those areas where intensive agriculture has been pursued longest, and the evidence, at least tentatively, supports our expectations.

While we are also tempted to venture speculations on other changes which the future may bring, we shall here forego that temptation and leave such speculations to a later section. In the next chapter we shall attempt to summarize the relationships between the changing selective forces and the effects that they have exerted during the course of human evolution from the australopithecines to twentieth-century humans.

Suggested Readings

BRACE, C. L. *The Stages of Human Evolution.* Prentice-Hall, Englewood Cliffs, N. J., 1967.
An expansion of the coverage in the present chapter.

———, H. NELSON, AND N. KORN. *Atlas of Fossil Man.* Holt, Rinehart and Winston, N.Y., 1971.
Accurate drawings of the more important hominid fossils.

CAMPBELL, B. *Human Evolution: An Introduction to Man's Adaptations.* Aldine, Chicago. 2nd ed., 1974
An excellent integrated account of man's evolution.

GARN, S. M. (editor). Culture and the direction of human evolution, *Human Biology,* vol. 35, 1963, pp. 219–311.
Seven studies.

HOWELL, F. C. *Early Man.* Time-Life, N.Y., 1965.
A well-illustrated popular account.

HOWELL, F. C., AND F. BOURLIERE (editors). *African Ecology and Human Evolution.* Viking Fund Publications in Anthropology, No. 36, 1963.
Contains some fine papers on cultural factors in the evolution of man.

HOWELLS, W. W. *Evolution of the Genus Homo.* Addison-Wesley, Reading, Mass., 1973.
A gracefully written version of the standard view.

JOHANSON, D. C. Ethiopia Yields First "Family" of Early Man. *National Geographic*, vol. 150, 1976, pp. 790–811.
A vivid account of the Ethiopian discoveries of Australopithecine and hominid fossil remains.

KOENIGSWALD, G. H. R. VON (editor). *Neanderthal Centenary 1856–1956*. Kemink en Zoon, Utrecht, 1958.
Thirty valuable contributions on various aspects of Neanderthal man, celebrating the centenary of the discovery of Neanderthal man.

MONTAGU, ASHLEY (editor). *Culture and the Evolution of Man*. Oxford University Press, New York, 1962.
Twenty contributions toward the understanding of the role cultural factors have played in human evolution.

———— (editor). *Culture: Man's Adaptive Dimension*. Oxford University Press, New York, 1968.
Additional contributions supplementing the preceding volume.

———— (editor). *The Origin & Evolution of Man*. Thomas Y. Crowell, New York, 1973.
Readings covering a wide range of material.

Origin and Evolution of Man. Cold Spring Harbor Symposia on Quantitative Biology, vol. 15, 1950.
A classic symposium dealing with a wide range of topics, especially relevant to those discussed in the present chapter.

ROE, A., AND G. G. SIMPSON (editors). *Behavior and Evolution*. Yale University Press, New Haven, 1958.
A synthesis of evolutionary facts and principles as they bear on behavior, with behavioral facts and principles as they bear on evolution.

SPUHLER, J. N. (editor). *The Evolution of Man's Capacity for Culture*. Wayne State University Press, Detroit, 1959.
Six essays.

WASHBURN, S. L. (editor). *Social Life of Early Man*. Viking Fund Publications in Anthropology, No. 31, 1961.
A highly informative and stimulating series of contributions.

WOLPOFF, M. H. *Human Paleontology*. W. H. Freeman, San Francisco, 1977.
The most complete account available.

Interpretive Summary of the Fossil Record

Our examination of the evidence for human evolution has led us to the genetic arrangement of the fossil record in four representative stages: Australopithecine, Pithecanthropine, Neanderthal, and Modern. In the first edition of this book, we considered subdividing the Australopithecine stage and we included all the stages in the genus *Homo*. But if all the specimens we have reviewed qualify for the designation "hominid" by virtue of the fact that they all rely on culture as their primary adaptive mechanism, we feel that the changes that followed the development of hunting and the control of fire at the beginning of the Middle Pleistocene distinguish those and subsequent hominids from their predecessors at the generic level. The members of the Australopithecine stage we then return to the genus *Australopithecus*. All subsequent hominids, pithecanthropines, neanderthals, and moderns, we include in the genus *Homo*.

The major morphological changes that have occured since the beginning of human evolution can be focused on four areas.

This must have occurred at the very beginning of human evolution, since it was evidently a characteristic of the earliest australopithecines yet discovered. The well-developed arms of one recently discovered but very early specimen suggest that we have gotten back to near the pongid-hominid split, but the pelvis is that of a fully adapted biped. From a functional point of view, the loco-motor adaptation of the australopithecines works exactly the same way as it does in later hominids. The evident bipedalism of the australopithecines is one of the indications that points to their essentially hominid status, since a tool-less biped on the savannas of Eastern and Southern Africa could not have lasted a single genera-tion. The success of the australopithecines points to the likelihood of their use of culture as a major means of adaptation. We have also noted that the increase in size of the later australopithecines doubt-less was of survival value, but since this is not quite the same thing as a change in form, we have not equated it in rank with the other three changes.

The Increase in Brain Size

The australopithecines, as the earliest hominids, had brains no larger than those of some living anthropoid apes, but while living apes with brains of such size range in the neighborhood of a quarter ton of gross body weight, the australopithecines go on down to fifty or sixty pounds total. Relatively speaking, the australopithecines were much brainier creatures than any living ape. While the evidence for cultur-al development as seen in the archeological record reveals only a moderate increase by the time of the second glaciation when the pithecanthropines began to flourish, the selective advantage con-ferred by the possession of more brains was apparently powerful enough for the average brain size to double in volume while body size remained effectively unchanged since the late Australopith-ecine stage. A doubling of brain size represents a profound evolu-tionary change. This coincides with the change from a gathering and scavenging hominid to a true hunter, and we suspect that cerebral expansion was the consequence of the selective forces overcome in converting an advanced terrestrial primate into a true member of the genus *Homo*.

By the Neanderthal stage, the brain had almost tripled in size when compared with the original australopithecines, while again culture had shown only a moderate increase in tangible complexity.

From this point on, however, culture develops at an ever-increasing rate, while cranial capacity does not change at all. We can only infer that some sort of threshold had been passed and that the efficiency of culture in transmitting information among individuals and across generational boundaries was sufficient so that beyond a certain point, marked increases in individual intelligence conferred no particular survival advantages upon the possessors.

Various Reductions in the Dentition

The nonprojection of the canines, even in the earliest australopithecines in whom these were still relatively large teeth, is another reason why all the fossil stages considered are regarded as proper hominids. Lacking such anatomical means of controlling the environment, we must conclude that the creatures in question relied upon a nonanatomical instrument, i.e., culture. Certainly changes in diet resulted in reduction of the canines, especially since tools began to be employed deliberately to perform, more efficiently, the functions of these teeth. Throughout human evolution, the canines have fulfilled the same function as have the incisors.

The molar teeth underwent a sharp decrease between the Australopithecine and Pithecanthropine stages, and this is tentatively correlated with the evident increase in hunting efficiency of the pithecanthropines. Protein foods do not require the same amount of crushing and mixing with salivary enzymes as do carbohydrates and starches, and it is reasonable to associate the significant increase of meat in the diet with a reduction in the amount of heavy duty mastication required. Furthermore, the addition of fire to the cultural repertoire indicates that the use of heat to break down the more resistant parts of the utilized foodstuffs would lead to a further reduction in the amount of required chewing, allowing the probable mutation effect to produce a reduction in the size of the molar teeth. This reduction proceeded at an even greater rate after the end of the Pleistocene among those peoples who developed pottery.

The incisors remained large until manufactured tools could be more effectively utilized for specific tasks. This started in the Mousterian. With the pressure taken off the front teeth, the accumulation of random variation results in their reduction, with the result that the large heavy face of the Pithecanthropine and Neanderthal stages reduces to the form recognizable in modern humans. Changes in eating habits and further reduction produce the overbite generally present in modern *Homo sapiens*.

Figure 154 shows graphically the features wherein the major stages of human evolution differ from each other and conveys some

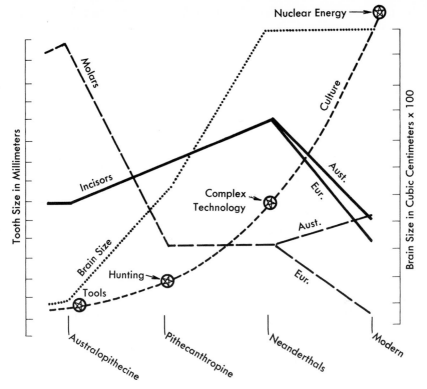

Figure 154. Brain, tooth size, and cultural relations in the Pleistocene. Summary chart of the major changes that have taken place in human evolution with their suggested cultural causes. The drop in molar size to the Pithecanthropine level indicates the addition, with the development of effective techniques, of quantities of meat protein to the diet. The increase again to a maximum of tools which assume tasks formerly performed by the teeth. This has been less so in the Australian aborigines, reflected in the fact that the incisors do not decrease so markedly and the molars decrease not at all—technology being at its minimum development in Australia, the burden falls on the teeth. Australopithecines belong to the Villafranchian, the Pithecanthropines to the Middle Pleistocene, Neanderthals to the Upper Pleistocene, and Moderns to Post-Pleistocene times. The spaces allotted are not to scale.

hint of the changes in selective pressures that result in the morphological responses indicated. Doubling of the brain and reducing the molars changes the australopithecines into the pithecanthropines. A further simple increase in brain size produces the neanderthals out of the pithecanthropines, and finally the reduction of the nean-

Interpretive Summary of the Fossil Record

derthal dentition, particularly at its forward end, and the accompanying adjustments by the supporting facial architecture accounts for the final development of modern form.

Changes in Sexual Dimorphism

The first hominids can be expected to have resembled their pongid relatives in displaying a marked male/female difference in size and robustness. The earliest hand-held implements can hardly have been much more effective than pongid-type canine teeth and almost certainly required a good deal of effort on the part of the wielders in order to have played a significant role in group defense. At the beginning of hominid evolution, then, we should expect to find that males were twice the size and robustness of females.

With the adaptation to hunting in the Middle Pleistocene, selective pressures acted to maintain and increase the muscularity and robustness of the male physique. The problems of coping with large game animals when armed only with hand-held implements led to the strengthening of arm and leg joints and the reinforcement of the bones of the cranial vault. In spite of this, sexual dimorphism decreased from its australopithecine level, although it remained far more pronounced than is true today. The reduction during the Pithecanthropine stage was due to an increase in female body size. This in turn, we suggest, was the result of the selective pressures related to bearing a large-brained baby and then carrying it and caring for it through an increasingly prolonged period of infant dependency and juvenile immaturity.

As implements and techniques were refined particularly after the Neanderthal stage, hunting put less of a burden on the male physique and it ceased to be maintained at its previous level of robustness. The disparity in size and robustness between males and females then declined, a trend that has proceeded to its greatest extent among those peoples whose ancestors were the first to abandon a hunting and gathering for a horticultural mode of subsistence.

Treated in this way, the changes that have taken place in the human physical form since the first record of its existence are actually less dramatic than they would at first appear to be. This is because in our intimate familiarity and concern with human morphology we tend to magnify our perceptions of the difference between the several manifestations of human form. As a counteraction to this pardonably egocentric tendency, it is possibly a healthier exercise to reduce the differences to their proper perspective. This we have attempted to do. Differences still remain and they are unquestionably important ones, but, related to the selective pressures and adaptive mechanisms that called them into being, they take their place in the proces- **363** sual continuum of development that is human evolution.

Suggested Readings

BAKER, P. T., AND J. S. WEINER, (editors). *The Biology of Human Adaptability.* Oxford University Press, New York, 1966.
On the problems of man in his natural environments and his adaptive responses to them.

DOBZHANSKY, TH. *Mankind Evolving.* Yale University Press, New Haven, 1962.
On the evolution of man from the genetic point of view.

DILL, D. B., E. F. ADOLPH, AND C. G. WILBER (editors). *Handbook of Physiology, Section 4: Adaptation to the Environment.* American Physiological Society, Washington, D. C., 1964.
The fundamental treatise on the adaptation of mammals, and especially man, to the environment, containing sixty-five contributions by the authorities in their fields.

DAMON, A. (editor). *Physiological Anthropology.* Oxford University Press, New York, 1975.
Thirteen admirable studies, on the effects of nutrition, disease, environmental stimulation, light, noise, cold, heat, altitude, and much else. Indispensable.

HARRISON, G. A., J. S. WEINER, J. M. TANNER, AND N. A. BARNICOT, *Human Biology.* Oxford University Press, New York, 1964.
A fine introduction to human evolution, variation and growth.

ROBINSON, J. T. *Early Hominid Posture and Locomotion.* University of Chicago Press, Chicago, 1973.
Of the australopithecines.

TUTTLE, R. (editor). *The Functional and Evolutionary Biology of Primates.* Aldine-Atherton, Chicago, 1972.
Nineteen contributions covering a wide range of subjects.

WEINER, J. S. *The Natural History of Man.* Doubleday, Anchor Books, New York, 1973.
An excellent account of the evolution of human populations and their precursors in the setting of the total environment

Part Three

Living People

Race: The History of the Concept

chapter 11

The urge to divide mankind into fixed types and races is evidently endless. Each attempt only illustrates anew how race groupings have been shaped not by nature but by the mode of thought or the stage of mechanical efficiency that mankind valued at the moment.

JACQUES BARZUN

On The Race Concept

If, then, race is not a useful concept when applied to humans how then did we get "stuck" with it? It should be instructive to spend some time and consider the development and history of the concept. As we shall see, the firm conviction that humanity is naturally divided into three, or four, or whatever number of clearly delimited groups to which the label races can be applied is of quite recent origin. As a facet of general belief, the concept of race did not gain currency until the beginning of the nineteenth century, although it was then much less specific than now since it included differences in language, nationality, and assumptions of morality.

Even now, strong remnants of this pre-scientific view are to be encountered in socially and intellectually backward areas. For instance, in many parts of the South, it is widely believed that Blacks are congenitally immoral, unteachable, and lazy. These attitudes bolster feelings of comparative personal superiority in their non-Black holders and elicit such a satisfying emotional response that no amount of contradicting fact can negate them. How splendid it is to know that one is "better" than others. And if science can provide no basis in fact for such attitudes, so much the worse for science and the facts.

The survival of the concept of race among some biologists and anthropologists is due not to the satisfaction it may provide for invidious racial comparisons, but because of their conviction that race is in fact something real. The assumption that humanity is divided into biologically meaningful groups is taken as axiomatic, and only after such an assumption is any justification offered. This initial conviction in the reality of "racial" configurations has provided a certain amount of ammunition for those who use race to justify discriminatory behavior, and it has been a matter of such embarrassment to well-meaning social scientists that there has been a near cessation of studies focusing on innate human differences. Frank racists have pounced on this with evil glee and twitted the anthropological profession, suggesting that the reason for the reduction in the number of studies of human differences is really that anthropologists are afraid they might discover that races really do have different abilities — and are hence of different worth. The charge has just enough truth in it to cause a considerable amount of discomfort and not a little bluster in reply.

The practicing racist can point to studies showing large differences in racial intelligence, for instance. The anthropologist, on the defensive, is left with the retort that it is nearly impossible to measure innate intelligence since such a large element of sociocultural background influences performance on "intelligence tests," and there is, as yet, no way to correct for differences in such backgrounds. While this retort is perfectly valid, it is nevertheless a negative and defensive answer — never very effective as a debating ploy.

A much more effective counter is that while there may be average group differences in innate ability (noting that there is no present means of demonstrating this), it is quite unjustified to treat an *individual* as though he or she were an averaged member of his or her group. Even the Army, which has a well-earned reputation for treating individuals as though they were all the same — warm bodies — recognizes that it is unprofitable, to say the least, to require all recruits to wear the same size shoe. The anthropologist's answer to the racist focus on average group difference, then, is to state that the only fair and democratic procedure to follow is that which assures each individual the maximum opportunity to realize his or her full potential as a person, so long as this does not conflict with the potential realization of any other individual.

At this point, biological anthropology comes right up and meets with social science proper, and it is just as well for our purposes to leave it there. We may point out, however, that the biological anthropologist can make an additional contribution that will deprive the racist of any scientific basis for his or her views. This is to deny the very existence of race as a valid biological category. Part of the trouble social scientists have had in dealing with mentally agile racists is based on the fact that both groups have assumed the existence of races as valid, and, hence, comparable categories. If, as can be shown, races do not exist as coherent biologically based categories, then the racist is left without a valid cause other than a desire to demonstrate worth on grounds unrelated to individual achievement.

If races do not have any biological coherence, why, then, were we all brought up to believe in them? Why did the concept take such a hold on both the popular and the educated mind? Certainly part of the reason why race as a concept has been so unshakable and persistent is related to the categorical way humans have of dealing with the world of their experience. One of the secrets to the success of human survival has been the ability to reduce the graded variation of the perceived world to a finite number of categories. These are symbolically rendered by assigned labels, which allow people to compare and recombine the dimensions of their experience in a manner unique in the animal world. In a word, this is the advantage of language.

As symbol-making and symbol-using animals, humans have a behavioral adaptability that is approached by no other creature. At times, however, this symbol-making behavior makes humans prisoners of their own verbal constructs, even when these are oversimple or grossly inaccurate renderings of the actual world. Because people are frequently least rationally objective about matters in which they are most emotionally concerned, it is possible to suggest that the categories people apply to themselves and to their fellow humans include some of the least valid human efforts at category creating. Among these are many of the frequently invoked national, ethnic, and racial stereotypes. In fact, the very assumption that a label invoked by one given discernible trait difference can also serve to characterize a collection of others is itself an example of unwarranted category creation.

Naming

In the early-mid eighteenth century, Linnaeus considered it an act of piety to discover and label the categories of divine creation. At the time, this was an end in itself. Not only did this have orthodox Christian sanction, but it also appealed to a surviving strain of pre-Christian belief that equated the power of human control over the various

components of the world with the ability to call them by name.   **369**
Whether this was the "open sesame" of Near Eastern mythology or
the power to command the Devil by pronouncing his name attributed to Medieval magicians, it was simply the survival of a version of
sympathetic magic. Written for another context, but really quite appropriate, are the words of the late British prehistorian, V. Gordon
Childe:

> It is an accepted principle of magic among modern barbarians as among
> the literate peoples of antiquity that the name of a thing is mystically equiva-
> lent to the thing itself; in Sumerian mythology the gods "create" a thing
> when they pronounce its name. Hence to the magician to know a thing's
> name is to have power over it, is — in other words — 'to know its nature.'

And in biology from Linnaeus on up to the "New Systematics" of
Julian Huxley and others in the early 1940s, one of the principal activities of professional practitioners was the giving of names. Even
now, a goodly percentage of professional biological anthropologists
may sympathize with most of the principles discussed in this book,
yet, in the end, put to us the question, "But how do you propose to
build a subspecific taxonomy?" The implication clearly is that the
power of biological anthropology is determined by its ability to give
names.

Ideal Types

Another dimension involved in the temptation to end the task of biological anthropology with name giving is the conviction that diversity in natural science is best understood by naming and also describing ideal types. This may differ somewhat from the feeling that
power resides in name giving, but it too is ultimately derived from
the human tendency to categorize.

Writing in the fourth century B.C., Plato suggested that the spectrum of varying individuals that we can see in this world is actually
an imperfect rendering of perfect ideas that exist in the divine mind.
Since that time, there has been a persistent tradition that regards the
variation of the visible world as imperfection and illusion. The only
true reality, according to this view, is that of the divine and practically unattainable ideal type. Such was the power and prestige of
Plato that this tendency to what can be called "typological thinking"
has continued to the present day. The stress that the modern racist
puts on "average" differences, even when they cannot be demonstrated, is a perfect example of typological thinking. An individual is
evaluated by the assumption that he or she is an approximation to a
supposed type.

The "modern" appraisal of the spectrum of human diversity by means of a given number of named races, each perceived as stereotyped ideal configurations, received accidental support by the way in which knowledge about the world grew during and after the Renaissance. The discovery of exotic plants, animals, peoples, and places by exploring Europeans was largely accomplished as a result of maritime activity. A ship and its crew, officers and men, put out to sea from northwest Europe and, for a space of several months, saw nothing but water. Eventually when landfall was made, there was a good chance that the people and ecology encountered were quite different from those at the port of origin. As a result, a very particular categorized and discontinuous picture of human variation was reported back to Europe by those who had the broadest first-hand experience in the ways of the world. We can suggest that it is no accident that the first organized accounts depicting the spectrum of variation among the peoples of the world took, as the framework for the organization, the stereotyped appearance of human populations in the major ports of call of the sixteenth and seventeenth century mercantile empires.

Many of the racial stereotypes still assumed — African Negroes and American Indians, for instance — involve the configurations of characteristics encountered in the first European contacts with non-European peoples. These first impressions have survived with extraordinary persistence, in spite of the fact that they were not based on particularly representative samples of the major geographic areas from which they were drawn. With seamen's reports of their discontinuous experience relating to human variation, and the scholar's rendition in terms of divinely created Platonic ideals, it is not surprising that there has been almost no serious questioning of the actual reality of human racial types.

The Fixing of the Race Concept

For several reasons, the Western Hemisphere played a crucial role in the fixing of the race concept as it is now generally if erroneously assumed. Accounts of human variation by the most prestigious and literate eighteenth century Euopeans, for instance that of Linnaeus and, later, the expansion of it by Blumenbach, were still largely academic exercises based on second-hand information. Linnaeus, in fact, fixed on the number four as sufficient to represent the human races, not because it was his experience that such was the case, but because, traditionally, there were four quarters to the world. For the educated European-derived denizen of the New World, however, the

question was a far less academic one. The consciousness of sharp **371**
human differences was reinforced by daily encounter. Moreover, the
gradations that originally occurred between the differing manifestations of human form were not perceived since the groups that faced
each other had been summarily uprooted, transported from the areas
in which they had developed, and artificially juxtaposed.

Americans of European origin included, by virtue of cultural and
educational background, as well as the leisure granted by privileged
socioeconomic position, the only individuals of the confronting
populations who could speculate in writing on the significance of
the encounter. Practices such as slavery and Indian exterminating
were initially carried on without qualm, because, of course, the victims were not Christians. In time, however, both the Indians and the
imported slaves became Christians themselves. But the Christian
Negroes were still slaves and the Christian Indians were still being
run off their land and shot down if they objected, all of which forced
the educated White American to re-examine the nature of visible
human differences.

One of the most disturbing things to be considered was the very
fact of strikingly visible human physical difference. The biblical
account deriving all humankind from a single pair in the Garden of
Eden provided little help. A careful counting of the "begats" in the
seventeenth century had produced a variety of estimates for the
length of time that presumably had elapsed since creation, and these
were in the neighborhood of six thousand years or less. Although
this seemed like a very long time to many, it was uncomfortably
short to those who contemplated the black skin and woolly hair of
African aborigines and tried to imagine how this had developed
from the fair features of Adam and Eve rendered in the religious
paintings of the Old World.

Samuel Stanhope Smith: The First American Anthropologist

The first elaborated attempt to account for the differentiation of
human form following the expulsion from the Garden of Eden was,
not surprisingly, produced by an American scholar, Samuel Stanhope Smith (1751–1819), professor of moral philosophy at the College of New Jersey. In 1794/5 Smith became president of the college,
which, more than a century later, changed its name to Princeton University. As were nearly all college professors at that time, Smith was
an ordained minister, and, as such, he clearly had a vested interest in
reconciling scripture with reality. Reality showed people of very different appearance inhabiting the world, and scripture spoke of all
people having been descended from the original pair. Smith had

Figure 155. Samuel Stanhope
Smith (1751–1819). Author
of *An Essay on the Causes
of the Variety of Complexion and Figure in the Hu-
man Species*, (1787); second
and definitive edition, 1810.

served parishes in the South, the majority of Princeton students was
drawn from the South, and the problem of accounting for human differences was very much in mind.

His account, *An Essay on the Causes of the Variety of Complexion and Figure in the Human Species*, first published in
1787, suggested independently but very much in the same manner as
his German contemporary, Blumenbach, that variations in human
appearance such as skin color, face form, and body build were related to the environmental conditions prevalent where their possessors lived. Some of the argument sounds surprisingly modern, although he did make the almost Lamarckian assumption that the
environmental pressures themselves produced the adaptive responses visible in various human populations—in contrast to the
view we now have of the environment simply selecting those favorable variants that the processes of mutation occasionally generate.
Even so, Smith's book was a remarkable and thoughtful production
considering that it was written more than seventy years before
Darwin's *Origin*.

Humane and thoughtful innovation by a college president, then as
now, however, is a personally risky business, and, shortly after the
second and revised edition of his book was published in 1810, Smith
was forced to resign. The situation has striking parallels to the one in
California more than a century and a half later where a reactionary
and anti-intellectual Board of Regents, instigated by a hostile gover-
nor, fired the university president. "We cannot afford to subsidize
intellectual curiosity" was the guideline in the latter case.

At Princeton in the years immediately following the American

Living People

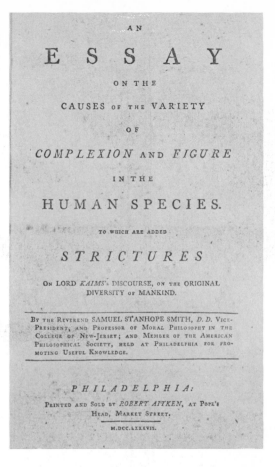

Figure 156. Title page of the First Edition (1787) of *An Essay on the Causes and Variety of Complexion and Figure in the Human Species*, by Samuel Stanhope Smith.

Revolution, Smith presided at a time in which the rigid bonds of traditional orthodoxy were being exposed to the scrutiny of free inquiry. Smith even went to the then-extraordinary length of trying to introduce "science" to the curriculum by hiring John Maclean, a distinguished Scottish chemist. The atmosphere of student ferment and, as a result of his controversial book, questions concerning Smith's orthodoxy led the Board of Trustees to dismiss Professor Maclean, suspend a substantial portion of the students, and force Smith's own resignation. The repression was so successful that, to this day, there are no biological anthropologists at Princeton.

Explanations of Human Diversity

Actually the position defended by Smith, that the human diversity we observe developed from original unity, was identical to that held

374

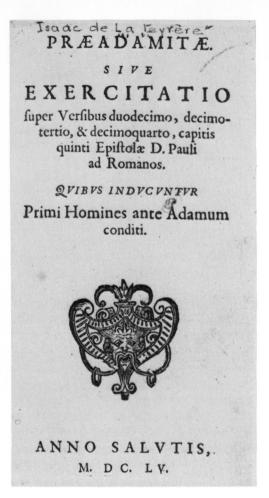

Isaac de La Peyrère

PRÆADAMITÆ.

S I V E

EXERCITATIO

super Versibus duodecimo, decimo-
tertio, & decimoquarto, capitis
quinti Epistolæ D. Pauli
ad Romanos.

QVIBVS INDVCVNTVR

Primi Homines ante Adamum
conditi.

ANNO SALVTIS,.
M. D C. L V.

Figure 157. Title page of Isaac de la Peyere's (1594–1676) *Praeadamitae*, 1655, the pamphlet which preceded publication, in the same year, of the author's *Systema Theologicum.*

by most thoughtful people at that time. Occasionally during the two preceding centuries the notion was raised that not all the people of the world were descended from the "original pair." Some of the arguments were essentially theological—where did Cain's wife come from, for instance. Such questions first achieved public notoriety in the middle of the seventeenth century when in 1655 Isaac de la Peyrère (1594–1676) published a book entitled *Systema Theologicum ex Praeadamitarum hypothesi.* In this work Peyrère argued that there must have been humans before Adam. There was a great outcry against the book among both the orthodox and the learned. Innumerable works were written in condemnation of its heresies. Peyrère himself was seized by the inquisition and forced to publish a recantation in an apology addressed to Pope Alexander VII. In Paris it was ordered that his book be burned by the common

Living People

Figure 158. William Lawrence (1783–1867). Anatomist, surgeon, and physical anthropologist, whose *Lectures on Physiology, Zoology, and the Natural History of Man*, first published at London in 1822, represents one of the classics of physical anthropology.

hangman. The English translation of the book, *A Theological Systeme Upon that Presupposition That Men were before Adam,* appeared some months later in the same year, 1655. In the eighteenth century Voltaire observed that only a blind man could maintain that all humanity had a single origin. From his various writings it is clear that had he lived today Peyrère would have been a distinguished anthropologist.

A number of other French and German authors and scholars in the eighteenth century had maintained views claiming that human diversity could best be explained by multiple creations. In spite of this, however, the most serious and respected students of human physical form, Blumenbach, Smith, and the able English anthropologist James Cowles Prichard (1786–1848), all started with the unquestioned assumption that all humankind could be traced back to the single pair in the Garden of Eden. During the first several decades of the nineteenth century, however, the increase in natural historic knowledge made it increasingly difficult to reconcile the Biblical account of the origin of animate nature with the number of living creatures

376 known. The brilliant English surgeon William Lawrence (1783–1867), in his book *Lectures on Physiology, Zoology, and the Natural History of Man*, 1819, contemplating the gathering of all living creatures at Eden to be named by Adam, their dispersal to the remote corners of the world, and their supposed reassembling to be crammed two by two on the Ark, declared it "zoologically impossible."

While few other scholars were sufficiently daring or impious to state things quite so bluntly — and Lawrence himself was forced to recant under threat of the ruin of his career — nevertheless many were quietly suggesting alternatives to the Biblically sanctioned single time and place for creation. Paris in particular, heir to the sophistication of the "Enlightenment" of the eighteenth century, was a center of innovation. Increasing knowledge of the varied and differing creatures in geologically prehistoric times led Cuvier to suggest that there had been several creations, each at a different time in the past, and that humanity was the product of the last one, the one mentioned in the Bible. Others, more concerned with the variety of creatures in the living world, sought to explain this by postulating that there had been separate creations in each of the major geographic provinces of the world. According to this view, humanity had multiple origins since human populations of different appearance could be roughly associated with the major geographic divisions of the world.

Polygenism

This was an approach to the explanation of human difference that came to be known as "polygenism." French, German, and English writers of the eighteenth century had presented schemes that can qualify them for the label polygenists, but the polygenist movement only gained real strength toward the midpoint of the nineteenth century. Once again, it was in America, where populations from different areas of origin confronted each other, that the thoroughly developed exposition of polygenism was worked out. This is attributable to the influence of the Philadelphia anatomist and physician, Samuel George Morton (1799–1851).

SAMUEL GEORGE MORTON

As a result of his comparative study of prehistoric skeletal material excavated from mounds in the Ohio Valley, Morton came to the sound conclusion that the hitherto mysterious Mound Builders were indistinguishable from more recent American Indians. At least this put an end to the claims that the stockades, earthworks, and other evidences for former civilizations along the Missis- sippi River and its tributaries had been the handiwork of one of the lost tribes of Israel or perhaps Malays or Tartars. These and other explanations had been offered by some who simply could not accept the fact that the remains of sizable former settlements had been pro- duced by the "benighted" Indians.

Morton's work put an end to the guessing, but, in this and in a sub- sequent work on the ancient Egyptians, he demonstrated that for a period of time roughly equivalent to that of the extent of recorded history, human form had undergone no major changes. Of course, it was impossible to judge the precise antiquity of the ancient Mound Builders, but even then archeologists recognized that their towns had extended so far back in time that the inhabitants could not easily have gotten there from the Garden of Eden. Of course, there are those who claim that the Garden of Eden had been located in Western Mis- souri of all places, but this then raises the problem of populating the Old World from there. The case for the antiquity of the Egyptians was much more precise. When Morton was writing his *Crania Aegyptiaca*, enough of the hieroglyphic writing was understood to allow the year by year tracing of Egyptian history back almost to the date that Biblical scholars had fixed for creation. In fact, the person who had furnished Morton with his collection of Egyptian skulls enjoyed confounding the orthodox by demonstrating archeologically that civilization was flourishing in the valley of the Nile before the supposed date of creation.

Be that as it may, Morton had demonstrated in his *Crania Ameri- cana*, 1839, and his *Crania Aegyptiaca*, 1844, that the same human types observable in his day extend back in time to very near the point of assumed creation without exhibiting any signs of convergence. This rendered the monogenist interpretations of Smith, Blumenbach, and Prichard increasingly unlikely and led Morton to favor a polygenist, multiple-center-of-creation interpretation.

Morton's first work (1839), dedicated to Prichard, was hailed as a landmark in anthropology and earned him widespread recognition as the successor of Blumenbach. It was an admirable scholarly ac- complishment comparing human crania by means of more than a dozen carefully performed measurements and marred only by the fact that he allowed an appendix to be attached, written by an avowed phrenologist. The second work (1844) confirmed his repu- tation and earned him the praise of the most distinguished sci- entists in Europe and America.

Morton is largely unknown today, or, if he is remembered, it is in connection with his polygenist views or the taint of phrenology that he did not really accept (although he did not explicitly reject it). His admirable metric and comparative approach to understanding human physical form has been forgotten, and, while there has been much talk about population resemblances and differences, few subsequent investigators have tackled the subject with the systematic and quantitative approach used by Morton.

NOTT AND GLIDDON

By the middle of the nineteenth century, the monogenist opposition was relying more on piety and less on science. Polygenism — separate creations — seemed to be the most reasonable explanation to account for observed human physical differences. But Morton died unexpectedly and prematurely in 1851 and what was offered as the continuation of his ideas in America was the work of two self-styled disciples of a somewhat dubious if flamboyant nature. These were the expatriate British opportunist George R. Gliddon and the racist physician Josiah Clark Nott from the intellectual center of Mobile, Alabama. These two claimed to offer the authority of the late Samuel George Morton in support of the institution of slavery, at that time an explosive issue in the United States. Following the explanation of separate creation for the races of the world, they added the by-no-means-new suggestion that different relative worth was its inevitable concomitant.

In the half dozen years following Morton's death, Nott and Gliddon collaborated on two sprawling tomes that purported to show that slavery, as it was practiced in the American South, was justified by the latest findings of "science." There are two little ironies associated with this. One is that the social and political leaders in the South rejected the support supposedly offered by "science," since the claim of multiple centers of creation was not strictly in agreement with the Biblical story of creation. Slavery was considered all right, but questioning the authenticity of the Biblical account of creation was morally indefensible. The other little irony lies in the fact that the South, having rejected the testimony of "science" in the support of its cherished inhumanity, has turned around in the twentieth century and attempted to use a modified version of the very arguments it originally rejected to condone the continuation of racial discrimination. For whatever small comfort it might offer, at least the present version is couched in somewhat less sophisticated and effective verbalizations than was the case a century ago. In general, the modern racists are somewhat less literate than those of a bygone era, although the theme is the same and they continue to constitute a disruptive and deplorable element.

Polygenism as a recognized explanation for observable human differences, particularly where uprooted human groups faced each other out of context, was dealt two fatal blows within the space of just a couple of years — at least, as far as the English-speaking world was concerned. First was the publication of Darwin's epoch-making

Origin, which displayed a vista of relatively unlimited time and the **379**
slow working of natural forces that completely cut the scientific
ground from beneath polygenism. The second blow was the fact of
the American Civil War. Any use of science that tended to support
the exploitative and racist political philosophy in the American
South was naturally suspect in the emotional climate of the North.
And with Darwinian evolution completely changing the way in
which organic diversity was appraised, it was evident to many that
the only excuse for the continuation of polygenism was the desire to
base differences in privilege and status on differences in human
appearance alone.

Polygenism died in America with the end of the Civil War. It died
in England at about the same time and for much the same reasons.
Not that the British were actively involved in the American conflict,
but the issues were debated in the British press with both pro- and
anti-slavery factions holding forth vigorously, although slavery and
slave trading had been abolished a generation and more before that
time in Britain and her possessions, and majority feelings were reinforced by the outcome of the war.

JAMES HUNT

Scientists in Britain were split on the issues, just as they were in the
United States. One of the most explicit attempts to justify differences
in human treatment solely on differences in appearance was that of
the founder of the *Anthropological Review*, James Hunt (1833 –
1869). In reaction to Thomas Henry Huxley's *Man's Place in Nature* of 1863, which was an extension of the Darwinian thesis to
humans, Hunt used his position as president of the Anthropological
Society of London to deliver an address entitled "On the Negro's Place
in Nature." Since he was an enthusiastic racist, it is not hard to imagine what he thought the Negro's place should be. Within just a few
years, he died quite prematurely, although his passing was still being
mourned in Nazi Germany in the 1930s, where one of the most indefatigable students of race remarked concerning Hunt's death that
"English anthropology also foundered with him." The German judgment was correct if one equates a polygenist form of racism with
"anthropology." Certainly such a manifestation thoroughly deserved
to founder. Suitably enough, the death knell of English polygenism
was sounded by Darwin himself, when he wrote in *The Descent of
Man* (1871): "when the principles of evolution are generally accepted, as they surely will be before long, the dispute between the mono-
genists and the polygenists will die a silent and unobserved death."

While this more or less finished polygenism in England and America, and to a lesser extent in Germany, the alternative was not clearly
perceived and developed. Darwin backed off from a full-scale and

systematic application of the principle of natural selection to humans, stressing rather the import of sexual selection. As we shall show in the next chapter, it is first necessary to break the idea that *configurations* of characteristics have evolutionary meaning — in fact, to abandon the race concept entirely — before a trait by trait evolutionary interpretation of human variation can be developed.

But in the late nineteenth century and continuing right up to the present time, the habit of perceiving human beings in a stereotyped manner was so strong that even Darwin was unable to break it in dealing with human variation. The self-satisfied and literate Victorian world persisted in the assumption that it constituted the pinnacle of cultural and moral excellence, ethnocentrically regarding other societies as inferior to the relative extent of their difference. Likewise, biological inferiority tended to be equated with physical difference from those literate Victorians who pronounced judgment. This tendency survived right up into the twentieth century, where it was reunited with a strain of undiminished polygenism.

Gobineau

One might ask how, following the events of the 1860s and Darwin's statement of 1871, a strain of undiminished polygenism had managed to survive. The answer is that it survived on the continent, particularly in France, where strong antidemocratic and royalist sentiments continued among the socioeconomically privileged, and where the scientific community explicitly rejected Darwinian evolution. The foundation for subsequent appraisals of relative racial worth — really for relative degrees of unworth — can be attributed largely to Count Joseph Arthur de Gobineau (1816–1882) whose principal work, his *Essay on the Inequality of Human Races* (1853, 1855), earned him the dubious distinction of being called "the father of racism," in the admiring words of German racists just before the Second World War. Although Gobineau was French, his Nordic Aryan idealization, really a mystical mixture of distorted culture history, philology, and biological ignorance, was most enthusiastically received in Germany. The composer Richard Wagner and many other influential public figures were strongly attracted; Gobineau societies sprang up toward the end of the century, and his theories found an equally enthusiastic reception in France.

Vocal adherents in England and America followed suit. The general impact on the twentieth century ranged from the race quotas and immigration restrictions legislated, in the mid-1920s by the United States Congress, to Hitler, "The Final Solution," and the horrors of Auschwitz, Dachau, and Buchenwald. Even now, a century later, Gobinism finds direct echoes in the justification for segregation being publicly applauded by White supremacists in the American

South. And as if racism at home were not enough to tarnish the aura of the American dream in the eyes of the world, the United States, for more than ten years, committed massive military support to the maintenance of a political *status quo* in what was part of the French colonial empire, Vietnam. Racism had been a major factor that contributed to the justification for establishing and maintaining political control and exploitation in the first place, and by continuing to shore up what France lacked the power to maintain, the United States was vulnerable to a charge of racism, which only the most self-deceiving rationalization can ignore.

JOSEPH DENIKER

If Gobinism is still apparent in the version of the white man's burden that continues to influence international politics, there is also a strain of polygenist thought that continues in the "scientific" study of race at the present time. Most present-day anthropologists who take seriously the task of creating racial taxonomies recognize that the scheme they eventually produce is, in fact, a modification of the list compiled by the French scholar Joseph Deniker (1852–1918) in his monumental *Races and Peoples of the Earth*, published in 1897. Almost all modern physical anthropologists juxtapose their schemes of classification with a consideration of evolutionary theory, and many of the recent studies on the adaptive significance of variation in individual characteristics represent meaningful contributions to human biology. In spite of this, however, the "evolutionary" study of race starts with groups—it is fashionable to call them "populations"—as a given. As a representation of individual mating probabilities, breeding populations are obviously the focal point for the study of human physical variation, but to assume that there is something significant in the association of, for example, particular manifestations of head form, skin color, and hemoglobin type—something which would warrant giving that particular configuration a name—is quite gratuitous.

PAUL BROCA

In spite of continuing attempts to support this gestalt approach by an overlay of evolutionary terminology, it is apparent that the assumption that there are such nameable configurations in the first place is based on the same world view that shaped the perceptions of Deniker and his contemporaries. It should be instructive to consider this world view for a moment. The logical starting point is with the works and thoughts of the person who has been called the Blumenbach of France, Pierre Paul Broca (1824–1880). As with so many powerful figures—Linnaeus, Cuvier, Virchow—the limitations in

Figure 159. Paul Broca (1824–1880). Neurosurgeon and physical anthropologist. Founded the first anthropological society in Europe at Paris in 1859.

viewpoint that Broca shared with his era have been enshrined by his followers and have continued to control the intellectual climate of the times long after his death. Today in attempting to correct this in retrospect, we should note that the lingering influence is not to be laid entirely at Broca's door.

On the positive side, it was due to Broca's energy and vision that France could be referred to as "the mother-country of physical anthropology," a title conferred with admiration by the American physical anthropologist Aleš Hrdlička. In the face of formidable government suspicion, Broca founded the Anthropological Society of Paris in 1859. The obstacles to its success will be appreciated when one realizes that the Prefecture of Police only allowed the society to meet so long as it did not touch on questions of a "theological, political or social" nature, and sent a plainclothes policeman to the meetings for more than five years to make certain that the organization really was not subversive (it is recorded that the poor policeman was bored to distraction).

Broca persisted and by the mid-1870s his Laboratory of Anthropology became the locus for a School of Anthropology that was recognized as a department of the Collège de France, headed conjointly by Broca and his disciple and successor, Paul Topinard (1830–1911). By the time of Broca's death, his school had grown to

Living People

formidable dimensions and, with the presence of archeologists, ethnologists, linguists, and other scholars, had begun to resemble the kind of rounded anthropology department that has come to flourish in the United States following the Second World War. As a center for the study of biological anthropology, it has not been equalled since.

Presiding over this was Paul Broca, and, while the full development of his views is best presented in the comprehensive tome of his colleague Topinard, *Eléments d'Anthropologie Générale*, 1885, it should be of interest to identify some of the currents of Broca's thought. He was a frank and enthusiastic polygenist, opposing Darwinian evolution. Accepting the conclusions of Samuel George Morton, he adopted the major skull measurements Morton had pioneered and added many more, inventing a battery of measuring devices and establishing a technique that has become the core of anthropometry to this day. Because of his admiration for phrenology, an entire century of subsequent anthropologists and racists has exhibited an almost perverted interest in the relative height of the forehead and size of the frontal lobes of the brain in human groups throughout the world. Attracted by the views of Gobineau, Broca was convinced that progress in civilization depended on race and that Whites, by and large, were superior to Blacks; although his contributions to the techniques of biological anthropology and much else should not be minimized, his contributions to the political power of racism should not be slighted either.

It was in Broca's School of Anthropology late in the nineteenth century that the race concept as it is now generally accepted was most explicitly formalized. And it was Topinard, Broca's pupil, colleague, and successor, who expressed it in its full Platonic form: "Race in the present state of things is an abstract conception, a notion of continuity in discontinuity, of unity in diversity. It is the rehabilitation of a real but directly unattainable thing." Attempting to use this as a guideline and apply Broca's techniques to elucidating the races of the world, Deniker concluded that "in reality, those peoples are almost undiscoverable who represent 'somatological units' (races) comparable to the 'species' of zoology."

WILLIAM Z. RIPLEY

Right at the turn of the century, American economist-sociologist-anthropologist William Z. Ripley tried to simplify the Broca-Topinard-Deniker approach, still using the same "logic," and to produce an easily usable scheme, which he did in his *The Races of Europe*, 1899. This established the Nordic-Alpine-Mediterranean scheme, which still has a grip on public (and alas professional) opinion. Noting that the more measurements one adds, the less likely it becomes that one will discover an individual who fits the racial stereotype, Ripley says, "Confronted by this situation, the tyro is here tempted to turn back in despair. There is no justification for it. It is not essential to our position that we should actually be able to isolate any considerable number, nor even a single one, of our *perfect* racial types in the life." At this point, not being a tyro, he quotes Topinard's definition of race. Following this he adds:

> In this sense alone do we maintain that there are three ideal racial types in Europe to be distinguished from one another. They have often dissolved in the common population; each particular trait has gone its own way; so that at the present time rarely, if indeed ever, do we discover a single individual corresponding to our racial type in every detail. It exists for us nevertheless.

And so typological polygenism, which largely vanished from American anthropology as a result of the Civil War, returned at the beginning of the twentieth century and has been with us ever since. As for the logic on which it is based, Topinard's concept of race could well qualify for inclusion in the appraisal of Bergsonian philosophy given by the historian of science Arthur O. Lovejoy. This he describes as " . . . a thing to be reached, not through a consecutive progress of thought guided by the ordinary logic available to every man, but through a sudden leap whereby one rises to a plane of insight wholly different in its principles from the level of mere understanding." Lovejoy notes that such an approach has great appeal under what he calls the "metaphysical pathos," "the pathos of sheer obscurity, the loveliness of the incomprehensible," and also under "the pathos of the esoteric. How exciting and how welcome is the sense of initiation into hidden mysteries."

We conclude our chapter, as we began it, with the words of Jacques Barzun: "For all purposes, the chief value of race worship is that it stimulates group conceit after paralyzing the critical faculties."

Suggested Readings

BARZUN, JACQUES. *Race: A Study in Superstition.* Revised edition. Harper & Row, Harper Torchbooks, New York, 1965.
    When it first appeared (1937) this brilliant little book was so far ahead of its time that it had less impact than it deserved. Now in its revised form, it is at least as timely and, we hope, more influential than before.

BIDDISS, M. D. *Father of Racist Ideology: The Social and Political Thought of Count Gobineau.* New York: Weybright and Talley, 1970.
    An admirable study.

Living People

GOSSETT, T. F. *Race, The History of an Idea in America.* South- **385**
ern Methodist University Press, Dallas, 1963.
 An excellent work.

HALLER, JR., J. S. *Outcasts From Evolution: Scientific Attitudes of Racial Inferiority, 1859–1900.* University of Illinois Press, Urbana, 1971.
 Scientific attitudes toward race and racial inferiority between the years 1859–1900, and their influence on popular culture. A fascinating book.

JENNINGS, F. *The Invasion of America: Indians, Colonialism, and the Cant of Conquest.* University of North Carolina Press, Chapel Hill, N. C. 1975.
 A benchmark book. Indispensable reading.

JORDAN, W. D. *White Over Black: American Attitudes Toward the Negro, 1550–1812.* University of North Carolina Press, Chapel Hill, N. C., 1968.
 Covers an enormous amount of ground with thoroughness, sophistication, and compassion.

MONTAGU, ASHLEY. *The Idea of Race.* University of Nebraska Press, Lincoln, 1965.
 Encapsulates the trend of our approach in a nutshell.

———. *Man's Most Dangerous Myth: The Fallacy of Race.* 5th edition. New York: Oxford University Press, 1974.
 The myth and the facts.

——— (editor). *The Concept of Race.* Free Press, New York, 1964.
 A critical examination of the concept of race.

OSOFSKY, G. (editor). *The Burden of Race: A Documentary History of Negro-White Relations in America.* Harper & Row, New York, 1967.
 An extraordinary and thorough compilation of excerpts illustrating the attitudes toward race by the great and not-so-great right up to the present time.

RIPLEY, W. Z. *The Races of Europe: A Sociological Study.* D. Appleton, New York, 1899.
 Based on the nonevolutionary and polygenist French viewpoint. This book established the model that has generally been followed by twentieth century English and American anthropologists dealing with race.

SMITH, S. S. *An Essay on the Causes of the Variety of Complexion and Figure in the Human Species.* (Reprint of the 1810 edi-

386 tion) Edited by Winthrop D. Jordan. The Belknap Press of Harvard University Press, Cambridge, 1965.

> This work with the excellent biographical introduction by Jordan is a splendid testimony to the energy, imagination, and devotion of a man who had been unjustly forgotten.

STANTON, W. *The Leopard's Spots: Scientific Attitudes Toward Race in America, 1815–59.* University of Chicago Press, Chicago, 1960.

> A brilliant and thorough job.

STOCKING, G. W., JR. *Race, Culture, and Evolution: Essays in the History of Anthropology.* Free Press, New York, 1968.

> The title is a little misleading since the focus is more on the development of American professional anthropology than it is on the study of race *per se*, but the history presented is fascinating and it does bear on the treatment of race both in legislation and scholarship during the first quarter of the twentieth century.

Human Variation and Its Significance

Chapter 12

The Task of Biological Anthropology

It is the task of biological anthropology to further the understanding of human evolution. The investigation and interpretation of the hominid fossil record is clearly one of the ways in which this may be accomplished, but another and equally important approach is through the consideration of biological diversity among the living peoples of the world. Superficially it might seem as though it would be easier to deal with the abundant evidence present in the form of living peoples, but actually this turns out to be somewhat more difficult.

The paleoanthropologist's approach begins with the arrangement of the known fossil record in time, after which the causal mechanisms postulated to produce the changes so observed can be discussed. To many, the analogous procedure on the part of the student of the living is to arrange the peoples of the world according to geographical location, and then to attempt an explanation for the population differences observed. In practice this is far less easy, since a number of problems immediately arise which greatly complicate the issues.

While it may appear simple, it is in reality extremely difficult to determine where one population ends and another begins. An arrangement of world populations based on such characteristics as stature and head form would differ radically from an arrangement based on hair form and skin color. The criterion for the delineation of living human groups is considered to be their breeding behavior, and a population is then considered to be that group of people whose members habitually choose their mates from among themselves. This approach to the identification of meaningful human groups enjoys considerable popularity at the present time since, following the insights that have come from that branch of the biological sciences called population genetics, the significant unit for the evolutionary survival of a species has been recognized as the breeding population. This works quite well in delineating meaningful groups in nature such as field mice or fruit flies. Zoologists have used the term "races" to designate breeding populations that share identifiable characteristics, and it has been assumed that a similar practice could be followed in dealing with human groups. When "races" are delineated for humankind by modern biologically oriented biological anthropologists, they are usually defined along these lines.

The use of such an approach as an attempt to discover biologically meaningful human groups usually does not take into consideration the fact that human breeding populations are determined by the dictates of culture rather than by specifically physical features. Certainly the most valid groupings of human beings are based on cultural criteria. This puts the biological anthropologist in the awkward position of having to base the analysis of human biological diversity upon groupings that are not primarily based upon morphological characteristics.

The result is that "race" has always been a troublesome issue for human biologists, altogether apart from the social and political problems that have been involved. This accounts for the fact that there is such widespread disagreement among anthropologists concerning the definitions of race and the identification of the races of humans. Definitions range all the way from the denial that races exist at all to the attempt to define race on an exclusively morphological basis, and, for the majority of anthropologists who recognize some division of *Homo sapiens* into constituent races, the number recognized ranges all the way from three to somewhere in the hundreds. Finally, once a given anthropologist has settled on a definition that suits him he then discovers there is relatively little that he can do with his races except to list them.

This is all in marked contrast to the convenience the social scientist finds in the term race. While individual sociologists may have slightly differing definitions, the differences are not significant and in fact disappear in practice. There is virtual unanimity among professionals in the applications and uses of the term. Even those anthropologists who have attempted to define race on biological grounds alone are forced to admit that the sociologist is quite properly within his own province when he studies the problems engendered by race relations. Obviously the concept of race is used in the same way by people concerned with a theoretical as well as an applied interest in politics, i.e., by political scientists as well as by politicians.

The Definition of Race

The definition of race that we offer is essentially that of the social scientist and is based on the perception of physical traits which are assumed to characterize human groups. We define a race as being:

A human group, members of which can be identified by the possession of distinctive physical characteristics.

The inclusion of the word "distinctive" in this definition is crucial, since the importance of race is primarily in human perception and of course the attitudes and actions of the perceivers. Unless differences are clearly and easily perceived, consistent attitudes and practices cannot be pursued and the race in question loses its identity as far as the people under consideration and also the social scientists are concerned. In some cases what are perceived as racial differences are in fact primarily cultural differences between people whose genetically based physical characteristics are not markedly distinguishable. For example, if one were to send a Sikh man to a barber, give him a shave and a haircut and dress him in a business suit he would be indistinguishable from, say, someone of Italian or any other Mediterranean origin. The same thing would be true for a Sikh woman in, for instance, a bikini and a bathing cap. However, the man in beard and turban and the woman in her sari are immediately recognizable as being racially distinct from people of European origin.

Because human breeding populations are delimited by culturally established boundaries, because of inherent defects in the meaning of the term, and because of the inhumanity that has been practiced in the name of race, it has occasionally been advocated that the term be entirely abandoned. One of us (Montagu) has suggested that the significant group to be considered is the human breeding population, noncommittally called an "ethnic group," and that the term race be abandoned for these reasons.

The Analysis of Human Variation

On the face of it, it might seem that race as we have defined it, namely, as a breeding population with the addition of physical differentiation, would be the most desirable grouping for the exploration of human physical differences. Actually the accumulating evidence from recent research shows to an increasing extent that neither the use of breeding population (ethnic group) nor race is sufficient for the understanding of human diversity. It has become apparent that the assumption that there is something significant in the association of traits in a single group of people obscures the factors influencing the occurrence and distribution of any single trait. *The most important requirement for the analysis of human variation is the appreciation of the selective pressures that have operated to influence the expression of each trait separately.* Since in many important cases the crucial selective factors have no reference to ethnic or population boundaries, obviously an approach that takes population as its unit for study will fail to produce an understanding of whatever is influencing the distribution of the characteristics in question.

At this point the reader will remember that the most significant changes in the human fossil record occurred as a result of changes in the selective pressures affecting particular features that followed improvements in the primary adaptive mechanisms in question. Since the primary human adaptive mechanism is culture, it may be legitimately asked why a culturally defined group should not be the proper unit for the study of adaptively determined human variation. The answer is that for some purposes the presence or absence of the crucial adaptive mechanism may indeed coincide with culturally determined population boundaries, but for most characteristics the adaptive mechanism, although cultural, is quite unrestricted by the boundaries of specific cultures. For instance, metal cutting utensils are as much the property of the Congolese pygmy as they are the property of the Viennese — or Roman or New Yorker. Clearly many adaptively important cultural features are not limited by the boundaries of specific cultures, any more than are the genetic characteristics of particular populations limited by their preferred, but not exclusively practiced, breeding habits.

Human physical variation can best be understood by relating the distributions of specific morphological features to the distribution and history (also the prehistory) of the rele-

vant selective and adaptive forces. In the section that follows we
shall discuss a few of the most obvious characteristics of humankind
where the distribution parallels the known or postulated distribution of the selective factors involved. Because of the stress that has
been placed on characteristics controlled by single genes it has been
assumed by many recent authorities that only the study of such traits
could produce any precise insight into human diversity. It is apparent, however, that most of the traits by which human races can be
easily recognized are not single gene traits, and yet, as we shall see,
their distribution is just as revealing as that of the traits which are
relatively simpler in their genetic background.

The traits we shall consider first are those that have been traditionally most important for racial recognition (or discrimination, depending on the purpose motivating the making of the distinction).
The first such trait that we shall examine is skin color.

SKIN COLOR

Figure 160 a and b shows the distribution of skin color throughout
the world just before European exploration and colonization so radically changed human distributions on the face of the earth. It can be
seen that dark pigmentation is only found among people who live
within fifteen to twenty degrees of the equator although not all people who live in the tropics are dark. Furthermore some people who
are generally accounted as being very dark may be partially exhibiting the effects of heavy sun tanning. The aboriginal inhabitants of
Australia, particularly those who did not live in the extreme northern part, frequently give evidence of the fact that their dark color is
sometimes due to living out in the sun without any clothing.

In some areas, however, it is clear that people living within twenty
degrees of the equator are distinctly not noticeably dark, as is the
case with the inhabitants of Indonesia and northern South America.
In these cases, the people in question apparently have not been there
for a sufficient length of time to have developed pigmentary protection.

The three main components involved in producing skin color are
the brown pigment melanin, which occurs in the lower layers of the
epidermis, the red pigment hemoglobin in the skin circulation, and
the yellowish pigment carotene.

Melanin. The most important pigment in the human skin is a
complex organic molecule called melanin formed by special cells,
melanocytes, at the boundary between the inner layer, the dermis,
and outer layer, the epidermis, of the skin. The number of melanocytes does not differ between the various populations of the world,
but the amount of pigment secreted clearly does. The metabolic

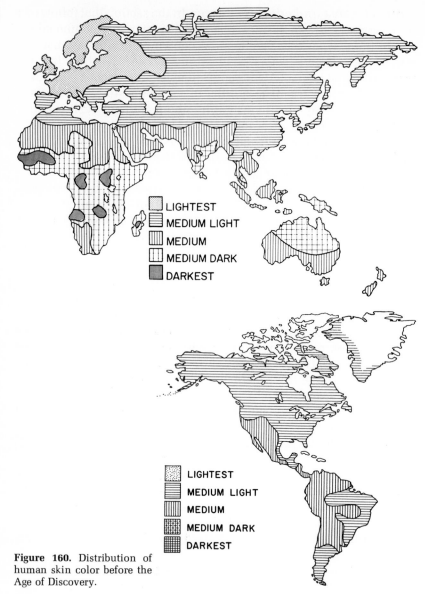

Figure 160. Distribution of human skin color before the Age of Discovery.

pathway by which the melanin particles, or melanosomes, are constructed has several enzyme-mediated steps, one of the most important being the oxidation of the amino acid tyrosine by the enzyme tyrosinase. For our purposes here, a precise knowledge of the steps involved in melanin production is not so important as knowing that a number of enzymes are involved. From our earlier discussion of basic biological processes, it will be recalled that enzymes are pro-

Living People

tein molecules, and that proteins are constructed by linking amino acid units in sequence. A typical enzyme, then, will have several hundreds to some thousands of amino acid units, and each such unit is under separate genetic control. And if it takes at least three nucleic acid base pairs to code one amino acid unit, then one must multiply the number of amino acids in a protein by three to get a minimum estimate of the number of genetic factors involved. In the case of the metabolic pathway by which melanin is constructed, there are several proteins involved, and the number of "genes" contributing to the end product must of necessity be in the thousands. This, basically, is why variation in human skin color appears to us as an infinite gradation, and why no simple Mendelian picture of its mode of inheritance has ever been worked out.

After the melanosomes are formed they migrate out to the tentacle-like tips or dendrites of the melanocytes. These tips are engulfed by the surrounding cells of the Malpighian layer at the base of the epidermis, which is how pigment becomes incorporated into the ordinary cells of the outer layer of the skin. It has been shown experimentally that melanin has the property of being able to absorb light, and, furthermore, that its maximum powers of absorption correspond precisely to the wavelengths that we refer to as the ultraviolet spectrum. Cell biologists are unanimous in their view that the primary function of melanin is the absorption of ultraviolet radiation.

Adaptive Value of Pigment. Where the ultraviolet component of solar radiation is strong, as it is in the tropics, the possibility of damage to the living cells in the dermis of the human skin is always present. Melanin in the outer layer of skin absorbs the harmful ultraviolet radiation and does not allow it to penetrate the living skin. As a result, physicians have long noted the much higher frequency of tissue injury and resultant skin cancer in relatively depigmented as opposed to relatively heavily pigmented peoples where the skin of both has been subjected to excessive amounts of sunshine. Dark skin, apparently, has distinct survival value in the tropics.

Against this it has been argued that many dark-skinned inhabitants of the tropics are not, in fact, much exposed to strong sunlight. The Congo Negroes spend large parts of their lives sheltered by jungle; nevertheless they are quite well endowed with melanin. The explanation is that these peoples have not been forest dwellers for very long. While this at first seems unexpected in view of the widespread belief that the Negro comes from the jungles of Africa, the fact is that this belief is largely a piece of modern folklore. For one thing, tropical rain forest is relatively restricted in extent, covering far less area than either dry grassland with scattered scrub trees or full desert. For another thing, survival in the rain forest depends on the

Figure 161. Albert Namatjira, the distinguished Australian aboriginal painter, and family. Left to right: Rubina, his two daughters, Albert, Oscar, second eldest son, and Tjinaputinga, elder of the Ngarilla tribe. (Courtesy Australian Department of the Interior.)

possession of iron tools and suitable jungle-adapted crops, both of which are relatively recent in Africa. Apparently the Congo area has only recently sustained the populations that now live there, and a consideration of the selective pressures that were important in determining the skin color of the Congolese inhabitants at the present and in the recent past must look instead to the areas from which these people came. There are no historic records placing their origins, but linguistic and cultural evidence all indicates that they came from the area where the grassland merges with the forest to the north and west of the Congo basin and just south of 20° north latitude. The assumption that dark skin has value for individuals who have been adapting for a long time to an environment characterized by an abundance of tropical sunlight is thus not contradicted by the pigmentary characteristics of the peoples of Africa, despite their present distribution.

In addition to the rain forest horticulturalists whom we have mentioned above, there are remnant groups of gatherer-hunters such as the pygmies of the Ituri Forest in the northeast part of the Congo basin. It is commonly assumed that the pygmies represent an older adaptation than the farmers and have been in their present location

Living People

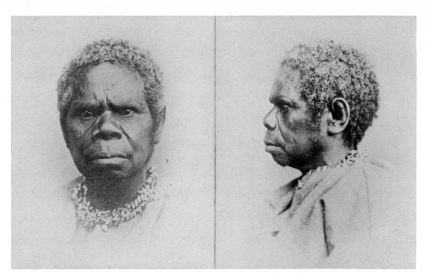

Figure 162. Truganini. Tasmanian aboriginal female, the last of her people to survive, dying 8 May 1976. (Courtesy of The Tasmanian Museum, Hobart, Tasmania.)

for a somewhat longer period of time. In the eyes of those who make such crude racial judgments, both the pygmies and their farming neighbors would be regarded as "black," but in actual fact, the pygmies are a distinctly lighter brown. Evidently their longer residence in the recesses of the forest and the consequent sheltering from the full effects of the tropical sun has resulted in a lessening of the selective pressure needed to maintain a maximum degree of skin pigmentation.

Pigmentation and Environment. While the equator passes several degrees south of the southernmost parts of India and Ceylon, the whole southern half of the Indian subcontinent from Bombay down lies below the twentieth parallel and one would expect, if our assumptions are correct, that the peoples who have inhabited these regions for the longest period of time, and hence who have been longest exposed to the selective effects of the environment, would exhibit the greatest amount of pigmentation in their skins. As is expected, the peoples who as present cultural and linguistic evidence suggests, were the most ancient inhabitants of the area (this is also supported by the myths, legends, semihistorical and historical writings of the ancient Aryan-speaking peoples) are, indeed, the darkest in color, for instance, the Munda-speaking people, as relatively northerly outposts in central India, and most particularly, backwoods "hill tribes" such as the Kadar of southern India and the Ved-

Human Variation and Its Significance

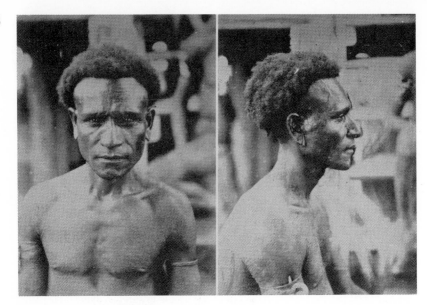

Figure 163. New Guinea male, aged 35 years. (Courtesy of the Musée de l'Homme, Paris.)

Figure 164. Veddas. (From C. G. and B. Seligman, *The Veddas*. Courtesy of the Cambridge University Press.)

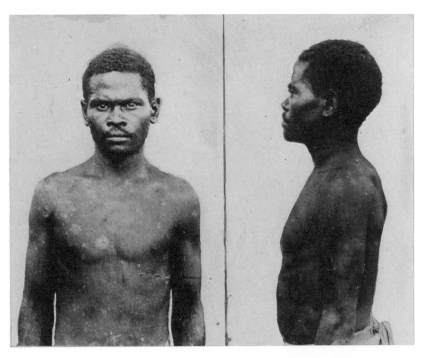

Figure 165. Negrito Aeta male, from Zambales, Luzon, Philippines. (Courtesy of the Musée de l'Homme, Paris.)

Figure 166. Fiji Islanders. Melanesians. (Courtesy of the American Museum of Natural History.)

398

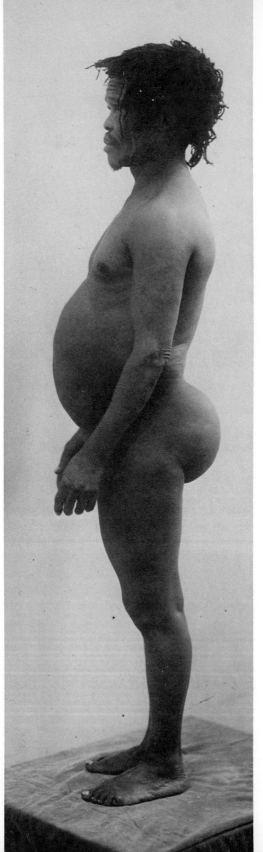

Figure 167. Bushman male. (Courtesy of the American Museum of Natural History.)

Figure 168. Three Hottentot girls. The steatopygia is already marked in the middle one; the one on the right is the offspring of a Hottentot mother and a white father. (Courtesy of the Musée de l'Homme, Paris.)

da of Ceylon. In general there is a north-south color gradient with the darkest people in the south. India then supports the generalizations that have been made on the basis of skin color distribution in Africa.

In southeast Asia, Indonesia, and the western Pacific, again, the initial impression is one of a great confusion of different colors. The

Human Variation and Its Significance

Figure 169. Bushman mother from in front (a) and in profile (b). Hybrid daughter of white father and Bushman mother from in front (c) and in profile (d). Her husband with their daughter (e). Mother, hybrid daughter, and hybrid granddaughter (f). Daughter of white father and hybrid mother (g) and (h), showing how virtually every trace of her Bushman ancestry has disappeared. (Courtesy of Professor P. V. Tobias.)

Living People

equator runs right through the middle of the big islands of Sumatra and Borneo, just south of the tip of the Malay Peninsula, and just north of New Guinea, and the area bracketed by 20°N. and 20° S. includes mainland southeast Asia, the northern quarter of Australia, and all of the islands in between extending far east into the Polynesian part of the Pacific. There are no really dark-skinned people in Sumatra or Borneo or the parts of Indonesia right on the equator, and it is not until one gets farther away from mainland southeast Asia, such as into parts of the Philippines, New Guinea, Melanesia, and northern Australia, that one finds the kind of really dark brown skin

Human Variation and Its Significance

Figure 170. West African Negro. (Courtesy of West African Information Services.)

that for purposes of social discrimination is called black. A few peoples in the refuge of the Malay jungles and the inhabitants of the out-of-the-way Andaman Islands between the Malay Peninsula and India also exhibit very dark skins, but with these exceptions the bulk of the people in Indonesia and southeast Asia range from brown in the south to yellow-brown toward the Chinese border.

The reason there is so little evidence of dark skin among the inhabitants of the western and northern parts of this area is connected with the history of population movements during the recent past. On the basis of the remnant peoples such as the Semang and Sakai of the Malay Peninsula, the Andaman Islanders, the Aeta of the Philippines and other less adequate indications, it is reasonable to regard the original inhabitants of the whole area as having been dark. Population was not dense because the basic means of subsistence was gathering and hunting, which requires large areas to support limited numbers of people. The development of efficient farming techniques farther north allowed these northern peoples to spread south into what must have been for them relatively unoccupied country, either absorbing or eliminating the few darker people who had formerly had the country to themselves.

Historical records amply confirm the north-south movements of the last two thousand years and the decrease in both cultural and physical resemblances to the mainland becomes more marked the farther east one goes until one reaches New Guinea. The inhabitants of New Guinea and Australia are clearly the most ancient populations of the area under consideration, and consistently have dark skins. It seems reasonable to regard the Polynesians who now spread far to the east of New Guinea as being the end product of the first great push from mainland southeast Asia, having passed north of New Guinea itself. If we are correct in regarding the whole area as having been thinly populated with dark-skinned peoples before the migrations, then the present descendants of the first light-skinned people to come from the mainland should show the effects of having absorbed darker elements on the way. This certainly is supported by the appearance of the present Polynesians.

In our consideration of the distribution of the various shades of

Figure 171. Nilotic Negro. Nuer. (From Evans-Pritchard, *The Nuer*. Courtesy of the Oxford University Press.)

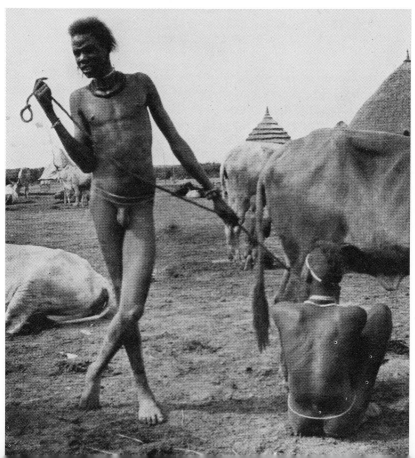

Figure 172. Pygmies. Belgian Congo. (Courtesy of the American Museum of Natural History.)

human pigmentation we have made no mention of the Western Hemisphere. In general it appears that the American Indians have not been across the Bering Straits for a long enough time for selection to have had much affect on skin color, even in the most tropical parts of Central and South America. The color of the Indians then, like that of the Indonesians, betrays their eastern Asiatic origin.

So far, much of our account has been concerned with light-skinned people moving down into tropical areas where dark people had prevailed. Of course in Africa the formidable barrier of the Sahara desert and the swamps of the upper Nile prevented any such population movements and in the New World there were no preceding dark tropic dwellers, but this picture holds true for Arabia, India, and southeast Asia—Indonesia. This southern expansion of light-colored peoples has been recognized by many generations of geographers, historians, and anthropologists, but very few have grappled with the explanation for it.

There are two basic problems involved. First, what made these people light skinned in the first place, and, second, why did they press south? The problem of their southerly movement has been

Figure 173. Andamese Negritoes. Front individual carries palm leaf umbrella; second carries fire container in her right hand; third carries wooden bucket. Little Andaman Island, South of Big Andaman, Bay of Bengal. (Courtesy of the American Museum of Natural History.)

treated from time to time, but we shall defer it until we have discussed the source of their depigmentation. Some authorities have simply assumed that "white" was the original color for all humankind, although this still evades the question of what adaptive advantage it could have conferred in order to become originally established.

Vitamin D. Another suggestion has been advanced claiming that the reduction in epidermal melanin allows more ultraviolet radiation to penetrate the skin and aid in the formation of vitamin D. This presumably is an advantage in those parts of the north temperate zone where year round cloud cover so reduces the available amount of sunshine that every little bit absorbed is of value. This view runs into difficulty when one realizes that at the time of year when sunlight is at its rarest and weakest, the greatest amount of depigmented skin is securely covered with quantities of clothing. By the same token, the fur-covered members of the animal world

Human Variation and Its Significance

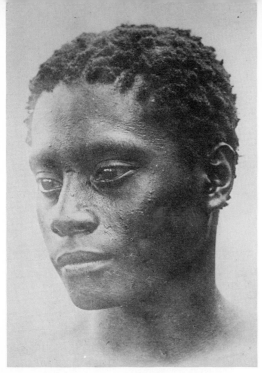

Figure 174. A young Andaman male. (Courtesy of the Musée de l'Homme, Paris.)

Figure 175. Polynesians. Group of Katiu islanders. (Courtesy of the American Museum of Natural History.)

Living People

should all be showing the effects of a severe vitamin D deficiency.

Not only that, but the claims that depigmentation among northern peoples is necessary for adequate vitamin D production have as a corollary the assumption that the presence of pigment in the skin of tropical peoples prevents the overproduction of vitamin D. But as we have mentioned, the chief problem encountered by depigmented people in the tropics is not overproduction of vitamin D but ultraviolet-induced skin damage and resultant cancer. Skin pigment may or may not play a vital role in controlling the synthesis of calciferol or Vitamin D, but there can be no doubt about its importance in controlling the possible damage caused by prolonged exposure to ultraviolet radiation.

Clothing. The mention of clothing brings us to what appears to be the real source of the reduction in skin pigment that is so apparent in peoples whose remote origins were in the neighborhood of 50° north latitude. From our foregoing discussion it seems apparent that a relatively great amount of skin pigment has been of value to a hairless animal living in the sunnier parts of the tropics, and since the fossil record points to precisely this area as the remote home for all humankind, there is some basis for the assumption that the remote human ancestors were dark in color. This being the case, our problem is how some of their descendants eventually became light.

While there can be no proof for it, this is how we believe it happened. The archeological record shows that relatively successful and

Figure 176. Indonesian. Young Javanese male from Bautam. (Courtesy of the Musée de l'Homme, Paris.)

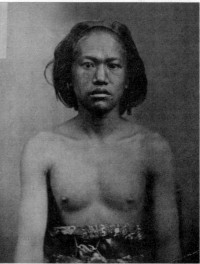

Human Variation and Its Significance

Figure 177. Asiatic Indian. Northwestern India. (Courtesy of Information Service of India.)

Living People

extensive human occupation of the north temperate zone as a permanent habitat did not occur until the last glaciation. During the previous glaciations, the onset of cold conditions had forced people back south, but by the end of the third interglacial, the technological facets of developing human culture had just reached the point where, with some refinement, they would allow people to adapt to the cold instead of having to flee from it. People stayed in the north, then, taking abundant advantage of the quantities of big game that lived there.

The archeological record reveals an abundance of scrapers appearing in Europe and the Middle East at the onset of the Würm glaciation, and this clearly shows an increasing preoccupation with the preparation of animal skins. Equally clearly the Neanderthals did not tramp through the snows in the loin-cloth type of garment pictured in the standard cartoon. One of the things that allowed them to survive was the use of adequate clothing. Humans presented something besides their own skin to the outer world, which meant that the presence or absence of melanin no longer possessed any importance.

With the adaptive significance of melanin substantially reduced, beginning with the onset of the last glaciation approximately seventy thousand years ago, the genetic background for melanin production was free to vary, with the eventual result that mutations opposed to melanin production occurred. Since these were not selected against because of the reduction in importance of the protective function formerly played by melanin, such mutations accumulated with the consequence that melanin ceased to be produced with the same efficiency. Thus the cultural factors that allowed human survival in the north temperate zone greatly reduced the survival value of a particular trait—pigmentation—and the resultant accumulation of random mutations meant that the trait was eventually reduced.

The degree of human depigmentation wherever it is found should indicate the length of time and the extent to which skin pigment has been reduced as an adaptive feature. This is, indeed, borne out by observation since the people with the palest coloring in the world today are those who can trace their ancestry back to the zone stretching from western through eastern Europe and on into southern Russia where the archeological record offers evidence that human survival depended on the use of clothing for a longer period of time than anywhere else in the world. We are tempted to suggest that perhaps this may also be related to why peoples with cultural backgrounds stemming from northern Europe have always been so stuffy about the idea of human nudity, but this is to trespass somewhat beyond the realm of biological anthropology.

It might be asked why the inhabitants of northern China (Manchuria) and Mongolia are not as light skinned as the Europeans of the

Figure 178. Amazonian Indian. (Courtesy of the American Museum of Natural History.)

Living People

Figure 179. Tierra del Fuegian Indians. Straits of Magellan. (Courtesy of the American Museum of Natural History.)

same latitude. The answer must be that they have not been where they now live for quite as long, and that their ancestors therefore were not dependent on clothing for survival for as long a time as the ancestors of the Europeans. The archeological record does not provide the same kind of confirmation for this view which can be seen in the West since the artifacts assignable to the early Würm are notably meager, although this is actually what one would expect if the area were not permanently inhabited at this time. The almost complete absence of evidence for human habitation at this time in the northern parts of the Far East is in marked contrast to the abundance of Mousterian remains in the West and suggests that the depigmentation process in Asia started substantially more recently.

Eventually the cultural mechanism was developed which allowed the inhabitants of eastern Asia to spread north, and which at the

Human Variation and Its Significance

Figure 180. Tierra del Fuegian Indians. Mother and three children. (Courtesy of the American Museum of Natural History.)

same time allowed for a reduction in their epidermal melanin. In this northward spread during the final stages of the Würm, they encountered the Bering Strait land bridge which then existed, and, as a result, populated the Western Hemisphere. With this background, the depigmentation of the inhabitants of eastern Asia and the New World should have started at the same time and it is no surprise to discover that they are approximately the same color.

Only two areas of the world suggest that the south temperate zone was inhabited in the Pleistocene for any length of time, one being South Africa and the other being the southern half of Australia. While neither area shows evidence that clothing was ever sufficiently used to reduce the significance of extensive skin pigmentation, significantly enough both areas are south of the tropics and the intensity of ultraviolet radiation is substantially reduced. We should expect that peoples who are long-time inhabitants of these zones would show at least a partial reduction in pigmentation from the deep pigmentation associated with the descendants of the ancient

Figure 181. Plains Indian. Holding Eagle of the Gros Ventre tribe. (Courtesy of the American Museum of Natural History.)

Figure 182. Eskimo. Alaskan seamstress chewing the sole of a sealskin boot she was making for the United States armed forces in the north. (Courtesy of the American Museum of Natural History.)

Figure 183. Group of Chinese. Staff of Peiping Union Medical College, with Professor Franz Weidenreich in front row center. (Courtesy of the American Museum of Natural History.)

dwellers in the tropics proper, and this we find, indeed, to be the case. The aborigines of the southern part of Australia are not as dark as the "blackfellow" in the north, and the South African Bushmen and Hottentots are lighter still, being a sort of yellow-brown, which accords with the inference, based on archeological evidence, that they have inhabited the southernmost parts of Africa for a longer period of time than the aborigines have lived in southern Australia.

The Relatively Depigmented Peoples. With this explanation of the factors that produced the differences in human skin color, it is now appropriate to consider the factors responsible for the extensive movements, in the recent past, on the part of the relatively depigmented peoples south into India and southeast Asia. Our explanation runs as follows: the technological and cultural changes that

Living People

Figure 184. Italians from Ischia. (Courtesy of the Italian State Tourist Office.)

allowed people to survive in the temperate latitudes during the cold of the last glaciation, and that led to their eventual depigmentation, started trends in cultural adaptation that culminated in the discovery of methods of controlling the food supply after the Pleistocene was over. The Neolithic revolution was a cultural development distinguished by the beginning of human endeavors to control the propagation of plants and animals.

The success of this food-producing way of life in contrast to the previous hunting and gathering kind of existence can be seen in the vast increase in numbers of the peoples whose cultural heritage stems from this source. The food-producing revolution occurred earliest in the Middle East, commencing about ten thousand years ago, and before long the area had almost as many people as the existing subsistence techniques could support. Cultural elaboration, including the improvement of farming, was one result, but another was the actual movement of populations producing the kind of color dis-

Figure 185. Scandinavian. A Swedish fisherman. (Courtesy of the American-Swedish News Exchange.)

tributions we see in the world today. An independent manifestation of the food-producing revolution occurred at almost exactly the same time in the Far East, possibly in southern China, and somewhat later in Mesoamerica in the Valley of Mexico. The consequences for the shaping of subsequent biological developments among the peoples in these areas follow the course one would expect.

HAIR

The form and color of the hair of the head is often given an importance second only to skin color by those who feel impelled to make racial discriminations. The geographical distribution of hair color follows the distribution of skin color without exception, and, in spite of the numerous individuals in whom the two traits appear to be unrelated, it is apparent that this is the one instance where two traits vary together for a biological reason. Pigment in hair itself has no particular significance, but hair is a structure derived from the epidermis and will necessarily share in the processes of the same system for melanin production.

Living People

Figure 186. Eastern European Russian stevedores on the Volga, province of Yaroslav. (Courtesy of the American Museum of Natural History.)

Hair Color. For individuals whose forebears had become adapted to survival in areas of strong sunlight, the well-developed melanin production system of the epidermis will certainly ensure that the hair too has its fair share of melanin. Because of the structure of hair and the arrangement of the melanin granules within it, hair with only a moderate amount of melanin will appear black, which is why so many people in the world whose forebears underwent slight to moderate epidermal depigmentation still have predominantly black hair. Where depigmentation has been allowed to become advanced, the hair is affected, and, depending on the degree, all shades can be seen from brown through blond.

Red hair is something else, the existence of red pigment in the skin and hair being not well accounted for as yet. Red hair appears to be due to a deficiency of melanin, with carotene predominating. The deficiency is also seen in the skin, in which the melanin tends to aggregate in numerous small islands as freckles. Owing to the deficiency in melanin the skin of redheads is highly vulnerable to the

Human Variation and Its Significance

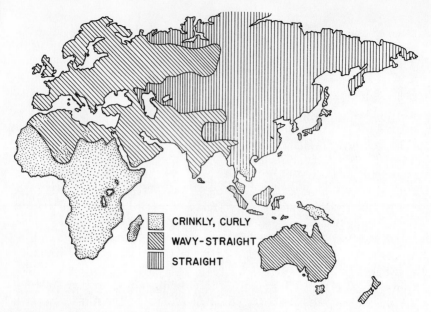

Figure 187. Distribution of human hair form before the Age of Discovery. (Drawing by Mary L. Brace and Richard V. Humphrey.)

effects of what would be considered a normal exposure to solar radiation. With respect to the distribution of melanin, redheads appear to stand intermediate between albinos and brunets. It seems likely that redness in hair and skin arose as the result of random changes in a different part of the enzymatic substrate normally responsible for melanin production, but this must be accounted an educated guess. The highest frequency of red hair, 11 per cent, occurs among the highlanders of Scotland.

Hair Form. Unlike hair color, hair form apparently has had definite adaptive significance. The top of the head is very vulnerable to blows, scratches, burning, and overheating from direct sunlight. There is only a thin layer of subcutaneous fat beneath the skin. A good hair covering not only affords protection to the soft tissues and bone, but serves as protection against mechanical and radiation injury to that rather vital organ, the brain.

The most striking thing about the distribution of hair form is the tendency for the extremely kinky forms of hair to occur among the same populations in which the very darkest skin pigmentation is to be found. There is no direct correlation between skin color and hair form as is shown by the presence of the most extreme hair form among the only moderately pigmented Bushmen of South Africa, so the suspicion is raised that tightly spiral hair may be an adaptive feature and the reason why its distribution parallels that of dark skin color is that both traits may be responses to related conditions. If dark skin is the adaptive response to high levels of ultraviolet radiation, and the insulation provided by woolly head hair is a response to high levels of solar heat radiation, then it is obvious that both adaptations are responses to different problems raised by living in an area characterized by an excessive amount of sunlight.

In the past, observers have noted the presence of dark skin and kinky hair in Africa, traces of it in southern Arabia, stronger traces among the hill tribes of India, the jungle peoples of the Malay Peninsula, the Andaman and Philippine pygmies, and finally its full development in the inhabitants of Melanesia, and have offered a number of theories involving vast migrations for obscure reasons. It is much simpler, however, to regard these instances of the simultaneous occurrence of extremes of human variation in both skin color and hair form as essentially adaptive responses to similar selective pressures. The sunlight at Rabaul in New Britain (Melanesia) is just as intense as that in Kuala Lumpur, Malaya, or that in Kampala, Uganda (Africa), and we should expect to find that similar biological adaptations among the aboriginal inhabitants of these areas developed independently. It is unnecessary to postulate inherently unlikely migrations over half the circumference of the earth in the absence of any evident driving force.

Baldness and Grayness. One more thing can be added in considering variations related to the hair. If our argument relating to depigmentation is generally applicable, then among those people who have provided cultural means for the protection of the head for the longest period of time, we should find the greatest amount of reduction in the biological adaptations aimed at such protection. The same people who were the first to use clothing extensively may be assumed to have provided protection for the head, i.e., hats, and this assumption receives support from the fact that it is among their descendants today that we observe the highest proportion of deficiencies in the normal head protective mechanism. Not surprisingly, it is among people of European derivation that the highest frequencies of gray hair and baldness occur.

And if, as we have argued, the evidence for pigment reduction in China and adjacent parts of the Orient is due to the fact that the use of clothing there has been in effect only somewhat less long than has been the case in Europe, it should also follow that the frequency of gray hair and baldness should approach that of Europeans more closely than is true for any other population in the world. Such indeed is the case.

So far our discussion of human biological variation has dealt with extremes in adaptation that are responses to purely environmental selective forces. To be sure these forces are limited by latitude and not by specific geographic province or breeding population, which means that no nice explanation can be offered which starts with the breeding population as the significant unit. The next facet of human variation that we shall consider will clearly show the futility of beginning one's analysis with "races" or breeding populations, since that variation cuts right across population and even geographic boundaries, and as in the characteristics discussed above, it follows the dictates of selection or its absence.

FACE FORM

Besides general pigmentation and hair form, the characteristics long considered of greatest importance for racial diagnosis are connected with the form of the face. Although the previously discussed characteristics are not merely controlled by single genes or even by the various alleles of a single locus, they are genetically much simpler than the complex of anatomy we call the face. Nevertheless despite the complexities and unknowns that surround the genetic background of face form, an investigation of the variations in the human face shows that the differences can be associated with relatively clear differences in selective factors.

There are two aspects of the face each associated with a different major function subject to important differences in selective forces affecting human survival. These are the parts particularly associated with the respiratory passages and those associated with the whole chewing apparatus. It might be argued that the face is also the locus for the organs of sight, which of course is true, but on the other hand the microscopic complexity of the visual machinery does not allow any gross anatomical differences to occur. Variations in the color of the eye, in color vision, visual acuity, and even in the size of the eyeball can occur without affecting the skeletal housing called the eye socket and without any influence on the anatomy of the adjacent areas. This cannot be said for variations in the nose area and in the jaws and teeth, and it is our intent here to consider such variations and the selective pressures which produce them.

The Teeth. Because variations in the dental apparatus are most clearly related to differences in selective pressures, we shall consider these first. Apart from the existence of an edge-to-edge bite in some peoples but not in others, which is largely a matter of the characteristic mode of usage and hence wear, the primary differences in the human masticatory apparatus are simple differences in size. Some peoples have big teeth and others have small teeth, and of course the whole tooth-bearing part of the face is related to the size of the teeth themselves. Not surprisingly, the people in whom the growth process produces large teeth also tend to have large jaws, large chewing muscles, and other evidences of exuberant bone growth associated with the skull and face.

Good studies on the dimensions of human teeth are surprisingly rare in the scientific literature, but enough information is available to enable us to arrive at a quite satisfactory understanding of the relationship between the size of the dentition and the selective factors influencing it. The smallest teeth are to be found among the peoples of central and eastern Europe, the Middle East, and China; the largest teeth are those of the Australian aborigines. Not only are Australian teeth the largest in the world, but under pre-European conditions they regularly showed the most extreme degree of wear.

This amount of abrasion points in a direct and simple manner to the selective forces operating to maintain large teeth. With the largest of human teeth being worn to the gums by middle age, it is easy to imagine what would happen if the teeth had been any smaller. Obviously smaller teeth would wear down at an earlier age leaving the possessor effectively toothless in the prime of life. A toothless person in the Australian "outback," before the advent of European technology, had a relatively reduced chance of surviving, and if these circumstances occurred before the normal end of reproductive life, the opportunities for transmitting the traits involving small tooth size to the next generation were materially decreased. The operation of the forces that maintained large teeth in pre-British Australia offers one of the clearest pictures of natural selection at work influencing human form and survival.

Since there are great differences in the amount of tooth wear to be seen among the different peoples of the world, and since extremes of tooth wear can influence the chances for survival, it is instructive to consider the causes for wear in its most pronounced form. Clearly the most important function of the masticatory apparatus is to reduce food to the appropriate form and size for swallowing. The teeth, as the bearing surfaces of this crushing machine, are worn, at least in part, by the abrasive content of the food they are made to chew. In the case of the Australian aborigines, the game they catch is singed by being rolled in the ashes of an open fire, briefly roasted, and then eaten—ashes, grit, and all—with a minimum of assistance from a manufactured cutlery. Of course, the products of the hunt provide only a portion, and even so not the major portion of the aboriginal diet, although it was certainly large enough to account for a substantial amount of dental abrasion. The rest of the diet included varying amounts of seeds, nuts, fruits, berries, insects, roots, and vegetable products most of which were eaten without any further preparation or baked uncovered in hot ashes. Obviously the eating of the proverbial peck of dirt was more of an annual experience for the

Human Variation and Its Significance

Australian aborigines and not something that took a lifetime to accomplish.

Although the immense variety of their diet might not qualify the Australians as a literal example of grinding poverty, there can be no question that such a regimen can produce a great deal of tooth wear. There is, however, another important source of tooth wear to be considered that has nothing to do with the diet, and this involves the observation, also made on other peoples who show similar kinds of tooth wear, that the aborigines use their mouths like a third hand. When first discovered, the Australian aborigines possessed a culture of a technological poverty more striking than that of any other people in the world, being on a par with what we believe the most advanced human technology was like some time during the Upper Paleolithic. There was actually quite a spectrum of sophistication in aboriginal Australia ranging from a level equivalent to the Mesolithic in the north to the Mousterian in the south, but there was nothing that could qualify for the designation of technological elaboration. With such a rudimentary tool kit they frequently avail themselves of the convenient all-purpose tool that heredity has provided in the form of their large and powerful jaws and teeth. As a vise, clamp, or pliers, the dentition is frequently used to hold objects, which are then manipulated with the hands. The wear thus produced occurs in most pronounced form on the front teeth in contrast to wear produced by heavy-duty food chewing, which affects the molars, and it is interesting to note that it is the front teeth that show the most extreme degrees of wear by early middle age.

This being the case, one would expect an inverse correlation between the amount of wear on the front teeth and the level of technological development among the peoples of the world, and to a certain extent this holds true. The simplicity of the picture is somewhat spoiled by the discovery that a people such as the Eskimo, with a relatively complex technology for a nonliterate nonindustrialized culture, exhibit a quite similar degree of wear on the incisors definitely limiting the chances for survival of the aging Eskimo. The special problems that survival in the Arctic raise mean that, despite the greater technological development, the Eskimo use their teeth extensively in manipulating their environment—untying knots, chewing frozen boots, and, most important of all, preparing skins for clothing. Among most of the peoples of the world, however, the greater the technological complexity of their culture, the less the front teeth are worn and the smaller these teeth tend to be.

Technology and Teeth. It is apparent that where the teeth are extensively used as tools a premium is placed on large incisor size. Furthermore, small front teeth are distinctly disadvantageous and are actively selected against by the early deaths and failures to reproduce of their possessors. We have no problem then explaining the existence of large teeth wherever they are found. The existence of small teeth at first seems somewhat less easy to account for, but a little reflection will show that their occurrence follows the same principle governing the distribution of depigmentation. Specifically, where technological development has resulted in the production of tools designed to execute the tasks formerly performed by the teeth, the presence of large front teeth ceases to be important for human survival. Random mutations affecting the teeth can occur without disadvantage, and since, generally, random mutation in reference to any structure eventually results in its reduction, the affected teeth are reduced. As would be expected, the people with the smallest teeth in the world are those whose remote ancestors first developed a complex technology.

Technological complexity, however, is not limited by race, and, as a result, that part of face size which is contributed by the dentition varies across population boundaries in a manner that would be quite inexplicable if racial group were taken as the starting point for analysis. Any chart attempting to trace the distribution of differences in human dentition size is plagued by two problems. Published information exists for only a few human populations, and second, other things being equal, big people should tend to have big teeth. Figure

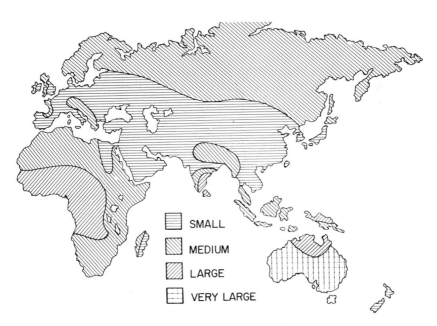

Figure 188. Distribution of relative tooth size before the Age of Discovery. (Drawing by Mary L. Brace and Richard V. Humphrey.)

Human Variation and Its Significance

188 is based on the available information crudely corrected for body size by showing the relative size of the teeth in proportion to body bulk. For instance, the Bushmen of South Africa have always been cited as having small teeth since their dental dimensions are approximately the same as those of Europeans, but then no consideration is given to the fact that Bushmen are noticeably smaller in gross bulk. In proportion to their body size, Bushman teeth are actually relatively large, although not in the same category as those of the Australian aborigines.

We shall offer a few words of interpretation for Figure 188. The smallest teeth belong to those people whose forebears first enjoyed the benefits of the food-producing revolution. Food producers with their sedentary existence generally accumulate more possessions and can therefore develop a more elaborate technology than gatherers and hunters. One of these aspects of technological elaboration is pottery. While we have noted that the development of cooking techniques such as earth ovens and stone boiling may well have led to the beginnings of dental reduction as far back as the Neanderthal stage, it was not until the development of pottery that people could easily reduce food to drinkable form and thus totally suspend the adaptive value of having any teeth at all. But pottery is heavy and it is breakable, and hence is more of a nuisance than a benefit to a nomadic gathering and hunting people. Not surprisingly, the development and regular utilization of pottery does not occur until subsistence technology allows a sedentary way of life. In conformity with expectation, then, a broad band extends from central Europe through the Middle East, across northern India into the Far East and Southeast Asia corresponding with the areas where the food-producing revolution has exercised its effects for the longest period of time.

Shovel-Shaped Incisors. Plotting the distribution of relative gross tooth size in this manner obscures the fact that there is something of a West-East gradient in *effective* incisor size that is not expressed by simple length-width dimensions alone. This is due to a change in the form of the front teeth. Some years ago the American anthropologist Aleš Hrdlička noticed that the incisors of American Indians possessed raised margins on the tongue (lingual) side in such a manner that, considering the root to be the handle, they looked like miniature coal shovels (Figure 189). These "shovel-shaped incisors" were then recognized as characteristic of the inhabitants of eastern Asia, a discovery that gave further support to the view that Asia was the area from which the American Indians originated. Subsequently the shovel shape was recognized in the teeth of Sinanthropus, a fact taken by Weidenreich to indicate that Sinanthropus was the direct ancestor of the modern Asians. However, it

Figure 189. A shovel, a shovel-shaped incisor, and a non-shovel shaped incisor. (Drawing by William H. Price.)

was shown following re-examination of material found before shovel-shaped incisors were recognized as significant that not only the European Neanderthals but also their Upper Paleolithic descendants possessed shovel-shaped incisors, although most modern Europeans do not.

The problem is less the explanation of the origin of shovel-shaped teeth than the explanation of the causes of their disappearance in the areas in which they are not absent. Following our principle of attempting to understand the causes for the existence of specific traits, rather than taking the recognition of difference as a datum of sufficient importance by itself, the significance of incisor form assumes a somewhat different meaning. Instead of constituting an indication of ancestry as was formerly believed, the raised lingual margins of the incisors are in fact an indication that the teeth were formerly (or still are) subjected to heavy usage and great wear. The addition to the total amount of incisor enamel by the elevation of the lingual borders represents a simple adaptive response to increased wear without the increase of overall tooth size and hence increased jaw size.

Although the available material is insufficient for a definitive judgment, it seems likely that all Middle Pleistocene hominids possessed large shovel-shaped incisors. As technology developed and the value of large incisors decreased, particularly in that part of the temperate zone in which the food-producing revolution occurred, selection pressures were relaxed and the teeth were free to vary, with the inevitable result that reduction occurred. There are two ways in which a large shovel-shaped tooth can undergo reduction. One is by the reduction of the overall dimensions, which in our chart (Figure 188) is shown to have occurred all the way across the middle latitudes of the Old World. The other method of reduction is the elimination of the extra enamel in the form of the raised lingual margins. As a reflection of the fact that technological elaboration, in the form of Upper Paleolithic cultures and subsequently the earliest food producers, occurred earliest in the area from the Middle East through central Europe, it is understandable how it has come about that the absence of shoveling makes the effective amount of enamel less among the peoples of these areas than among the peoples farther east whose teeth, in gross dimensions, are of similar size.

A comparison of the tooth-dimension chart (Figure 188) with that representing the distribution of variations in pigmentation shows that the two distributions do not coincide. In fact, starting in the Middle East, where teeth are smallest, and going north and west, it can be seen that teeth in fact increase in size while pigment decreases, with the largest teeth in Europe occurring at the extreme north and west fringes. Evidently while clothing was an ancient feature of cultural adaptation in these areas, the kind of technological complexity associated with a food-producing type of subsistence came much later, a statement supported by an abundance of archeological evidence.

Facial Form. The extent of a band of medium-large dentitions down the east part of Africa reflects the spread of effective stone cutting tools, of the sort which allowed the Neanderthal face to change into a more modern form. This occurred more or less contemporaneously with the Upper Paleolithic in the north. This form of technological advance failed to penetrate the edges of the forest region in West Africa and around the Congo drainage basin, perhaps because of a lack of sufficient suitable raw materials; the effect of this was that the dentitions of these peoples remained relatively larger. People with these larger teeth then multiplied in great quantities following the acquisition of farming techniques and suitable food crops, allowing them to spread into the previously unoccupied African rain forests. Extending outward to the south and east, these people moved into the regions in which a moderately large lower face had been characteristic, in this manner creating, so far as the student is concerned, a somewhat confused picture for this trait in the southern parts of East Africa and the eastern parts of South Africa. The relative size of the lower part of the face in Africa remains the same across the boundaries of skin color, hair form, subsistence economy, and geographic province while at the same time varying within each of these. Clearly hair form or skin color or geographic province has no particular biological or adaptive association with the size of the dentition so that any appraisal of human facial variations that begins with sociologically defined races as its basic units will fail to understand the distribution or the meaning of such variations. *It is only by plotting the distribution of such variations in relation to the relevant selective factors that it is possible to appreciate the problems involved.*

Dental variation elsewhere in the world follows the same principles. The parts of India and Southeast Asia in which live remnants of gathering and hunting populations show a relative enlargement of the lower face. When New Guinea and Australia are added to the areas considered, the results are exactly what one would expect with the relative increase in face size exhibiting a close correlation with the areas in which technological elaboration has been present for the shortest period of time.

The Western Hemisphere is something of a blank, so we have omitted it from our picture of the distribution of human dentitions. There is every indication, however, that it follows our principles very nicely, but the lack of precise published studies means that we cannot check the evidence for the kind of correlation we have found elsewhere. Judging from photographs of Indians from both North and South America, it would appear that the smallest faces in the New World are confined to an area running from the highlands of Peru in western South America north through Middle America to somewhere just south of the boundary between Mexico and the United States. Significantly enough this corresponds with the area in which food-producing cultures have been in existence for the longest period of time in the Western Hemisphere.

From the scant published accounts of actual tooth dimensions among American Indians, the smallest known belonged to the Aztecs of Mexico just before contact with the Spanish. At the same time, the teeth of the Pueblo Indians from the American Southwest were somewhat larger, reflecting the fact that their practice of sedentary agriculture was of more recent origin than that of their Mexican contemporaries. Likewise, the teeth of the Indians at the northern fringes of New World agriculture were larger still.

The distribution of variations in the size of the human dental apparatus apparently follows the distribution of the factors affecting it in an expected manner despite the sketchy nature of our information for many populations. Skin color also behaves in a similarly predictable manner, but the distribution of dental size bears no relation to that of skin color since the important operative factors vary quite independently.

The Nose. With two of the most prominent traits in which people can be seen to vary evidently showing no relation to each other, it is not surprising to find that other traits, the operative selective factors of which are known, are also independent. While the shape of the lower part of the human face is determined by the development of the masticatory apparatus, variations in the upper face are dominated by the shape of the nose.

The history of human face form, commencing with the prehuman ancestors of humans and proceeding to the present day, has been one of varying degrees of reduction. The dental apparatus has undergone reduction as its manipulative functions have decreased, and the whole supporting facial skeleton has correlatedly decreased along with it, with the exception of its respiratory portion. The result has been the preservation of a relic of the former extent of facial development that juts out from the face like a peninsula, and that we now identify as the human nose.

To a certain extent then, the degree of nasal prominence is a reflection of the amount of reduction of the rest of the face. Nose form is also, in part, determined by the relative degree of development of the immediately adjacent parts of the face; for instance the peoples who are noted for the possession of particularly broad noses all have particularly large incisors, meaning that the whole facial skeleton in the area where the nose is widest is noticeably spread. People such as the Australian aborigines and various other peoples from New Guinea to western Africa where, for the reasons mentioned above, the incisors are particularly large clearly show a widening of the whole lower face including the external form of the nose.

In addition to the differences in the width of the lower part of the nose, there remain outstanding differences in the length of the nose and in the height of the nasal bridge which cannot simply be explained by citing different degrees of reduction in the rest of the face. The distribution of nose form in the world is shown in Figure 190 as reflected by the various values recorded for the nasal index. A low index indicates a long narrow nose, whereas a high index describes a relatively short wide nose. However, since nasal width is at least partially accounted for by another trait that is distributed in correlation with the effects of its own selective pressures, it is evident that the nasal index is not the best criterion of nasal length and height. It is, however, the best measure we have and will have to serve in lieu of a better one as the basis for tentative interpretations.

Like dental size, the form of the nose does not correspond very closely to population boundaries and, apart from that portion of its variability directly related to the size of the lower face, it appears that nose form responds to another set of influencing forces. A quick glance at Figure 190 will show that the relatively shortest noses occur only in the tropics and observation confirms the fact that the nasal bridges of the peoples in question are low as well as being short. At first it seems as though no consistent sense could be made from such an observation since such people as the inhabitants of East Africa right on the equator have appreciably longer, narrower, and higher noses than the people in the Congo at the same latitude. A former generation of anthropologists used to explain this paradox by invoking an invasion by an itinerant "white" population from the Mediterranean area, although this solution raised more problems than it solved since the East Africans in question include some of the blackest people in the world with characteristically woolly hair and

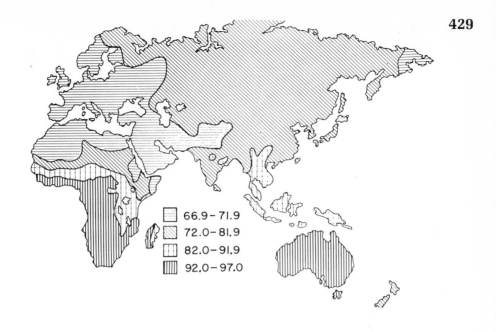

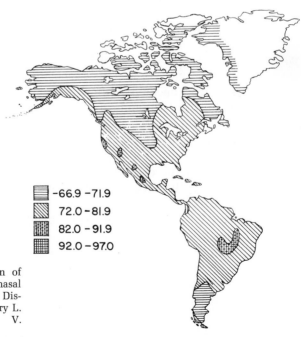

Figure 190. Distribution of different values for the nasal index before the Age of Discovery. (Drawing by Mary L. Brace and Richard V. Humphrey.)

Human Variation and Its Significance

a body build unique among the world's populations for its extreme linearity and height.

While the full answer to the problem of nose form distribution is yet to be given, a good attempt supported by some significant research has been made. The point of departure, as with the other traits, for which distributions have been sensibly explained, has been the consideration of the possible functions differences in nose shape might serve. A long nose lengthens the passage through which inspired air must pass before it reaches the lungs, and this appears to have benefits in two quite different kinds of environments. Where the humidity is extremely low, an elongated respiratory passage serves to moisten the air before it reaches the lungs, and, in an area where the temperature is extremely low, a similarly long passage serves to warm the air before it can desiccate the delicate and functionally highly important mucous membranes. Respiratory function requires a very specific temperature and humidity, and if these are not maintained, the exchange of oxygen and carbon dioxide is inhibited. Drying out of the mucous epithelium of the pulmonary bronchi and bronchioles, for example, results in a cessation of ciliary function and death will follow in only fifteen minutes or so. Eskimos and northern Indians admonish their children to breathe through their noses and keep their mouths closed when exerting themselves in the winter cold. Evidently they recognize the vital role played by the nose in the face of the stresses provided by the climate in which they live.

If this air-conditioning explanation is correct, the distribution of big noses should indicate the areas where people have had to cope with either extreme dryness or extreme cold, and by and large the actual distribution more or less fits expectations. The relatively long noses of East Africa become explicable then when one realizes that much of the area is extremely dry for parts of the year. The long noses of the dry Middle East and those of the cold northwest fringe of Europe fit expectations, but a number of cases seem less obvious at first glance.

The Bushmen of the extremely dry Kalahari desert in southern Africa possess greatly reduced noses seemingly uncorrelated with their habitat. This becomes less of a paradox when it is realized that the Bushmen have only recently been forced to take refuge in the desert by the settlement of the temperate southernmost parts of Africa by peoples possessing more efficient subsistence techniques and weapons. Likewise the inhabitants of the dry central Asiatic plains have only been there for the last few millennia. The Eskimos, also, can be viewed as relative newcomers to the Arctic, and although they do indeed possess long narrow nasal passages, the nasal bridge is not as high as might be expected — perhaps in part due to the fact that the heavy stress placed upon the dentition has meant that the

Living People

rest of the face has undergone relatively less reduction than among the cold-adapted peoples of northern and western Europe.

The Australian aborigines are the final apparent exception to the presumed association of nasal length with lowered humidity. The Australian desert is one of the driest areas inhabited by humans, yet the nasal index is relatively high. In this case, the actual length of the nose is in fact overshadowed by its great width, and this width is probably a function of the fact that the whole lower face is greatly broadened to accommodate the largest incisors possessed by modern *Homo sapiens*. Within Australia itself, however, nose form varies in conjunction with humidity precisely as one would expect, the longest and highest noses occur in the central desert, while the shortest and lowest noses occur in the tropical and humid north.

It remains to be noted that the air-conditioning function of the nose plays an important role in the protection of the individual against all sorts of diseases to which he or she might otherwise fall victim. Maintenance of the moistness of the nasal mucosa forms the first wall of defense against disease by enabling its viro-and bacteriolytic glandular secretions (especially lysozyme) to do their work. Dry mucous membranes lose their ciliary and secretory functions and becoming permeable admit every kind of germ into the circulation, frequently with lethal consequences. At best, the slightest loss of ciliary function results in failure of the mucous trapping of dust particles and the like, again with quite possibly life-threatening results. Hence, the form, structure, and air-conditioning functions of the nose are of the first order of importance.

A final comment on nose form concerns the explanation of the tendency for short low noses to occur among peoples dwelling in the humid parts of the tropics. This again represents an example of the reduction of a character that confers relatively little benefit on the possessors. Long nasal passages are of no particular advantage where the inspired air need be neither moistened nor warmed, so that any variation arising in relation to nose form would be equally likely to survive. Since most naturally occuring variations will tend to reduce the size of the affected structure, the accumulation of their effects in time results in the reduction of the noses of the long-time denizens of the moist tropics.

Body Build

Before turning our attention to a brief discussion of a few of the characteristics for which the mode of inheritance and the genetic basis are known, there is another grossly observable human morphological characteristic that may be considered from the standpoint of its adaptive value. This is body build.

Studies of a generation ago concentrating on variations in human physique tended to attach much importance to human stature. It was eventually shown that there was an inverse relationship between stature and temperature — the colder the habitat the taller the people tended to be. More sophisticated recent studies have shown that if that part of stature change which can be associated primarily with weight change is omitted, then there is no important variation of stature due to changes in temperature alone. Weight, however, does turn out to have a significant negative association with temperature — going up in areas where the temperature drops, and going down where the temperature rises.

There is more to gross variation in human body shapes than simple changes in average weight, and it has become apparent that variation in human body form may well be related to the problems posed by life under conditions that put stress on the ability of the organism to survive.

Body Heat and Body Form. One of the problems we must consider is that concerned with body-heat preservation and body-heat loss. Obviously in a cold climate it is desirable to use the heat generated by metabolic activity as efficiently as possible. Conversely it is equally apparent that for people to sustain activities in very hot climates, the major functional development must be some kind of mechanism that promotes the dissipation of the heat generated in metabolizing enough fuel to produce the activity in the first place. Since heat loss occurs at the surface of the body, it is clear that bodies which have different relative amounts of surface area will differ in the speed with which heat dissipation occurs, as a simple example will demonstrate. If one hundred pounds of copper is shaped into a sphere and heated, it will hold its heat for a much longer period of time than one hundred pounds of copper stretched out in a wire a half mile long and heated to the same temperature. As the example illustrates, a sphere presents a minimum amount of surface area per unit mass and thus is the ideal heat-preserving shape.

Not only does shape influence the relationship between surface area and bulk, but as a little reflection will serve to show, differences in gross size can also play a part. It is easiest to envision these relationships in a cube. The surface area is computed by multiplying the area of one side by the number of sides. The surface area of a single side is calculated by multiplying the width by the length and since these are equal in a cube and the number of sides is constant, changes in the total surface area of the cube will be proportional to the square of any linear dimension. Changes in the volume, however, will vary as the cube of any linear dimension, so it is obvious that as the object gets bigger the volume increases much more rapidly than the surface area, although the shape remains the same.

Nineteenth-century biologists noted that these principles can be **433** applied to animal distributions. Other things being equal, members of a species living in the colder parts of the species range will tend to be larger. It was also noted that those parts of the body that present an extensive surface to the air—noses, ears, limbs—tend to be reduced among the members of the colder parts of the species range. These principles also apply to humans.

Although there are many individual and group exceptions, it can be said that, on the average, human bulk decreases in the hotter and increases in the colder regions inhabited by humans, and the inference has been made that this is related to the greater heat-conserving properties of larger bodies. As examples one can cite the Indians of North America from the plains area on north through the Canadian woodlands and those of the southern Argentinean pampas and Tierra del Fuego. The Indians of these regions tended to be large and bulky. The southernmost of the aboriginal Australians, as also the northernmost of the native Europeans, were relatively large people. But not only are there size differences, there are also differences in shape. Long slender arms and legs are clearly associated with desert-living peoples, while short limbs and heavy bodies can be seen in the Arctic. A number of objections have been raised against considering the short limbs of Arctic peoples as adaptive, but it seems quite clear that the danger of frostbite makes long arms and legs considerably less desirable in cold climates. An example of this can be seen in the fact that the frequency of severe frostbite suffered by soldiers in the trenches during the First World War was far higher among those from Africa than it was among their French allies. And among the American troops on the front lines during the bitter winters of the Korean War, frostbite among Black Americans was many times that observed among White Americans. The difference in body proportions between those of more recent tropical origin and those whose ancestors had been forced to adapt to a climate with frequent and prolonged below-freezing temperatures evidently has considerable significance.

Surface Area and Body Size. Against the adaptive value of specific body form in the tropics, the fact has been cited that the tallest as well as the smallest peoples in the world live cheek by jowl right on the equator in east central Africa. It can, of course, be argued that both extremes in body build are different ways of handling the heat dissipation problem. One way of presenting a maximum amount of surface area to the air is to stretch a given mass into an elongated shape, and certainly the immensely tall East Africans of the Upper Nile area are about as linear and elongated as people can get. The other way of influencing the mass-surface area ratio is to change the size. Increasing gross size without changing form was seen greatly to increase mass in proportion to surface area. This being true, the converse evidently is that a decrease in size will greatly decrease the mass (proportionate to the cube root of any linear dimension) in relation to the surface area, thus accomplishing the same effect as modification of shape.

Adaptive Value of Body Size. The pygmy simply by being small acquires the same surface-mass ratio achieved by the Nilotic African who is normal in bulk but greatly elongated in shape. Since both are equally efficient heat-dissipating mechanisms, the factors influencing the appropriate adaptation will stem from sources other than a simple response to heat regulation. The tall East Africans generally are food producers whose subsistence is derived from their cattle. This means that the food supply is relatively assured and that they obtain regular amounts of protein from their diets. Pygmy subsistence, however, is less assured, and there may be long periods when food is not plentiful and little protein is eaten. This kind of problem would be particularly hard on people who are large enough so that they require a regular and substantial food intake and, of course, would be especially difficult for the rapidly growing child. A people having low nutritional requirements as adults, and whose members grow less rapidly during the critical phases of development, will have a better chance of surviving as marginal gathering and hunting populations in the fringes of tropical forests.

With small size being both efficient for heat dissipation and the best assurance for survival in an area characterized by periodic nutritional bottlenecks, it becomes possible to understand why peoples within the pygmy stature range exist in such places as the eastern edge of the Congo basin, southern India and Ceylon, the Andaman Islands, Malaya, the Philippines, and the remote parts of New Guinea. With the limited amounts of big game in these areas and before the recent advent of iron tools and weapons in many of them, the survival value of being small was considerable.

Former explanations for the distribution of pygmies relied on postulations of vast migrations of a single stock of small-statured people throughout the tropics of the Old World, but it makes much better evolutionary sense simply to regard the pygmies, wherever they occur, as size adaptations made *in situ* by the local populations of the areas in question. The Congo pygmy is simply the small end and remnant of a distribution of gathering and hunting peoples that extended, prior to the diffusion of an agricultural subsistence base into sub-Saharan Africa, around the edges of the Congo forest and on through the edges of the West African forest where it merges with the savanna. In southern India, Ceylon, and Southeast Asia the peoples of pygmoid stature are the remnants of gathering and hunting populations that, because of the great southward push of food-producing techniques and peoples into the more desirable areas, are confined to the more inaccessible and heavily forested areas. Only in the Andaman Islands did pygmies remain unaffected by the unequal competition with food-producing peoples, although here the only choice for habitat was necessarily tropical forest with no big game and the same sort of occasional nutritional bottlenecks that plague gathering and hunting peoples in the tropical forests elsewhere.

For the reasons discussed in our treatment of skin color and hair form, the remnants of the ancient inhabitants of southern India and Southeast Asia are all very dark in color and possess very tightly curled hair. In contrast to this, some of the jungle inhabitants of central Borneo and the Philippines have the reduced coloring and reduced hair curl that is more characteristic of the peoples who have arrived from the north in relatively recent times. At the same time, they are of extremely small size, illustrating the selective effect that the problems of survival in such an environment exert on the human physique regardless of the differences in other traits which may have developed in diverse geographical areas. In the highlands of New Guinea, as well, there are people of pygmy stature but again with very different faces from those of the short peoples of either Africa, Southeast Asia, or Borneo, since they come closer to resembling smaller versions of the faces of the aborigines of Australia. Again the effects of this kind of environment have determined the pygmy physique despite the differences in technological selective factors which have resulted in marked facial differences in the areas considered.

Central New Guinea is a particularly interesting case since there has been no overwhelming invasion of peoples whose characteristics developed in response to selective pressures elsewhere, as was true for southeast Asia and Indonesia, nor have new subsistence techniques been in effect for a long enough time for a substantial change in the distribution of local groups to have been distorted beyond the possibility of recognizing its original form, as has been the case in Africa. As a result the New Guinea pygmy represents neither a discontinuous nor an isolated phenomenon, either culturally or physically, as is now general for the small peoples elsewhere in the world. Because New Guinea has been less overwhelmed either by invading peoples or by the effect of diffusing cultural features than other parts of the world, it is interesting to note that only here is there the completely gradual cline, i.e., the gradient of differences, from the local normal-sized peoples to the pygmies without break in precisely the manner we assume was once the case for all the regions that now give shelter to isolated pygmy populations.

Before leaving the subject of the significance of variations in human physique, another set of influencing factors must be considered. While the pygmies appear to represent a response to problems stemming from both periodic food shortages and the necessity for the efficient dissipation of metabolically generated heat, and other differences in physique appear to be adaptive, there seems to be another factor affecting human survival in parts of the north temperate zone. A belt of chronic overpopulation and undernourishment extends from Egypt through India and into southern China and Southeast Asia, but the people, while small, have not become pygmoid in size. We suspect that their appearance reflects a relatively long-time adaptation to the problems engendered by the intensive cultivation of a single major subsistence crop. The physique of the inhabitants of Mesoamerica was almost certainly shaped by a similar set of circumstances. While it is impossible to do anything more than suggest the answer, it would appear that any further reduction in size would decrease the potential for the amount of work and nourishment people must produce in order to survive. These people seem to be able to produce a maximum amount of work on the smallest possible number of calories per day. If they were larger they would eat more than they could cultivate, if smaller they could not sustain the amount of labor necessary to support a family, so a close adjustment is made, and, despite the different origins of the peoples in this belt, there is a remarkable similarity in bodily proportions.

We have said enough about the gross morphological variations visible in humankind. Others exist that we have not treated, and much of what we have said has been obvious but undocumented by the kind of solid evidence usually demanded of biological interpretations. Our purpose has been not only to touch on the major observable variations in humans, but also to demonstrate that the various traits in which people differ are distributed in accordance with the selective factors responsible for their expression, and not as a result of any association with socially delimited boundaries such as the perception of "race." Where the selective factors are related or happen to vary together, then the traits they influence will likewise vary together, but as we have shown, it is more common to see the selective forces and their corresponding traits varying more or less independently of each other and crossing geographical and population boundaries without regard to the supposed limits of human gene pools or areas of mating preference.

If this approach to understanding human variation is clear when gross morphology is the subject under consideration, it is at least as obvious when characteristics are investigated for which a precise knowledge exists concerning the genetic background. In fact, in much recent biological thinking there has been the feeling that morphological variation is difficult to appraise, since the precise mode of inheritance of morphology is so poorly known. The result has been the abandonment of morphology as a valid area of investigation by many recent students. This in part explains the reason why the

based were collected primarily a generation or more ago and remain so incomplete.

SINGLE GENE TRAITS

Within the last two to three decades there has been a belief among biologists, and particularly biological anthropologists, that the simple understanding of the genetics of a trait was sufficient reason for acquiring information concerning its occurrence in different human populations. Accordingly, the energy that had previously been devoted to morphological trait gathering in generations gone by has recently been transferred to genetic trait gathering. The result has been the collection of an enormous amount of information relating to human characteristics with a simple mode of inheritance. If one recalls the role of the basic genetic material in the production of protein molecules, it is not unexpected that many of the features inherited as single gene characters turn out to be proteins or closely related molecules.

Within the last few years the realization has grown that the distribution of some of these traits corresponds with the distribution of recognized and important selective factors. Now at last some evolutionary sense can be made out of what formerly seemed to be merely biochemical oddities.

Color Blindness. The first such primarily physiological trait that we shall consider is color blindness. The exact biochemical deficiency that produces failures to see colors is unknown, but the mode of inheritance is clear and simple. Contrary to popular assumptions, failure to see red and failure to see green are not due to the same genetic deficiency, although the genes controlling each type of vision occur at loci on the X chromosome and hence are examples of the phenomenon of ordinary genetic linkage as well as sex linkage. Apparently there are at least two alleles at each locus.

While genetically these are actually two separate traits, as far as the individual possessing either is concerned, failure to see colors, whatever the genetic source, is subject to the same kind of selection and for purposes of distribution studies there is some justification for lumping the two. Furthermore, many studies have failed to recognize the differences and have lumped them anyway. It seems obvious that visual acuity, including color vision ability, is highly desirable for a people depending on gathering and hunting as a mode of subsistence. As pointed out by Richard H. Post of Michigan, any deficiency in vision in such a group would be detrimental and would be selected against. For people at a food-producing level of subsistence, the penalties for poor color vision would be less severe,

Human Variation and Its Significance

and one would expect mutations affecting vision to accumulate in time, and eventually result in a reduction of visual efficiency in the same manner in which skin depigmentation occurs following the relaxation of the significant selective pressures.

Theoretically, then, the highest percentage of deficiencies of color vision would be expected to occur among people whose forebears were the first to forsake a foraging for a food-producing mode of subsistence. It would, therefore, also be expected that the distribution of increasing color vision deficiency would be correlated with the cline of dental reduction. In most cases the expectation is completely fulfilled, with the highest percentages of color blindness occurring among people of European and Middle Eastern origin followed closely by Chinese. This, of course, is quite to be expected since, as with the slightly lesser degree of dental reduction in the Far East, the food-producing revolution occurred slightly later in China than it did in the Middle East.

The lowest percentages of color vision deficiency occur among modern gathering and hunting populations, although there is some confusion in the evidence where the samples tested are too small to be reliable. Clearly, then, the distribution of color blindness frequencies, in cutting across boundaries of socially perceived racial differences, behaves in the same manner we have already demonstrated for morphological features. Again, the most important criterion to consider is the distribution of the selecting factor.

Abnormal Hemoglobins. One of the classic cases of the interaction of biological and cultural selective factors can be seen in the distribution of abnormal hemoglobins, in spite of the first impression that this must be something difficult and obscure. This trait was first recognized more than half a century ago with the description of a form of anemia that was usually fatal. At first it was thought to occur only among people of African descent and that it was, therefore, an African "race marker." This view is still widely held among the medical profession and in the American Black community, but subsequent work has shown the trait to be more widely distributed, and that it probably did not arise in Africa in the first place. Not only is the sufferer afflicted with severe anemia, but when a sample of his blood is placed in a low oxygen environment, the red blood cells become twisted into a variety of angular shapes, many of which suggested the form of tiny sickles to the early observers. This latter characteristic, frequently encountered when samples were prepared on slides under glass covers for microscopic examination, earned the disease the name "sickle-cell anemia."

Sickle-cell anemia was eventually shown to be a single gene characteristic determined by the form of hemoglobin carried on the red blood cells. Hemoglobin is the complex organic molecule that forms a temporary bond with free oxygen, enabling the red blood cells to **439** pick up oxygen at the lungs and deliver it to the tissues where it is needed to burn (oxidize) the fuels that run the machinery of the body. Like so many other characteristics whose form is controlled by single genes, hemoglobin is. basically a protein molecule, and, as such, it is chiefly made up of a series of amino acid units. Recent analysis has shown that normal hemoglobin differs from the hemoglobin that produces sickle-cell anemia at the location of only a single amino acid. At a specific point in the amino acid chain, normal hemoglobin has glutamic acid, whereas sickle-cell hemoglobin has the amino acid valine.

Although there are now about two dozen kinds of abnormal hemoglobins known, our primary concern will be for the normal form and for the kind responsible for sickle-cell anemia. Normal hemoglobin is designated hemoglobin A, whereas sickling hemoglobin by convention is called hemoglobin S. Since chromosomes are double structures, the locus for hemoglobin always has two genes. The genotype for normal hemoglobin is AA, the genotype for a person who is afflicted with sickle-cell anemia is SS. This makes the cross between the two—the heterozygote—AS, which also can be induced to show the sickling phenomenon in blood samples but which in the carrier does not show the anemia symptoms. The heterozygote AS is said to show the "sickle-cell trait," and, since the homozygote SS generally dies in early childhood, most of the hemoglobin S in existence is that possessed by heterozygotes.

This brings us to the puzzling problem that has only recently been solved, namely, why the percentage of abnormal hemoglobin should be so high in some parts of the world. High frequencies for hemoglobin S occur in parts of Africa, southern Europe especially Sicily, southern Italy, Greece, Asia Minor, southern Arabia, India, and Southeast Asia; and in some places in East Africa the gene frequency rises as high as 20 per cent. Since almost all the occurrences are in the form of heterozygotes, that should mean that as much as 40 per cent of the people in such a population are heterozygotes. By chance matings, somewhat less than 5 per cent of the next generation should be SS, but since this is not viable, the genes should be eliminated from the common pool. The problem is why, with this constant drain, is S maintained at a 20 per cent level.

Selective Advantages of Sickling Trait. Recurrent mutation is obviously not a factor, since even the most extreme mutation rate is many thousand times too low. To maintain such a frequency, something must be eliminating the homozygote AA at a rate which balances that for the elimination of SS. The answer to this puzzle began to emerge when it was suspected that the heterozygote AS might confer some adaptive advantage in the presence of malaria.

Certainly the highest frequencies of hemoglobin S, all present in heterozygous form, occur exclusively in areas where falciparum malaria is a major hazard for human survival. While it is true that no high frequencies of hemoglobin S persist for long outside malarial areas it is also true that people with very low percentages of abnormal hemoglobin exist in the tropics and in areas where malaria is a severe problem. Since the proof of an adaptation can only stem from the correlation between the selective force and the presumed biological response, the spotty occurrence of hemoglobin S through the malaria belt of the Old World led to some skepticism concerning the proposed association.

Many important aspects remain to be accounted for, but the principal lines of the solution were worked out as a result of the brilliant work of Frank B. Livingstone at Michigan. Livingstone's studies have revealed the relationship between the spread of malaria and the impact of human activities in shaping the environment at present and during the recent past in Africa.

The most serious and widespread form of malaria is caused by the parasite *Plasmodium falciparum*, which is spread among the human hosts by the mosquito *Anopheles gambiae*. Curiously, these mosquitoes do not thrive in the tropic rainforests, since environments lacking sunlight and standing water are among the few in which they cannot thrive. The deep shade produced by uncut tropical jungle and the highly absorbent humus of the forest floor discourage the breeding of *Anopheles gambiae*, and it appears that falciparum malaria must therefore be a recent introduction to much of tropical Africa. Hence the pygmies of the Ituri forest in the eastern Congo and the remnants of former gathering and hunting populations of the Ivory Coast of West Africa have been until recently much less troubled with malaria than the Africans who practice slash-and-burn agriculture.

The practice of chopping down a patch of forest and burning it means that a rich harvest can be reaped after planting in the ashes. The heavy tropic rainfall soon dissolves the nutrients in the topsoil and within a very few years the ground is leached out and unproductive. Furthermore the disappearance of the absorbent humus leaves a soil impervious to water, so that the rain collects in puddles under the open air providing an ideal mosquito breeding ground. As slash-and-burn farmers move from plot to plot over the years they create an environment in which malaria thrives, and it is clear that, despite the high cost in human mortality, the incidence of Hemoglobin S has been spreading in the rain-forest areas because of the protection it gives to the heterozygotes.

The spotty distribution of Hemoglobin S in West Africa and the Congo is due to the fact that slash-and-burn agriculture as a means of subsistence is very recent. The simple business of cutting down the enormous jungle trees would be unprofitably laborious with stone axes and depends on the availability of iron tools. Iron apparently was used and worked in the savanna land south of the Sahara as long as almost twenty-five hundred years ago, but the invasion of the forest has occurred only within the last thousand years. The kind of farming that spread to the savanna land from Egypt was based on grains that yield very poor returns in the wet forest areas, so it was not until the domestication of the West African yam that Africans possessed both the tools and the crops necessary to enable them to penetrate the rain-forest environment.

Livingstone, by piecing together information from linguistic and cultural distributions and what historical accounts there are, has managed to reconstruct the history of the recent past for West Africa. The percentages of Hemoglobin S correspond exactly according to expectation. The peoples who are believed to have invaded the West African rain forest, bringing slash-and-burn agriculture and malaria, possess the highest percentages of Hemoglobin S. The peoples indigenous to the coastal area that have acquired slash-and-burn agriculture, and hence malaria, by diffusion also seem to have had sufficient contact with the invaders to have acquired the abnormal hemoglobin, for while its frequency is not as high as among the newcomers, it is decidedly higher than among the few remaining representatives of the original gathering and hunting forest dwellers where it apparently had been absent.

Of the nearly two dozen known abnormal hemoglobins, several others now appear to be associated with resistance to malaria conferred by the heterozygous state, with other types of malaria parasites and other kinds of mosquitoes implicated.

Malaria has been regarded by epidemiologists as the most serious single threat to human well being and even survival, affecting more people than any other single problem. A number of biological adaptations have arisen in response, and most of them consist of some kind of modification of the functioning of the red blood cell, whether this be an alteration of the hemoglobin molecule or something else. The focus on modifications of the red blood cell or erythrocyte clearly is related to the fact that this is the primary site of infestation by whatever kind of *Plasmodium* the transmitting mosquito introduces into the blood stream. The *Plasmodium* takes over the machinery of the red cell for its own purposes, which consist principally in manufacturing copies of itself. When it has reproduced many times over and its offspring have expanded to take up all the space within the cell, they then burst the cell walls and sally forth to infect other cells and begin the process over again. In a person suffering from malaria, a "crisis" occurs when a new generation of malarial parasites bursts forth from the red cells that had harbored them all at about the same time.

Glucose-6-Phosphate Dehydrogenase Deficiency and Thalassemia. In addition to the abnormal hemoglobins, malarial adaptations include glucose-6-phosphate dehydrogenase deficiency and Thalassemia (also known as Mediterranean anemia or Cooley's disease). The reader will note that many of the adaptations to malaria are associated with anemia. There is a relatively simple reason why this should be so. Anemia simply is the lack of the normal complement of red blood cells and hemoglobin. In the case of the adaptive anemias associated with resistance to malaria, it is not simply that red blood cells are produced in inadequate amounts, but rather that the life span of the average red cell is considerably less than normal. For one reason or another, the red cell undergoes dissolution or hemolysis prematurely. Since the red cell is the principal locus of the growth of the infecting parasite, this means that the immature parasites are dumped into the blood stream before they are ready to fend for themselves. There they are prey to the normal disease-eliminating cells within the blood serum, the phagocytes, which ingest and destroy them. Adaptive anemias, then, help keep down the level of malarial infection, although it should be noted that they do not confer immunity on their possessors nor do they combat the effects of the parasites that are present. Severe anemia, of course, interferes sufficiently with oxygen transport, which, along with a number of painful and unpleasant side effects, is why those who are homozygous for any of the several kinds of abnormal hemoglobins have such a poor prognosis for survival, rarely living past infancy in societies lacking professional medical care. In the heterozygotes, however, the attendant mild anemia is less of a threat to health than the unchecked ravages of malaria. It does pose some problems, however, and a heterozygote for sickle-cell anemia, for instance, can undergo the kind of painful and debilitating sickling attack, normally the lot of the homozygote, when faced with the stress of prolonged partial oxygen deprivation as for example at high altitudes or following extended periods of heavy exercise.

Deficiency in glucose-6-phosphate dehydrogenase, or G-6-PD, does not produce its malarial inhibiting effect through the mechanism of an anemia. Rather G-6-PD deficiency interferes with the ability of the infesting *Plasmodium* to synthesize protein, and if it cannot make protein, it cannot make copies of itself and use the resources of the red blood cell for purposes of its own reproduction. In this manner, G-6-PD deficiency minimizes the impact of the malaria parasite on the infected individual.

Anti-Malarial Traits—When and Where? Adaptive anemias and other such antimalarial traits can be studied among living peoples. The ecological conditions under which malaria becomes a problem can be explored and, with the aid of archeological and historical research, some understanding can be gained concerning the development of such circumstances and the probable role that humans played in creating them. But we can have little direct evidence for the existence of malaria in prehistoric times or when and where adaptive anemias arose to combat it. We know from the contemporary situation that endemic malaria requires a large enough host population so that someone always has it within mosquito transmission range of someone else. Endemic malaria, as with many of the other communicable diseases, could only become a threat to human survival after the population expansion made possible by the food-producing revolution, and at that, it could only occur in areas where conditions were favorable for mosquito propagation.

As we mentioned above, adaptive anemias do remove red blood cells from circulation prematurely. The blood-manufacturing tissues of the body are then pressed into service to replace what was lost. Among the blood-producing tissues are the spongy portions within the ribs and finger bones, the diplöe between the inner and outer layers of the skull, and even the marrow cavities of the long bones in extreme cases. When an individual is chronically short of red blood cells and the blood-producing tissues are continually at work, these portions of the skeleton become hypertrophied or enlarged. Thus, by the analysis of prehistoric skeletal material, we can actually see where anemia had been present. Care must be taken, however, not to confuse an adaptive anemia of genetic origin with anemia caused by a shortage of iron in the diet. The latter is particularly evident in the skeletons of children in their most rapid stages of growth and in women of child-bearing age during which pregnancy and lactation constitute a heavy drain on the female physique. But where both male and female adults show similar enlargements of the diplöe of the skull, we have good reason to suspect the presence of an adaptive anemia.

Analysis of this kind has been done by J. Lawrence Angel, curator of physical anthropology at the Smithsonian Institution in Washington. He has shown that adaptive anemias were present in Bronze Age populations inhabiting the low-lying and swampy areas of Greece and Asia Minor, whereas populations living in drier areas at the same time lacked such indications of disease. This can be taken as evidence that malaria was present in the area of the eastern Mediterranean some five thousand years ago, long before the techniques and consequences of the food-producing revolution had spread into sub-Saharan Africa. We cannot tell, of course, just which kind or kinds of adaptive anemia were present, but we have reason to suspect that most of the known ones had already been developed. The fitness values for the various genotypes can be calculated for the different anemias, and we can figure just how long it would take to reach gene frequency equilibrium. Work of this sort has led to the suspicion that the mutation for sickle-cell anemia may have arisen in the Arabian peninsula, subsequently spreading east into India and west into Africa, but our means of knowing this are somewhat indirect. However, the widespread conviction that it is a trait of African origin is one of the least likely of the several possibilities.

The case for Hemoglobin S, however, remains the best worked out and best documented. It represents something more important than a trait for which the distribution in relation to the selective factors is known, although that is important enough in itself. Of greater interest is the fact that through Livingstone's careful work we now have a well-documented picture of the spread of a trait not only by actual population movement but across population boundaries as a result of the inevitable genetic exchange adjacent populations practice, and the subsequent selective advantage that it confers. Since the genetics of this trait are simple and the selective forces involved are so strong, it can be quantified in a way that is not possible for the morphological traits we have previously discussed. Because of this, Hemoglobin S can serve as a model for understanding the mechanisms underlying the distribution of any trait whose expression is subject to natural selection, whether it be a single gene character or one controlled by an unknown number of genes and loci.

The Blood Groups. With the insights gained from the successful interpretation of the various conditions relating to the abnormal hemoglobins, it is now becoming possible to foresee the explanation of some other characteristics which have been known for some time. Specifically, the near future may produce an understanding of the distribution of the various human blood groups. Information concerning blood groups began to accumulate in 1900 at which time it was discovered that, when the blood from one person was mixed with that from another individual, a clumping or agglutination reaction occurred in some cases. Where agglutination occurred the blood samples in question were said to be of different types.

Blood types remained a minor medical curiosity until the First World War when it suddenly became of vital importance to the military to know the blood types of combat personnel. If transfusion were needed, it was most desirable not to introduce blood of an incompatible type to the recipient since a fatal reaction could occur. Continued research and discovery following the war demonstrated that the various blood types had a simple mode of inheritance, and since they have been identified as mucopolysaccharides, which are organic molecules closely related to proteins, this makes good sense. As the genetics were worked out, it was discovered that the blood types discovered were all the result of three different alleles at the same chromosomal locus. This was the famous ABO blood group system.

Because of its importance in transfusion, an enormous number of blood type determinations has been made during the last third of a century and today more is known about the distribution of the various allelic frequencies in the ABO system than for any other human trait. Somewhat paradoxically, virtually nothing was known about the significance of the distribution. Part of the reason why no effort was made to understand the meaning of blood groups lay in the erroneous assumption that some of the major biological differences between men were nonadaptive in character. The anthropologists who made this assumption were primarily interested in traits that they could use to distinguish what they believed to be the races of mankind. For this purpose they used traits that they assumed were uninfluenced by environmental or selective forces and that were presumably established in remote antiquity. Since blood groups seemed quite removed from the action of selective influences and since they were so clearly inherited, they were seized upon with enthusiasm as the best of racial markers.

There were two consequences of this approach to the study of human diversity. First, the fact that biologists commenced with the assumption that racial groups (breeding populations) were the significant units for analysis provided fuel for those individuals and groups who for their own profit wished to believe that human races are of different innate worth, hence justifying existing practices of racial discrimination. The second consequence was that by restricting consideration to breeding populations it was difficult to appreciate the covariation of selective factors and the respective human adaptations where these crossed population boundaries, as they do in so many cases. This meant that a full understanding of human variation and how it arose was not possible.

Recently, however, there has been a change in the orientation of students of human diversity. It has been realized that a simple naming of human groups or races has no particular significance as a biological aim, although the study of human group relations and hence group identification has real significance for the sociologist and for other social scientists. In addition, human biologists have increasingly realized that their primary task is the explanation of how human variations arose, and it is obvious that the assumption that human differences are nonadaptive defeats any such effort before it is begun. If human form is the product of evolution, then human differences must represent evolutionary responses to different selective pressures. It should, therefore, be possible to explain differences in the frequencies of what were once considered the least adaptive of nonadaptive characters, the various blood types.

With this revitalized evolutionary view in mind, some effort has been made to discover what selective factors could account for the marked differences in allele frequencies, which the ABO system

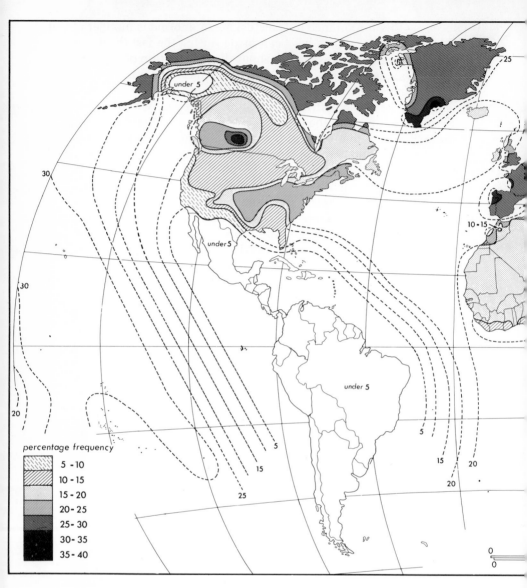

Figure 191. ABO Blood Group System. Distribution of the *A* gene in the indigenous populations of the world. (Courtesy of Dr. A. E. Mourant and Oxford University Press.)

exhibits in the various parts of the world (Figures 191 – 2 – 3). Among other things, it has been noted that there is a slightly higher than expected chance that people with blood type A will suffer from intestinal cancer, and there is a slightly higher than expected chance that those with blood type O will develop peptic ulcers. Neither

Living People

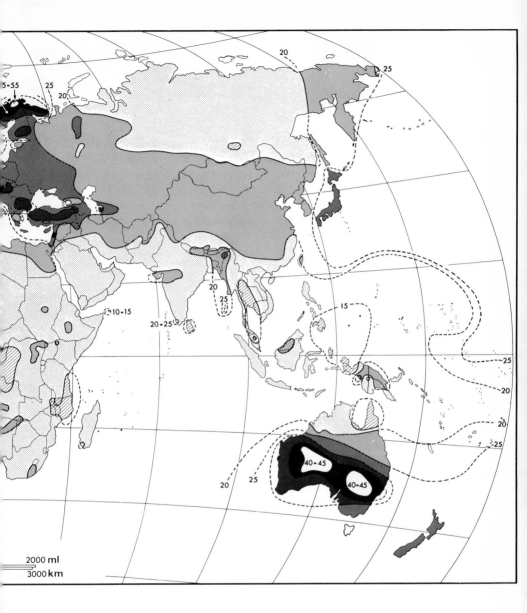

condition is important enough to account for the evolution of the
various differences observed and clearly some other factor must be
sought.

Recently the suspicion has arisen that ABO differences may be
related to characteristic differences in diet. With the immunological
techniques by which blood types are recognized, testing primarily
for incompatibilities in closely related proteinoids, it seemed probable that the various blood types may have something to do with adjustments to other complex organic molecules frequently encoun-

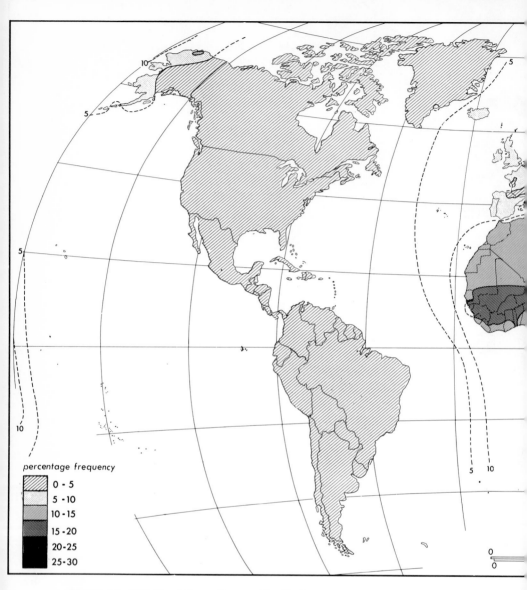

Figure 192. ABO Blood Group System. Distribution of the *B* gene in the indigenous populations of the world. (Courtesy of Dr. A. E. Mourant and Oxford University Press.)

tered during daily life—for instance in eating. The fact that both A and O types are in some way related to problems of the digestive system lends support to this suspicion. Preliminary research shows that there is indeed a suggestive association between various frequencies of the ABO system and major population differences in characteris-

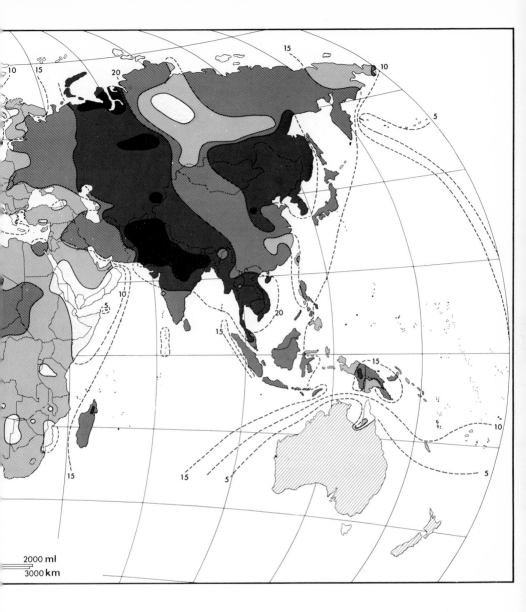

2000 ml
3000 km

tic amounts in fat, carbohydrate, and protein intake. Further work
may show that different kinds of protein may correspond to particular ABO frequencies — for example, some peoples may derive most of
their proteins from animals, while others obtain the greater quantity
from such vegetable foods as beans or lentils. This research, however, has only been initiated recently, and while it is most exciting
and suggestive, nothing has been proven yet. There also is some published work that indicates an association of gene frequencies within
the ABO system and the distribution of smallpox in the recent past.

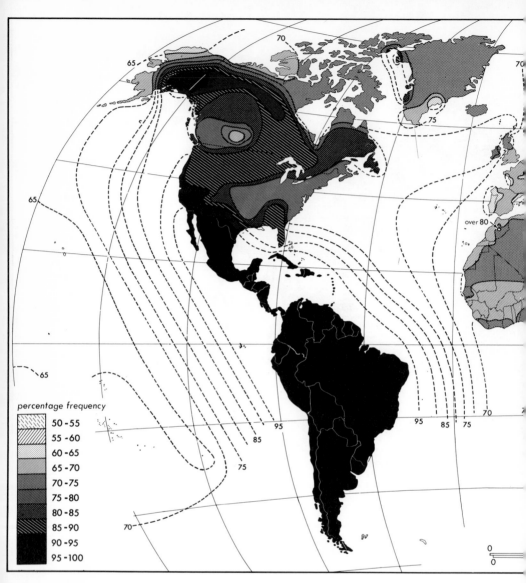

Figure 193. ABO Blood Group System. Distribution of the *O* gene in the indigenous populations of the world. (Courtesy of Dr. A. E. Mourant and Oxford University Press.)

This too is interesting and suggestive, but to date nothing conclusive has been demonstrated.

Other Blood Groups. For the first time, however, investigation is proceeding along fruitful lines, and we can foresee vast increases in the understanding of facets of human diversity in the near future.

Living People

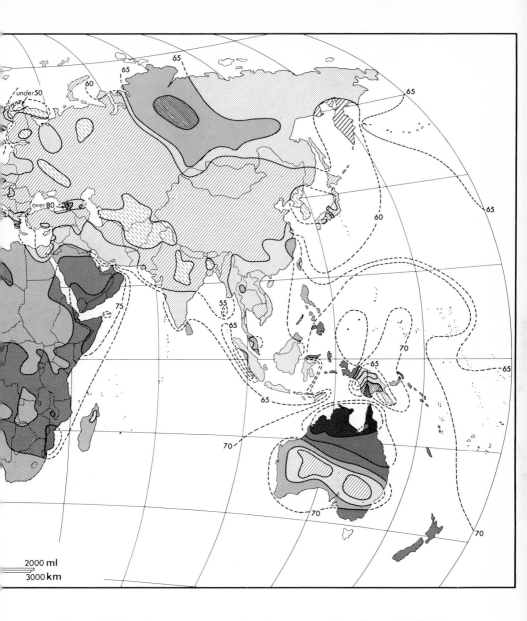

The ABO blood group system has been mentioned especially because we seem to be on the verge of a solution, but we should note
that there are many other blood group systems as well. The Rh system is another for which a great deal of information exists. The reader should not suppose that one is either ABO *or* Rh-something.
There are separate loci for each system and every individual has one
or another of the alleles for both. The Rh system has been considered
important because of the effect Rh incompatibilities can have on the
fetus during pregnancy, but the reasons for the existence of differ-

Human Variation and Its Significance

ences in the system in the first place remain entirely unknown. Other systems include MNS, Duffy, Kell, Diego, and a host of others whose number is limited only by the ingenuity of people interested in their discovery. Everyone has alleles for one or another type within each of these systems, but the selective conditions for the existence of these different types and for the significance of all these blood group systems remain as yet undiscovered. However with this new approach to understanding human diversity, we can look forward to an enormous increase in our understanding of human physical variation in the very near future — in fact, the research is being carried on at this moment and new insights are being reached even as this is written.

Hemophilia. Many other traits wherein people vary are controlled by genes at a single locus, but for most of these, the evolutionary significance remains obscure. Many of these involve failures in one or another metabolic step. Their possessors are at a distinct disadvantage when compared with normal people and have a lesser likelihood of living full productive lives together with a reduced chance of passing the particular trait involved on to subsequent generations. An example of such a trait is hemophilia, or the "bleeder" phenomenon. This is the inability of the blood to clot, a serious handicap to the possessor since it converts a scratch, a bruise, or a nosebleed into a potentially lethal occurrence. This is a sex-linked trait controlled by a single recessive gene on the X chromosome. Because it is so disadvantageous, it is relatively rare, and when it appears it is usually apparent in males only. Males possess a single X chromosome, and if the gene for hemophilia is present, it will be expressed. Females, with two X chromosomes, will usually have the gene for hemophilia masked by the compensatory effect of the dominant normal gene on the other X chromosome. A female, then, can be a "carrier" without knowing it. Half her children will receive the affected X chromosome. If the children are female, they will also have received an X chromosome from the father with a normal gene for clotting (unless the father happens to be a hemophiliac or "bleeder" himself). The single X chromosome present in each male is inherited from the mother, so half the sons of the woman who is a carrier will in fact be hemophiliacs. Queen Victoria, the nineteenth century English monarch, was a carrier and a prolific parent. Her daughters were widely distributed by marriages into the titled families of Europe and carried the potentiality for hemophilia in many instances, thus hastening by genetic means the demise of a system of governance that was already in decline.

Phenylketonuria. Another trait under simple genetic control is the inability to metabolize alanine, an amino acid naturally present in most foodstuffs. Unless this is recognized very early in infancy and countered by a controlled diet, it results in progressive visual and mental deterioration and, ultimately, death. This trait, like many others known to be under the control of a single gene, is an inherited metabolic deficiency. In this instance it is called phenylketonuria, and the observable consequences are referred to as amaurotic idiocy. As with hemophilia, phenylketonuria reduces the chances of individual survival and reproduction. Mutations toward such traits, then, are eliminated within a few generations if not sooner unless extraordinary medical efforts are devoted toward the survival of the afflicted. Because of the severity of the defect, such traits cannot be said to characterize one population as opposed to another. As individual phenomena they can tell us little about the adaptations of populations. Unfortunately, this is true for many of the traits for which genetic information is available.

Genetic and Environmental Interaction

The Face. There are a number of aspects of human biological variation where the interplay between the shaping forces of the environment and the genetic potential of the individual is so complex that it is extremely difficult to tell to what extent one or the other is responsible for the observable end product. We have already discussed the matter of the overbite, which is evidently largely due to the effects of culturally induced habits of tooth usage during the period of facial development. But differences in the kind and intensity of tooth use influence more than just the form of the bite. To be sure, tooth form and size and nose form and size are under pretty strict genetic control, even if these are complex polygenic traits. Other portions of the face, however, are much more malleable and can be greatly influenced by forces that impinge on them during the growth process. For example, heavy-duty chewing emphasizing the prolonged application of force between the molars is accomplished by the use of the masseter muscles, which run from the sides of the cheek bones to the gonial angles (or back corners) of the jaw. In individuals where this kind of activity is regularly performed, lateral growth of the cheek bones and expansion of the gonial angles of the mandible are stimulated during the maturation process. Regular heavy chewing also literally slows down the process of tooth eruption. A person raised under such conditions will have a broader and heavier but shorter face on reaching adulthood, although there may be no genetic difference from others with longer and narrower faces who were raised on a soft-food regimen.

Altitudinal Adaptations. The interplay between genetic potential and environmental shaping is relatively obvious where face form is concerned, but in a number of other traits the matter is more complex. The adaptation to living at high altitudes is an example. Anthropologists and physicians have long recognized the fact that the inhabitants of the Himalayas and the Andes from above 10,000 feet display regular differences from otherwise similar people living at lower altitudes. The barrel-chested appearance is visible evidence of what tests demonstrate to be a considerable enlargement of lung capacity. Red blood cell number is increased as is an alternative oxygen transport mechanism involving diphospho-glycerate. Much investigation has been devoted to the understanding of what it is that allows people to live and work at high altitudes, but it is still uncertain how much if any of the observed adaptations represent genuine genetic differences between high- and low-altitude populations.

Lactose Intolerance.   In the case of differences in the ability to digest milk, there clearly is a genetic component involved, and the doubts revolve around how much if any environmental influence is present. It is an interesting issue, and we shall discuss it briefly. After the age of weaning, most mammals are not faced with the necessity of digesting milk and in fact lose the ability to do so. As informed cat fanciers are aware, the picture of tabby at a saucer of milk is a harbinger of incipient indigestion and not one of contentment. What is true for cats is also true for dogs, horses, monkeys, apes, and most people as well. In recognition of this, milk is excluded from the cuisine that many recognize as the most developed and elegant in the world with respect to variety, subtlety, and overall excellence, i.e., that of the Orient. The Chinese, for example, find the idea of milk in their food repulsive. In their eyes, those who use it are barbarians. The reason, as we shall see, is not uncharacteristic oriental ethnocentrism but simple biology.

On the other side of the coin, ignorance of the same biological facts has ensured that American attempts to aid areas of the world suffering from malnutrition have been misconstrued. The idea that "what is good for America must be good for the world" resulted in the shipment of tons and tons of powdered milk to various "developing" nations long before the milk lobby did its bit to create the ethos of Watergate. Since milk produces cramps and diarrhea in most adult humans, many of the recipients came to regard American milk shipments as an insidious capitalist plot to poison them. In one Latin American country, the people, instead of throwing away the powdered milk "poison," used it as a whitewash for painting their houses.

The portion of milk that creates the digestive problem for so many people is lactose, a sugar that must be broken down into its monosaccharide components before it can be absorbed through the intestinal wall. Children, prior to weaning, possess an enzyme, lactase, which

performs the task of splitting the sugar, lactose, into digestible form.
Normally lactase ceases to be secreted some time during the juvenile years, after which milk can no longer be ingested with impunity.

Students of this phenomenon have referred to it as lactase "deficiency," as though people who exhibit it have something wrong with them. However, since it is the normal adult human condition, perhaps the term "lactose intolerance" would be preferable.

When we mentioned the problems that normal human lactose intolerance have created for American foreign aid, we used the phrase "what is good for America must be good for the world," but we should note that implicit in this statement is the unspoken assumption that the America being described is "White America." As it happens, most Americans of African origin have difficulty digesting milk when they are grown. When this was first recognized, it was thought that differences in lactose tolerance/lactose intolerance might be "racial" in nature. But if the reader has followed us in our discussion of sickle-cell anemia and the other traits once thought to be "racial" in nature, the suspicion should naturally arise that something else must be involved. This is indeed the case.

As it happens, the enzyme lactase continues to be secreted in the majority of adults of northwest European heritage. Since the initial studies of lactose intolerance were made by people of northwest European extraction, they assumed that their condition represented the norm and that departures from it were the exception. However, subsequent study has shown that, while the ability to digest milk is present in the majority of western Europeans, it decreases as one goes south and east in Europe until it becomes the rare exception by the time one reaches the eastern Mediterranean. But in certain peoples in Africa and India, again, lactase is normally present in the adult.

The key is to be found in the long-term adult use of milk in certain societies. The complication, on the other hand, is in determining just how much of the preservation of adult lactase secretion is determined by continued stimulation of enzyme secretion and how much is due to a genuine genetic difference between populations. Some individuals continue to possess lactase as adults whether they need it or not. Others lose the ability to secrete it regardless of the stimulation. But there are still others who continue to produce lactase so long as they are regularly exposed to milk during the years of childhood through adulthood; however, they lose this ability if they cease drinking milk for a period of time. Of these cases, some regain the ability to secrete lactase (and hence digest milk) after being reintroduced to milk and suffering stomach upsets for varying lengths of time, but there are others who cannot regain this ability once the stimulus has stopped.

In some individuals, lactase clearly acts like an inducible enzyme whose presence depends on continued stimulation. In others, the presence or absence appears to be principally under the control of heredity. At the moment, we do not know if this represents a genetic polymorphism. We suspect that this might be the case, but so far we lack the controlled studies that could demonstrate it.

It is clear, however, that the presence or absence of a functioning enzyme in adults is closely correlated with cultural practice. In the African and Indian societies in which adult lactase frequency is similar to that in northwestern Europe, milk and dairy products are staple foods. In such societies, it is possible that those who cannot digest milk have a lower fitness, and that the high lactase figures represent an actual evolutionary change, but until we know the extent to which lactase is an inducible enzyme we cannot be certain. All we can say at the moment is that adult lactase frequency levels are highly correlated with the use of milk as a staple food; that lactase presence is genetically controlled in some individuals; and that environmental induction appears to be important to differing degrees in other individuals.

Cold Adaptation. We have spoken repeatedly of humans as being tropical mammals, but we have noted that, at least where body proportions are concerned, there is evidence for some kind of difference in the adaptations of populations living in cold as opposed to warm climates. As with some of the other adaptations we have mentioned, there remains the problem of how much of the observed adjustment is due to acclimatization and how much is due to a genuine genetic difference between human groups. Let us turn, for a moment, to the evidence for physiological adaptations to temperature differences.

The Alaskan Eskimos maintain the highest known rate of metabolism, being matched only by the female divers, the Ama, of Korea and Japan. The maintenance of a high rate of metabolism, however, is considerably influenced by the extraordinarily high fat and protein intake, and, so far, the amount of genuine genetic difference, if any, has not been determined. In controlled studies, it has been shown that it takes more cold stress to induce shivering in an Eskimo than in other subjects studied, and that Eskimos maintain higher skin temperature and peripheral circulation for longer periods of time when tested with hands immersed in an ice-water bath. In these tests, White American soldiers, matched for age and body composition, appear slightly less adapted to survival under cold conditions than Eskimos, but the difference is small and may represent conditioning of some sort on the part of Eskimos. What is most interesting about these tests is the fact that Black American soldiers, matched for age and body composition, shiver sooner and show a much more marked drop in skin temperature and peripheral blood flow. If we cannot say whether the difference between Eskimo and White is of genetic origin, we certainly *can* say that the difference between White and Black represents a genuine genetically controlled case of adaptive distinction. Anyone whose hands have been thoroughly chilled in winter time is familiar with the difficulty this can induce in handling buttons and zippers. Admittedly the use of zippers has not itself been important during the thousands of years in which Eskimo physiology was being shaped to its current status, but almost certainly the ability to perform manipulations requiring a similar degree of strength and dexterity was of great and sometimes of crucial value. The ancestors of the White American soldiers, with an evolutionary background in glacial Europe, may well have been subjected to selective forces of a similar nature. The same, however, could not be said for the ancestors of the Black American soldiers.

Another kind of cold adaptation has been observed among Australian aborigines. This involves the drop in temperature of the skin and the extremities, while, without the onset of shivering, body core temperature is maintained. Such an adaptation enables an aborigine to sleep unclothed but comfortable during the winter nights of central Australia and yet burn a minimum amount of calories. This may seem to be a more efficient solution to the problems induced by temperature drop than the one evolved by arctic peoples, but it must be realized that the conditions faced in the two areas are really quite different. In the middle of the Australian desert, where daytime temperature may be 120° in the shade, winter night temperatures may drop appreciably below freezing, but the chance of freezing to death or even the possibility of the loss of fingers or toes by frostbite is virtually nonexistent. Of far greater importance is the maintenance of bodily functions with the minimum of caloric expenditure since food is rarely abundant and often in critically short supply. On the other hand, although starvation is always possible for the Eskimo and is known to have occurred, generally when food is available it is present in quantity with an abundance of fats and protein, while death by freezing is an ever present danger. For the Eskimo, bitter cold is the principal danger and calories can be squandered to meet its threat, while for the Australians, starvation is the greatest menace and caloric expenditure can be reduced by a lowering of peripheral temperatures at night simply because there is no danger of freezing to death. As with the Eskimo, however, there is still a good deal of uncertainty surrounding the question of how much of the Australian form of adaptation is genetic and how much is due to acclimatization.

Heat Adaptation. If populations faced with the stress associated with severe cold can be seen to demonstrate adaptive responses, we should expect to find some sort of adaptation to extreme heat.

458   Again, such indeed appears to be the case. In 1942 the summer was particularly hot in India, and there were more than fifteen hundred cases of heat prostration and nearly fifty deaths among the soldiers in the British army. But incapacitation among soldiers from the British Isles was between thirty and fifty times greater than among Indian troops. Subsequently it has been shown that there is far less salt (sodium chloride or NaCl) in the sweat of tropical populations than in that of White Europeans.

Profuse sweating causes dehydration and, in addition, where there is an appreciable amount of salt in the sweat, salt depletion can also occur. With the salt level of the blood thus lowered, the osmotic balance is upset. At this point, the body makes an attempt at adjustment by excreting more water via the kidneys to raise the salt concentration of the blood, but this causes still further dehydration and contributes to the danger of heat exhaustion and circulatory collapse. At this point, simply ingesting water cannot restore the balance, for in addition to the nausea and vomiting induced, this would result in a further dilution of the blood. Unfortunately, in human beings, there is no such thing as a specific craving for salt comparable to that which drives herbivores to salt licks. As a consequence, as physiologists have found, salt deficiency in tropical countries is possibly the most common deficiency state.

The deliberate addition of salt to food evidently is a product of the focus on plant foods that followed the food-producing revolution. The herding peoples of the world and the remaining hunters use no salt in their food, while agricultural people virtually all do. Plant eaters, whether human or not, ingest in their foods a quantity of potassium that must be excreted via the urine. Inevitably salt is lost as well, and this must be made up in some way. Herbivorous mammals do this by visits to salt licks, and agriculture-dependent human populations deliberately add condiments to their foods. Carnivores, on the other hand, get enough sodium chloride in their diet in the first place and are not faced with the problem of excreting excess potassium in the second.

Where copious sweating is necessary to control body heat, as in the tropics, some means of retaining salt within the body tissues is obviously desirable. This is particularly true for tropical agriculturalists where the salt lost through urine as well as sweat must be made up, and where table salt is a precious and often rare commodity. Body salt retention is promoted by the steroid hormone aldosterone, secreted by the adrenal cortex. In people who have become acclimatized to heat stress, aldosterone levels are significantly higher than for people in cooler areas. But while all people possess the capacity to adjust aldosterone output to the demand of circumstances, it is also clear that there are population differences of genetic origin.

In some populations, it appears that aldosterone levels are congeni- **459**
tally higher than in others.

This evidently is advantageous where body salt conservation is
needed to counter the threat of possible heat exhaustion, but under
other conditions it can pose something of a problem. Salt retention is
accompanied by a rise in blood pressure, and this, in cool climates
and on a diet high in salt, can lead to hypertension and its attendant
threats to health and well being. For example, during the last several
decades, medical authorities have become aware that American
Blacks have higher blood pressure, more hypertensive disease, and
higher mortality from hypertension at every age level than do American Whites. Differences in acclimatization are not involved, and differences in diet do not seem sufficiently important. Evidently there
is a genuine genetic difference in the level of aldosterone production
between American Blacks and American Whites. In a hot climate in
which sweating is profuse and salt intake limited, a high aldosterone
level promoting salt retention by the kidneys is desirable, and since
the high air temperature is accompanied by dilation of the peripheral blood vessels, blood pressure is not elevated. But a cooling of the
environment is accompanied by vasoconstriction, which produces a
rise in blood pressure, and this, along with a diet that is rich in salt,
creates a potential problem for people with a high aldosterone level.
French fries, potato chips, and that gastric disaster, the American hot
dog, can create hypertension in some individuals simply by the
powers of suggestion, but if aldosterone levels are already high, they
constitute a threat to more than the powers of digestion alone.

Intelligence.   The final topic we shall treat in our consideration
of traits that have both an environmental and a genetic component is
perhaps the most controversial of them all—intelligence. Things get
sticky even before we consider what evidence there is—if any—for
differences in intelligence because it is hard to find any consensus
on a definition for intelligence. There are many warnings about what
intelligence is not: it is not rote memory; it is not speed in problem
solving; it is not poetic creativity; it is not the ability to identify with
other people's problems; and it is not good manners or the capacity
to hold one's liquor. Nor is it any help to quote the old psychologist's
cliche, "intelligence is what intelligence tests test," since the reasoning behind the phrase is completely circular. Since no two intelligence tests are alike, what is being tested in each instance must itself
be different, which leads us to suspect that there is no identifiable
thing that can constitute a trait called intelligence. Like the concept
of "race," intelligence appears to have its reality principally in the
realm of human assumptions before these have been subjected to any
systematic investigation. No one is really sure, for example, what is

indicated by IQ, the intelligence quotient. IQ test scores do constitute an excellent predictor of success in schools, but so do tests for fluency in the use of standard middle class English, and a good case can be made for the possibility that IQ scores tell more about the kind of dialect a child was raised to speak than they do about his or her capacities.

Alfred Binet, the originator of the first intelligence tests, warned that differences in test performance were meaningless unless one were assured that the sociocultural background of those being tested was substantially the same. Others have noted that test performance cannot measure a capacity fixed by heredity at birth. Years of practice in the language and protocol of test-taking are necessary before a good performance can be achieved. Innate abilities are shaped by exercising them until they are completely altered. Raw capacity becomes practiced performance only after years of nurturing, and at the end, what is measured is principally the effect of that nurturing, at which point an attempt to measure the genetic contribution to that performance is at best completely irrelevant.

Yet the lives and futures of millions of children each year are determined by the measure of what is uncritically assumed to be innate capacities. An army of professional testers regularly decides who shall be allowed to learn what, effectively deciding years in advance who shall eventually be allowed to enter which special training program and consequently which career. The extreme of this form of determinism was practiced until recently in England, where a child's whole educational future was decided on the results of tests administered at age eleven.

From time to time, there have been attempts to prescribe treatment of whole population blocs on the basis of average test performance, rather than assessing each individual on his or her own merits. One of the most recent of these has been the attempt by California educational psychologist Arthur R. Jensen to draw conclusions from the average difference in performance between American Whites and American Blacks in IQ tests. The difference amounts to some eight points on a scale in which 100 is taken as "normal." Statisticians would call a difference of this magnitude "significant," although what it signifies is a matter of continuing debate.

It is claimed that, since IQ has a heritability of .8, presumably indicating that 80 per cent of one's test score is genetically determined, the lower average Black IQ is an indicator of innate intellectual inferiority. At this point the enthusiastic racial discriminator can say, "Aha!," or "I knew it all the time," or even "I told you so." Some might even go so far as to advocate segregation, reduction of funds for schools in Black districts, or disenfranchisement. But even if both the heritability and the IQ figures could be taken at face value, this would still constitute failure to treat an individual on his or her own merits. And as we have seen, there is more than just a little doubt about what is indicated by IQ figures.

Heritability also is a tricky concept. A high figure for the coefficient of heritability, the figure .8 for IQ, for instance, is often taken to indicate that genes are more responsible than environment in determining performance on intelligence tests, but there is a flaw in this common assumption. We can only demonstrate that heredity is important in determining the differences between individuals when the environment is not only uniform but also maximally favorable for the development of whatever is under genetic control. A high coefficient of heritability, then, is more an index of maximum environmental favorability than it is a measure of the importance of genes *per se* in the control of the development of a given trait. Intellectual attainments can only be fully realized under the most favorable of conditions, and if such conditions are provided, then individual differences will owe more to genes than to differences in environmental advantages. The figure of .8 for the heritability of IQ was derived from the study of upper middle class suburban school children, and it is more an indication of the favorable conditions that the upper middle class can provide for the intellectual development of their offspring than it is a disembodied measure of the importance of genes.

Where the coefficient of heritability for IQ is measured on the urban poor, the figure is below .4. In some instances, it is lower than .2 and not significantly different from 0. This, however, is more of an index of environmental deprivation than a demonstration of the unimportance of heredity. The coefficient of heritability, then, is evidently misnamed. At best, it can be taken as an indicator of environmental favorability. So far, the work in educational testing as indicated by both IQ and heritability data has demonstrated that Blacks in America have yet to be given the benefits that a large part of the White population has come to take for granted.

In spite of this, some very prominent people have chosen to interpret the results as confirming their assumptions about the intellectual inferiority of people of African origin. After citing average IQ differences, they then suggest that different intellectual capacities developed as adaptations to the pressures of living in different cultures, and some have claimed that the flowering of art, literature, and science in western civilization is the consequence of a superior average intellectual capacity. What this completely ignores is the fact that the average person played absolutely no role whatever in the celebrated florescence of Western Civilization. During the age of discovery in the Renaissance and until well after the Industrial Revolution was truly under way, the average European was an illiterate

462   peasant consigned to a life of hard agricultural labor almost exactly like that of the West Africans who were captured and brought to America as slaves. The climate may have been different, but the long-time adaptation to a life rooted in the soil, the care of crops, planting, weeding, harvesting, and the progress of the seasons gave them more in common with each other than either has with their descendants in the postindustrial America of today. If the argument that intellect is determined by adaptation to the long-term conditions of an ancestral civilization can be taken seriously, then there is every reason to expect that the inherited intellectual capabilities of the average American Black and the average American White should be absolutely indistinguishable.

Whatever the truth may be, there is no excuse for attempting to rank populations in terms of intellectual capabilities. We do not do so for strength, for the ability to make subtle taste distinctions, for the ability to determine pitch or color, or any of a wide range of other capacities. The prolonged public furor over possible racial differences in intelligence test scores, then, appears to be another attempt to reintroduce the old and discredited traditions of racial discrimination. No good can come of it, and the sooner it is allowed to relapse into the obscurity it deserves the better off everyone will be.

For those who persist in the feeling that it is somehow "important" to know what difference if any there might be in average intelligence, we can suggest that there is one positive benefit that might emerge. Such an assessment can only be made under equal conditions of maximum favorability. We recommend, therefore, that public energies be diverted from present invidious comparisons and focused on providing the greatest possible opportunities for the realization of individual potential. Only then can the issue of relative intellectual capabilities be posed with any chance for a fair answer. Although we suspect that the answer might prove to be as trivial under those ideal conditions as it most certainly is in our present less than perfect state, the achievement of such a future is well worth working for no matter what the initial motivation may have been.

Suggested Readings

BAKER, P. T., AND J. S. WEINER. (editors). *The Biology of Human Adaptability.* Oxford University Press, New York, 1966.
   An admirable series of studies,

BEALS, K., AND A. J. KELSO. Genetic variation and cultural evolution, *American Anthropologist,* vol. 77, 1975, pp. 567–579.
   A stimulating study of genetic variation in interaction with cultural evolution.

Living People

BLOCK, N. J., AND G. DWORKIN. (editors). *The I.Q. Controversy.* **463**
Pantheon Books, New York, 1976.
    An excellent book of readings.

BRACE, C. L. A non-racial approach toward the understanding of
human diversity, Ashley Montagu (editor). *The Concept of Race.*
Free Press, New York, 1962.
    A new approach to the study of human diversity.

————, G. R. GAMBLE, AND J. T. BOND. (editors). *Race and Intelligence.* American Anthropological Association, Washington,
D.C., 1971.
    An effort to put in perspective one of the most recent attempts to "prove"
    the supposed innate inferiority of non-Whites.

————, AND J. METRESS. (editors). *Man in Evolutionary Perspective.* John Wiley, New York, 1973.
    A selection of readings designed to support the views we present in the
    current book.

DAMON, A. (editor). *Physiological Anthropology.* Oxford University Press, New York, 1975.
    Excellent studies of human adaptations to climate, light, work, altitude,
    nutrition, disease, noise, and levels of stimulation and stress. Indispens-
    able.

FELDMAN, M. W., AND R. C. LEWONTIN. The heritability hang-
up, *Science,* vol. 190, 1975, pp. 1163–68.
    A critical examination of the misuse of heritability measures with espe-
    cial reference to IQ. A fundamental paper.

FRISANCHO, A. R. Functional adaptation to high altitude hypoxia,
Science, vol. 187, 1975, pp. 313–19.
    The most recent review of high altitude adaptation.

HARRISON, G. G. Primary adult lactase deficiency: A problem in
anthropological genetics. *American Anthropologist,* vol. 77,
pp. 813–35, 1975.
    An excellent review.

KATZ, S. H. [editor] *Biological Anthropology: Readings from
Scientific American.* W. H. Freeman, San Francisco, 1975.
    The *Scientific American* editorial style allows nonspecialists to read
    the results of experts in various fields.

LIVINGSTONE, F. B. Anthropological implications of sickle cell gene
distribution in West Africa, Ashley Montagu (editor). *Culture and
the Evolution of Man,* Oxford University Press, New York, pp.
343–54.

464   A demonstration of the manner in which genetic differences become established in adaptation to environmental pressures.

————. *Data on the Abnormal Hemoglobins and Glucose-6-Phosphate Dehydrogenase Deficiency in Human Populations.* Museum of Anthropology, the University of Michigan, Technical Reports, No. 3, Ann Arbor, 1973.
Everything you always wanted to know about hemoglobins but did not know enough to ask.

LOEHLIN, C. J., G. LINDZEY, AND J. N. SPUHLER. *Race Differences in Intelligence.* W. H. Freeman, San Francisco, 1975.
An unbiased, balanced, and noninflammatory treatment.

LOOMIS, W. F. Skin pigment regulation of vitamin-D biosynthesis in man, *Science,* vol. 157, 1967, pp. 501–506.
On the possible mechanism of skin color differences in man.

MOLNAR, S. *Races, Types, and Ethnic Groups: The Problem of Human Variation.* Prentice-Hall, Englewood Cliffs, N. J., 1975.
An up-to-date treatment of the material covered by the present chapter.

MONTAGU, ASHLEY. (editor). *Race and IQ.* Oxford University Press, New York, 1975.
An anatomy of the claims for the relation between IQ and race.

———— Natural selection and the origin and evolution of weeping in man, *Journal of the American Medical Association,* vol. 174, pp. 392–97, 1960.
Also provides an account of the anatomy and physiology of the air-conditioning functions of the nose and associated structures.

MOURANT, A. E., KOPEĆ, A. C., AND K. DOMANIEWSKA-SOBSCZAK. *The Distribution of the Human Blood Group Polymorphisms.* 2nd ed. Oxford University Press, London & New York, 1976.
The fullest and most authoritative presentation of the subject.

NEWMAN, M. T. The application of ecological rules to the racial anthropology of the aboriginal new world, *American Anthropologist,* vol. 55, 1955, pp. 309–27.

———— Adaptations in the physique of American aborigines to nutritional factors, *Human Biology,* vol. 32, 1960, pp. 288–313.

Newman, R. W. Why man is such a sweaty and thirsty naked animal: A speculative review, *Human Biology,* vol. 42, pp. 12–27, 1970.

————, AND E. H. MONRO. The relation of climate and body size **465** in U.S. males, *American Journal of Physical Anthropology*, vol. 13, 1955, pp. 1–17.
  Four papers on the relation between climatic factors and form and size of the body.

POST, R. H. Population differences in red and green color vision deficiency, *Eugenics Quarterly*, vol. 9, 1962, pp. 131–146; vol. 10, pp. 84–85, 1962.

———— Population differences in vision acuity, *Eugenics Quarterly*, vol. 9, 1962, pp. 189–212.

———— Hearing acuity variation among Negroes and whites, *Eugenics Quarterly*, vol. 11, 1964, pp. 65–81.
  Three papers indicating some of the factors probably operative in the evolution of certain functional differences between populations in vision and hearing.

ROBERTS, D. F. Body weight, races, and climate, *American Journal of Physical Anthropology*, vol. 11, 1953, pp. 533–556.

———— AND D. R. BAINBRIDGE. Nilotic physique, *American Journal of Physical Anthropology*, vol. 21, 1963, pp. 341–370.
  Two papers on climate and physique.

Weiner, J. S. *The Natural History of Man*. Anchor Books, New York, 1973.
  Highly readable, and especially good on adaptation and variation.

WILLIAMS, B. J. *Evolution and Human Origins: An Introduction to Physical Anthropology*. Harper & Row, New York, 1973.
  Especially good on the treatment of genetics and variation in recent human populations.

YOUNG, J. Z. *An Introduction to the Study of Man*. Oxford University Press, New York, 1971.
  A monumental survey of basic human biology, and a great deal more.

Continuing Evolution

Chapter 13

Culture and Development

The most remarkable thing about human beings is the cultural adaptive mechanism which they have created in order to increase their chances for survival. The realization of this fact constitutes the justification and the basis for the fascination exercised by the social sciences and humanities. In the preceding pages we have attempted to give some indication of the role that culture has played in not only ensuring humanity's survival but also in altering the selective pressures that have operated on humans and thereby influenced the course of their physical evolution.

Initially culture provided the tools and verbal means of coordinating group activities which served to increase the chances for group survival in the face of possible predation by carnivores, and which increased the efficiency of the acquisition and distribution of food. With culture as humanity's principal adaptive mechanism, it was important that individuals be able to acquire an adequate command of their culture before it became their responsibility to nurture the next generation. Up to a point, there was a selective advantage in favor of those individuals best able to master the necessary cultural adaptations.

Intelligence

Making a rough correlation between brain size and learning ability, it is obvious why cranial capacity increased during the greater part of the Pleistocene. Eventually a level was reached where the efficiency of the cultural adaptive mechanism was such that it benefited even those individuals who were not completely able to master it. At such a point, individuals who were just up to acquiring the necessary requirements of their culture would have just as good a prospect for survival and transmission of their characteristics to the next generation, as were those who could master their culture with ease. With no adaptive advantage inherent in further increases in learning ability, brain size ceased to increase and has remained effectively unchanged since the Middle Pleistocene. This also is the basis for the fact that there exists no demonstrable difference between the average intelligence of the various groups of people present in the world today.

One might even go a step further and offer the prediction, admittedly a speculation, that if any differences in intelligence are discovered in the future they will be inversely proportional to the efficiency of the cultural adaptive mechanism of the group in question. Highly effective cultures ensure that even the dull-witted shall survive and enjoy their opportunity to reproduce, provided they are at least capable of mastering the rudiments of their language and the mechanics of their social system. This provides a mental minimum, and, although modern technology has succeeded in lowering this somewhat, there is a limit below which effective participation in one's culture is so severely reduced that the chances for genetic perpetuation become negligible.

In literate cultures with an elaborate division of labor, it is distinctly possible that the "average" level of intelligence necessary for effective survival may be somewhat lower than is the case for those cultures where the problems involved in simple survival are much more immediate, and the advantages in the possession of a large store of accurate information about one's environment are much more apparent. The premium placed on human intelligence in the face of prolonged scarcity in the Australian desert or at the edge of the polar ice cap, where the penalty for stupidity is death, is almost certainly greater than it is for even the most downtrodden inhabitants of western Europe or North America. Even the most irresponsible and basically incompetent denizen of the slums of Chicago or Naples or Liverpool is capable of reproducing a dozen times over or more with a good chance that the greater part of the offspring will survive to do likewise.

While this situation has been frequently viewed with alarm by "racists," advocates of strict eugenics (control over who shall breed and in what number), and other alarmists, the consequences are certainly less serious than is often feared. For one thing, intelligence is such a complex phenomenon and under the control of so many genes that the genetic reshuffling which necessarily accompanies sexual reproduction makes it more probable that the offspring of the mentally semicompetent will be closer to the population average than their parents were. Despite the high rate of reproduction of members of the lower socioeconomic strata, the basic biological nature of the population remains relatively unchanged.

Increased intelligence apparently had adaptive value up to the Neanderthal stage. Since that time, however, a balance has been maintained with, if anything, a slight reduction of the premium placed on "brains" and a possible slight reduction in the average intelligence particularly of the members of the more effective cultural systems. Unless humans discover a means of manipulating their genes in a way that is as yet unforeseen, the future should certainly see no increase and probably a slight decrease in basic intellectual ability, however it is defined. Ultimately this should be relatively unimportant because of the social limit imposed on total mental incompetence.

The Dentition

From the very beginning of human evolution, the reliance on cultural rather than anatomical means for the manipulation of the environment meant that the significance of large projecting canine teeth had been suspended. As a result of the probable mutation effect, the accumulation of random mutation produced a reduction in canine tooth size until these teeth were functionally the same as incisors. Throughout the record of human evolution afforded by the known fossils, the canines have responded to the same forces that have influenced the form of the other teeth in the forward part of the dental arch, although they still retain a vestige of their prehuman importance in the fact that their roots are distinctly larger than is the case for the incisors, and their tips usually project beyond the occlusal level of the other teeth.

As culture took over the roles formerly performed by the teeth alone, the dentition underwent concomitant reductions. The increase in animal protein in the diet and possibly the use of fire by the Pithecanthropine stage meant that the burden placed on the molars was greatly reduced, and the operation of the probable mutation effect assured the subsequent reduction of both molar size and crown pattern complexity. The advent of specialized tools for cutting, chiseling, gouging, and scraping starting with the Mousterian had the same effect on the incisors. While all this has resulted in the transformation of the more than horsey Middle Paleolithic face into that relatively reduced anatomical complex that sets the standards for modern "beauty," the prospects for the future, while somewhat un-

certain, are not calculated to generate quite so much enthusiasm, **469**
except perhaps in the members of the dental profession.

Two centuries ago, rotting teeth exposed a person to the possibility of all kinds of secondary infections and distinctly lowered one's chances for survival. With the perfection of the technology of dentistry, all sorts of abnormalities can now be ameliorated to the detriment of nothing more than the owner's pocketbook. Reflect for a moment on the effect that would follow the complete cessation of dental care. How many among us reach voting age without a cavity? Admitting that the diet of the American teenager is rapidly approaching "one vast milkshake" and that the quantity of refined sugar ingested is partially related to the incidence of dental decay, nevertheless the suspension of all dental repair work would result in the untimely demise of an appalling number of people. One may surmise that the probable mutation effect is operating at this very moment to reduce the quality of the teeth of civilized peoples. The prophet of gloom could project this into the future and foresee a toothless species in another half-million years, but by that time there will have been enough other changes accumulated so that our present standards of what is "good" will not apply, and our remote descendants may be able to look back with pity on us their ancestors who had the misfortune to grow up with thirty-two unnecessary sources of potential pain in the permanent teeth, not to mention the twenty milk teeth. Even now, some individuals never develop lateral incisors, and many more fail to acquire third molars (wisdom [sic] teeth), while the dental profession becomes ever more adept at repairing or replacing the crumbling teeth that remain to us.

Other Traits

Other parts and functions of the human body can also be predicted to undergo reduction: pigmentation for the darker immigrants into the temperate zone, head hair for men and women everywhere, visual acuity, resistance to various diseases, and general physical robustness. The adaptive value of these features will be more or less cancelled out and replaced by clothes, hats, lenses, medicine, and power tools. Differentiation of this kind has been proceeding among the peoples of the world depending on precisely how long the adaptive value of the traits in question has been reduced, and it seems inevitable that the future will see further changes in the directions indicated. Unquestionably the people of 1,000,000 A.D. will be radically different from the people of today — possibly different enough to warrant a new specific designation within the Genus *Homo,* should we say *Homo durabilis?*

There is one other change that has been occurring recently and in which a somewhat misguided pride has been taken. This is the undoubted increase in size that has occurred during the last century and has occasioned the unwarranted feeling that the twentieth century is generating a better breed of people. While all the reasons for this change are not fully understood, most of it can be accounted for by two main factors. First is the undoubted increase in both the quantity and the quality of the diet. Second and often overlooked is the fact that under most of the conditions that have prevailed during human history, extraordinary size has been a distinct handicap. Imagine the despair of a family in the Middle East, southern India, or China attempting to meet the nutritional requirements of a child genetically destined to grow to a height of 6 ft. 8 in. with a weight of 250 pounds. Imagine further the despair of said growing child during the lean years when the per capita consumption averages eight hundred calories a day or less for an appreciable length of time. Furthermore, individuals who become especially large must necessarily grow more rapidly during youth than others, a fact that makes them particularly vulnerable to a variety of diseases that are less serious for those who grow at a more normal rate.

Until recently, both health and nutritional problems were more serious for the youngster destined to be large. At least part of the recent increase in overall size visible in modern populations is due to the fact that improved standards of food and medical care have allowed genetic combinations to survive which would have been selected against in ages past. Not only do modern humans tend to be larger and somewhat softer than was the case in days gone by, but the cessation of the survival value of physical performance has allowed the survival of a degree of variation in human physique and proportions that did not formerly occur. The number of individuals who sport wide hips and narrow shoulders, big hands and thin arms, heavy legs and lean trunk, and other such dysplasias is much greater among "civilized" peoples than is true for, say, the inhabitants of central New Guinea who, small though they may be, possess uniformly imposing and well-proportioned physiques.

What this all portends for the future is not altogether clear, although it seems apparent that, at the moment, the suspension of stringent physical selection and the improvement of medicine and nutrition is permitting a general increase in size, an increase in the variability of physique, and a reduction in muscularity. For the distant future, however, the crystal ball grows hazy and the picture dims. There are simply too many unknowns, and we feel that we have already extended our speculations far enough.

One thing is certain. There are going to be too many people. It is estimated that the present population of over four billion includes fully one third of all the people who ever trod the earth. At the present rate of increase, world population bids fair to multiply some fifteen times within the next century. By the year 2050, the number of people alive would be five times the entire cumulative total of all the people who have ever existed since the beginning of human history. Perhaps the efficient utilization of our present food resources could feed double our present population. Increased food-producing efficiency might feed triple the number of people in the world, but no conceivable development will enable the world to support fifteen times its present population. While we may be venturing into the territory of the cultural anthropologist, the sociologist, and the moral philosopher, yet, in the perspective of human evolution, it seems inevitable that humans who have exerted increasing control over the conditions of their survival—including the regulation of the rate of reproduction of many of the plants and animals of the earth—will have to take some responsibility for the regulation of their own reproduction simply to ensure their survival. Birth control is a necessity simply to keep human numbers manageable. Perhaps in the future the science of genetics will provide the means whereby some control can be exerted over the quality of human reproduction, but, at the present time, birth control is necessary simply in order to ensure the probability that there will be any future at all.

Suggested Readings

BRESSLER, J. B.(editor). *Human Ecology.* Addison-Wesley, Reading, Mass., 1966.
  A collection of readings on the effect of environmental factors on the development of man.

DANIELS, F., JR. Man and radiant energy: solar radiation, D. B. Dill *et al.* (editors), *Handbook of Physiology, Section 4: Adaptation to the Environment.* American Physiological Society, Washington, D.C., 1964, pp. 969–987.
  A good discussion of the effects of solar radiation on the skin of man.

DUMOND, D. E. The limitation of human population: A natural history, *Science,* vol. 187, 1975, pp. 713–723.
  A highly stimulating discussion in favor of the view that the demographic transition of modern times represents a return familiar to our hunting ancestors.

HARDIN, G. (editor). *Population, Evolution, & Birth Control.* Freeman & Co., San Francisco, 1964.
  An excellent collage of stimulating and controversial readings.

Continuing Evolution

472 HARRISON, G. A., AND A. J. BOYCE. (editors). *The Structure of Human Populations.* Oxford University Press, New York, 1972.
On biosocial interactions in influencing demographic structure covering a broad spectrum.

MONTAGU, A. (editor). *Culture and the Evolution of Man.* Oxford University Press, New York, 1962.
Fundamental and fascinating studies on the interrelations between culture and physical evolution.

———. *Man's Most Dangerous Myth: The Fallacy of Race.* 5th ed. Oxford Univesity Press, New York, 1974.
An examination of the fatal difficulties inherent in any attempt to use a concept of "race."

———, (editor). *The Concept of Race.* Free Press, New York, 1964.
A critical examination of the anthropological concept of race.

SIMONS, R.D.G.PH. *The Colour of the Skin in Human Relations.* Elsevier Publishing Co., Princeton, N.J., 1961.
An interesting monograph on the behavioral effects of skin color upon whites.

SPOONER, B. (editor). *Population Growth: Anthropological Implications.* The M.I.T. Press, Cambridge, Mass., 1972.
A valuable exploration of the interrelationships between population growth and decline and changes in technology, culture, and social organization.

Glossary

Adaptation A trait of the organism which, in the environment it inhabits, improves its chances of leaving descendants.

Adaptive radiation Evolution, from a primitive type of organism, or from a basically successful adaptation, of divergent forms adapted to distinct modes of life.

Aggression A term difficult to define because there are many forms of aggressive behavior. A working definition as good as any is: the actual or intended imposition of an individual's or group's wishes on others against their will.

Allele One of the two or more forms of a gene.

Amino acid One of a number of organic acids from which proteins are formed.

Anthropoidea Suborder of the Order Primates. Includes the monkeys, anthropoid apes, and man.

Apes Members of the family Pongidae, consisting of the gibbons, orang, chimpanzee, and gorilla.

Arboreal Adapted for living in trees.

Australopithecine A member of the African hominid forms of the Villafranchian.

Bacteriophage A virus that destroys bacteria.

Brachiation Progression in trees by swinging by the arms from branches.

Buccal Toward the cheek side.

Carbon 14 dating A method of determining the age of material by determining the amount of radioactive Carbon 14 which has been lost.

Catarrhine The taxon that includes Old World monkeys, apes, and humans.

474 **Cell** The living active unit of all plants and animals consisting of many specialized parts.

Cenozoic The geologic era that began some 70 million years ago, and in which we still live.

Cerebrum or **Cerebral hemispheres** The brain.

Chromosome One of a number of double-thread shaped bodies possibly made of protein, situated in the nucleus of the cell and carrying the genes. A code center.

Clactonian Lower Paleolithic flake-tool industry of northwest Europe dating from the Middle Pleistocene Mindel-Riss interglacial. Characterized by choppers, scrapers, and knives. A wooden spear is also known from this culture, a culture probably associated with the first inhabitants of Britain.

Cline A gradation of form differences or in the frequency of a trait within a species over a geographical area.

Codon A set of three bases that codes one amino acid. The *bases*, in DNA, are adenine, thymine, guanine, and cytosine.

Competition The process whereby those organisms possessing the adaptive fitness, in the environments they inhabit, are able to leave a larger progeny than those not possessing such fitness. Neither conscious "struggle" nor "survival of the fittest" is implied, but survival of the fit.

Conspecifics Members of the same species.

Cranial capacity The volume of the brain-bearing portion of the skull, hence a good measure of the volume of the brain.

Cranium The skull minus the lower jaw.

Cretaceous The final period of the Mesozoic. (See Figure 45.)

Crossover The shifting of genes from one chromosome to another.

Culture The part of the environment that is learned, shared, and transmitted in society. The man-made part of the environment.

Cytology The study of cells.

Deoxyribonucleic acid, DNA The principal constituent of the gene, believed to be the material of heredity itself. DNA carries the master plan or code containing the information that determines the order in which the amino acids fall into place in the protein molecule for which it is responsible.

Devonian The fourth period of the Paleozoic era. (See Figure 45.)

Diastema The gap between two adjacent teeth, e.g., the premaxillary diastema between the canines and the lateral incisors.

Dominant gene A gene that expresses itself, i.e., produces an observable effect in the offspring, when present, even though the gene pair also contains a recessive gene. Dominance and recessiveness are not properties of the genes *per se*, but the result of the total reaction system of the particular genotype. Both may be modified in degree by environmental influences including other genes.

Glossary

Dominance   In ethology dominance is the establishment of hierarchical relationships between the members of a group.

Dryopithecine   A taxon of Miocene apes which may be ancestral to both the later apes (pongids) and humans (hominids).

Ecological niche   The position occuped by an organism in relation to its total environment, but more especially to the particular situation of the environment which it actually occupies.

Ecology   The study of the interactions between organisms and their environment; the economics of organisms.

Endocranial   Referring to the inner aspect of the skull, the walls of which enclose the cerebrum and its meninges.

Environment   The conditions acting upon the organism. Such conditions may be internal as well as external.

Enzyme   Any of various organic compounds secreted by the body cells that act as catalysts causing the chemical processes of the body to be carried on.

Entropy   The tendency of any system to dissipate heat, decrease in organization, and increase in randomness. That part of the heat or energy invested in the body or any system which cannot be taken out and is therefore unavailable for work.

Eocene   Geological period, subdivision of Tertiary, lasted approximately from fifty-five to thirty-five million years ago.

Epicanthic fold   A fold of skin from the upper eyelid that covers the inner angle of the eye.

Estrus   The cyclical period of maximum receptivity and fecundity in most female mammals, with the possible exception, among the primates, of woman.

Ethology   The comparative study of behavior.

Euhominid   Used by some authors to refer to the stages of man immediately above that of the Australopithecines, e.g., *Homo (Pithecanthropus) erectus*, and *Homo sapiens*.

Evolution   Development, by descent, with modification

Falciparum mosquito   *Plasmodium falciparum* is the parasite that produces a particularly virulent form of malaria. It is transmitted by the mosquito *Anopheles gambiae*.

Family   A taxon consisting of a number of similar genera. The name of a family ends in *-idae*.

Fossil   Remains of an organism or direct evidence of its presence preserved in rocks.

Gene   The physical unit of heredity, a small region in a chromosome consisting mainly of DNA. The minimal hereditary unit determined by crossover. Possibly a section (codon) of a DNA molecule.

Gene flow   Relating to the dissemination of genes from one population to another.

Gene frequency   Relating to the frequency of certain genes in certain populations.

Genetic drift or the Sewall Wright effect   The nonselective random distribution, or extinction or fixation of genes in a population.

Genotype   The genetic constitution, determined by the number, types, and arrangement of genes.

Gene pool   The genes present within a given population.

Genosorption   The incorporation of the genes of one population into the gene pool of another.

Gonad   The sex gland; the ovary in the female, the testis in the male.

Grade   A general term referring to developmental level, e.g., the prosimian grade, the monkey grade, the ape grade, the hominid grade.

Grooming   Tactile communication in the form of searching in the hair and on the skin for skin flakes, debris, parasites, and so on. An important social bonding demonstration of amiability cementing relationships among primates.

Günz   The first of the four Alpine glaciations. (See Figure 74.)

Habitat   Place with a particular kind of environment where animal lives.

Hemoglobin   The red respiratory protein in red blood cells, serving to carry oxygen to and carbon dioxide from the cells of the body.

Heterozygous   Carrying different forms of a gene (allele) on both homologous chromosomes.

Hominine   Synonym of *Euhominine* (See *Euhominid.*)

Hominid   A member of the family *Hominidae.*

Hominidae   The family name of all species of man, including the Australopithecines.

Hominoidea   The superfamily including the Hominidae and the Pongidae, i.e., man and the apes.

Homo   The genus to which all forms of humans belong.

Homo habilis   Name given to a form of man, at present inadequately described, possibly an advanced Australopithecine, perhaps approaching the Pithecanthropine stage, with status at present undetermined.

Homo sapiens   The living species of the genus *Homo*, as well as several extinct forms of this species.

Homozygous   Having identical genes in the two corresponding loci of a pair of chromosomes.

Incest tabu   The prohibition of sexual intercourse between family members. The result of this is the promotion of outbreeding (exogamy) and gene flow.

Intelligence   The ability to make the most appropriately successful response to the particular challenge of the situation. The individual's total repertory of those problem-solving and thinking discrim-

The "usual and expected" response is one of which 65 to 75 per cent of the given population is capable.

Interstadial   The temperate or cool period between phases of a single glacial period. Interstadials are shorter and cooler than interglacial periods.

Isolation   The condition in which potential mating groups are separated by ecological or social barriers and thus prevented from mating.

Labial   Toward the lips.

Lactase   The enzyme that enables suckling mammals to digest milk sugar (lactose), but which is reduced in many adult mammals, including some human populations. This trait is probably under genetic control.

Latimeria   Crossopterygian fish, the Coelocanth, a living fossil from the Jurassic or earlier, thought to have been extinct since then, but discovered to have survived in 1954 when the first specimens were caught off the Comoro Islands (Madagascar). (See Figure 47.)

Lingual   Toward the tongue.

Linkage   Genes situated on the same chromosome are said to be linked. The linkage is broken by crossing-over.

Locus   A particular place on a particular chromosome that always contains one kind of gene or one of a particular set of alleles. Homologous chromosomes usually have identical sets of loci.

Mammal   A member of the class of Mammals, characterized by hair, milk secretion, diaphragm used in respiration, lower jaw made up of single pair of bones; presence of only left systemic arch, and three auditory ossicles in each middle ear connecting eardrum and inner ear.

Mandible   The lower jaw.

Maxilla   The upper jaw.

Meiosis   The two successive cell divisions from a cell containing the full complement of chromosomes (forty-six in man) preceding formation of the gametes. Both divisions resemble mitosis, except that while there are two divisions of the nucleus, in the second meiotic division the chromosomes are not duplicated, hence resulting in the formation of gametes with half the number (haploid) of chromosomes from the mother cells with the double number (diploid) or full complement of chromosomes.

Melanin   A complex, dark brown pigment, which in various concentrations affects the color of the skin, hair, and eyes.

Menarche   The first menstruation.

Mendel's laws   The three principles of chromosome behavior at meiosis: 1. *The Law of Segregation* refers to the behavior of one pair of genes. When the homologous chromosomes separate, the two alleles segregate into different gametes. 2. *The Law of Independent Assortment* or *Free Recombination* refers to the behavior of two or more pairs of alleles carried on different chromosomes. Each pair of chromosomes separates into different gametes independently of other pairs. The result is that the gametes contain all possible combinations of the genes constituting the different pairs. *Linked genes* are the exception to this law; recombination of such genes occurs through *crossing-over*. 3. *The Law of Dominance and Recessiveness* refers to the fact that some genes are capable of suppressing the expression of their alleles. Genes of the first class are called *dominant;* genes whose expression is suppressed are called *recessive.* Recessive genes do not or only minimally express themselves in heterozygous condition, but do, more or less, fully express themselves in homozygous condition.

Mesozoic   The era after the Paleozoic and before the Cenozoic. (See Figure 45.)

Metacarpals   The bones of the hand between the wrist and the fingers.

Metatarsals   The bones of the foot, between the tarsal bones and the toes.

Mindel   The second of the four Alpine glaciations. (See Figure 74.)

Miocene   Geological period of the Tertiary, lasting from about twenty-five to five million years ago. (See Figure 45.)

Mitosis   The process of cell division during which the genes and chromosomes duplicate, migrate to an equatorial plane, and separate to opposite poles, and the cell splits and forms two new cells.

Mongoloid   One of the major groups of humanity or a member of that group, generally characterized by a flattened face, high cheekbones, marked overbite of upper teeth, shovel-shaped incisor teeth, epicanthic folds, very slight yellowish tinge to the skin, and lank black hair.

Monkey   A grade of the Anthropoidea characterized by tails, comprising the New World monkeys (Ceboidea) and the Old World monkeys (Cercopithecoidea).

Morphology   The study of form, usually involving the study of the relation between function, structure, and form.

Mousterian   The dominant toolmaking industry of the Middle Paleolithic, associated with Neanderthal man. Dating from somewhat more than 80,000 to 35,000 years B.P.

Mucopolysaccharide   A carbohydrate containing a large number of compound sugars with their bases made up of repeating units that include an amino sugar.

Mutation   A change in the structure of a gene resulting in a transmissible hereditary modification in the expression of a trait.

Mutation pressure   The measure of the action of mutation in tending to alter the frequency of a gene in a given population.

Natural selection The fact that those organisms that possess a trait or traits that enable them to adapt better to the environment than those organisms lacking such a trait or traits are more likely to leave a larger progeny. As Darwin put it: "As many more individuals of each species are born than can possibly survive; and as, consequently, there is a frequently recurring struggle for existence, it follows that any being, if it vary however slightly in any manner profitable to itself, under the complex and sometimes varying conditions of life, will have a better chance of surviving, and thus be *naturally selected*. From the strong principle of inheritance, any selected variety will tend to propagate its new and modified form." *The Origin of Species*, 1859, p. 5.

Neanderthal man The man of Mousterian culture (in the Upper Pleistocene) prior to the reduction of the face and teeth of the Middle Pleistocene.

Neanderthaloid Possessing some features resembling the true Neanderthals.

Neolithic The period of appearance of ground stone tools, pottery, and the domestication of plants and animals. The time of the Neolithic varies: 10,000 years B.P. in Southeast Asia, the same in Southwest Asia, and 6,000 B.P. in Europe.

Nucleic acid Family of substances of large molecular weight, of double helical form, composed of nucleotides, found in chromosomes, viruses, etc.

Nucleotide One of three units of which nucleic acids are composed. Consists of a phosphate and a sugar with an organic base attached to the sugar. There are four different kinds depending on the nature of the base (adenine, guanine, cytosine, thymine). (See Figure 14.)

Nucleus The structure of the cell containing the chromosomes.

Occlusion The relation of the upper and lower teeth to each other when the bite is closed or "occluded."

Occipital bone The bone at the back of the head.

Oldowan The earliest Lower Paleolithic cultural tradition, the type site of which is Olduvai Gorge in Tanzania and dates to more than 2 million years ago. Choppers, polyhedrals, discoids, spheroids, proto-bifaces, and utilized flakes are characteristic, and occur also in South Africa, the Near East, and Western Europe.

Oligocene Geological period of the Tertiary, lasting from about forty to twenty-five million years ago.

Order A systematic category embracing families, genera, and species, and their subdivisions, such as the order Primates, consisting of the lemurs, lorises, tarsier, monkeys, apes, and men, all characterized by a basic structural patterning of traits.

Oreopithecus An anthropoid genus of the Pliocene.

480   **Orthogenesis**   A not widely accepted theory of the tendency of groups of organisms to evolve consistently in the same direction over prolonged periods of time without any discoverable reason.

Paleocene   Geological period of the Tertiary, lasting from about eighty to sixty million years ago.

Paleozoic   The geological era between the Proterozoic and the Mesozoic, which covered a period between 600 million and 230 million years ago. (See Figure 45.)

Pangenesis   Darwin's outmoded theory that heredity might be accounted for by gemmules, set free from all the cells of the body, to be aggregated in ovum and sperm, so that in conjugation of the latter all the elements of the body would be recombined.

Paleontology   The science that deals with the life of past geological epochs.

Phenotype   The manifest characteristics of the organism; the product of the joint action of environment and genotype.

Phylogeny   The study of the historical development of the line or lines of evolution in a group of organisms.

Pithecanthropine   Resembling *Homo erectus.*

Pithecanthropus   Preferably now known as *Homo erectus,* extinct form of man of Middle Pleistocene age.

Platyrrhine   Broad-nosed. A term sometimes used to refer to the monkeys of the New World.

Pleistocene   The sixth epoch of the Cenozoic, which lasted from about 3.3 million years to 10,000 years B.P. The Lower Pleistocene or Villafranchian is dated by some authorities as far back as 5 million years. The Middle Pleistocene begins about 700,000 years ago, and the Upper Pleistocene begins some 75,000 years ago.

Pliocene   The fifth epoch of the Cenozoic lasted from 5 million to about 3 million years ago. (See Figure 45.)

Pliopithecus   A fossil Primate with gibbonlike teeth which lived during the Miocene and Lower Pliocene.

Pluvial   A rainy period.

Polymer   One of two or more isomeric substances (i.e., having same percentage composition, but differing in their physical properties), usually of high molecular weight, made up of a chain of repeated units.

Population   The group of individuals which forms a single interbreeding community.

Polymorphism   Individual variability, having several different forms; the presence of two or more alleles at the same loci of homologous chromosomes ensures variability for specific traits in the same population.

Polytypic   A genus with several species or a species with several subspecies or varieties.

Pongidae   The family of apes, orangs, chimpanzees, and gorillas.

Potassium-Argon dating A method of determining the age of fossils by measuring the transformation of radioactive potassium into argon.

Preadaptation A term not really possessing any significantly different meaning from the term *Adaptation (q.v.)*. Here taken to mean the reapplication of structures or functions to life in a new environment.

Primate A member of the order Primates, consisting of the lemurs, lorises, tarsiers, monkeys, apes, and men.

Probable Mutation Effect The effect of accumulated randomly produced mutations. Where selective forces are relaxed, this results in structural reduction.

Proconsul A no longer useable name given to an apelike form from the Lower Miocene of East Africa before it was identified as a member of the genus *Dryopithecus*.

Propliopithecus An Oligocene anthropoid, which may be ancestral to the hominoids.

Protein Any of certain nitrogenous substances consisting of a complex union of amino acids, a chief constituent of chromosomes and of plant and animal bodies.

Proteinoids Proteinlike substances.

Race Used in many senses, by geneticists to mean any population that differs from other populations in the frequency of one or more genes, and by anthropologists to mean a population whose physical characteristics distinguish it from other populations, and finally, by the layman, in any sense in which he desires to use the term. A term that has outlived any dubious use it may once have had.

Ramapithecus A late Miocene Early Pliocene probable ancestor of the australopithecines and of *Homo*.

Recessive gene A gene that fails to express itself phenotypically in the heterozygous genotype.

Rhinarium The moist patch present at the tip of the snout, as in lemurs.

Ribonucleic acid or RNA The form of nucleic acid (see DNA) synthesized in the nucleus on a DNA template, and responsible for directing protein synthesis.

Ribosome A morphologic unit of the cell machinery in the cytoplasm where amino acid units are linked together to form proteins.

Riss The penultimate glacial period, in the roughly upper two-thirds of the Middle Pleistocene.

Ritualization The modification of a behavior pattern to serve a communicative function.

Savanna A grassland characterized by scattered trees, especially in tropical and subtropical regions, a cross between a woodlands and a desert.

Selection The maintenance of certain genotypes having adaptive value in contrast with others that do not, and which therefore are not likely to do as well by way of leaving a progeny.

Selection pressure   The measure of the action of selection in tending to alter the frequency of a gene in a given population.

Selective advantage   The genotypic condition of an organism or group of organisms that increases its chances, relative to others, of representation in later generations.

Sexual dimorphism   Marked morphological differences characterizing the sexes of a species.

Sexual selection   Conscious selection on the basis of some preferred sexual trait as a factor of evolution. A widely discredited theory once held by Darwin.

Sickle cell   A red blood cell which in the absence of oxygen assumes bizarre shapes often resembling those of a sickle.

Sicklemia   Sometimes known as *sickle cell anemia*, due to sickle cells in the blood inherited as incompletely recessive, and homozygous in the sicklemic, the sicklemic rarely survives beyond childhood.

Sinanthropus   Preferably now known as *Homo erectus pekinensis*, fossil hominid of Middle Pleistocene age, found at Choukoutien, S.W. of Peking in China.

Skull   The bony framework of the head, composed of the cranial bones and the bones of the face.

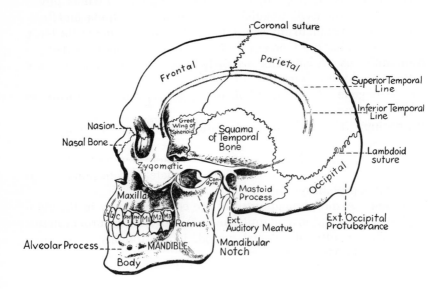

Specialization   A much overworked term, used relative to an actual
or presumed ancestral form to mean the development of special
adaptations to a particular habitat or mode of life, thus resulting in
divergence of characteristics from ancestral forms.

Species   A group of actually or potentially interbreeding natural
populations, which is more or less reproductively isolated from
other such groups.

Suture   The edges at which the different bones of the skull come
together, and with age mostly unite.

Taxon   A taxonomic unit or category.

Taxonomy   The science of classification of organisms.

Territory   An area that is defended, among different animals from
many different motives, for different purposes. A concept with different shades of meaning.

Tetrapods   Four-footed animals; all the essentially land-living vertebrates characterized by two pairs of pentadactyl limbs. Includes
amphibians, reptiles, birds, and mammals.

Therapsida   Mammal-like reptiles; extinct groups of reptiles that
lived from the Permian to the Triassic. The main reptile group until the appearance of the dinosaurs. Therapsids were ancestral to
the mammals.

Variation   The occurrence of differences in characters. *Discontinuous variation:* gradations that are perceptible in the phenotype. *Continuous variation:* gradations of difference that are
imperceptible in the phenotype.

Villafranchian   The earliest part of the Pleistocene before the first
glaciation (Günz).

Virus   A minute living parasite composed of nucleic acid and protein that can be seen only by the electron microscope.

Würm   The fourth and last of the Alpine glaciations.

Zinjanthropus   An australopithecine of the Lower Pleistocene age,
found in Olduvai Gorge, Tanganyika.

Zygote   The fertilized ovum, the product of the union of the ovum
and the spermatozoon.

Index

489